Creative Stitches

for Contemporary Embroidery

VOLUME 2

114 More Essential Stitches for Stunning Designs

Sharon Boggon

C&T PUBLISHING
Another Maker Inspired!

Publisher: Amy Barrett-Daffin

Creative Director: Gailen Runge

Senior Editor: Roxane Cerda

Copy Editor: Nordvest LLC

Cover/Book Designer: April Mostek

Production Coordinator: Tim Manibusan

Photography Coordinator: Rachel Ackley

Front cover photography by Jerry Everard

Photography by Jerry Everard, unless otherwise noted

Published by C&T Publishing, Inc., P.O. Box 1456, Lafayette, CA 94549

Attention Teachers: C&T Publishing, Inc., encourages the use of our books as texts for teaching. You can find lesson plans for many of our titles at ctpub.com or contact us at ctinfo@ctpub.com.

 For your convenience, we post an up-to-date listing of corrections on our website (ctpub.com). If a correction is not already noted, please contact our customer service department at ctinfo@ctpub.com or P.O. Box 1456, Lafayette, CA 94549.

Library of Congress Cataloging-in-Publication Data

Names: Boggon, Sharon, 1956- author

Title: Creative stitches for contemporary embroidery, Volume 2 : 114 more essential stitches for stunning designs / by Sharon Boggon.

Description: Lafayette, CA : C&T Publishing, [2026] | Includes index. |

Summary: "Discover 114 more contemporary surface-embroidery stitches in this essential follow-up guide by Sharon Boggon. With step-by-step photos, innovative variations, and inspiring samplers, beginners and experienced embroiderers will confidently explore texture, asymmetry, modern fills, and creative adaptations for contemporary embroidery and crazy quilting projects"--Provided by publisher.

Identifiers: LCCN 2026001821 | ISBN 9781644035566 trade paperback | ISBN 9781644035573 ebook

Subjects: LCSH: Embroidery | Stiches (Sewing) | BISAC: CRAFTS & HOBBIES / Needlework / Embroidery | CRAFTS & HOBBIES / Needlework / General

Classification: LCC TT770 .B6425 2026 | DDC 746.44--dc23/eng/20260206

LC record available at https://lccn.loc.gov/2026001821

Printed in China

10 9 8 7 6 5 4 3 2 1

◊ Chained bullion knot used around a Suffolk puff (yo-yo) in slow-stitch project

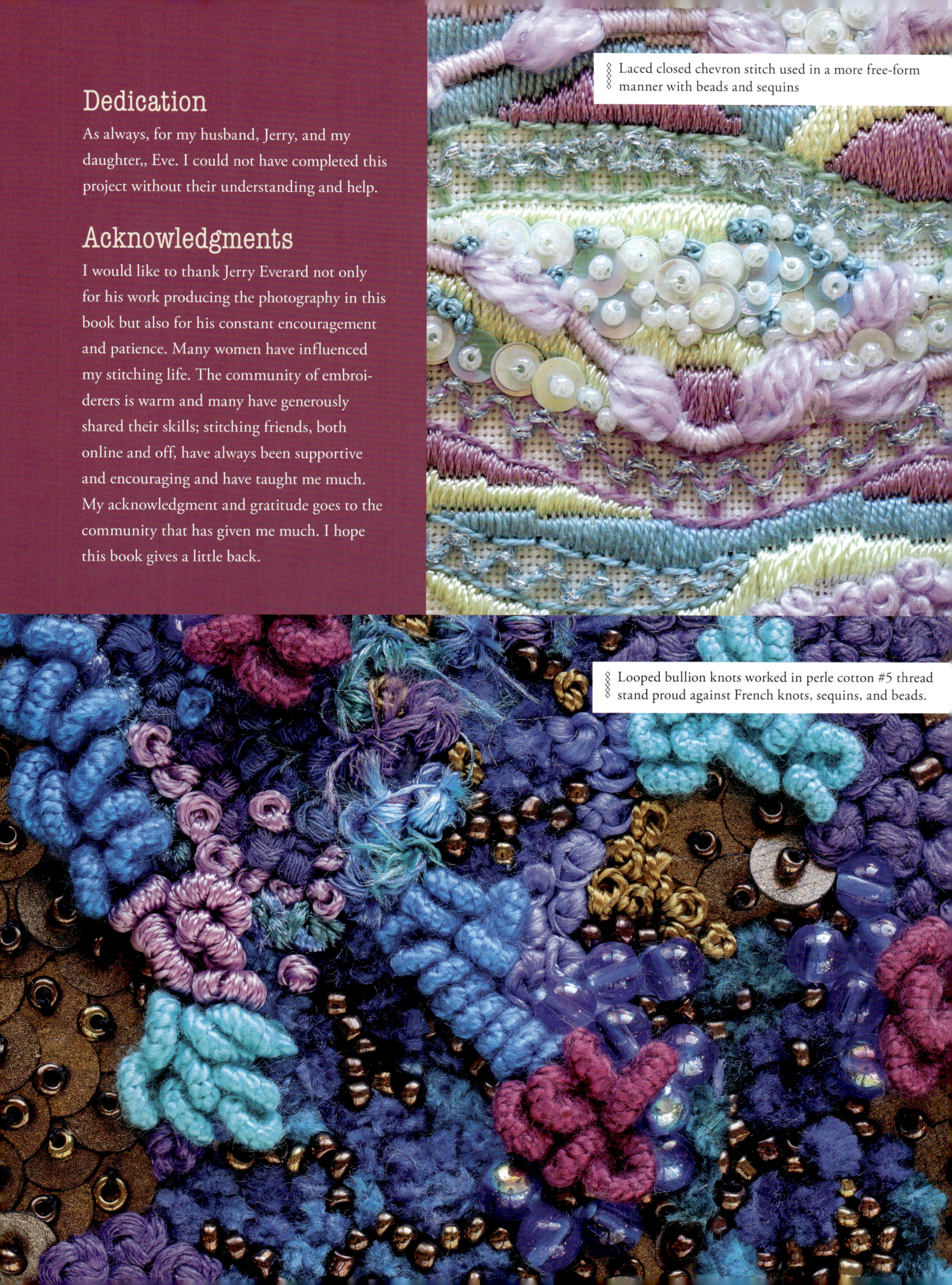

Dedication

As always, for my husband, Jerry, and my daughter,, Eve. I could not have completed this project without their understanding and help.

Acknowledgments

I would like to thank Jerry Everard not only for his work producing the photography in this book but also for his constant encouragement and patience. Many women have influenced my stitching life. The community of embroiderers is warm and many have generously shared their skills; stitching friends, both online and off, have always been supportive and encouraging and have taught me much. My acknowledgment and gratitude goes to the community that has given me much. I hope this book gives a little back.

Laced closed chevron stitch used in a more free-form manner with beads and sequins

Looped bullion knots worked in perle cotton #5 thread stand proud against French knots, sequins, and beads.

Contents

◊ Detail of wall piece

THE STITCHES

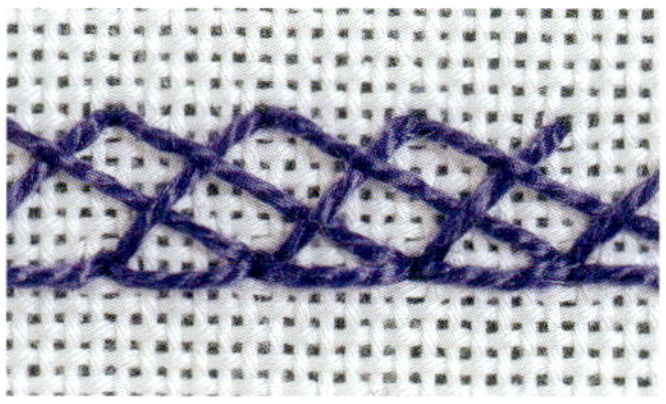

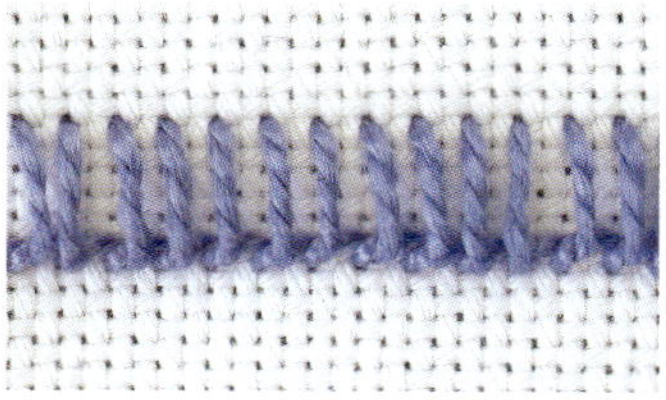

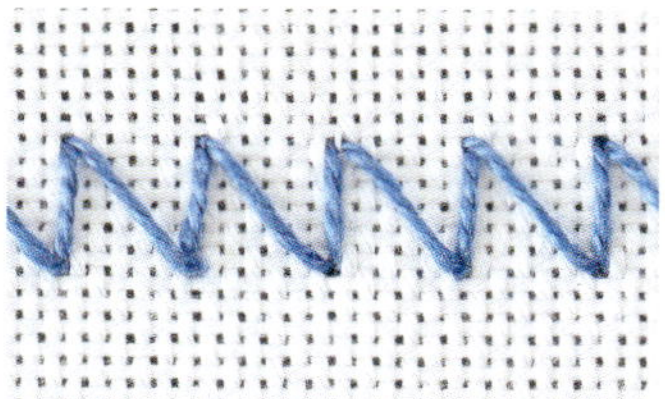

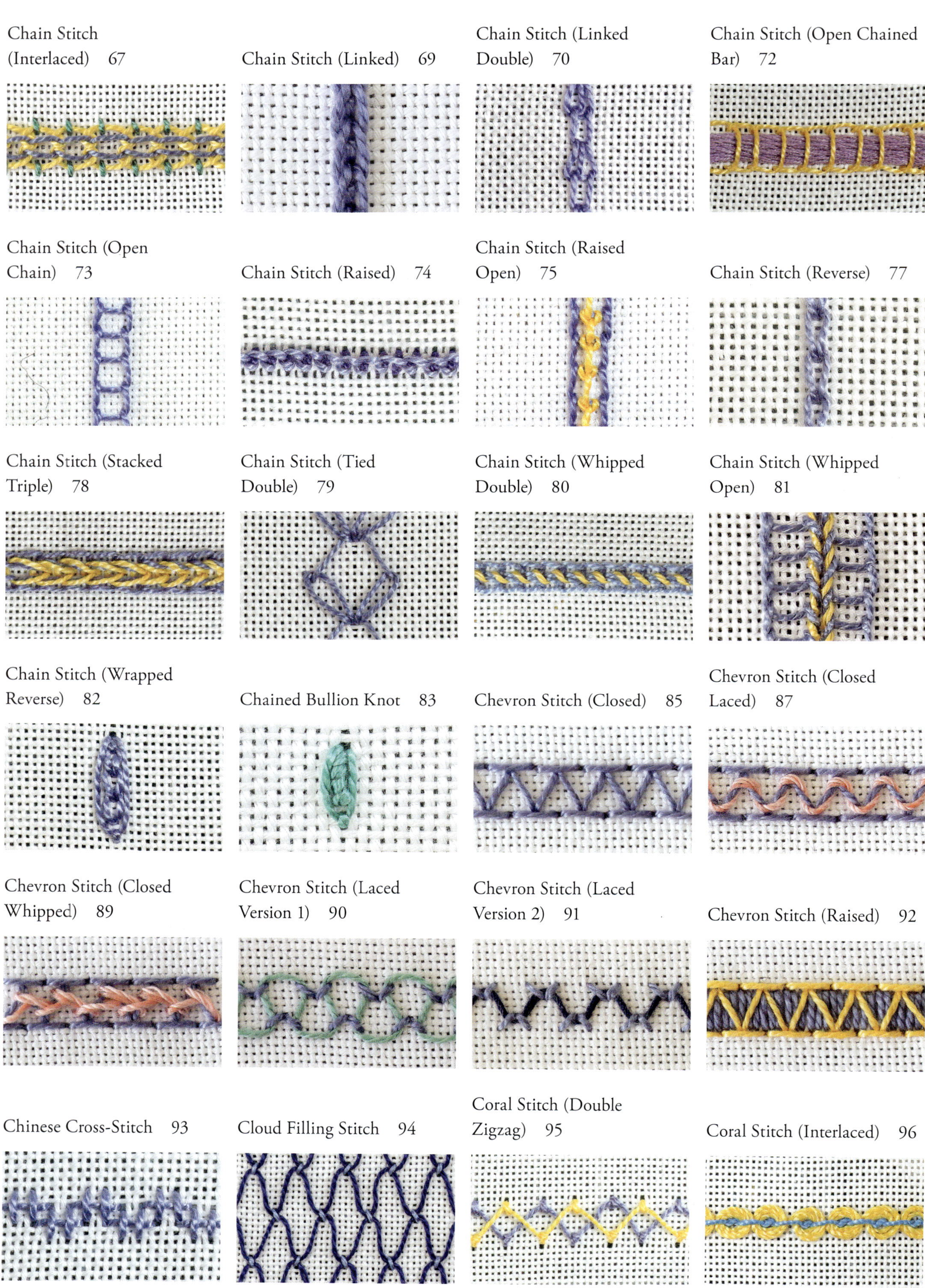
Chain Stitch (Interlaced) 67
Chain Stitch (Linked) 69
Chain Stitch (Linked Double) 70
Chain Stitch (Open Chained Bar) 72
Chain Stitch (Open Chain) 73
Chain Stitch (Raised) 74
Chain Stitch (Raised Open) 75
Chain Stitch (Reverse) 77
Chain Stitch (Stacked Triple) 78
Chain Stitch (Tied Double) 79
Chain Stitch (Whipped Double) 80
Chain Stitch (Whipped Open) 81
Chain Stitch (Wrapped Reverse) 82
Chained Bullion Knot 83
Chevron Stitch (Closed) 85
Chevron Stitch (Closed Laced) 87
Chevron Stitch (Closed Whipped) 89
Chevron Stitch (Laced Version 1) 90
Chevron Stitch (Laced Version 2) 91
Chevron Stitch (Raised) 92
Chinese Cross-Stitch 93
Cloud Filling Stitch 94
Coral Stitch (Double Zigzag) 95
Coral Stitch (Interlaced) 96

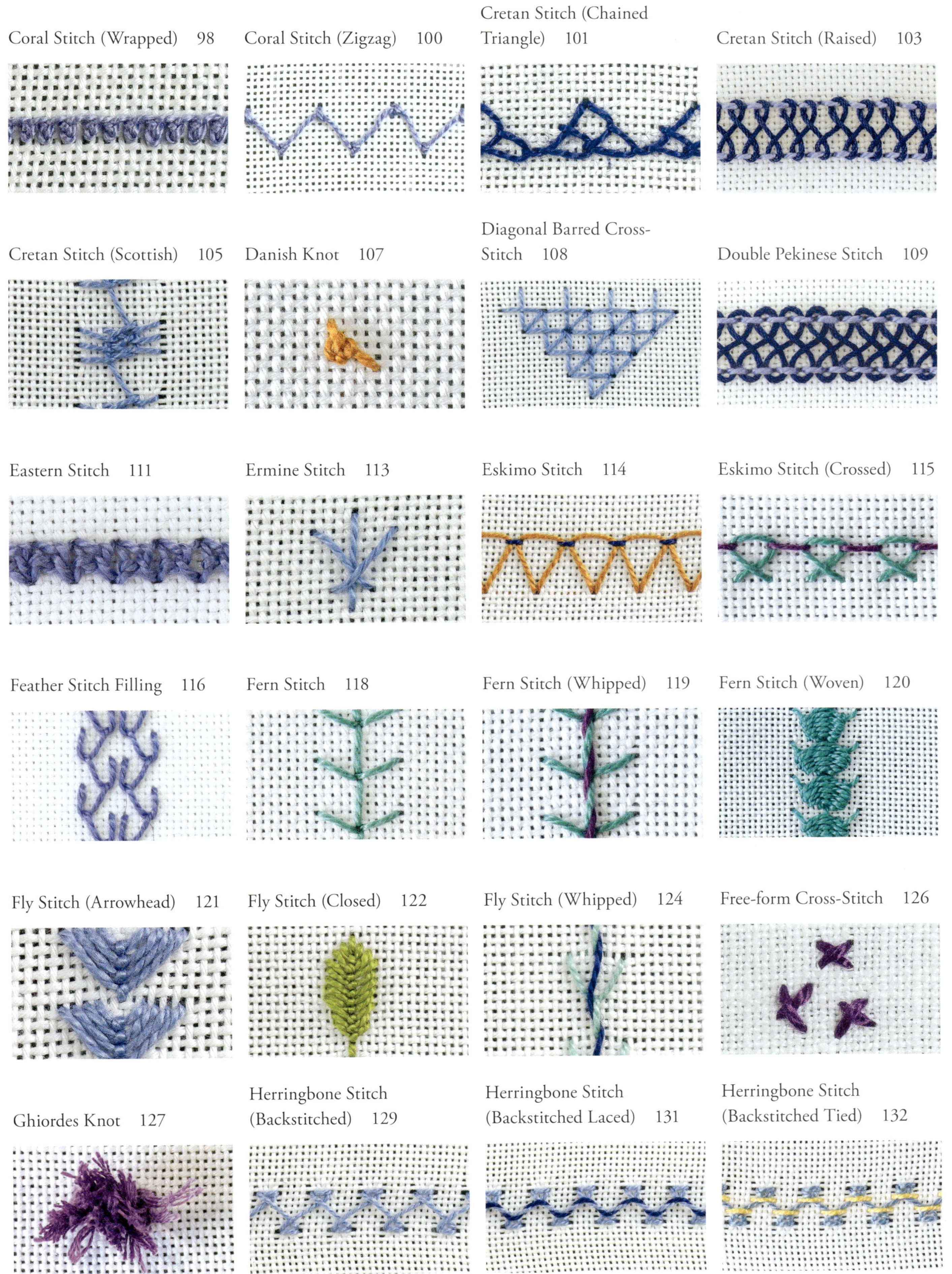

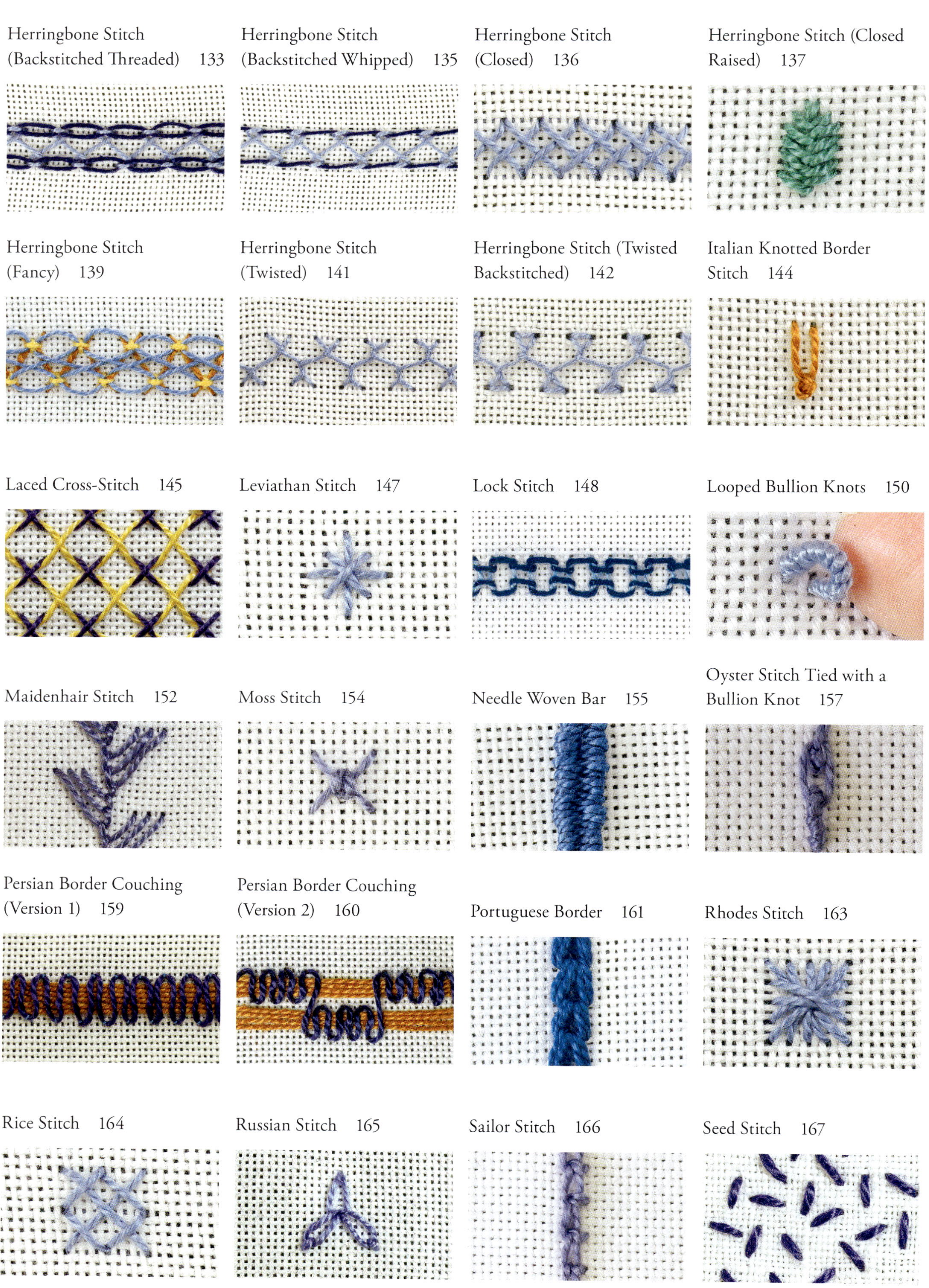

Introduction

We all live busy time-poor lives. With this book, I invite you to slow down, take some time for yourself, and explore self-expression via creative embroidery. I aim to introduce you to more hand stitches so that you can add variety and interest to the pieces you stitch.

We stitch as a form of self-expression. Hand embroidery runs counter to mass-produced items that are manufactured to precise uniform standards. Manufactured items look and feel machine-made. Handmade items are a little bit wobbly, a little uneven, and you relate to them because they leave a trace of the hand that made them. They are human rather than perfect. I encourage you to explore these stitches, thinking about what it is to be human rather than what it is to be perfect.

With any project, you will make dozens of choices, such as choosing the dominant color, the weight and type of fabric, and which stitches will embellish the project. These are your unique choices. Through these small personal decisions, you express yourself. It is my aim to give you more stitches to choose from. Many of these stitches are hundreds if not thousands of years old, from many cultures around the globe. I hope some at least give you another way to express yourself, and most of all, you have fun exploring them.

◊ Detail of slow-stitch project

Supplies, Tools, and Equipment

Hand embroidery is an enjoyable pastime, but it can quickly become frustrating if you don't have some basic supplies suitable for the job.

Fabric Choice

Tip When you start a project, choose your fabric first, your thread second, and your needle last.

When selecting fabric for a project, think about how you'll use the item you're making. For instance, for a tote bag, pick out a fabric that will take a little wear and tear, such as a sturdy cotton rather than a fine silk. For a baby's bib, make sure both fabric and thread are machine washable. I think you see my point. When you choose your fabric, think about the life it will have. Does it need to be easily laundered? How much wear and tear will it receive? If I am making something to be hung on a wall, I have more freedom in fabric choice.

You can use most fabrics for hand embroidery, but (yes, there is a but) the fabric you choose can significantly affect the quality of your embroidery.

When looking at fabric for embroidery, you have a choice between even-weave and non-evenweave fabrics. Even-weave fabrics are woven with the same number of threads per inch in both directions. This means you can easily stitch on a grid. Cross-stitch and many other techniques, such as whitework, drawn and pulled threadwork, blackwork, and needlepoint, are stitched on a grid. Most of the stitches in this book are used in surface embroidery and do not need a grid to work well. However, I worked many of the samples in this book on even-weave fabric, which means that, in order to work a straight line, I followed the line of the threads instead of marking guidelines on the fabric.

Even-weave embroidery fabrics come in a variety of thread counts, meaning the number of threads per inch of fabric. You can find options as fine as 42 or the far more course 18 count, and everything in between. These fabrics are woven in a number of different fibers. Most common are cotton and linen, which are strong and easily laundered. Linen is lovely to stitch on. Some linen is woven with a slightly rougher texture, with slubs or little bobbles of linen fiber left in the weave to create a natural, rustic look.

◊ Selection of even-weave fabrics

◊ Selection of plain garment, thrifted, hand-dyed, eco-dyed, and linen fabrics suitable for hand embroidery

Other garment fabrics can also be used as a foundation for embroidery, including common fabrics such as cotton muslin, quilting cotton, cotton/linen blend, bamboo, and cotton/bamboo blend. Wool of all weights is great to stitch. Denim is good to stitch on, particularly if it is worn and soft. Or you can choose more exotic fabrics such as silk or some of the newer silk and wool blends on the market. You will notice that most of these fabrics are natural fibers.

You can also use synthetic fabrics, but being synthetic, they are made of very strong fibers. In some cases, those fibers will create friction as you stitch. The action of constantly passing the thread back and forth through synthetic fabric can rub your working thread and cause it to shred, making for frequent knots and fluffy, shabby work. This is particularly true if you are stitching with silk thread or silk ribbon. For this reason, I tend to prefer natural fabrics.

Thinner or more delicate fabrics may need to have interfacing applied so that they have enough strength to take the stitches. Other fabrics, such as knit fabric or stretch fabrics, are not ideal for hand embroidery. If you want to embroider on a stretch fabric the solution is to interface it, but I don't recommend stretch fabric for beginners.

You can also choose to embroider on vintage linen and upcycled items. When using old or thrifted items, wash everything, cut away any damaged, worn, or stained areas, and set aside the good portions to be used as needed.

Tip Prewash your fabric to avoid shrinkage. It is very disappointing to work patiently on a piece only to discover that after washing, it has shrunk, distorting your stitches.

A Doodle Cloth

A *doodle cloth* is a scrap of fabric used to test a stitch. It doesn't have to be big or even good fabric, because once it's covered with stitches, it has served its purpose and ends up in the bin. Doodle cloths are a great place to try out stitches because they aren't intended as anything other than a place to learn something new.

When learning a new stitch, break the learning process into two steps. Start with a free-form stitch on a doodle cloth. Focus on the rhythm of the stitch, but don't worry about making every single stitch the same size, the same spacing, or even keeping it on a line. Give yourself a chance to get in the swing of things and to understand the hand movements that produce a good rhythm, then move on to the second step. Once you have learned the stitch, aim to be more controlled and practice to master keeping the stitch the same size, spacing, and along a line.

Why work this way? If you start off with a free-form sample, you can learn the hand motion and rhythm of the stitch before trying to bring it under control. Trying to master both skill areas at once can be difficult, so break the learning process into two parts—free-form first, and then control. One step at a time is a walk, two steps is a jump. Walk first!

Threads for Creative Embroidery

Once you have chosen your fabric, select your thread. Most people reach for stranded cotton floss, which consists of six strands of thread twisted together. Stranded cotton floss is the most commonly used thread for embroidery because it is readily available and comes in a huge range of colors that are consistent from dye batch to dye batch. You can use all six strands together or separate them for finer stitching. However, this type of thread is not really designed for surface embroidery because, often, stitches worked in a stranded floss will lie flat against the fabric instead of sitting proud and showing the unique texture of the stitch.

My favorite is perle cotton, which is a non-divisible, twisted thread that gives a thicker, more textured appearance. Sizes #8 and #5 are my favorite; for fine work, I use #12. The lower the number, the thicker the thread. I often enjoy thicker threads as they create more volume and texture.

Wool is traditionally used for crewel embroidery, but it has some wonderful contemporary applications. Wool is more textured than cotton and has a bit more bounce, which means beads and other stitches can be nestled into areas covered in stitches worked in wool. If you want a soft, dimensional piece, try using some fine wool. Novelty and knitting yarns can also be used for lacing, threading, and couching.

Silk threads can be quite expensive but are wonderful to work with. They come in a range of twists, types, and thicknesses. You can buy silk threads that are stranded, like stranded cotton floss, which are easy for people to start stitching with because they've likely used stranded cotton floss in the past. I prefer silk threads that are twisted like perle cotton as they produce a lovely texture. The sheen from silk can be very beautiful. Silk can be tricky to work with, but don't hesitate to try some once you have a little stitching experience.

Rayon threads are sometimes sold as artificial silk. They have a wonderful sheen and are economical but can be tricky to use. There are both stranded and twisted rayon threads on the market. Rayon ribbon floss looks like a small thin ribbon of silk but is actually made of rayon; it has a structure that makes it pliable and less likely to twist when stitching.

Tip Rayon threads can be difficult to use. The trick is to run the thread over a damp sponge just before stitching.

◊ Perle cotton #5 threads

◊ Silk threads

Metallic threads are available in different thicknesses and textures and can add a lot of sparkle to your work. When buying metallic threads, look carefully at the thread to see if the metallic fiber is twisted together. Avoid the spools labeled as "blending" threads—these filaments are meant to be used with a second thread because they aren't strong enough to be used on their own.

Tip If you are experimenting with a tricky thread, use shorter lengths. Cut threads the same length as the distance between the tip of your thumb and elbow. This is the maximum pull of your arm. You'll have fewer knots because, with a shorter thread, fewer loops are created during the stitching process.

You can choose from hundreds of different commercial threads. I am not exaggerating. I love the variegated hand-dyed threads, and I constantly experiment with threads containing bamboo, rayon, and Tencel. Some novelty and synthetic threads can be difficult to stitch, but they are worth the patience because they add a lovely texture and sheen to your work.

◇ Variegated over-dyed perle cotton #8

◇ Perle cotton #8 threads

Needles for Creative Embroidery

Tip Whenever you buy needles, just remember that the smaller the number, the larger the needle.

With your fabric and thread chosen, next choose your needles. When choosing a needle, make sure that your thread can pass through the eye with some ease. If the thread is too thick for the eye of the needle, choose a larger needle. Test to see if the needle slides through your fabric easily. Fabric with a tight, firm weave will need a finer needle, whereas fabric with a loose weave will allow larger needles.

When you are stitching, the needle is what makes the hole in the fabric, not the thread. If the thread starts to fray and become fuzzy, change to a larger needle. If you have holes in your fabric, the needle is too large, so switch to a finer needle. I suggest purchasing a mixed packet of needles that contains a range of needle sizes.

◇ Selection of needles used in hand embroidery

Embroidery or Crewel Needles

Invest in a mixed packet of crewel needles, which some manufacturers call embroidery needles. These have a sharp point and slightly larger eye to accommodate embroidery threads. Be aware that not all manufacturers have the same numbering system. Needles made in different parts of the world have different sizes, so it's good to develop the skill to choose your own favorite needle size for a particular project. When choosing embroidery or crewel needles, I mainly use sizes 6–10, but test them for yourself.

Straw or Milliners Needles

For stitches that involve wrapping the thread around the needle multiple times, such as French and bullion knots, you will need a needle with an eye that is the same thickness as the shaft of the needle, such as a straw or milliners needle. On other types of needles, the wrapped thread is caught where the eye of the needle bulges slightly, making it difficult to ease the thread along the needle shaft. With a straw or milliners needle, the wraps of working thread will slide over the eye of the needle and not be caught up. These needles come in sizes 3–10. Have a range of sizes on hand so you can easily work textured stitches in different types of thread.

Tapestry Needles

Tapestry needles are short, blunt needles designed to take thicker threads through their long eye. They come in sizes 18–28 and can be purchased in mixed-size packets. For threaded and whipped stitches, to avoid splitting the foundation row during the lacing, use a blunt tapestry needle to weave a second thread through the foundation stitches.

Chenille Needles

Chenille needles may appear the same as tapestry needles, but chenille needles have a sharp point. Think of them as being thicker and longer crewel needles. This means they have larger eyes that enable you to use a heavier thread. Chenille needles are used in silk ribbon embroidery as they have a sharp tip and a large eye. They are commonly available in sizes 13–26 and can be purchased in mixed packs.

Tip Add a needle threader to your sewing box—it can be a real time-saver. They are not absolutely necessary, but they can help prevent frustration.

Embroidery Hoops or Frames

Embroidery hoops and frames keep your fabric taut, which ensures even stitching. Both hoops and frames come in various sizes; choose the size hoop that will accommodate your project. I prefer wooden hoops for nearly all my embroidery. Wooden hoops come in a range of different sizes and are easily adjustable to keep fabric tight. For larger projects, scroll frames are ideal because they allow you to roll your fabric as you work.

Tip To avoid hoop lines on your work, remove your work from the hoop every time you take a break from stitching.

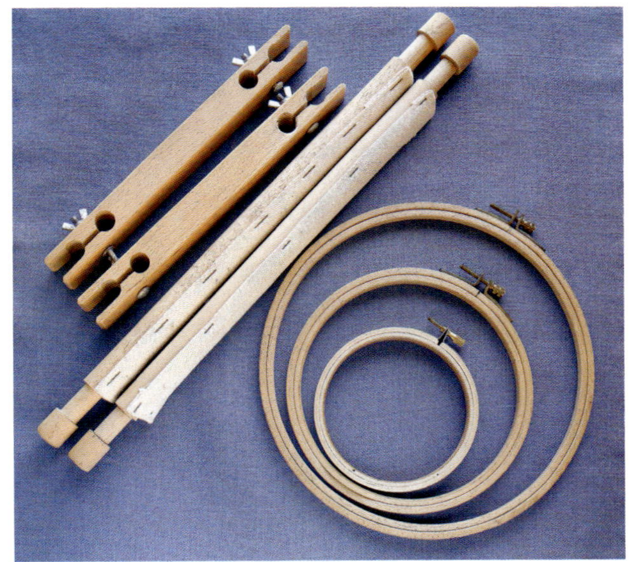

◊ Hoops and frames used in hand embroidery

Scissors

You'll need a good pair of sharp sewing scissors to cut fabric and embroidery scissors to make precise cuts in tight spaces. Embroidery scissors are small with sharp, pointed tips.

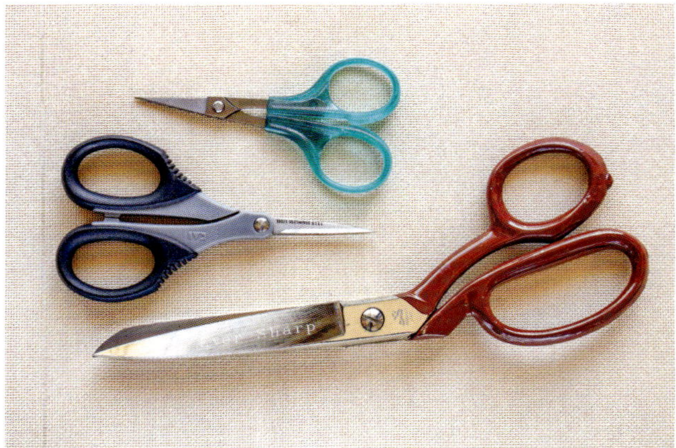

◊ Scissors used in hand embroidery

Plastic Canvas and Stencils

◊ Plastic canvas and stencils that can be used to mark guidelines for stitches

With even-weave fabric, to keep your stitches even, you can simply follow the weave of the fabric.

Plastic canvas is a lightweight plastic that can be purchased in needlework and craft stores in a number of different sizes and shapes. You can cut it easily with scissors, and it is cheap. A small piece tucks easily into your sewing box.

With plain-weave fabrics like denim, you can use the grid created by the plastic canvas to mark a series of dots that will act as a guide for your stitches. When I know the marks will be covered with stitching, I use a permanent pen to mark my guides. I use water-soluble pens or quilters pencils to mark fabric if they will be visible.

◊ Marking fabric using plastic canvas

◊ Marking fabric in circle using plastic canvas

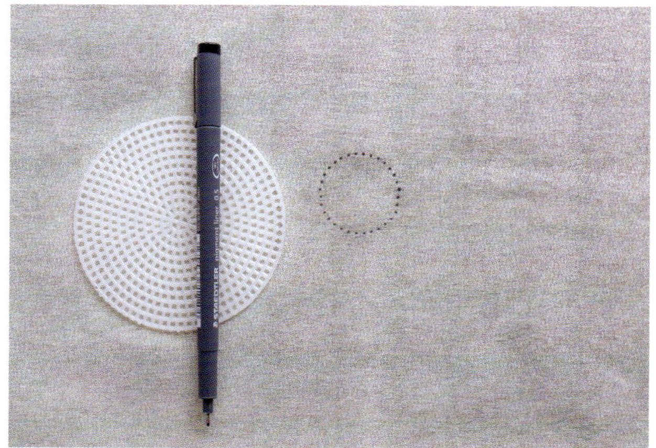

◊ Marked fabric ready to stitch

Not all designs are stitched on a grid. For designs made up of geometric shapes, such as scallops, or organic lines, such as those found in floral sprays, I often use a template to keep my lines even. I regularly use commercial stencils created for graphic designers to mark out geometric shapes. You can also use some scrapbooking stencils or cut your own from quilters template plastic or cardboard.

I have also designed sets of templates for creative embroiderers. They are a mix-and-match system you can use to create hundreds of patterns for your projects. They are easy to use and totally transparent so you can position them easily while seeing what is underneath. They are available from pintangle.com.

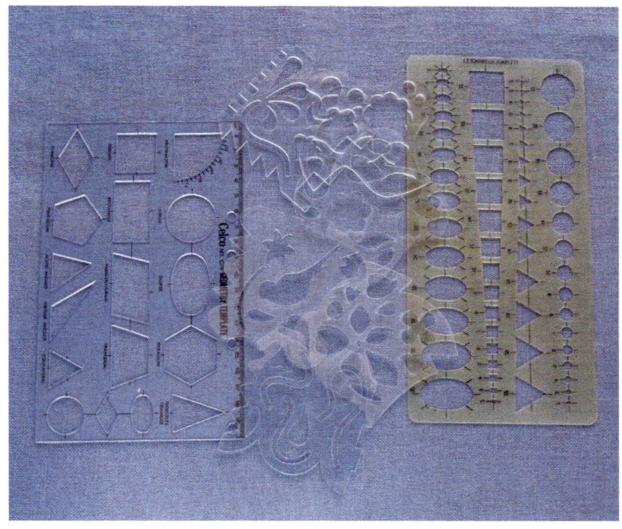

Readily available commercial stencils and the templates I have designed for embroiderers

Fabric-Marking Pens or Pencils

Marking pens and pencils come in numerous different colors and types. You'll find that what works on one piece of fabric will not show up well on another. Color is the main thing that will affect how useful a particular pen or marker is. However, the fabric weave and texture will also influence how visible a mark made by a particular pen or marker will be.

I mainly rely on water-soluble markers, as their marks are washed away with water after stitching.

I use a water barrel brush pen to remove marks made by water-soluble markers. Water barrel brushes are available in art supply stores. They are fine paint brushes with a water reservoir in the brush handle. They are portable and handy because you can dampen just the marked fabric area.

There are air-erasable markers on the market, too. Marks made with these pens disappear after a few hours. With these markers, you have to be able to stitch the design in one sitting.

Chalk pencils and quilters pencils make marks that are designed to be brushed away after stitching. These work well, but some delicate fabrics do not respond well to vigorous brushing.

◇ Water barrel brush (left) and fabric-marking pens and pencils

If I am sure that all the lines of a design will be covered with stitches, I use an artist's fine-point waterproof pen. You must be sure that all the lines of a design will be hidden as once these pens mark the fabric, the marks can't be washed off! The advantage is that they provide a very fine line that is useful for detailed designs.

Design Transfer Supplies

Dressmaker's carbon paper makes it easy to transfer patterns to fabric. It comes in a range of colors, and its success depends on the fabric color, type, and texture. Dressmaker's carbon has two sides. The right side, which is placed face down on your fabric, is the darker side. To transfer a design, place the carbon face down on your fabric. Place your design on top and, if necessary, pin in place. With a pen or stylus, firmly trace your design. Lift your design and dressmaker's carbon off to reveal your design transferred to your fabric.

You can also use a light box or window to trace your design onto your fabric. This method is very easy. Tape your pattern to a window or light box. Place your fabric over the top and tape it in place. Trace your pattern using a water-soluble marker or pen.

Notebook

Develop the habit of jotting down ideas in a notebook. Not only does this help you record ideas, but in doing so, you develop the practice of paying attention to your own good ideas! Note stitch combinations that you think of while sewing. Also, keep your notebook beside you when you are online, and record any good ideas you see.

◊ Small abstract design using sprat's head stitches sprinkled over the area.

The Stitches

Basket-weave Stitch

Basket-weave stitch, also known as *surface darning,* and *visible mending stitch,* is a woven stitch that creates a highly textured area that is great fun to work. Use a hoop—tension is important for a neat result. I've used a different color thread to weave so that you can see what is going on. You can use the same color thread as the foundation stitches, switch colors, or even shade with the weaving thread creating some interesting effects for your contemporary embroidered pieces.

Tip Use a tapestry needle to weave the foundation stitches.

1. Work a series of vertical straight stitches that become the foundation "bars" of your stitch. These foundation stitches will be the stitches you weave on. You can change the spacing of these bars. If you want an open, airy fill, space your foundation stitches further apart. For a solid woven filling, work your vertical stitches close together as I have done.

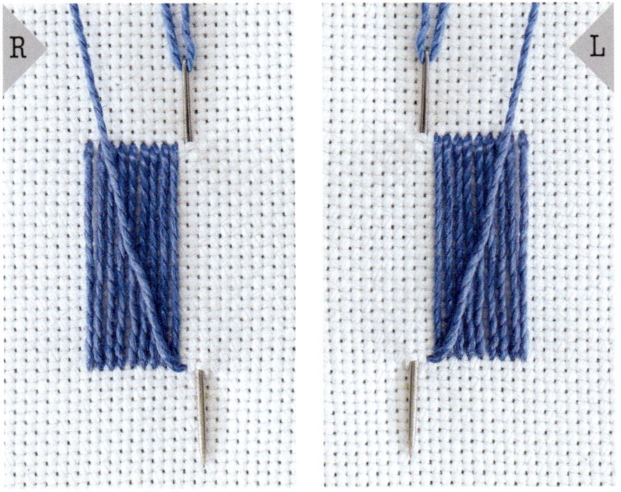

2. Bring your thread out at the base of the foundation stitches. Pass your needle under the first thread, over the second thread, under the third thread, and so on.

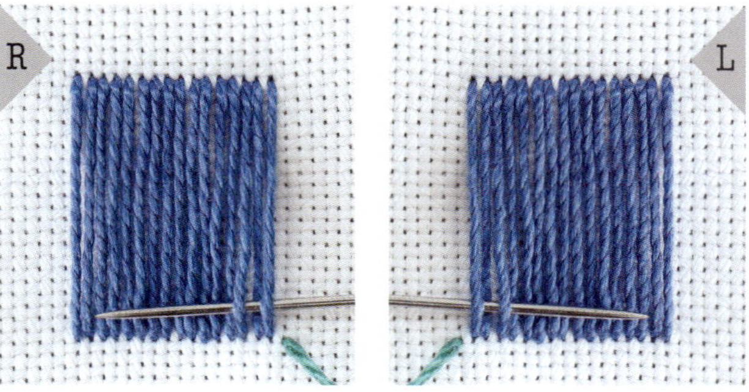

3. Continue in this manner, alternating moving over and under threads, until you reach the other side.

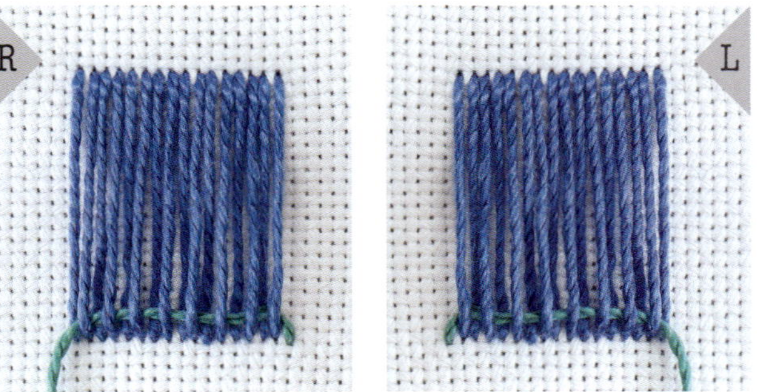

4. Turn your needle and weave a second pass by going over and under the alternating threads from your first pass. In other words, if on the first pass you went under the foundation thread, on the second pass go over the foundation thread.

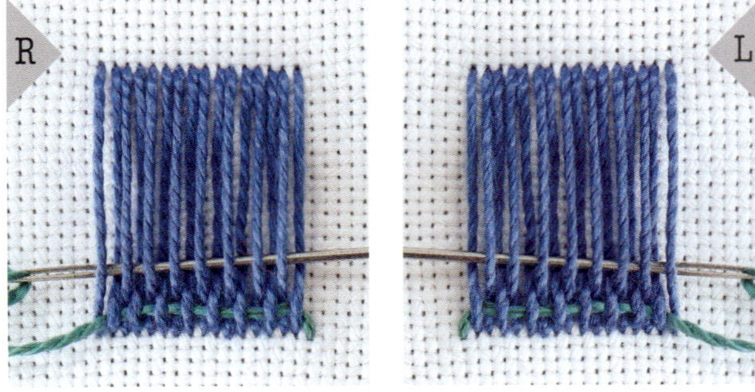

5. Continue to weave up your shape. As you weave, nudge your weaving down with your needle to pack the foundation threads. Do this quite frequently in order to keep an even tension on your weave.

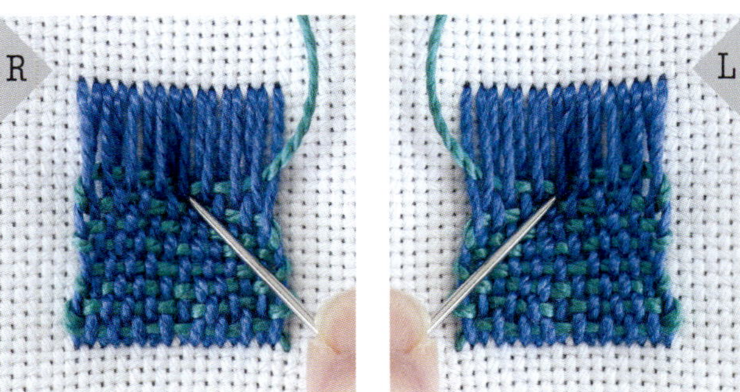

6. Fill your shape to the top. Take your thread to the back and tie off.

◊ Basket-weave stitch using different color and variegated perle cotton #8 threads

Belgian Cross-Stitch

Belgian cross-stitch is a variety of cross-stitch, but a line of straight stitches form along the base. This makes it ideal for borders and edges. Like most stitches in the cross-stitch family, it is worked on a grid.

Work over a grid of two, four, or six threads. In this demonstration, I have worked Belgian cross-stitch over six threads:

1. Imagine a square on your fabric and create a large diagonal backstitch with the needle tip emerging at the bottom of the diagonal.

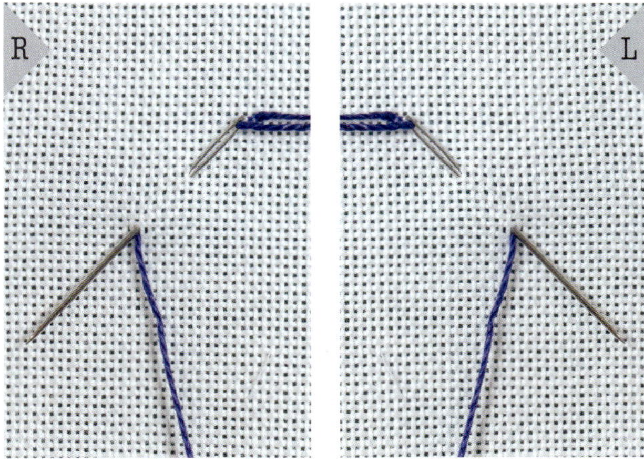

2. Pull your thread through the fabric.

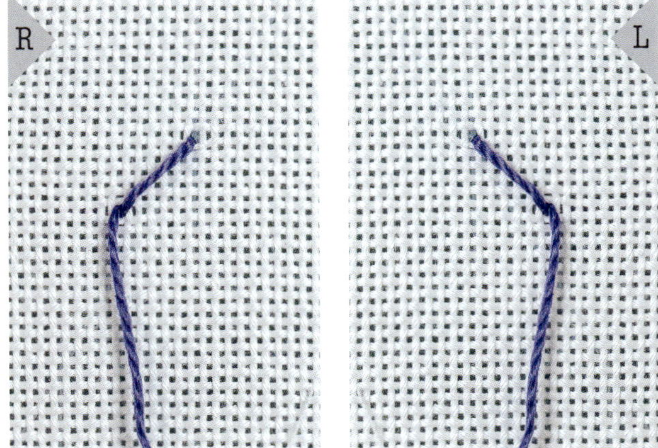

3. Make a horizontal straight stitch along the baseline. Position the needle to emerge in the upper-left corner of the imaginary square.

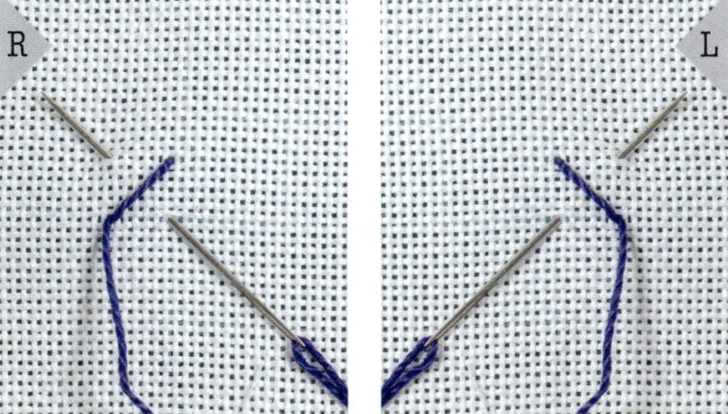

4. Pull the thread through. Imagine a second square next to the first.

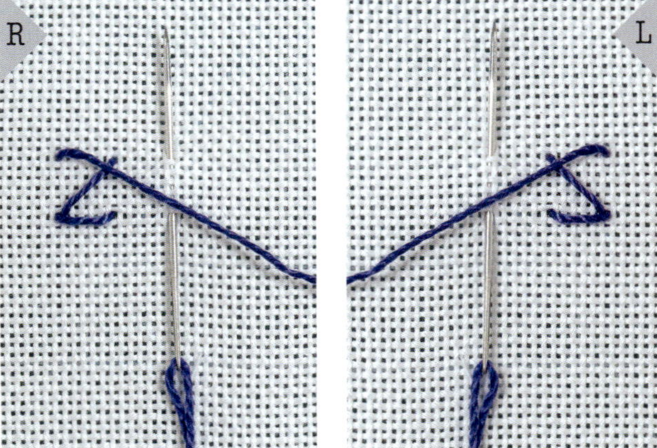

5. Make a long diagonal stitch that emerges on the top and enters the fabric at the bottom of the imaginary square.

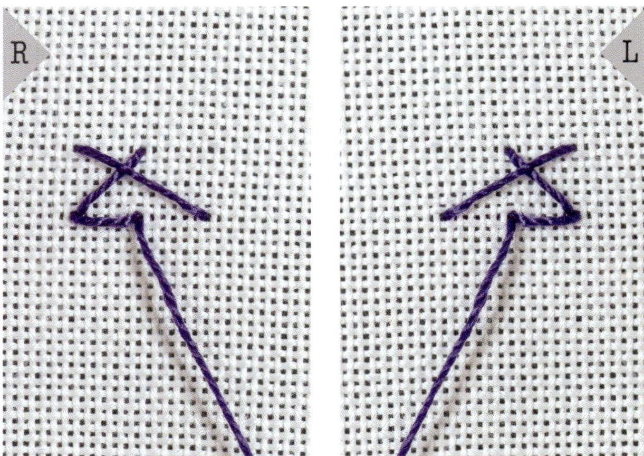

6. Create a shorter diagonal cross-stitch by placing the needle.

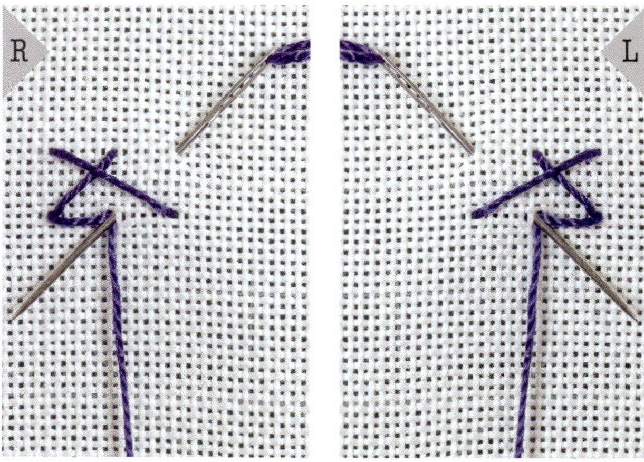

7. Work a second straight stitch that sits on the baseline.

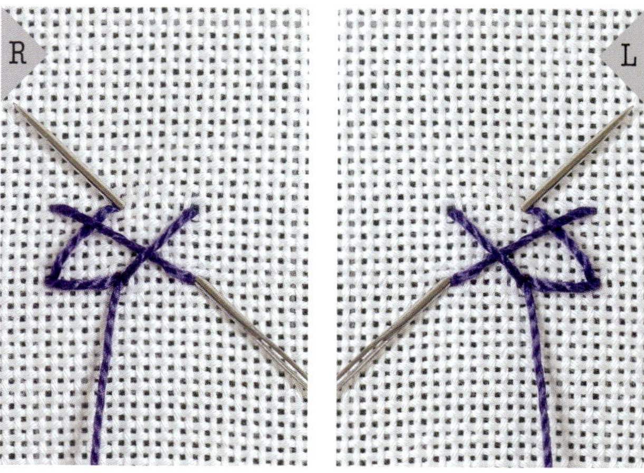

8. Make a second long diagonal stitch.

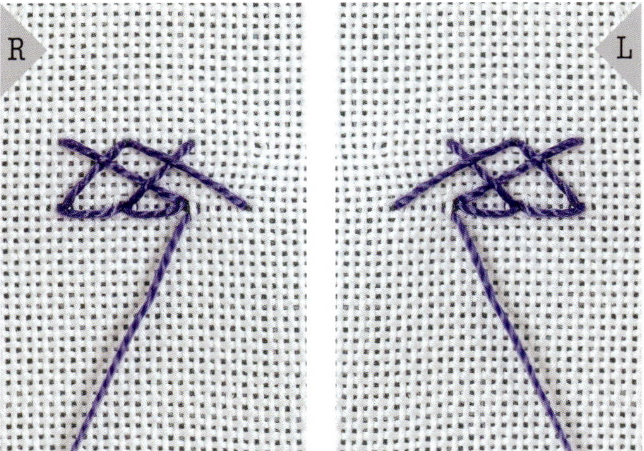

9. Continue in this pattern along the line.

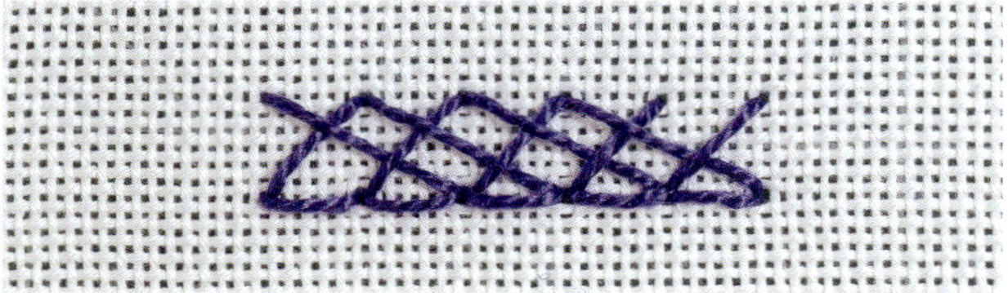

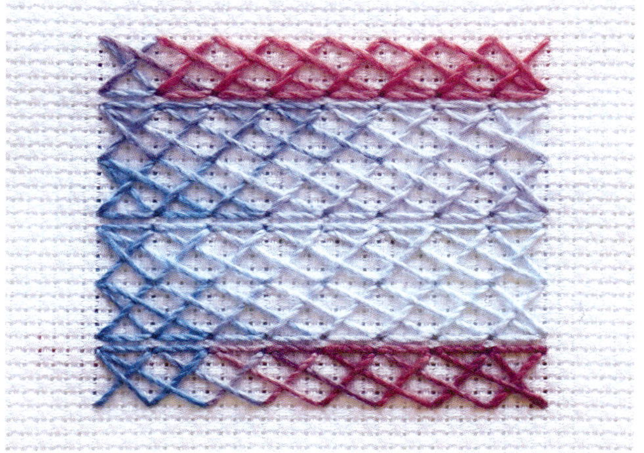

Spacing and your foundation fabric change the look of this stitch. Belgian cross-stitch worked on hand-painted Aida cloth.

◇ Belgian cross-stitch worked in variegated thread

Berwick Stitch

Berwick stitch produces a line that can look similar to buttonhole stitch, but it forms a neat edge. It can be used like buttonhole or blanket stitch but can produce an extra finish to a project.

Berwick stitch is a variety of buttonhole stitch that forms a line of upright stitches, each with a knotted base. Berwick stitch is also known as *looped edge stitch.* You can work it as a decorative stitch or along the edge of an item, and it will follow curves easily. Berwick stitch is equally effective with the knotted edge on the inside or outside of the curve. By changing the length and spacing of the spines, you can create patterns for borders. If you use a thread with a firm twist such, as perle cotton, the texture of the ridge at the base of the spine can be very effective.

Work Berwick stitch along two imaginary parallel lines. If you need to mark the lines on the fabric, use a water- or air-erasable pen.

1. Bring the thread out on the lower line, insert the needle in position on the upper line making a straight downward motion, and then wrap a loop of thread over the top and then to the back of the point of the needle. Pull the needle through the fabric to form a loop.

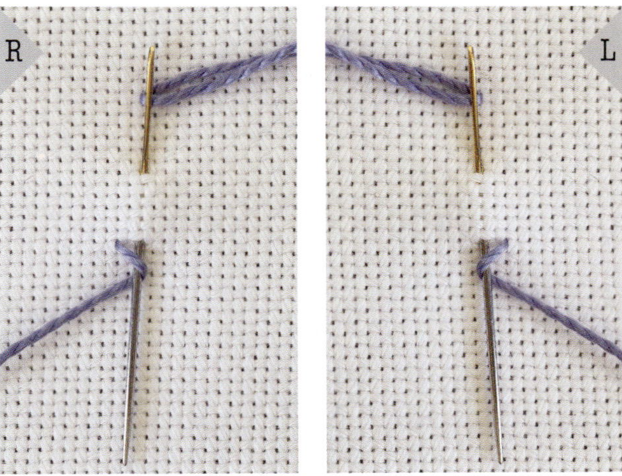

2. Pull the thread snug to tighten the knot slightly before moving to the next stitch.

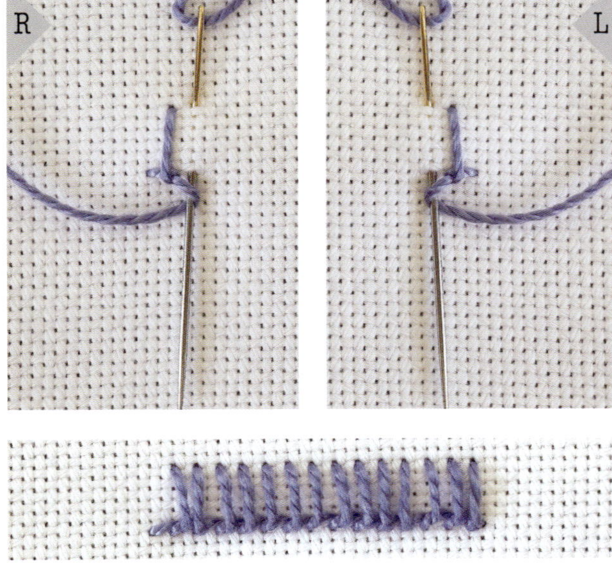

◊ Completed Berwick stitch

◊ Berwick stitch worked in perle cotton #5

Berwick Stitch (Buttonholed)

Berwick stitch is an ideal variety to adapt as it has a knotted base. In this variety, you buttonhole the arm of Berwick stitch, creating a line of bobbles at the base of the stitch. You can use this version to replace buttonhole stitch with a more decorative stitch variety along the edge of an item. It will follow curves easily. If you use a thread with a firm twist, such as perle cotton, the line of bobbles created by this stitch can be very effective. You can change the height and spacing of the spines of the foundation stitches—which means you can create patterns with rows of this stitch.

Work this stitch along two imaginary parallel lines. If you need to mark the line, use a water- or air-erasable pen.

1. Start the stitch as you would Berwick stitch (page 23), bringing the thread out on the lower line. On the upper line, insert your needle to take a bite of the fabric in a straight downward direction. Wrap the thread over the top of the needle, and wrap it back under the point of the needle.

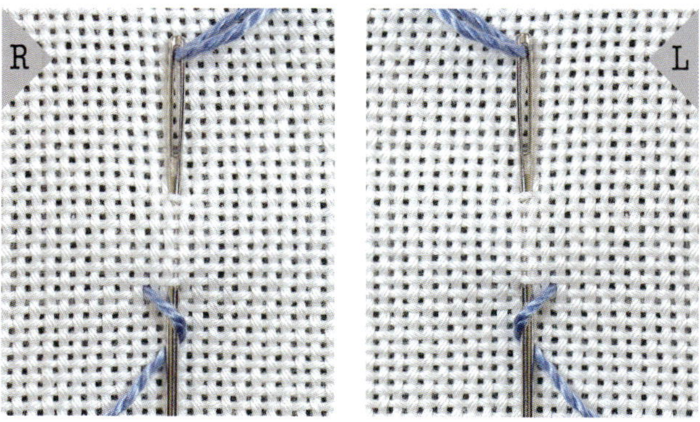

2. Pull the needle through the fabric to form a loop. This is a Berwick stitch and the foundation thread to which you will add buttonhole stitches.

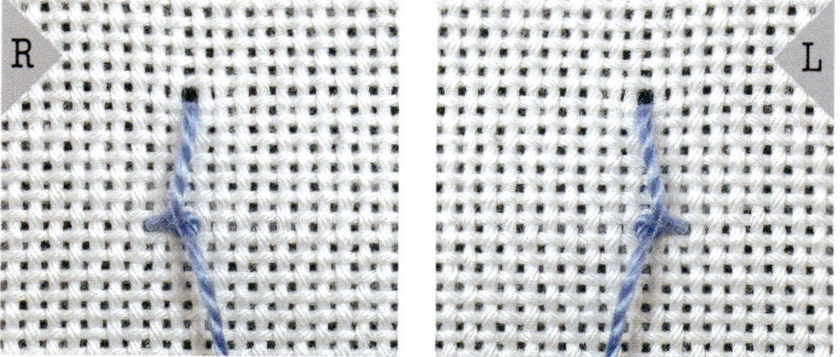

3. Where the thread crosses itself, pass the needle in a diagonal direction under the base of the stitch as shown. Make sure you are passing the needle under the thread, not through the fabric. At this stage, you are creating a knot, which will act as a stop when you snug the stitches against it. Pull the thread through and tighten the knot slightly so that it sits at the base neatly but does not distort the stitch.

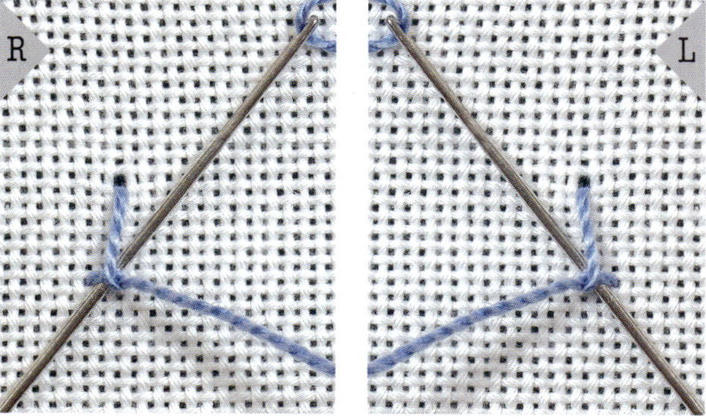

4. Pass the needle under the bar of the stitch and, with the thread wrapped under the needle as shown, pull the needle through. You are buttonholing the bar of the foundation stitch, so take care to work your stitches on the bar of the foundation stitch and do not take the needle through the fabric.

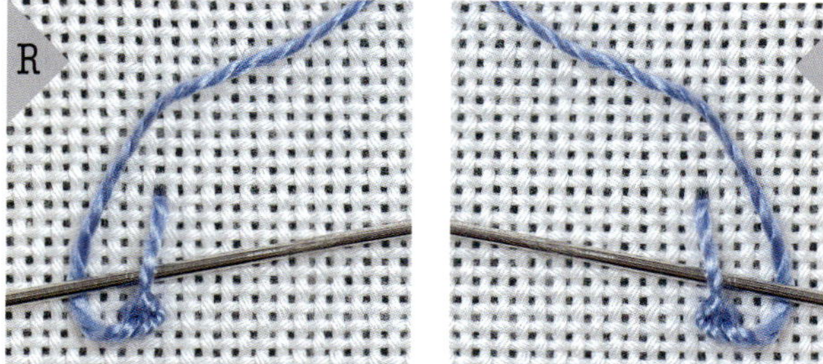

5. Pull the thread through to create the first buttonhole stitch.

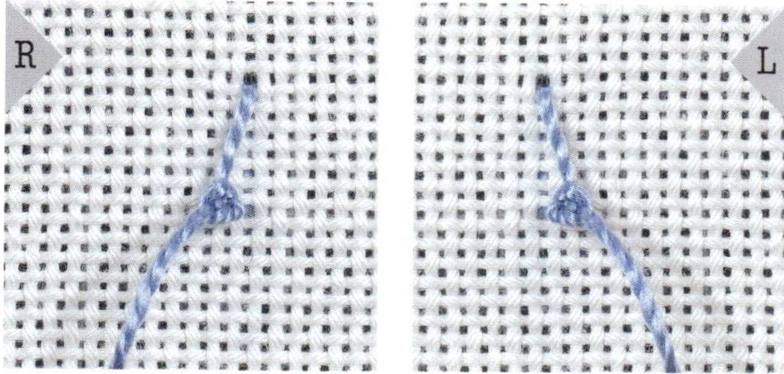

6. Do this for between 3–5 stitches. In each case, make sure you work the stitch next to the previous stitch, not on top of it. Once you have your required number of stitches on the bar, snug them down a little with your needle pushing them along the bar until they sit neatly.

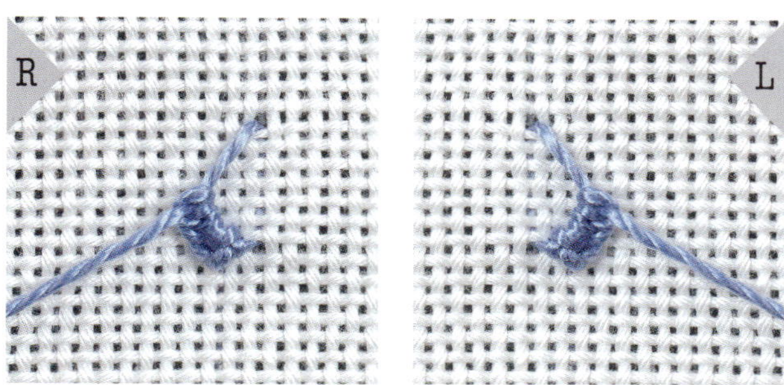

7. To create the next stitch, insert your needle vertically and wrap the thread over your needle as shown. At this point, the bobble will flip over and sit slightly proud. Continue repeating these steps along the line.

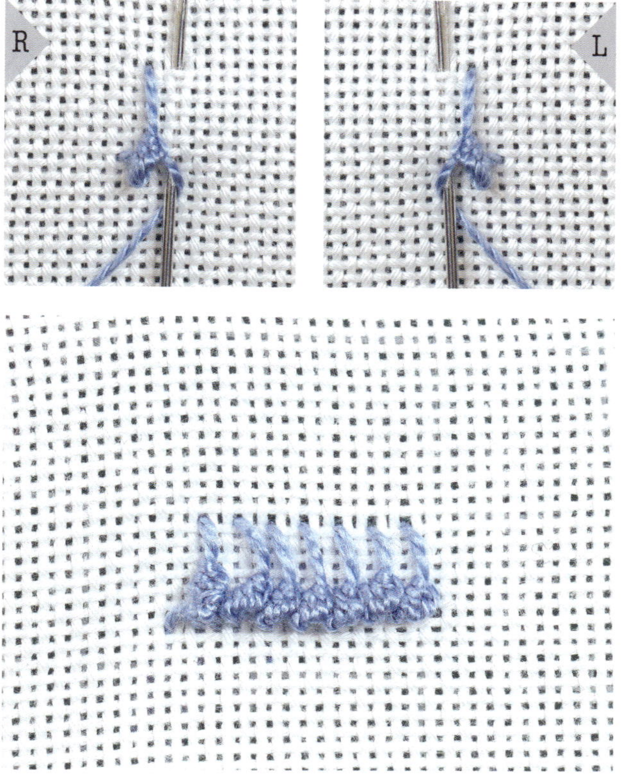

◇ Completed buttonholed Berwick stitch

◇ Buttonholed Berwick stitch worked along seam using hand-dyed perle cotton #8

Bonnet Stitch

Bonnet stitch forms a line of stitches that have upright twisted looped prongs. You can use this stitch on plain- or even-weave fabrics. It is quick and easy to work, looks best in a thread with a firm twist, and will follow a curve well.

Work bonnet stitch between two imaginary lines. If you need to mark the line, use a water- or air-erasable pen.

1. Bring the needle out on the bottom line. Make a small stitch on the top line.

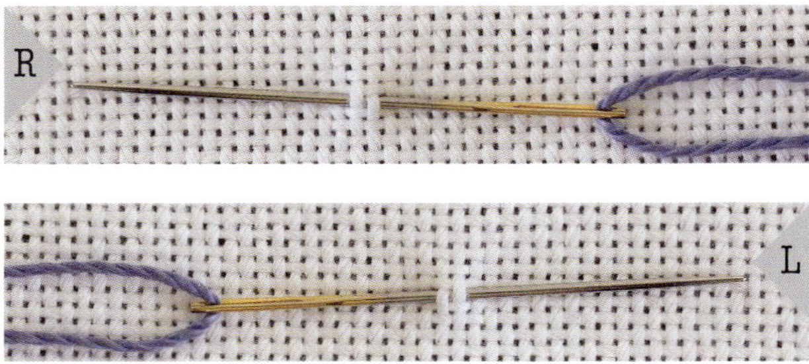

2. Slide the needle under the straight stitch you just made. Do not take the needle through the fabric—just slide it under the stitch. Pull the needle through.

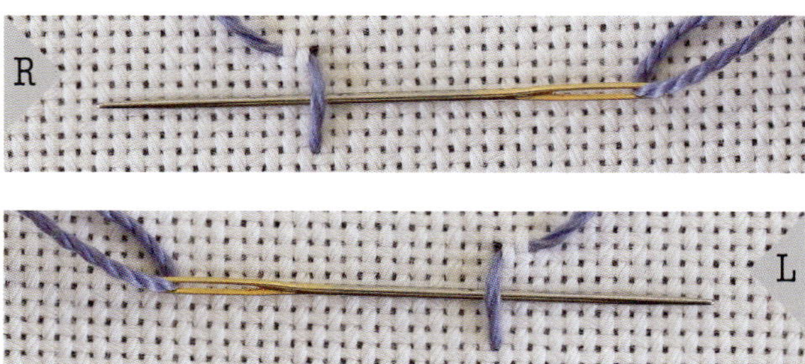

3. On the bottom line, insert the needle where you started to stitch. Wrap the thread under the needle, and pull the needle through.

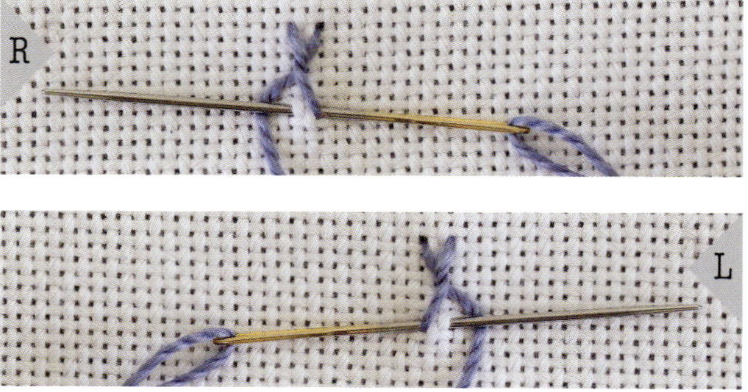

4. Take the needle to the top line, insert the needle a little along the line, and start the next stitch.

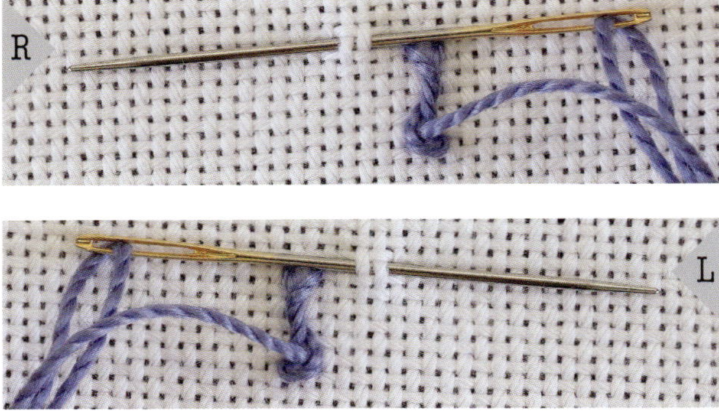

5. Continue along the line to complete the bonnet stitch.

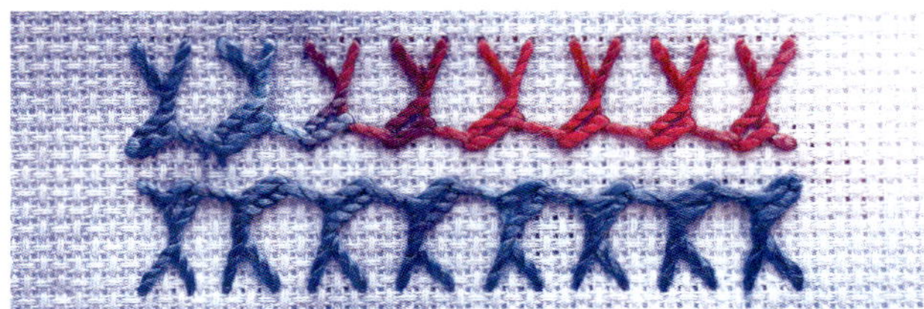

Two lines of bonnet stitch worked back-to-back on hand-dyed Aida cloth.

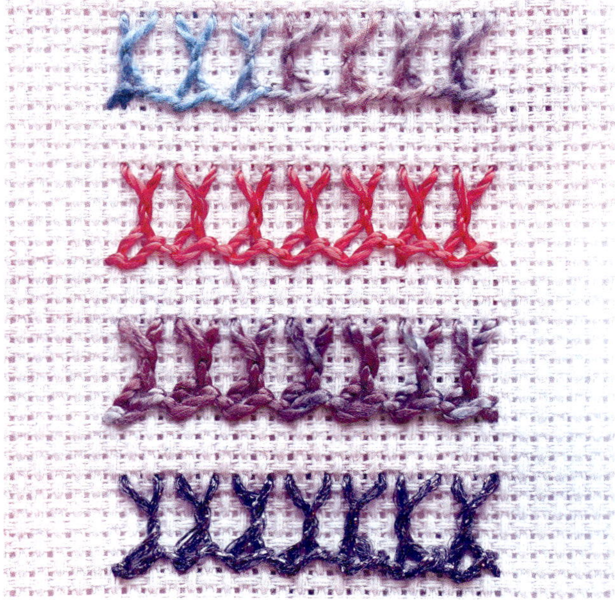

Bonnet stitch worked in different threads. Top line is hand-dyed perle cotton # 8, second line is rayon thread, third line is silk thread, and last line is rayon with metallic thread twisted in it.

Bosnian Stitch

Bosnian stitch is also known as *Bosnian filling, barrier stitch, fence stitch, French fence, Yugoslav border,* and *zigzag Holbein stitch.* This stitch can be used on borders and worked row upon row as a filling.

Work this stitch in two journeys:

1. Work a line of upright straight stitches.

2. Bring your needle out at the end of the line and make a diagonal straight stitch that connects the bottom of one upright straight stitch to the top of the next upright straight stitch.

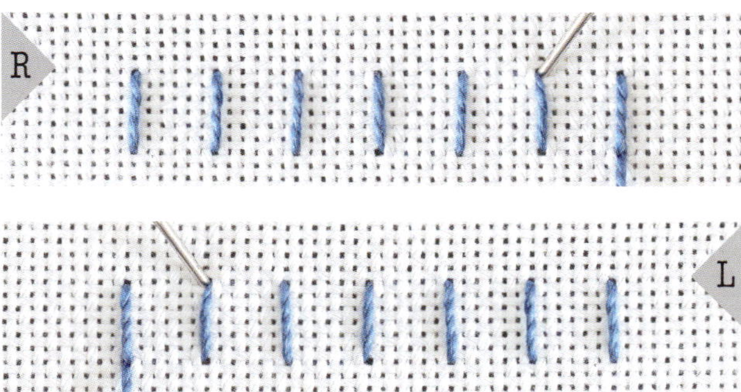

3. Make a return journey with a series of diagonal stitches.

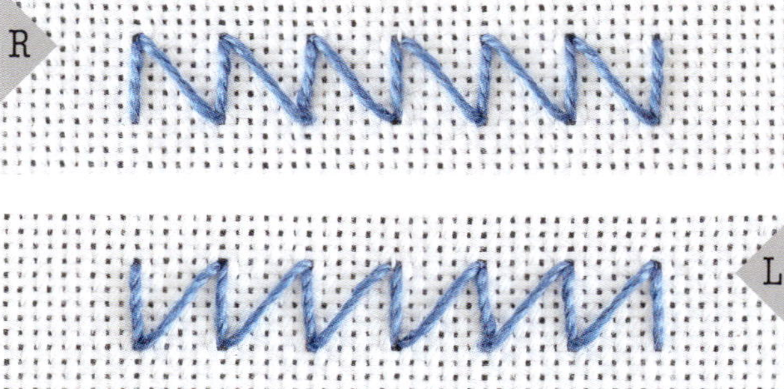

◊ Bosnian stitch worked in variegated perle cotton thread #5

Burden Stitch

Burden stitch is a type of couching that dates back to the Middle Ages when it was used as a grounding stitch, particularly in Italy and Germany. This stitch is named after Elizabeth Burden, the sister-in-law of the nineteenth-century designer William Morris. Miss Burden taught at the UK's Royal School of Needlework and revived this type of couching.

Burden stitch produces a solid filling with an interesting texture. It can be varied by experimenting with both the type of threads you choose to couch on and the threads you use as the couching thread. You can vary the stitches in size and spacing.

Tip: For a Neat Finish With this stitch, it helps to use a hoop and keep your piece under tension.

1. Create a series of evenly spaced, long, straight stitches to be couched down.

2. Bring your couching thread out on the second line as shown. Make a straight stitch.

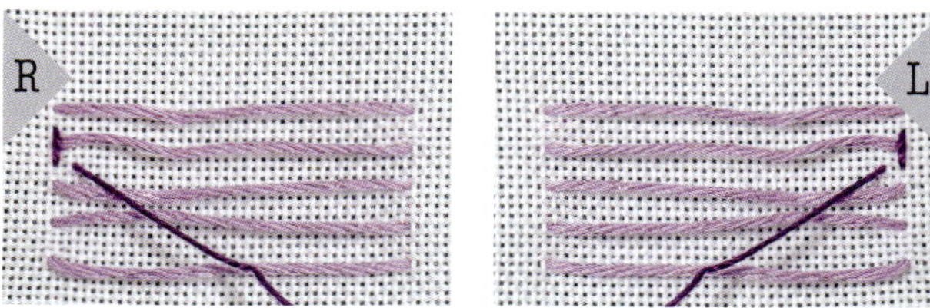

3. Continue along the line, creating evenly spaced straight stitches.

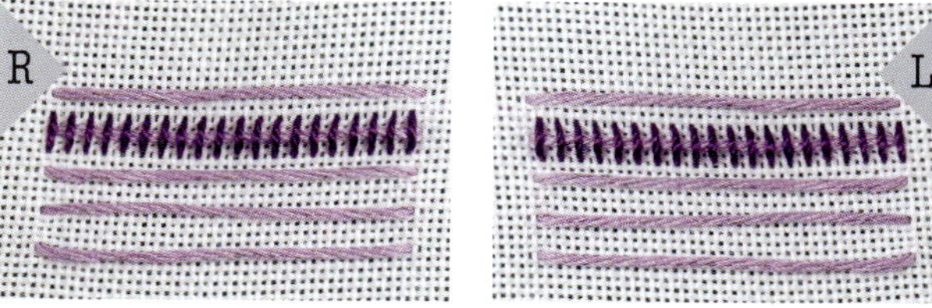

4. On the second journey, fill in the top line with straight stitches that are offset as shown.

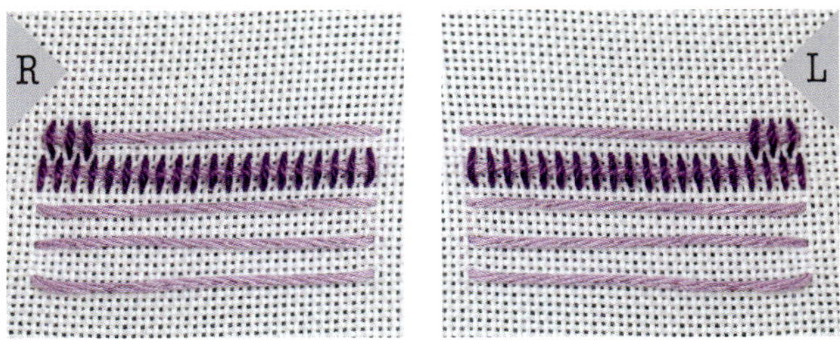

5. Continue, working every second row offset to fill the area.

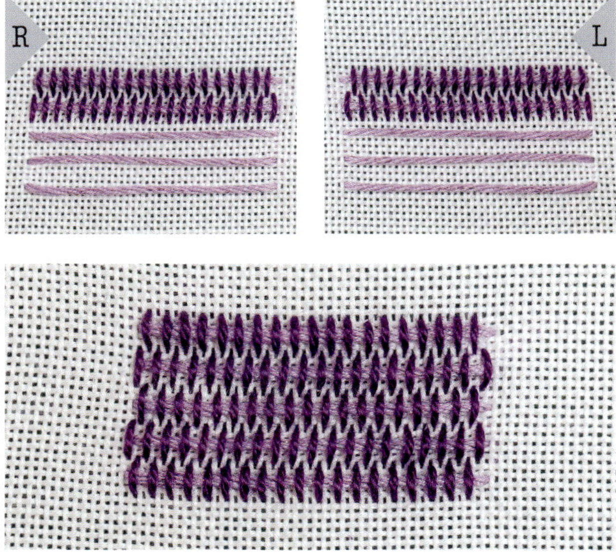

◊ Completed Burden stitch

◊ Burden stitch worked horizontally and vertically

Buttonhole Stitch (Closed Double)

Work closed buttonhole stitch over two parallel guidelines. If you need to mark the fabric, use a water- or air-erasable pen.

1. Bring the thread out on the lower line, insert the needle on the upper line, and make a downward diagonal motion with the needle emerging on the bottom line. With the thread looped under the point of the needle, pull the needle through the fabric.

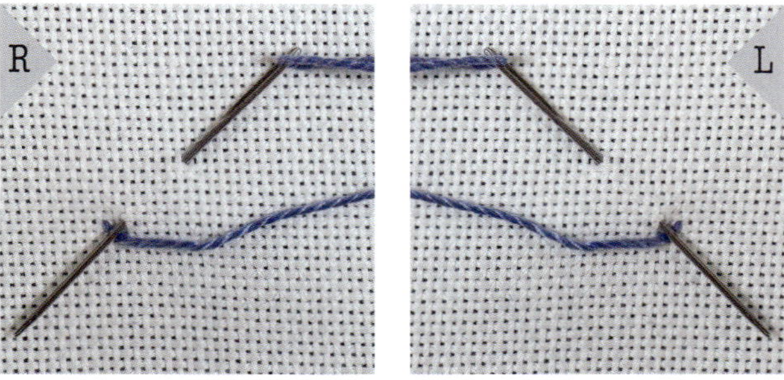

2. The second stitch is made the same way but a little smaller. Bring the thread out on the lower line, and insert the needle on the upper line under the first stitch. Make sure the insertion point is near the first stitchit is not the same insertion point. With the needle on a diagonal, emerge on the bottom line. With the thread looped under the point of the needle, pull the needle through the fabric. The 2 stitches should lay parallel to each other.

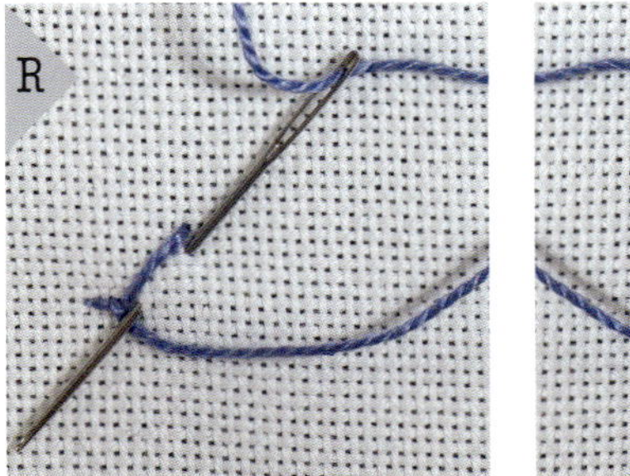

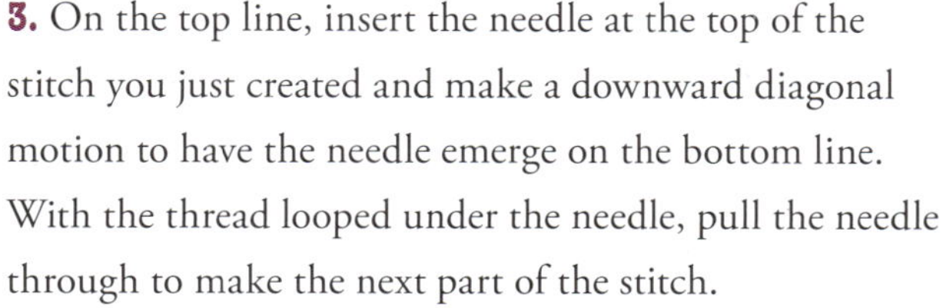

3. On the top line, insert the needle at the top of the stitch you just created and make a downward diagonal motion to have the needle emerge on the bottom line. With the thread looped under the needle, pull the needle through to make the next part of the stitch.

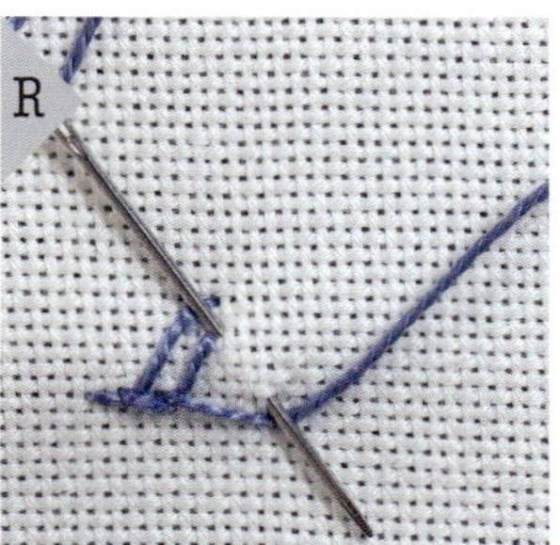

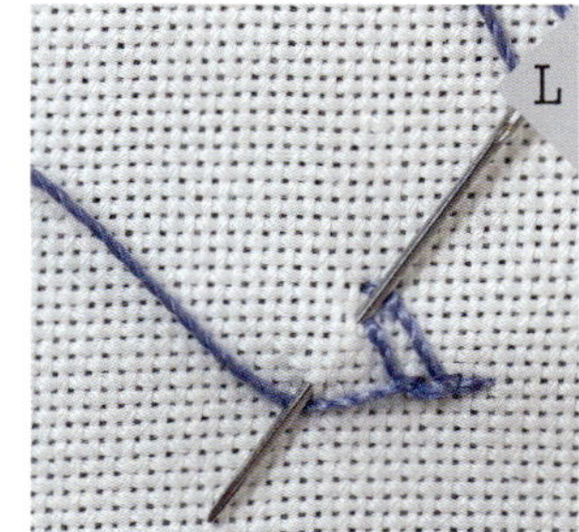

4. On the top line, insert the needle at the top of the stitch you first created and make a downward diagonal motion to have the needle emerge on the bottom line. With the thread looped under the needle, pull the needle through to make the next part of the stitch.

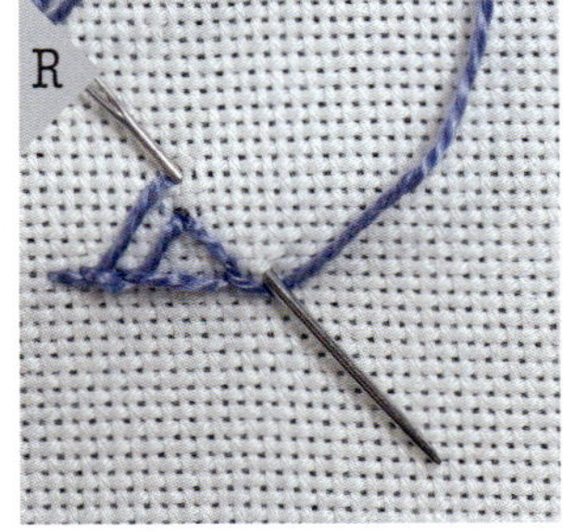

5. This completes the first unit of closed double buttonhole. Continue this process, sewing along the line.

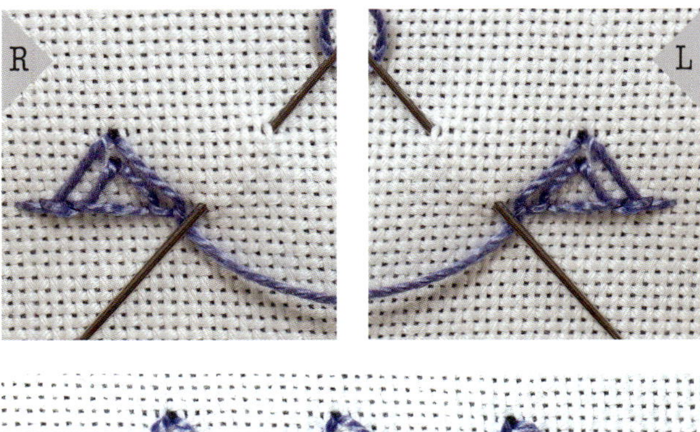

◊ Double closed buttonhole stitch complete

Two lines of double closed buttonhole stitch worked back-to-back.

Double closed buttonhole stitch is an interesting variation on closed buttonhole (page 183). It is easily worked and can be used as an edging or worked in multiple rows to create a patterned border.

Double closed buttonhole stitch used along seam in slow-stitch project

Buttonhole Stitch (Detached)

Detached buttonhole produces a lacy fabric that stands free of the foundation fabric; it can be used in 3-D embroidery. You can work this stitch over forms. With this stitch, you are actually constructing a layer of fabric over the foundation fabric, adding texture or high relief to a piece.

It is important to work this stitch at an even tension, so stretch the fabric in an embroidery hoop. In order to not pierce the foundation threads and fabric, use a blunt needle such as a tapestry needle of suitable size.

To work the stitch, you first lay down a line of foundation stitches. You can use any linear stitch that you can attach buttonhole stitches to, most commonly backstitch and chain stitch. When choosing your foundation stitch, think about how that stitch would follow the shape you want to create. Create shapes by adding and subtracting stitches as you would with crochet or knitting. To make the shape flair out, add stitches. Skip a stitch to make the shape pinch inward. These stitches should be worked closely together. For the best results, use a firm thread.

1. Work a line of backstitch.

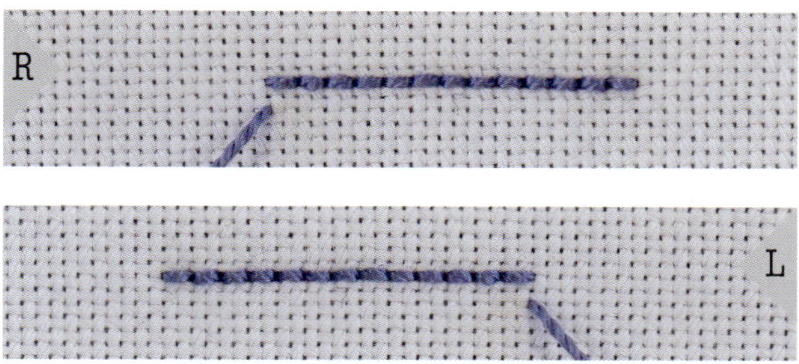

2. Bring your thread out just below the start of your foundation line of stitches. Pass your needle under the first stitch and, with the thread wrapped under the point of the needle, pull your needle through to produce your first freestanding buttonhole stitch.

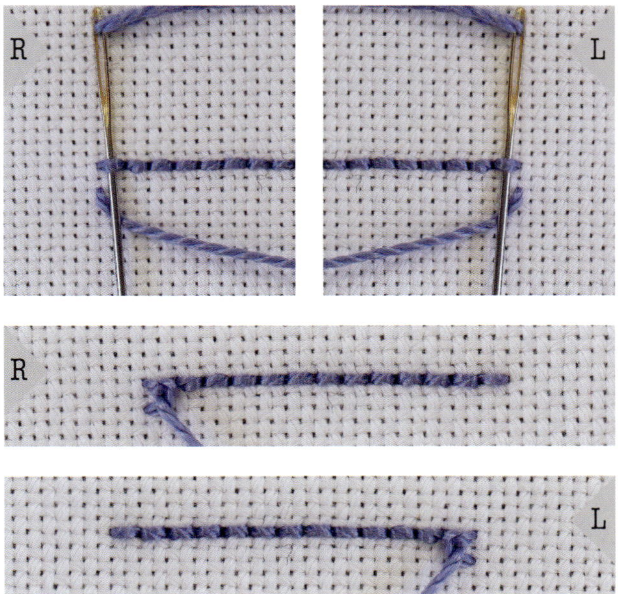

3. Continue along the line. At the end of the line, take your needle to the back of the fabric. If you want your piece to be totally 3-D, simply turn your work and continue to work row upon row. If you want a pocket-like shape, take your thread to the back and bring it out at the start of the row.

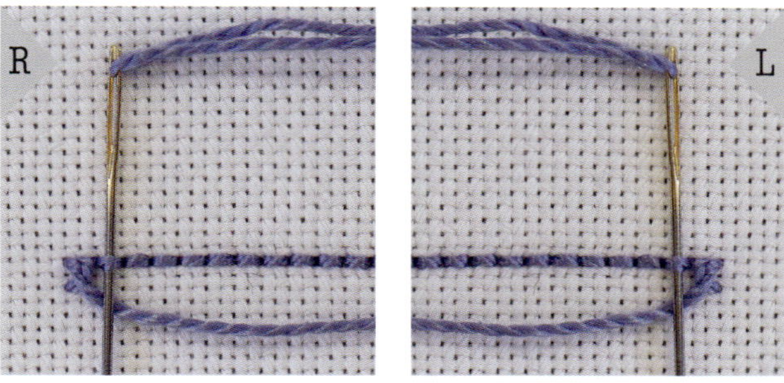

4. Bring your needle out at the start of the row and work a second row of detached buttonhole stitches into the loops of the first row. With each row, stitch without entering the foundation fabric.

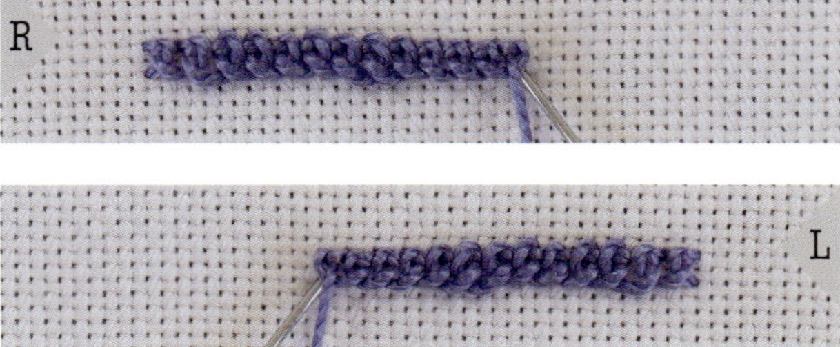

5. Continue in this manner, working from side to side, until you have filled the shape required.

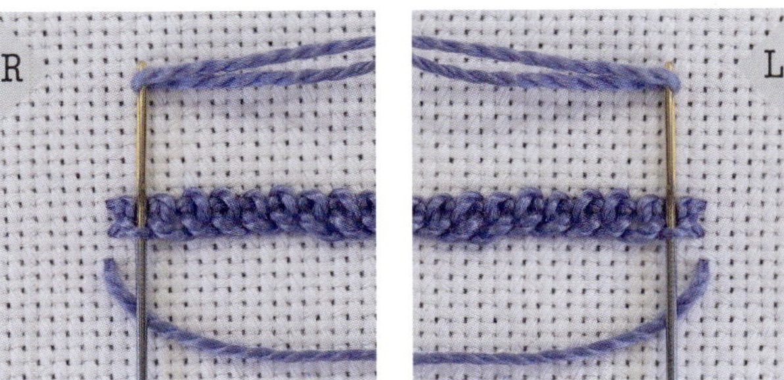

6. To create shapes in this stitch, you increase by working 2 stitches into 1 loop or decrease by not working a stitch into the loop at the end of each row.

◊ Completed detached buttonhole stitch

To produce a neat edge, the final row should be worked in a slightly tighter tension. When complete, use small straight stitches to secure the edge to the foundation fabric.

This sample is attached at the edges to create a pocket. However, you can work detached buttonhole in a free-form manner by building row upon row without taking the thread to the back at the edge of the shape. Another technique with this stitch is to work it over padding, such as felt. Cut the padding to shape but slightly smaller than the area you wish to cover. Stitch the padding into position before working detached buttonhole over the shape until it is covered.

◊ The base of these abstract flowers is worked in detached buttonhole stitch.

Buttonhole Band (Knotted)

In order to demonstrate this stitch, I have worked the steps in different color threads. Traditionally, you work this stitch in the same color thread, but if you want to play with various threads, you can. Many novelty yarns look good with this stitch. Fine metallic braids and threads also produce interesting effects. The only constraint is that the thread has to behave itself enough to be knotted twice and still sit proud.

If you have tension problems with this stitch, use an embroidery hoop.

1. Start this stitch by working a foundation of evenly spaced straight stitches.

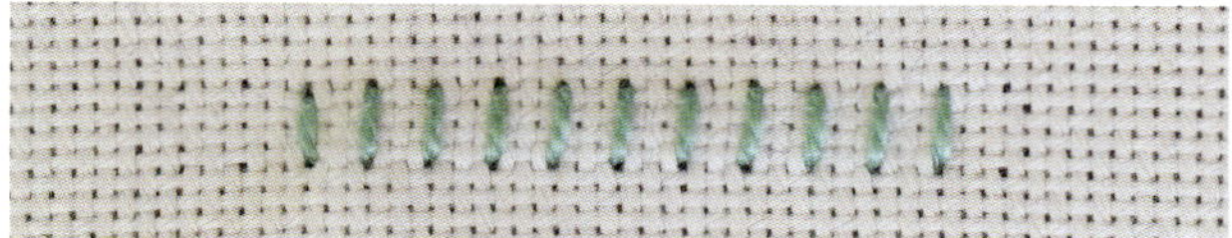

2. Bring your needle out at the base of the first foundation bar. Tuck the needle under the bar and wrap the thread under the needle as you would if you were working a buttonhole stitch. Make sure the needle is pointing downward as shown. Take the needle through.

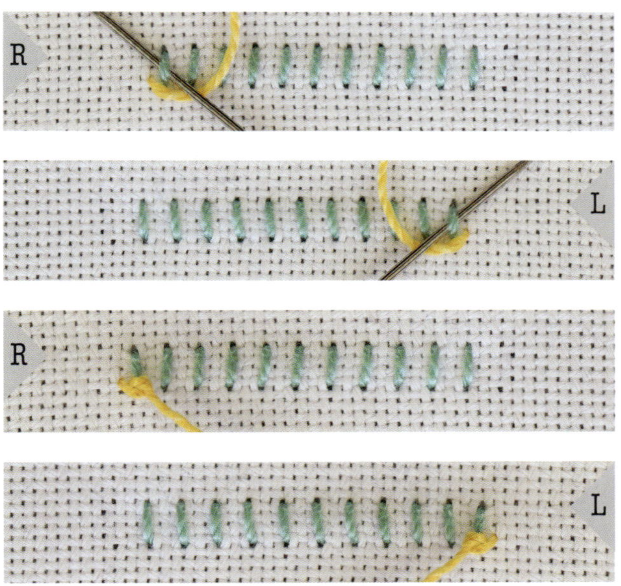

Note that you are not stitching through the fabric. You are working a stitch on a foundation bar.

3. Pass the needle through the loop on the bar that you have just created. Wrap the thread under the needle. Pull the needle through to create a second loop. It looks like a little knot on the bar; this is what causes the ridge along the stitch.

4. Move to the next bar and repeat this process along the line. Try not to distort the foundation stitch by pulling the knot too tight.

You now have the first side of the stitch. You can use the stitch like this as a half band.

5. Take your needle to the top of the line of foundation stitches. Repeat the process, only this time point your needle up as you make the loops.

◊ Completed knotted buttonhole band

◊ Knotted buttonhole band worked in variegated orange-red perle cotton #8 used in wall piece

Buttonhole Stitch (Laced Version 1)

There are many versions of laced buttonhole stitches. Lacing stitches is a great way to introduce more texture, particularly if you incorporate novelty yarns. When lacing, use a tapestry needle so you do not split the foundation stitches as you lace.

1. Start with 2 lines of buttonhole stitch worked in a pattern of 3 short stitches and 1 longer stitch. Work these rows face-to-face.

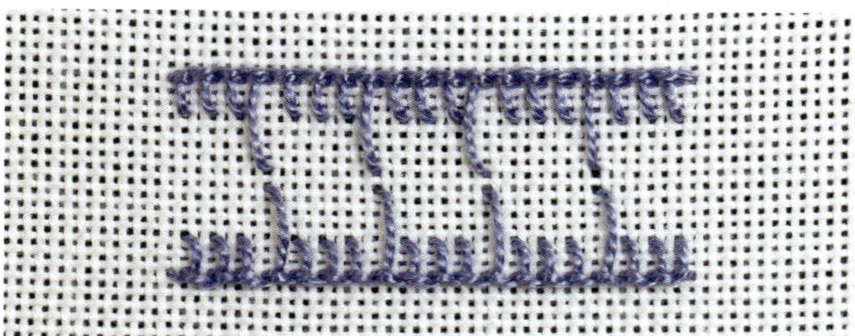

2. With your needle threaded with your lacing thread, bring it out on the bottom line. Thread your needle under the first 4 stitches. Note that you are not taking your needle through the fabric. Pull your needle through.

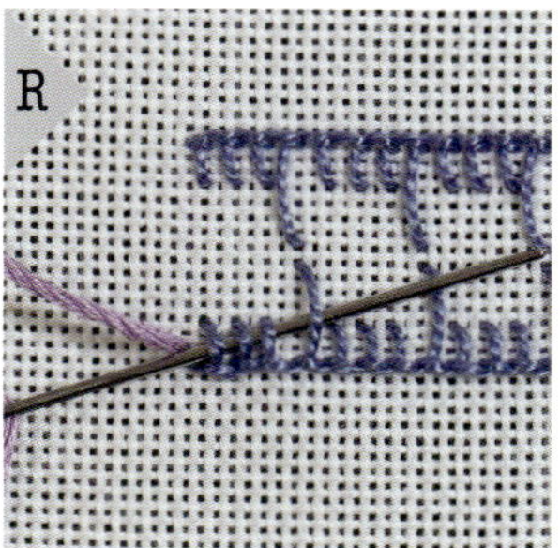

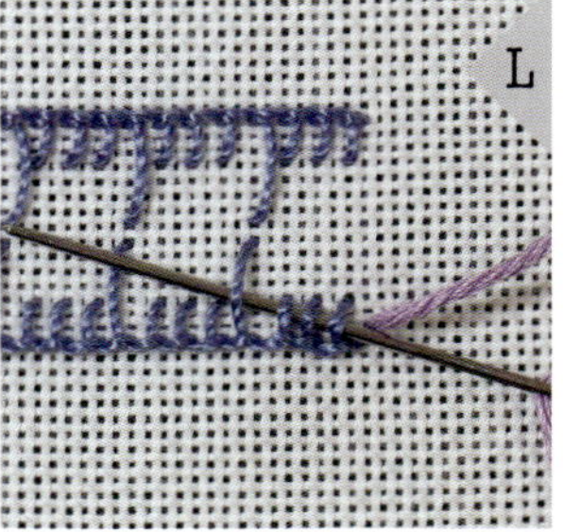

3. Take your needle to the top line of buttonhole stitches and pass it under the longest stitch. Pull your needle through. Do not pull your lacing stitches too tight.

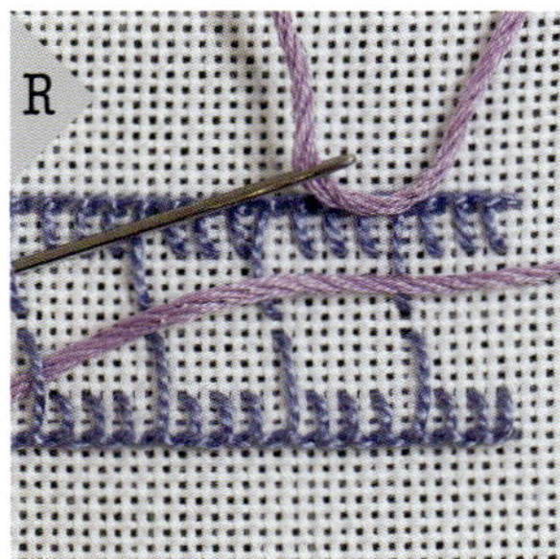

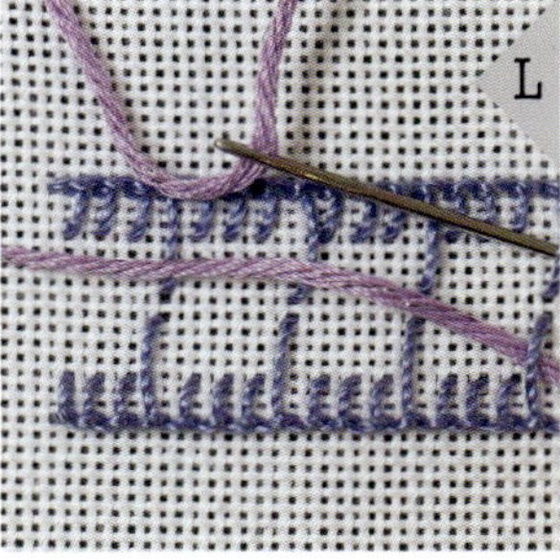

4. Take your needle to the bottom line of buttonhole stitches and pass it under the longest stitch plus the next 3 short stitches. Pull your needle through. Do not pull your lacing stitches too tight.

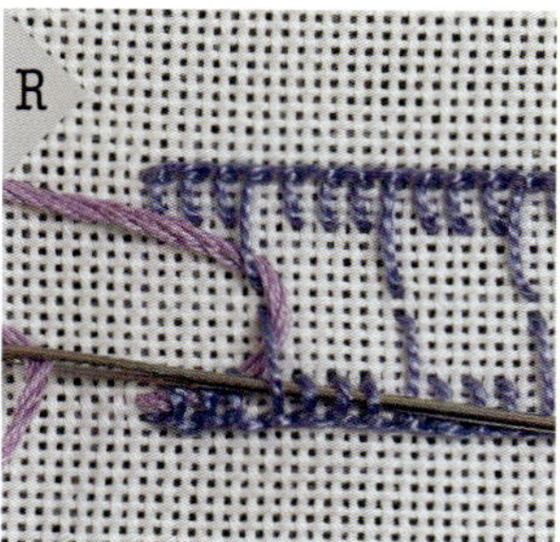

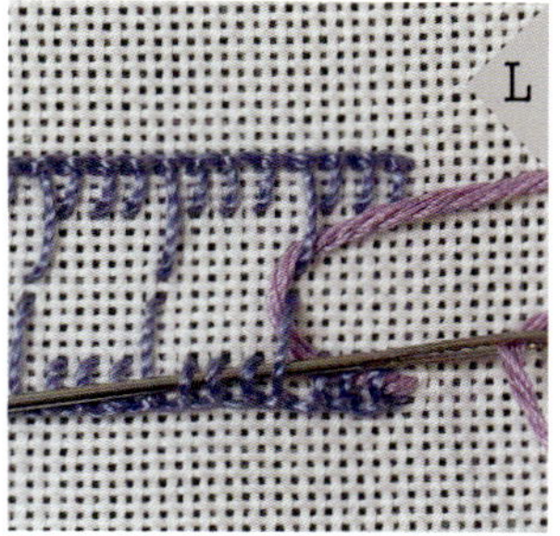

5. Continue this way along the line. You can lace just the base of this stitch.

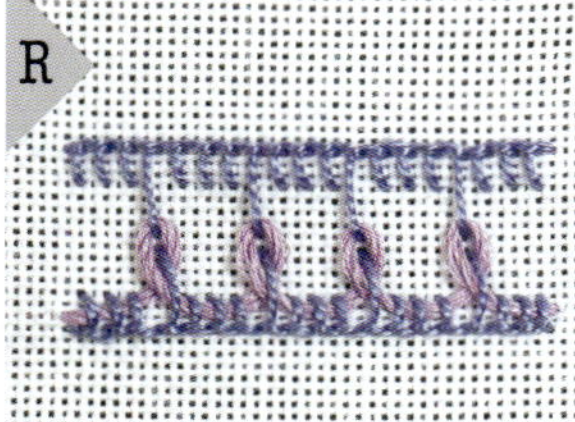

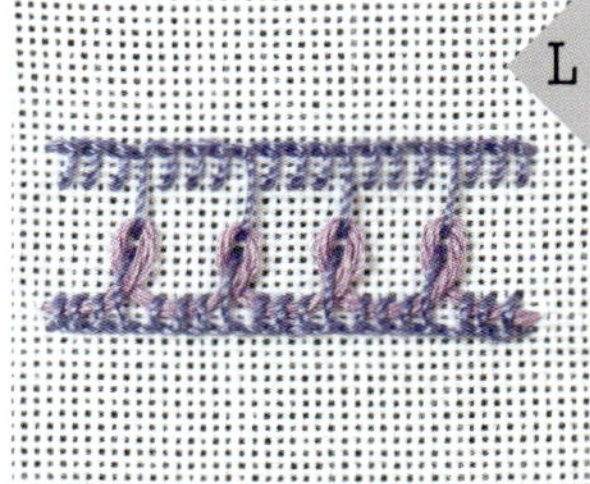

Or you can turn your work and lace the top line of stitches the same way.

Sample of laced buttonhole stitch version 1 worked with both foundation stitch and lacing done in hand-dyed perle cotton #5

Buttonhole Stitch (Laced Version 2)

This version of laced buttonhole has a foundation of two lines of buttonhole stitches. This variety is sometimes mistakenly called *raised Cretan stitch*. Your lacing thread can be the same as your buttonhole stitches or a thread of a contrasting color or texture. When lacing, use a tapestry needle so you do not split the foundation stitches as you lace.

1. Start by working 2 lines of buttonhole stitch a little apart and back-to-back.

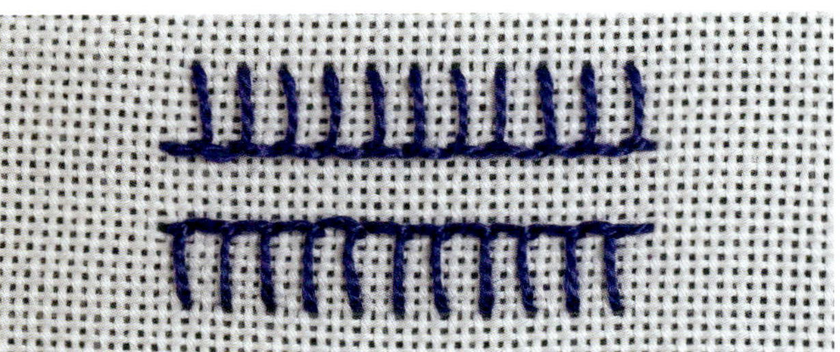

2. Bring your needle out between the 2 lines of buttonhole stitches and pass it under the base of the first buttonhole stitch on the lower line.

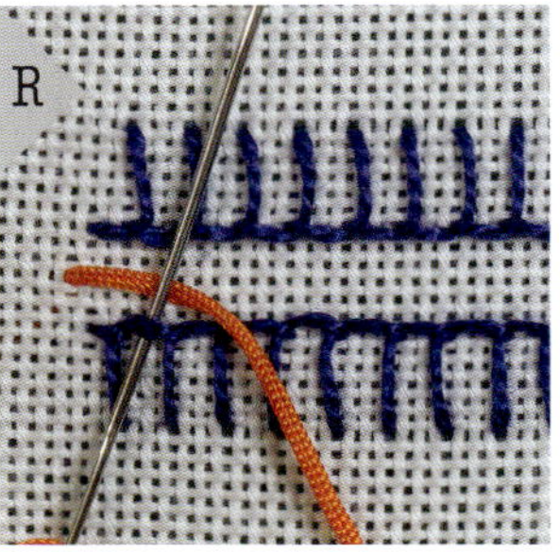

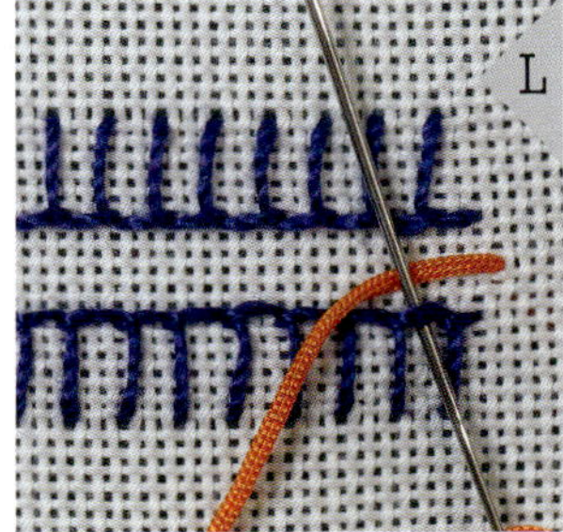

3. Pull your thread through. Note that you do not pass the needle through the fabric.

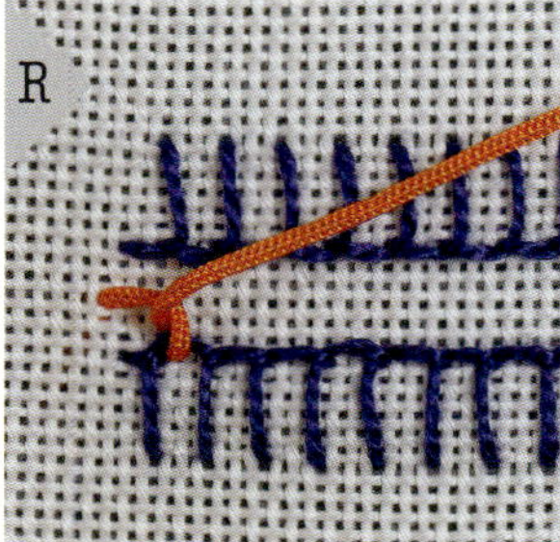

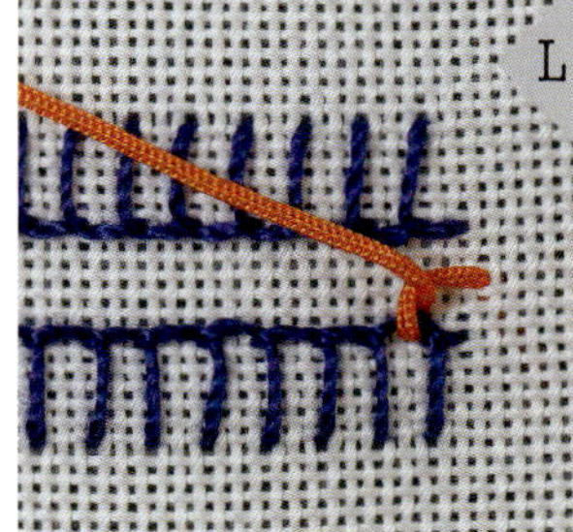

4. Take your needle to the top line of buttonhole stitches and, with the point downward, pass your needle under the first buttonhole stitch. With your thread under the needle, pull your needle through. Do not pull too tight.

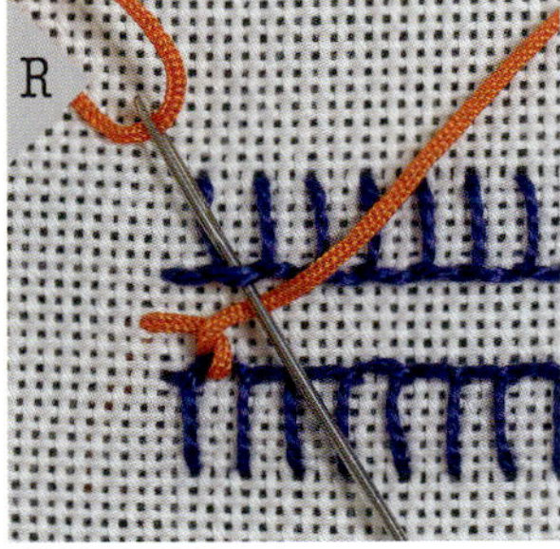

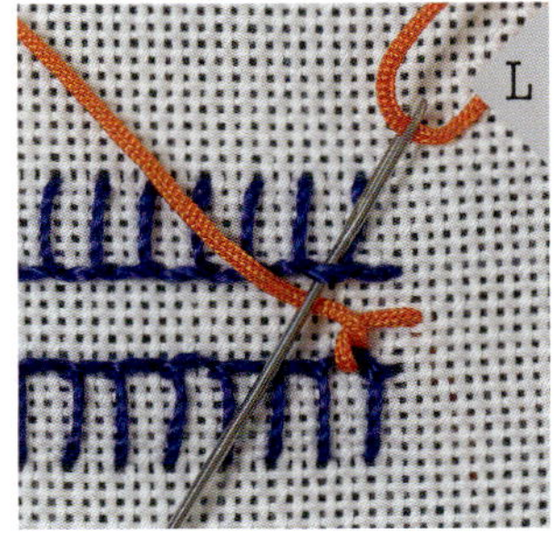

5. Continue in the same manner along the line.

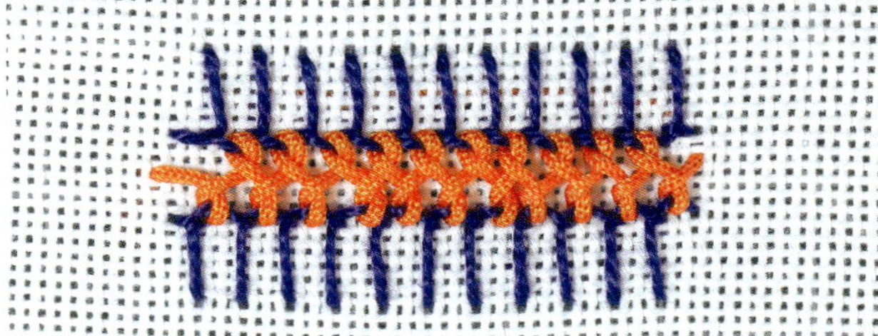

◊ Laced buttonhole worked in perle cotton #5

Buttonhole Stitch (Laced Version 3)

This version of laced buttonhole also has a foundation of two lines of buttonhole stitches. When lacing, use a tapestry needle so you do not split the foundation stitches as you lace.

1. Start by working 2 lines of buttonhole stitch a little apart and back-to-back.

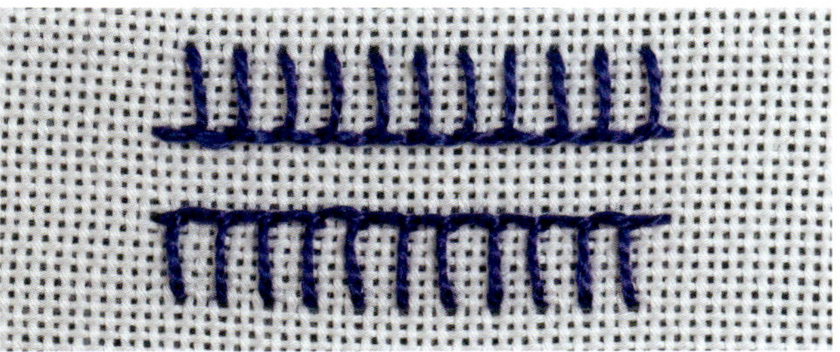

2. Bring your needle out between the 2 lines of buttonhole stitches. Pass your needle under the base of the second buttonhole stitch and then under the base of the first buttonhole stitch on the upper line. Pull your thread through so that it forms a loop. Do not pull too tight.

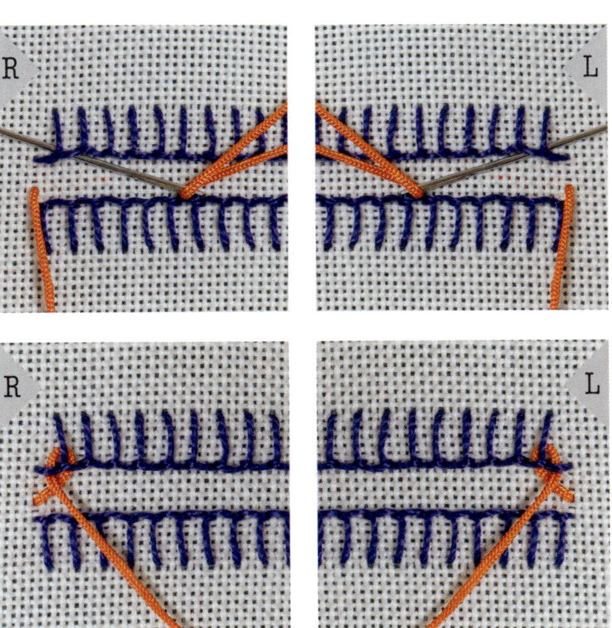

3. Take your needle to the bottom line, pass your needle under the base of the second buttonhole stitch and then under the base of the first buttonhole stitch. Pull your needle gently through.

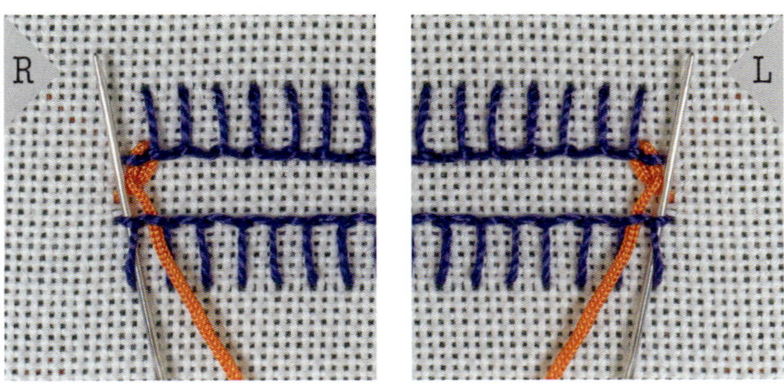

4. Continue along the line.

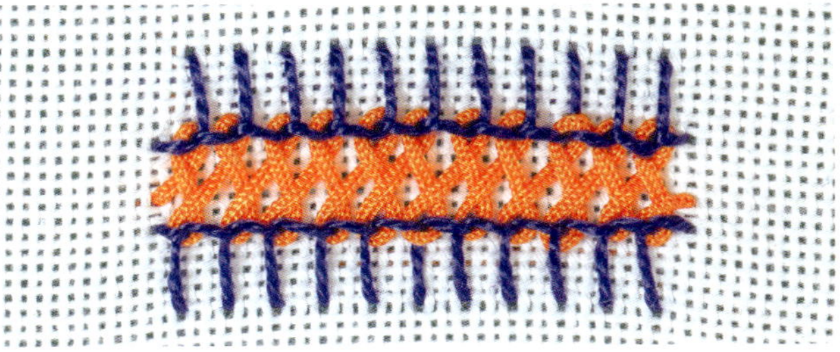

◇ Laced buttonhole worked in perle cotton #5

Buttonhole Stitch with Picot Bullion

Picot bullions can be added to buttonhole stitches. You usually see them spaced at regular intervals along a line.

1. Start with a line of buttonhole stitches. When you reach the point where you want to add a picot, start with the thread under the needle.

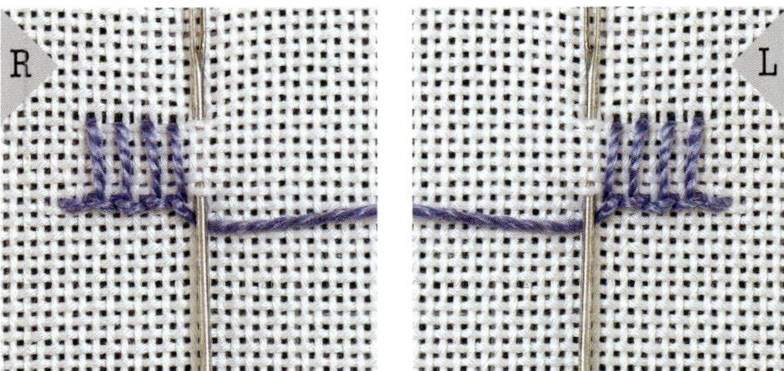

2. Wrap the needle 2 or 3 times.

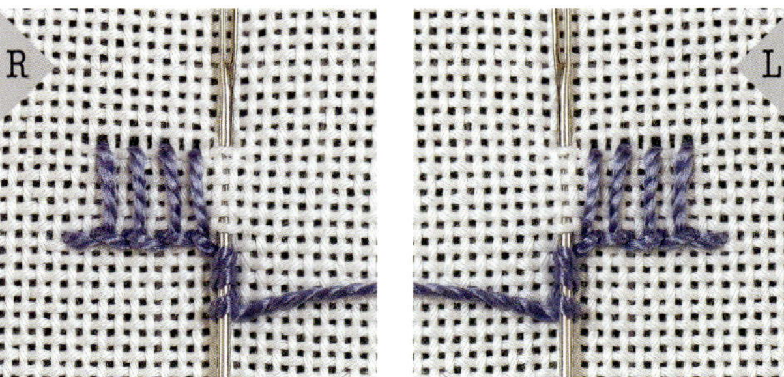

3. Nudge the knot wraps so they are snug to the buttonhole and pull the thread through in a downward motion. You may need to hold the needle flat to the fabric with your thumb as you pull through.

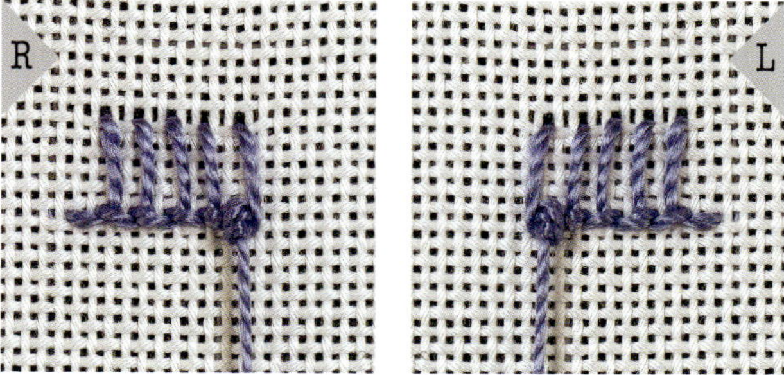

Tip If you find the bullions bunch up on themselves, use a straw or milliners needle, which has an eye and shaft of the same width; this makes sliding the wrapped bullion knot along the needle easy.

4. Slide your needle from left to right under the last stitch and, keeping the thread under the needle, pull it through. If you need to push the knot up snugly, do so with either your needle or thumb. Continue along the line, working the next section of buttonhole.

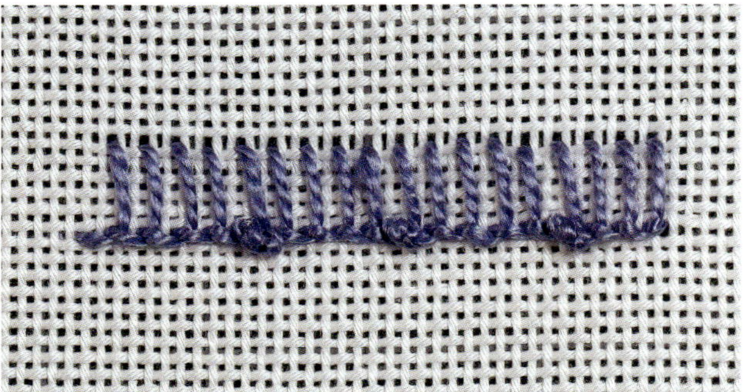

Buttonhole Stitch with Picot Chain

Space the picot knots as required along a line of buttonhole stitches. Usually the buttonhole stitches are worked close together, as an edging stitch. For the purposes of demonstration, I have spaced them a little farther apart so you can see how the picot stitches are worked.

1. Start with a line of buttonhole stitches, when you reach the point where you want to add a picot, slide your needle under the base thread of the last buttonhole stitch but not through the fabric.

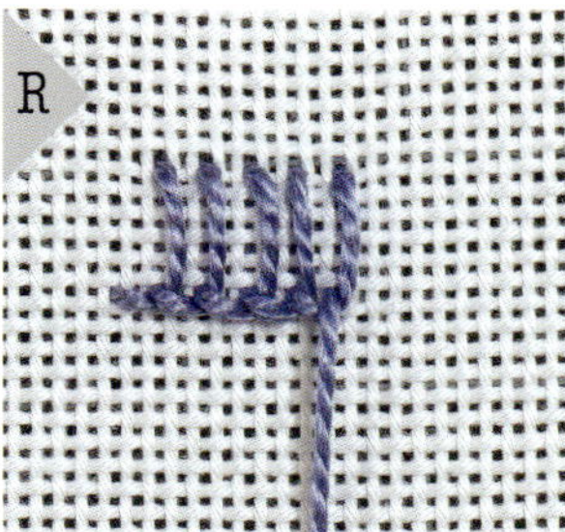

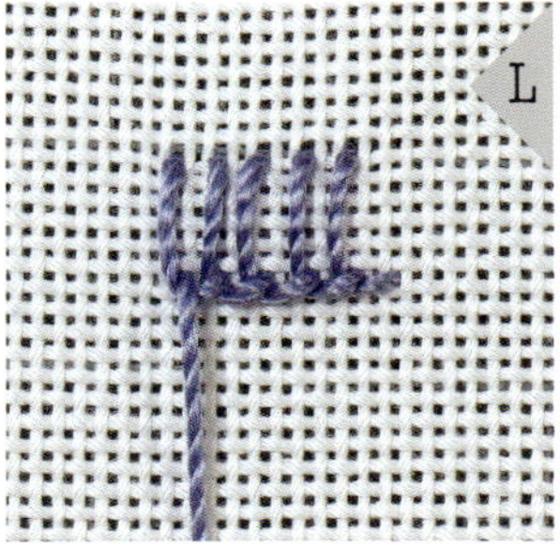

2. With the thread under the needle, pull your needle through so that you make a little chain stitch loop using the buttonhole as a foundation.

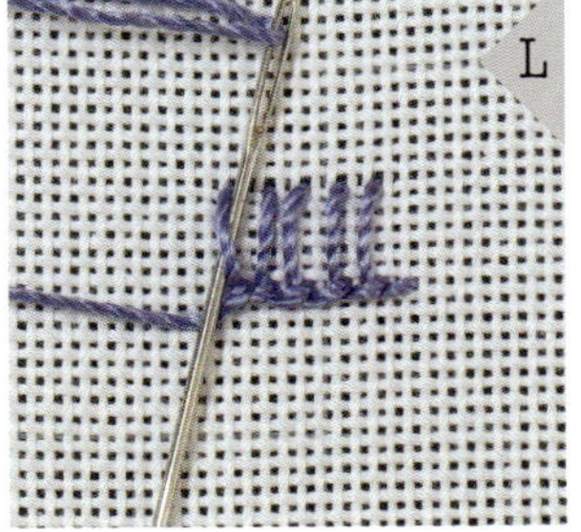

3. Pull the needle through to make a chain stitch.

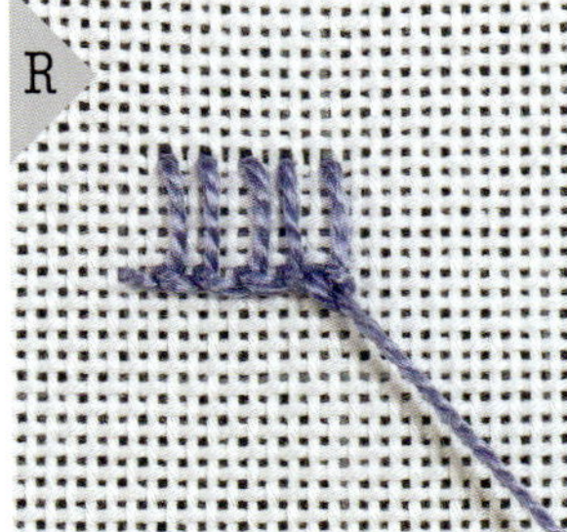

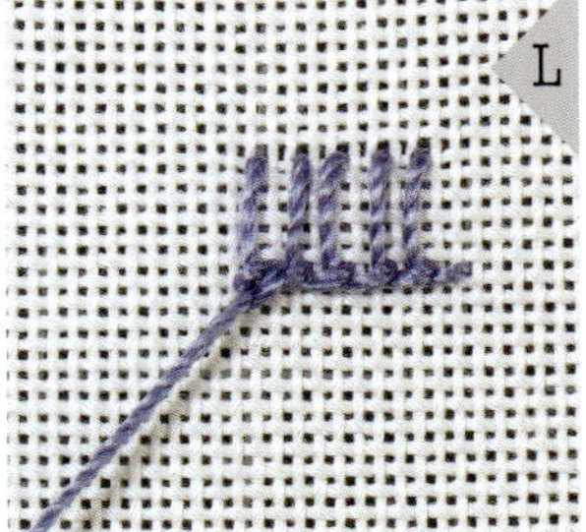

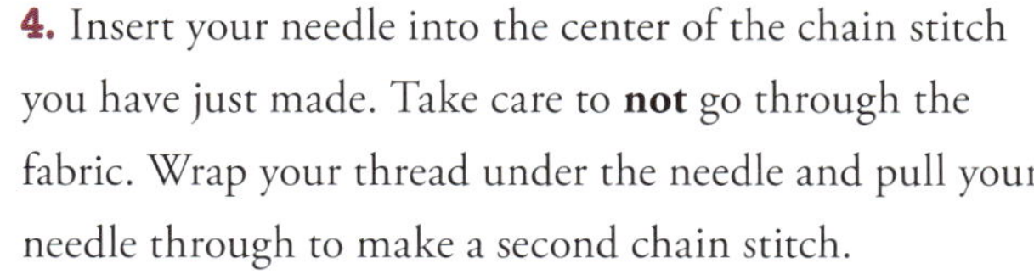

4. Insert your needle into the center of the chain stitch you have just made. Take care to **not** go through the fabric. Wrap your thread under the needle and pull your needle through to make a second chain stitch.

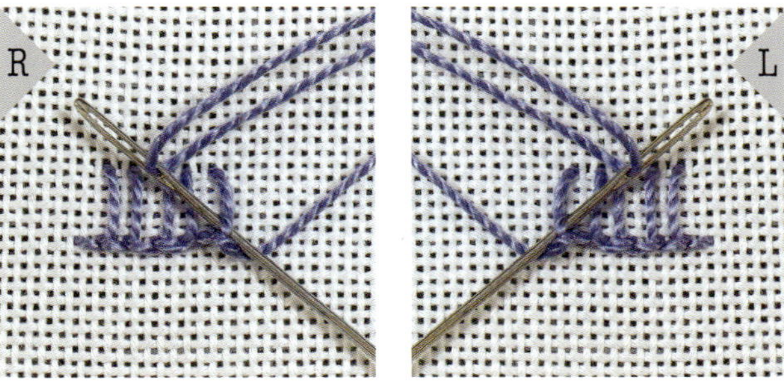

5. If you want a larger knot, you can make a third chain.

6. Slide your needle under the last stitch and, keeping the thread under the needle, pull it through. If you need to push the knot up snugly, do so with either your needle or thumb.

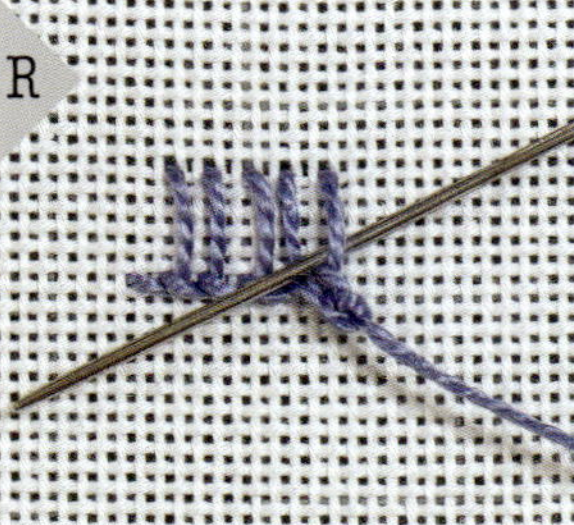

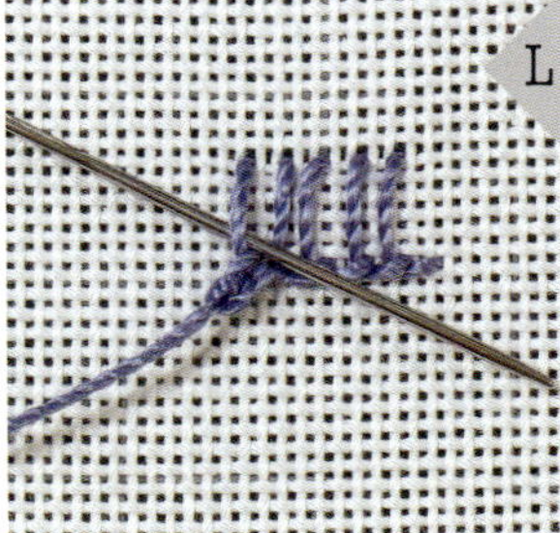

7. Recommence regular buttonhole stitch and continue along the line.

◊ Buttonhole picot chain worked in hand-dyed perle cotton #5 used in slow-stitch project

Buttonhole Stitch (Up and Down with Chain Stitch)

This stitch is an interesting combination of up and down buttonhole and chain stitch.

Work this stitch along two imaginary parallel lines. If you need to mark these lines use a water- or air-erasable pen.

1. Bring your needle out on the baseline, move along slightly and insert your needle on the top line and have your needle emerge on the bottom line. With your thread under your needle, pull your needle through.

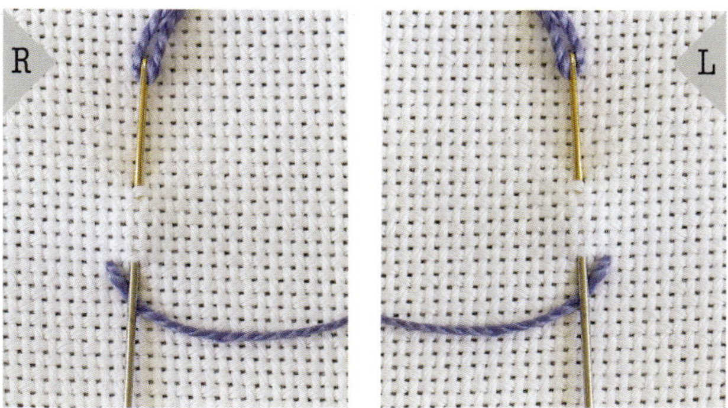

2. Move slightly along the line, insert your needle on the bottom line and have the needle emerge from the fabric on the top line. With your thread under your needle, pull your needle through.

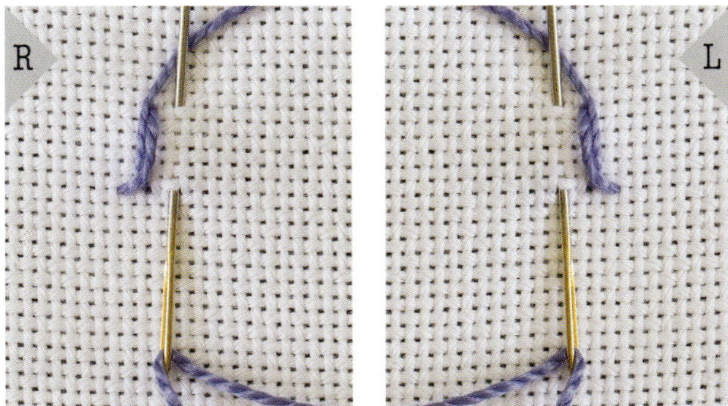

3. As you do this, with your free thumb, hold down the loop that forms to prevent it slipping. This loop forms the bar at the base of both stitches.

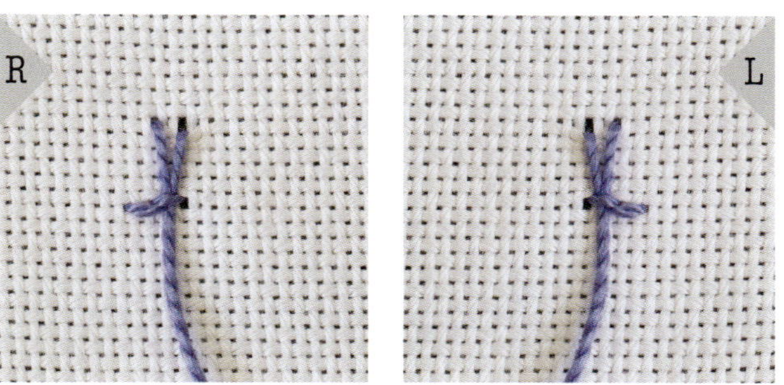

4. Insert your needle close to the bar and point it along the line. With your thread wrapped under the needle, pull it through to create your first chain stitch.

5. Create a second chain stitch.

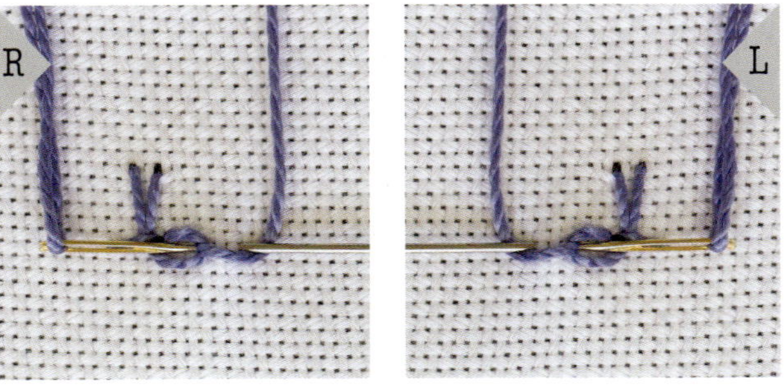

6. Make the third chain stitch.

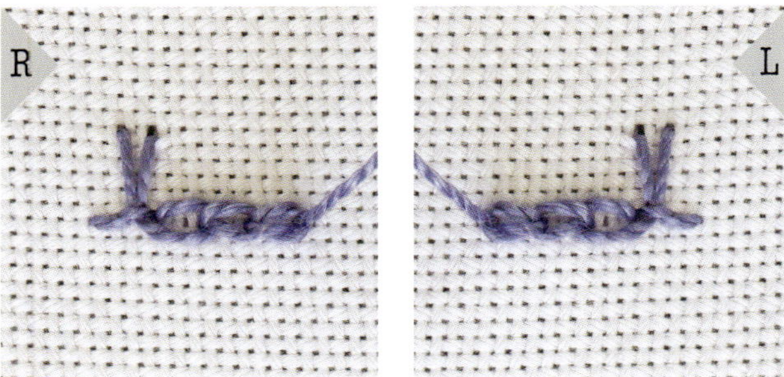

7. Move along the line and repeat the process pointing your needle from top to bottom. With the thread under the needle, pull it through.

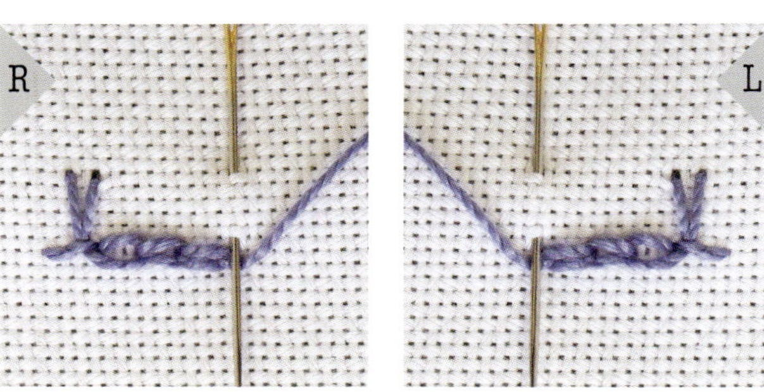

8. Insert your needle so that it points upward, and with the thread under the needle pull it through. Continue with 3 chain stitches.

◊ A completed line of buttonhole up and down chain stitch

◊ Up and down with chain stitch worked on a sun-dyed background in slow-stitch project

Buttonhole Stitch (Up and Down Feathered)

Up and down feathered buttonhole is a feathery line of twin stitches that look more complicated to work than they are. It is also known as *floral feather stitch* because it sits well as greenery and twiggy bits in floral sprays. It is worked in a similar manner to feather stitch and is easily worked on all types of fabrics.

1. When working this stitch, it is useful to imagine 3 parallel lines. Bring the needle out at the top of the line to be worked. Insert the needle along the line, bringing it out of the fabric below these 2 points in the center. Loop the thread under the needle and take the needle through the fabric. This first V shape creates the first of the tied pairs of stitches.

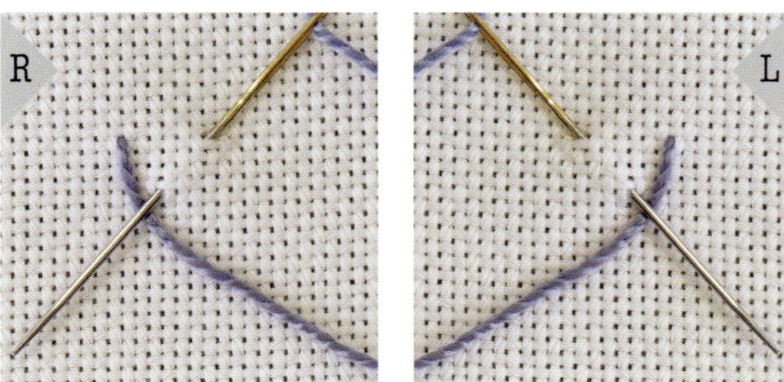

2. For the second stitch of the pair, insert your needle at the same angle as the side of the V that you have just created, with the point of the needle outward.

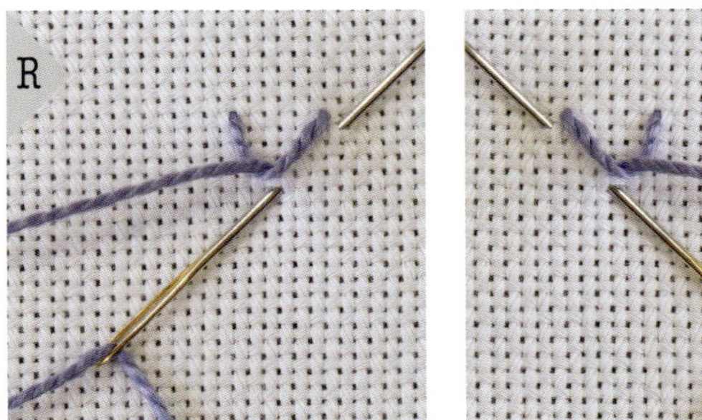

3. When you take the needle through the fabric, wrap the thread under the needle at the top. Pull the needle through the fabric. As you do this, hold down the loop that forms with your free thumb to prevent it from slipping. This loop forms the bar at the base of both stitches.

The first pair of tied stitches.

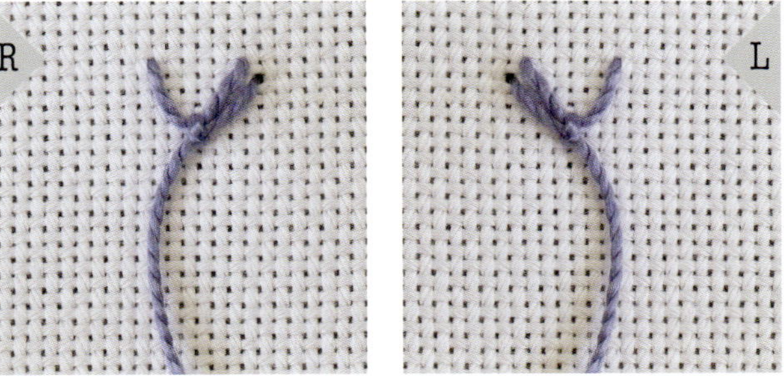

4. Take a diagonal bite of the fabric with the needle inserted on the same level as the tied stitches. Have the needle emerge from the fabric on the centerline. Keeping the thread under the needle's point, pull the thread through the fabric to make a V shape; this is the first part of the next pair of stitches.

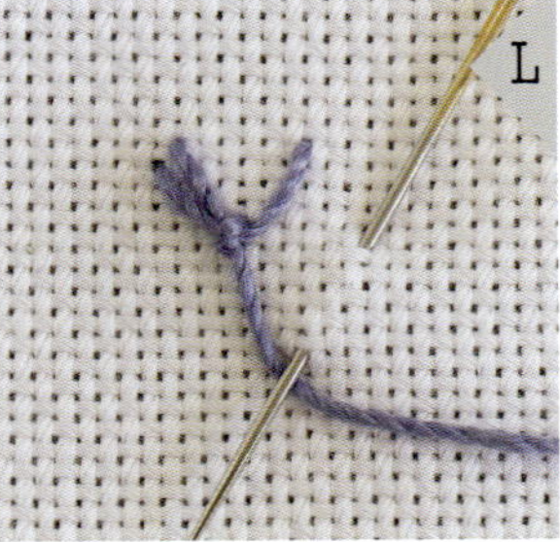

5. Make the second tied stitch.

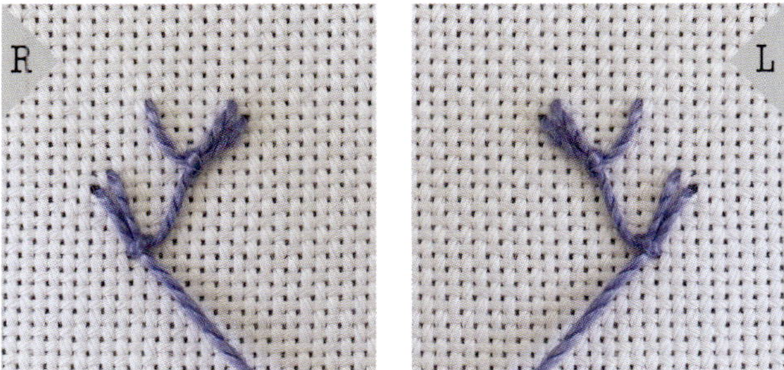

6. Work these movements from side to side down the line.

Up and down feathered buttonhole stitch worked in hand-dyed variegated perle cotton #5 on a crazy quilt block. Beads were added to the middle of each fork.

Up and down feathered buttonhole stitch worked on a crazy quilt block. The orange bugle beads were added to the middle of each fork after the stitch was worked.

Buttonholed Single Feather Stitch

Buttonholed single feather stitch is a textured stitch. It is created by buttonholing a foundation of single feather stitch. If your fabric will accept it, use a blunt needle so that you do not split the foundation thread in the second part of the stitch.

1. Start this with a single straight-sided feather stitch. Bring the needle out of the fabric and reinsert it a little space away. The distance between these 2 points will determine the width of the line you create with this stitch. Make a small diagonal stitch downward. Keep the thread under the needle's point, and pull the thread through the fabric to make the first stitch.

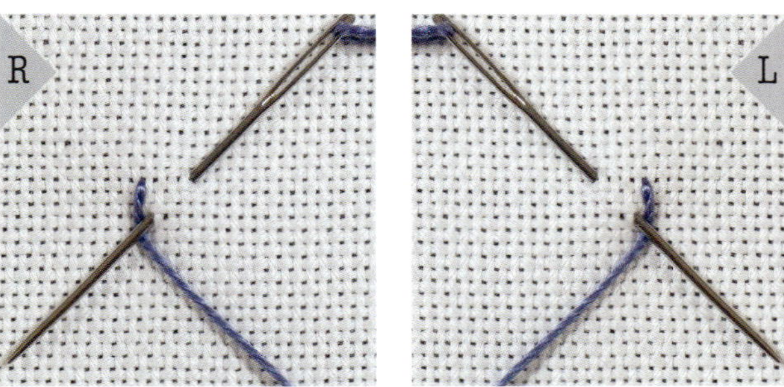

2. Wrap your thread under the needle and pass your needle under the bar of the stitch to create the start of a buttonhole stitch.

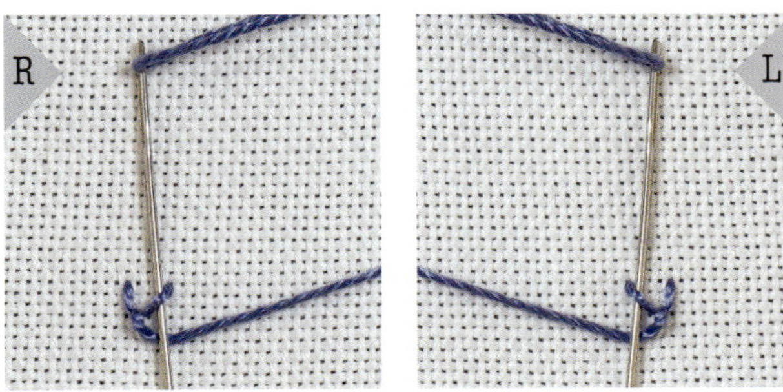

3. Pull your thread through. Note that you are working on the bar of the foundation stitch; you are not passing your needle through the fabric.

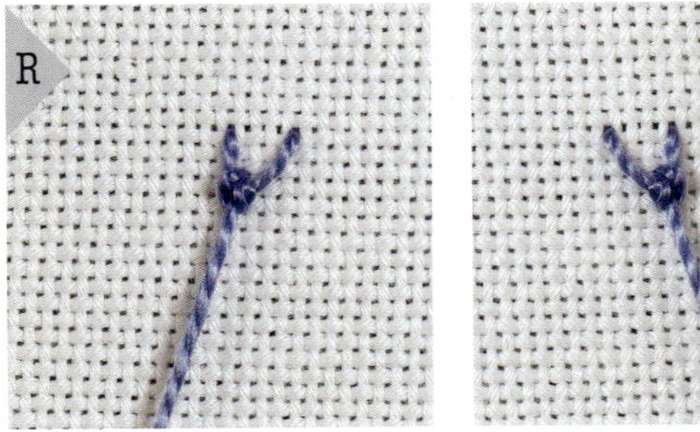

4. Pass your needle under the thread of your foundation stitch, wrap your thread under the needle, and pull your needle through to make the second buttonhole stitch.

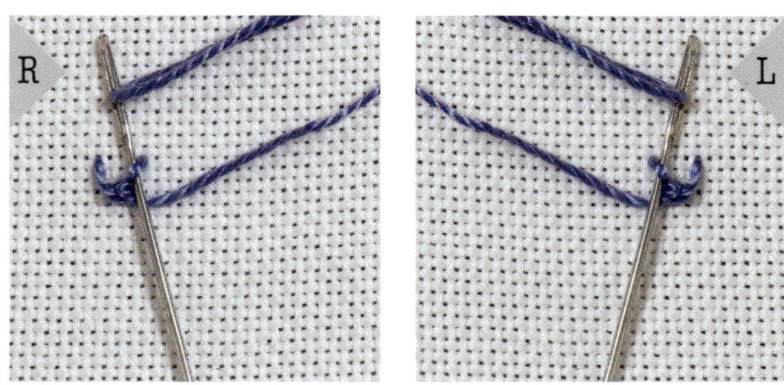

5. Continue buttonholing this way for the length of the foundation stitch. When the bar is snug with buttonhole stitches, take your needle to the back of your fabric, inserting it near the end of the foundation stitch. Have the needle emerge at the point where you started buttonholing.

6. Make your next foundation stitch by taking a small diagonal bite of the fabric. Keeping the thread under the needle, pull the thread through the fabric to make the next stitch. Continue to buttonhole this stitch and work the buttonhole stitches along the bar until they are snug.

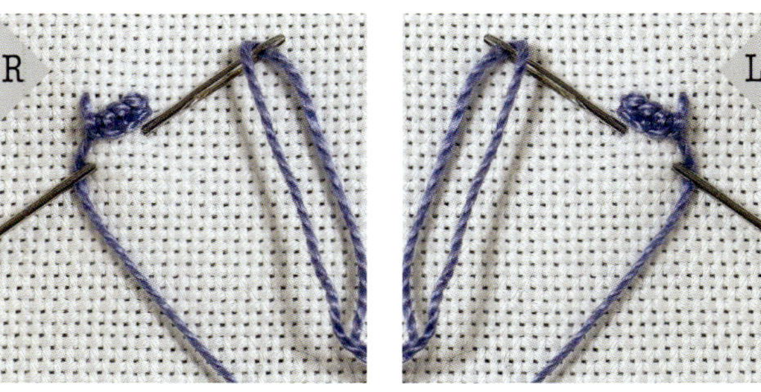

7. Continue in this way along the line.

You can change the thickness of your line by making the foundation stitch smaller so that only a couple of buttonhole stitches fill the bar.

◊ Buttonholed single feather stitch used to outline appliqué piece in slow-stitch project

Cable Chain Stitch (Interlaced)

Interlaced cable chain quickly creates a pretty, textured border, which is great fun to work in variegated threads. This is a very quick, easy, and yet dramatic stitch.

I have worked this stitch in two different colors so you can clearly see the cable chain foundation rows and the lacing. You can work it in the same color or lace with novelty threads and fine ribbons. When lacing, use a tapestry needle so that you avoid splitting the thread on the foundation rows.

1. Start with working 2 parallel lines of cable chain stitch (page 185).

2. Bring your needle up through the fabric at the midpoint of the 2 foundation rows. Slide your needle under the chain stitch on the top row, so that the needle emerges in the middle of the chain stitch. Take your needle through the loop of the stitch.

3. Slide your needle under your lacing thread.

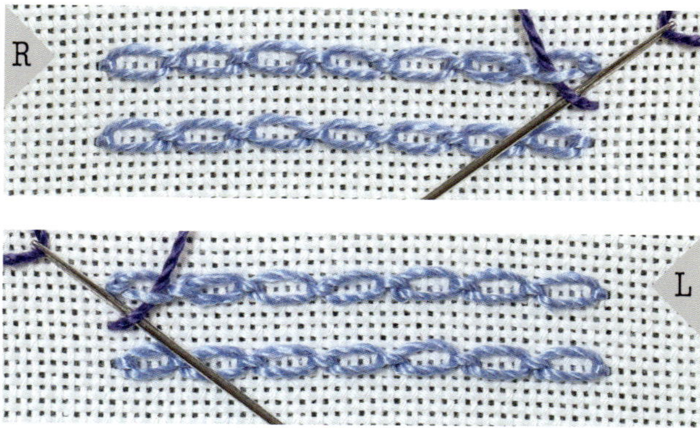

4. Angle your needle toward the bottom foundation row of stitches. On the bottom line, skip a chain, point your needle downward, and slide your needle under the stitch. Pull your thread through.

5. Angle your needle toward the top row of stitches. Then slide your needle under your lacing thread. Skip a chain stitch, before passing your needle under the inside loop of next chain stitch, on the top line. Pull your needle through.

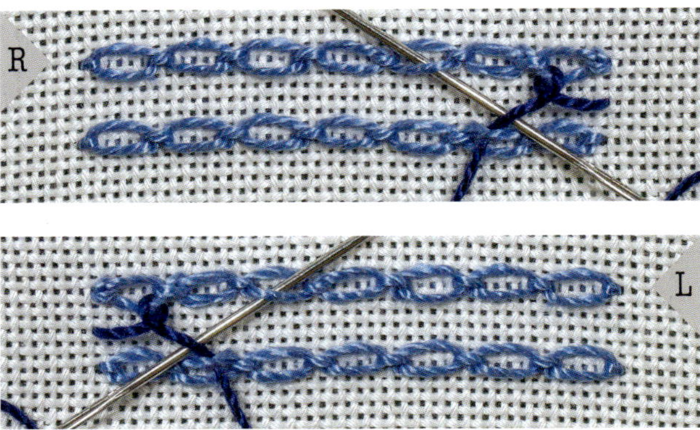

6. Continue along the line.

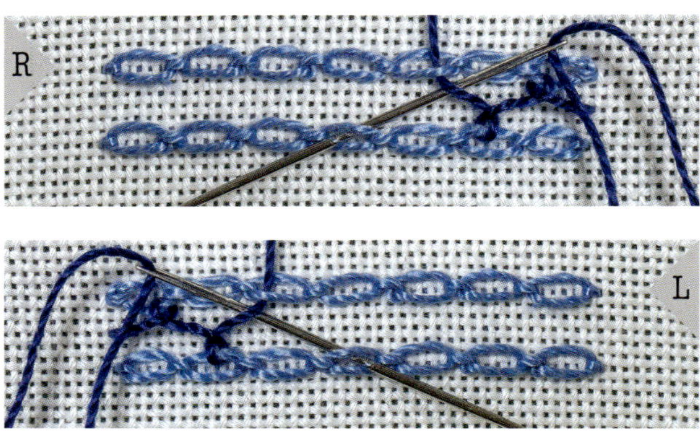

7. Lace every second chain stitch in this manner until the line is complete. Take the lacing thread to the back of the fabric.

8. Bring your lacing thread out of the fabric just below where it entered your fabric and make a return journey, lacing every second chain stitch.

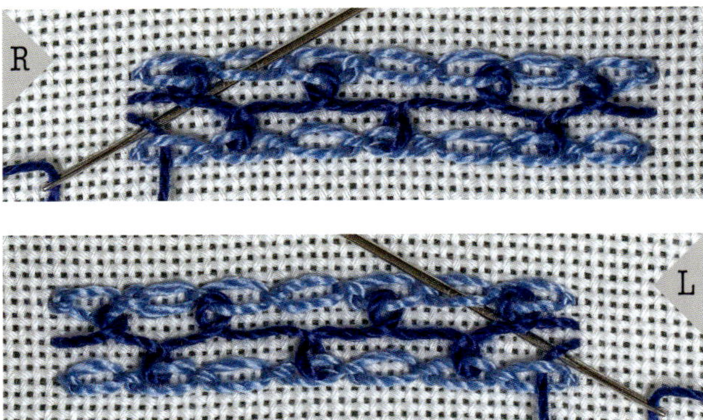

9. Work every second stitch as you did on the first journey.

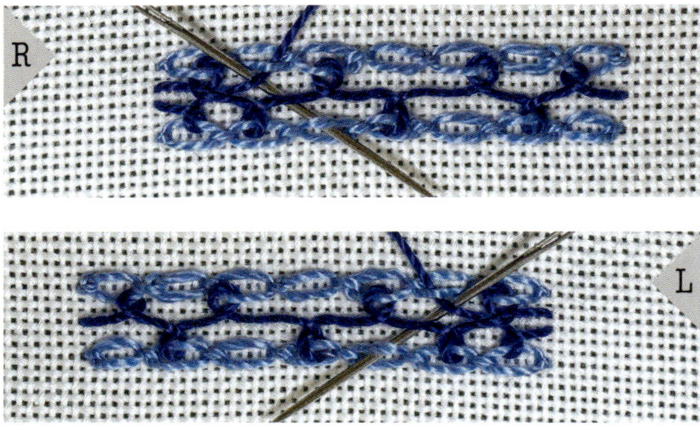

10. Take your thread to the back and tie off. You have created an interesting line or border for your projects.

Cable Chain Stitch (Slipped)

Slipped cable chain is a decorative linear stitch that starts with a foundation of cable chain stitch (page 184). The loop between chain stitches creates a space to weave other threads through. These threads can be of a different color, thickness, or texture, which means this stitch lends itself to experimentation.

1. Bring the thread out to the side of the cable-stitched line on a diagonal. Slide the needle under the bar of the bottom link. As you do this, take care not pick up any of the fabric.

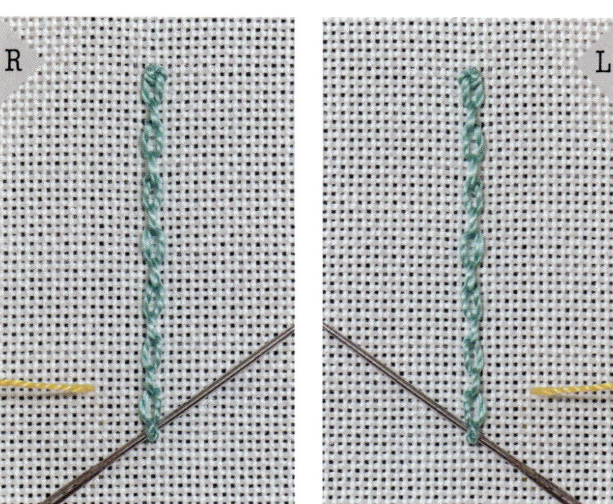

2. To complete the V, insert the needle back into the fabric on the opposite side of the foundation row of cable chain. Take the needle diagonally across the back of the fabric, and bring it out farther up the line. Repeat threading the second journey until you are at the top. You can just do 1 line of slipped stitches or choose to do 2.

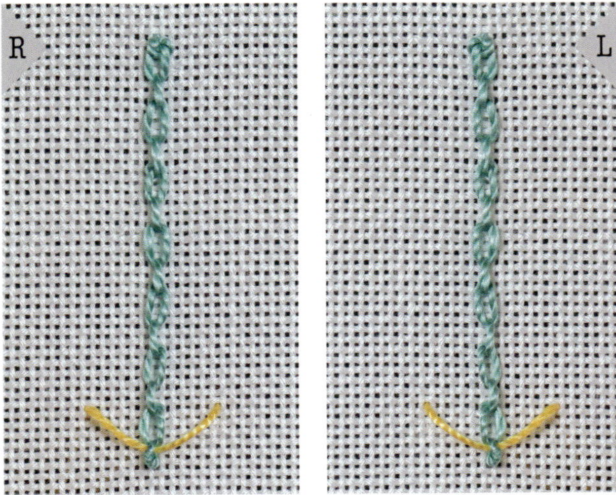

3. This is a very quick and versatile stitch, which is interesting on its own, but you can add more slip stitches.

Secondary slipped stitches can be added in the same thread, a different color, or a thread of a different thickness.

In this sample, secondary slipped stitches were added using perle cotton thread.

Detail of slipped cable chain used in slow-stitch roll

Cable Chain Stitch (Threaded)

Threaded cable chain is a fun stitch that is quick and easy to work, as it is a laced version of cable chain.

Work a foundation line of cable chain stitches (page 184).

1. Using a blunt tapestry needle so that the foundation threads do not split, bring your lacing thread out at the base of the line and pass your needle under the first cable chain stitch. Note that you are not going through the fabric at this point.

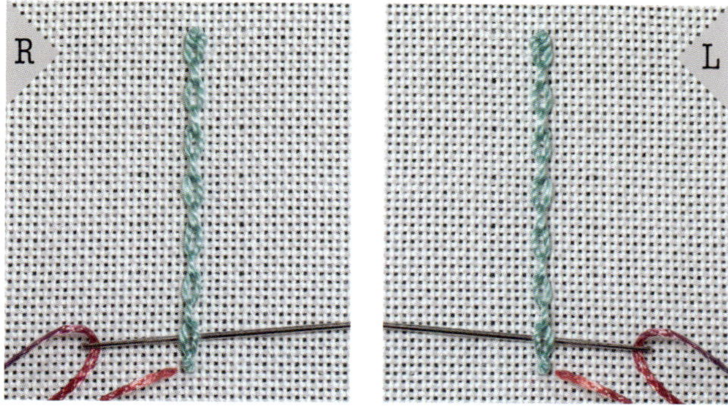

2. Turn your needle and pass your needle under the next cable chain stitch.

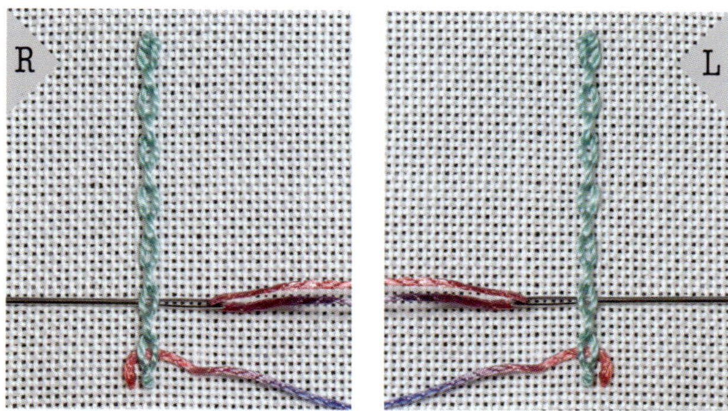

3. Lace the length of the row and take the thread to the back of the fabric. Bring the thread out on the opposite side for the return journey.

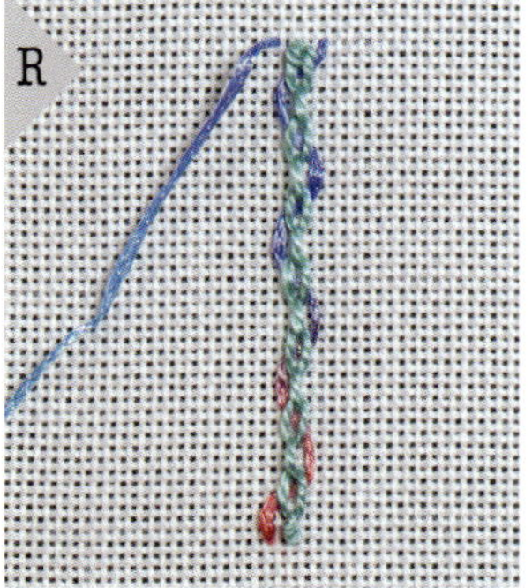

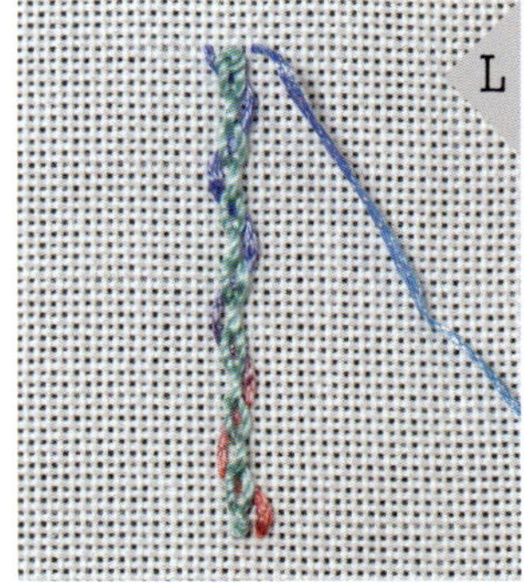

4. Continue to the end of the line.

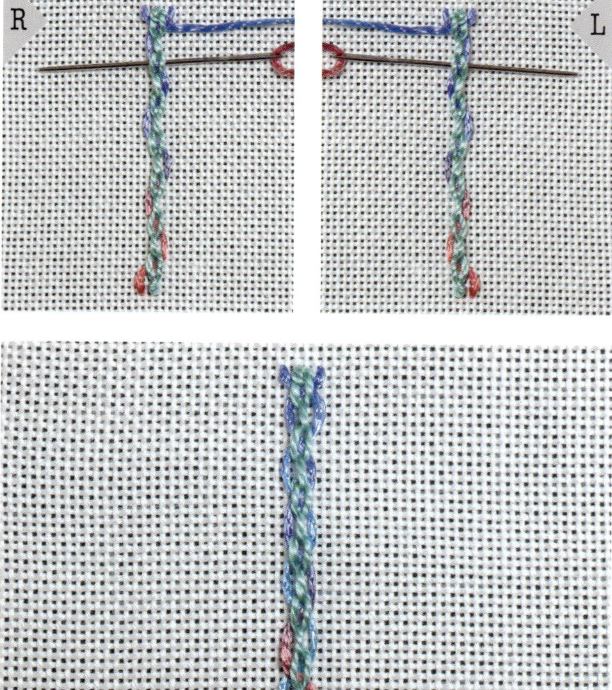

This stitch follows a curve well. You can add lots of variety by adding interesting threads or beads.

Detail of threaded cable chain worked in perle cotton #5 and laced with stranded floss

Cable Chain Stitch (Zigzag)

Zigzag cable chain is also known as *double cable stitch.* This is a very quick and versatile stitch that is interesting on its own but is also interesting when worked in combination with other stitches. You can take advantage of the angled structure of the stitch and create patterns by working it row upon row to make an attractive patterned filling. A bead can also be stitched to the middle of each chain.

1. Bring the needle up through the fabric. Slip the needle under the thread. With the needle under the thread, twist the thread around the needle once.

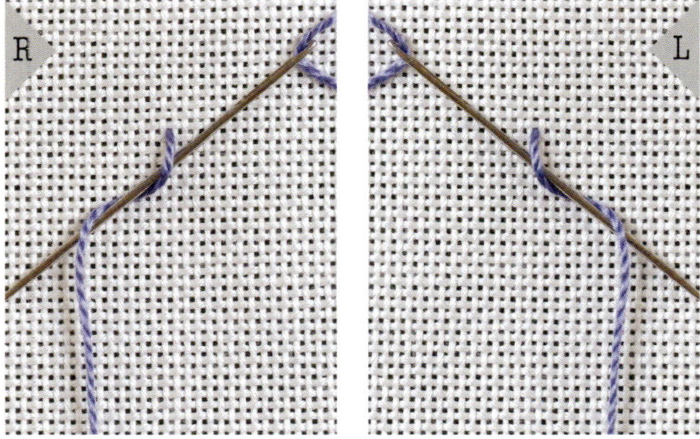

2. Point the needle back into the hole it emerged from. With the thread wrap sitting close to the fabric so it forms a firm loop around the needle, bring the needle out on an angle below the loop and wrap the thread under the point of the needle.

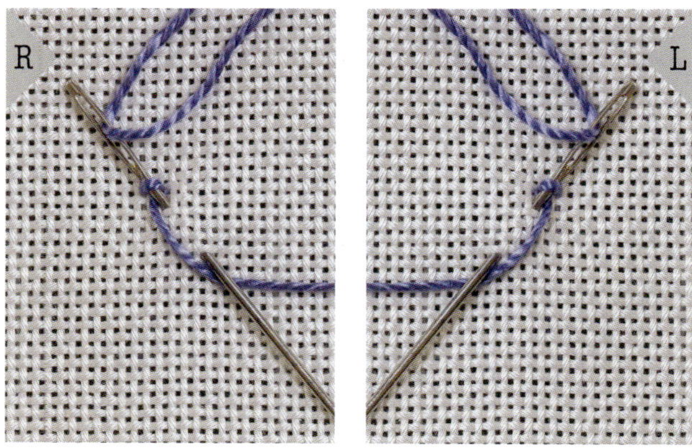

3. Pull the thread through the fabric.

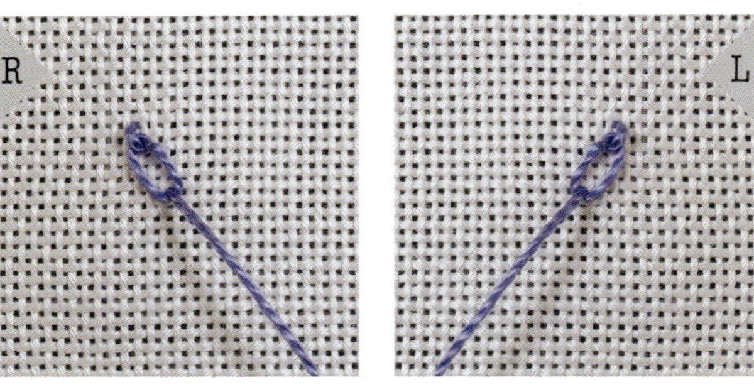

4. Repeat this process again but at the opposite angle. When you start at the top of the chain, make sure you wrap the thread around the needle once before inserting your needle to make the second part of the stitch.

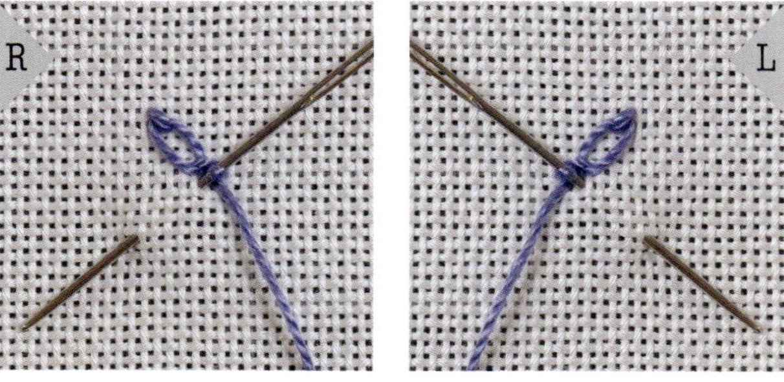

5. Wrap your thread under the needle and pull the thread through. Continue in a zigzag manner.

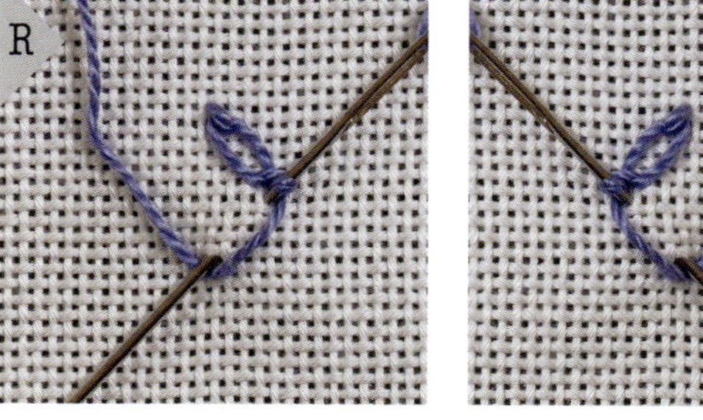

6. Continue down the line until complete.

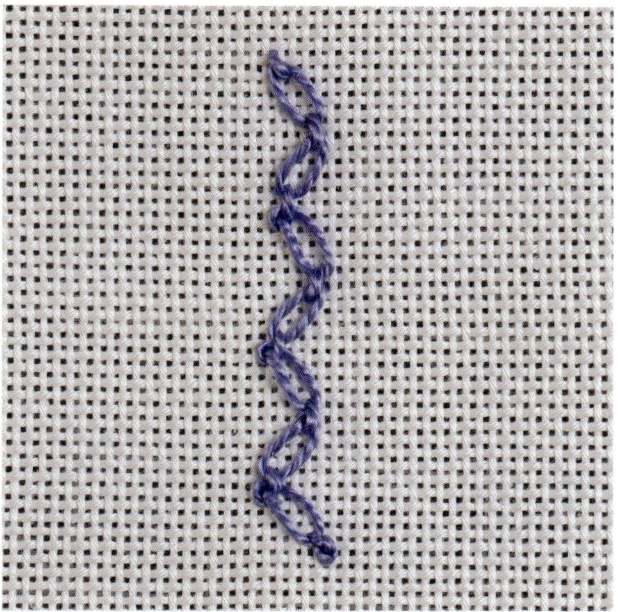

◊ Zigzag cable chain worked on hand-painted Aida cloth using perle cotton #8

Chain Stitch (Detached with a Picot)

This version of detached chain stitch adds interesting texture and variety. You can use it anywhere you would normally use a detached chain or lazy daisy stitch.

1. Start by making the loop of a detached chain. Instead of making a simple straight stitch to secure the stitch, insert your needle at the base of the detached chain stitch and have it emerge just below.

2. Wrap your thread under the needle to make a small chain stitch and pull the thread through.

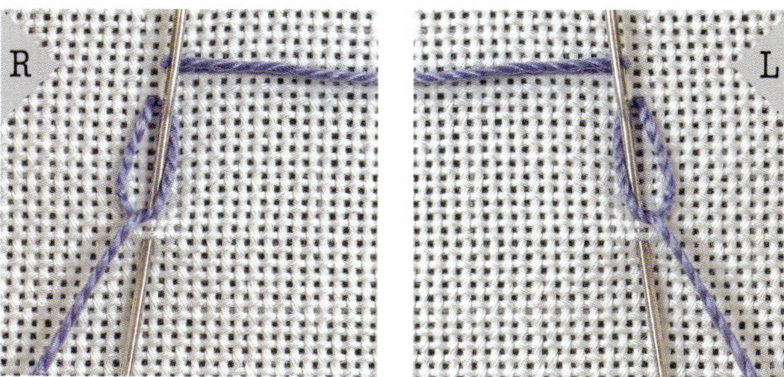

3. Slide your needle under the side of the small chain stitch you have just created. Wrap the thread under the needle and pull the thread through. You are not passing the needle through the fabric at this stage. You are creating a small freestanding chain stitch.

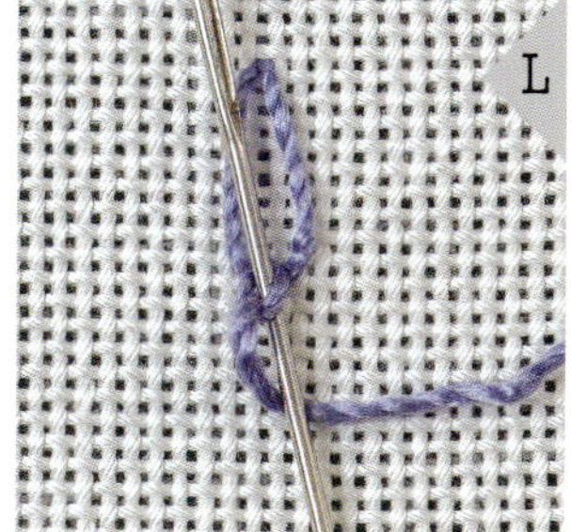

4. Repeat the process and make 2 or 3 freestanding chain stitches. All these stitches are free of the fabric. If you continued making these stitches, you would end up with a tiny, thin cord.

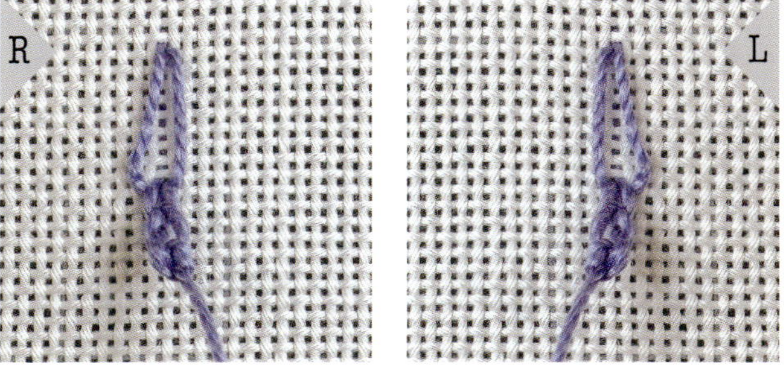

5. Once you have 2 or 3 chain stitches worked, insert your needle back into the fabric, in the middle of the detached chain stitch.

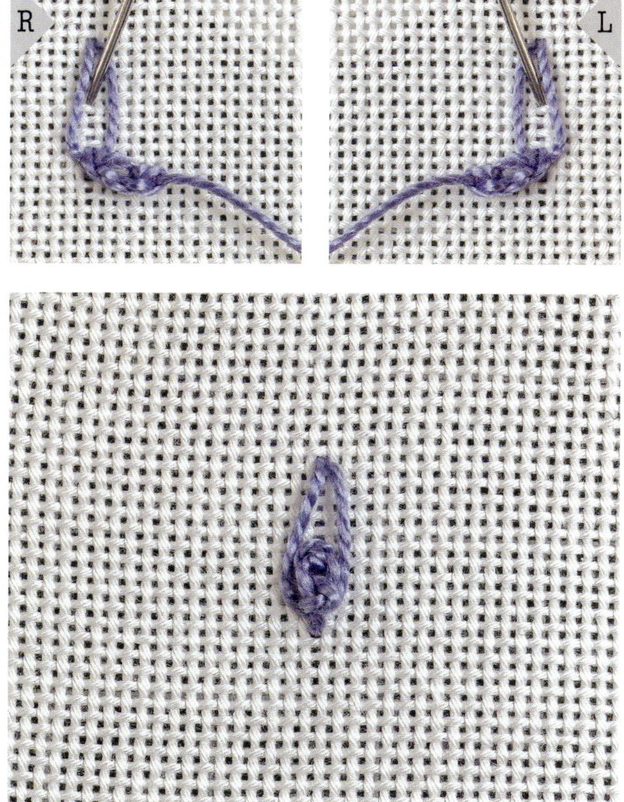

You now have a detached chain with a picot. The more freestanding chain stitches you work, the bigger the picot bobble.

◊ Detached chain stitch with three freestanding chain stitches create a picot (small loop).

Chain Stitch (Alternating)

This stitch looks good worked with a thread that has a firm twist, such as perle cotton. Alternating chain stitch can be used in numerous creative ways. It can vary greatly depending on the width of the space between the top of the V, the angle of your needle, the spacing, changes in the lengths of stitches, and the regularity of stitches—all these variations change the look of the stitch. It is easily worked on a curve, and it's great to use in organic designs.

1. Start with a chain stitch (page 185). Take a bite of the fabric with your needle so that the point emerges a short space along the line to be stitched.

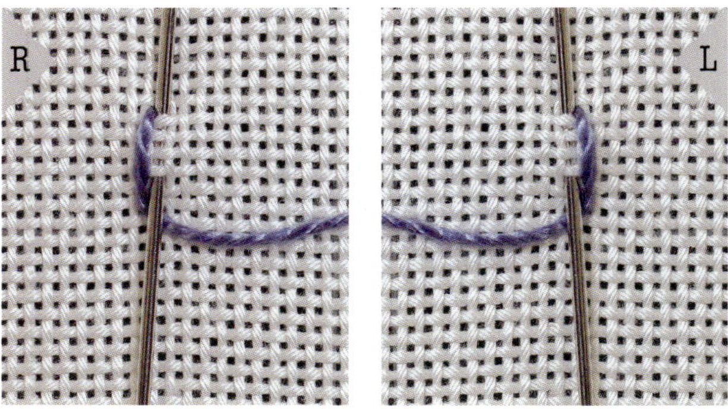

2. With the thread wrapped under the needle's point, pull the needle through the fabric to create a chain stitch.

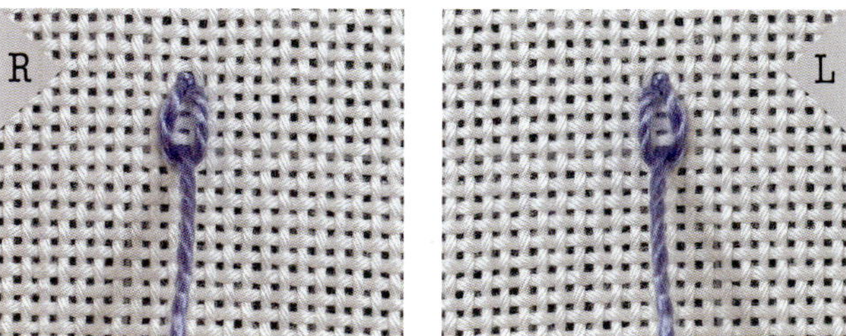

3. Insert the needle to 1 side of the chain stitch with the point of your needle emerging farther down the line. Wrap the thread under the needle.

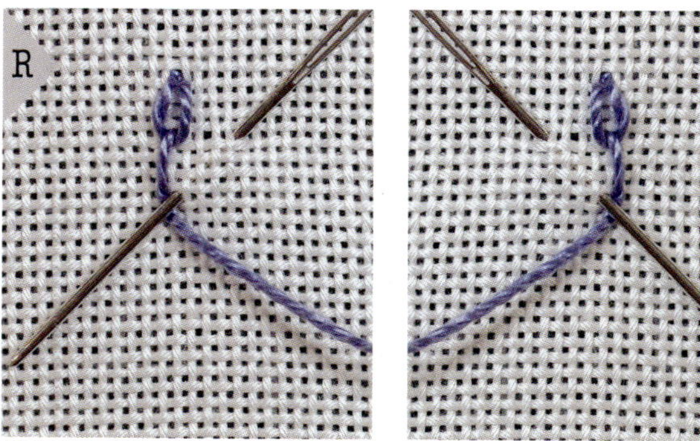

4. Pull through to form a stitch that looks like a lopsided V.

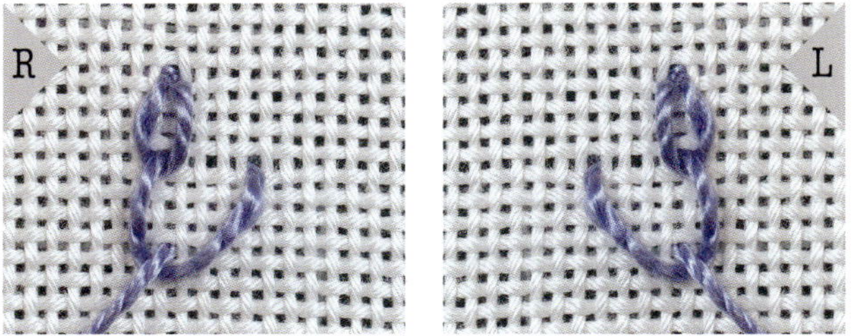

5. Work a chain stitch. Insert your needle at the base of the V, close to where your thread emerges. Wrap the thread under the needle.

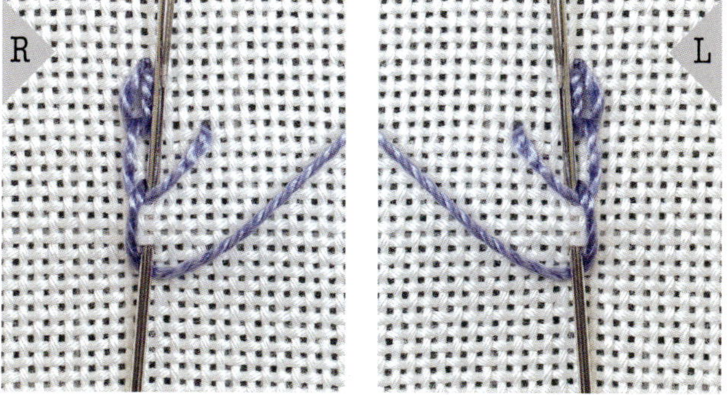

6. Pull your thread through to create a second chain stitch.

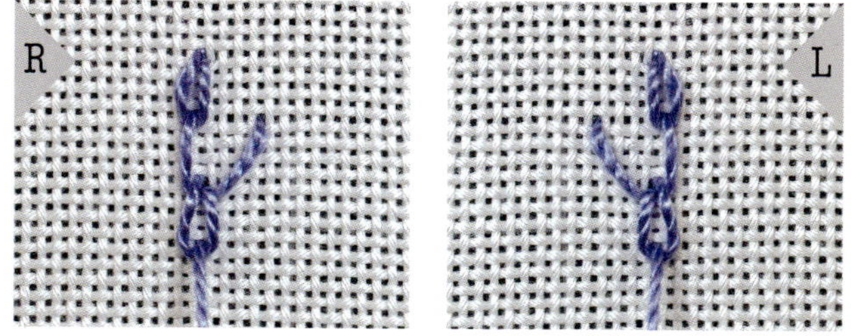

7. Take your needle to the other side and create another V. Keep it in line with the previous stitches.

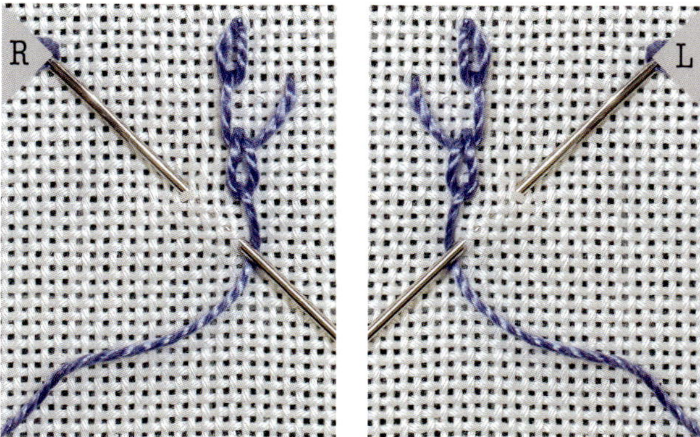

8. Continue along the line and tie off the last chain stitch with a small straight stitch.

Alternating chain stitch used alongside a seam in slow-stitch project

Chain Stitch (Broad or Heavy)

Broad chain stitch is also known as *heavy braid chain, heavy braid,* or *heavy chain.* It creates a solid sewn line, which looks like a fine braid. The difference between this stitch and reverse chain stitch (page 77) is that the needle is passed under the previous two chain loops; in reverse chain, the needle passes under just the previous chain. This stitch produces a thicker braid-like line.

1. Start by working a detached chain stitch (page 187) upside down. After this first stitch, bring the needle out of the fabric further along the line at the base of the detached chain. Leave enough space for 1 chain stitch.

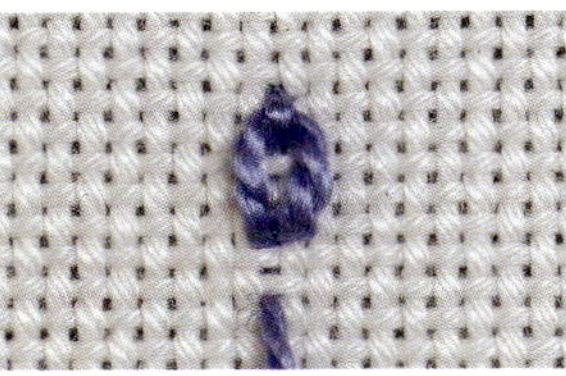

2. Slide the needle under the tie of the chain but not through the fabric and take the needle back down through the fabric where it came out.

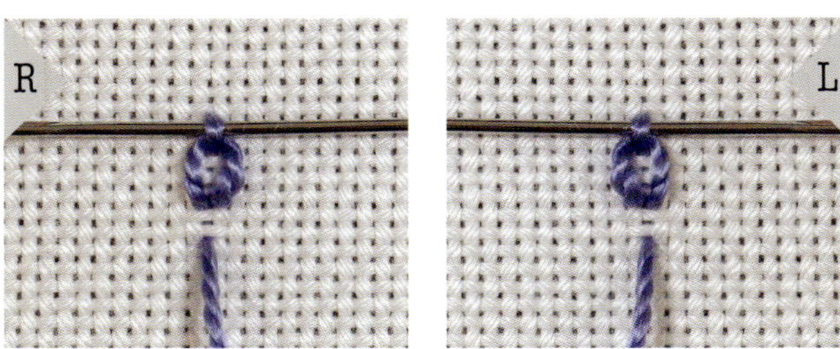

You should have 2 chains tied with the same stitch.

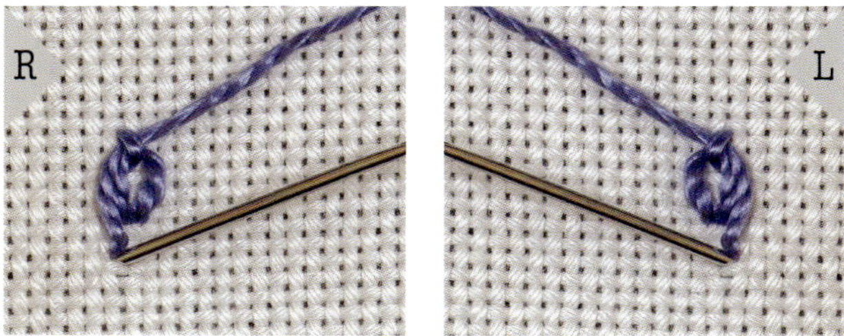

3. Bring the needle out of the fabric farther along the line, and slide the needle under the base of the first chain but not through the fabric.

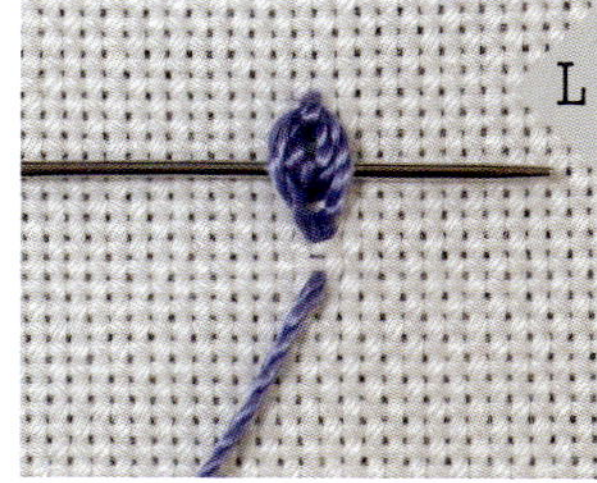

4. Bring your needle back down through the fabric where it came out.

Make sure when you pass the needle under the chains you do not pick up any fabric.

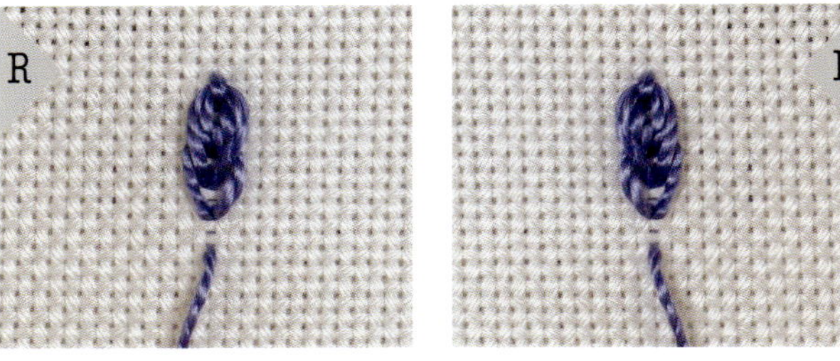

5. Repeat to finish the line.

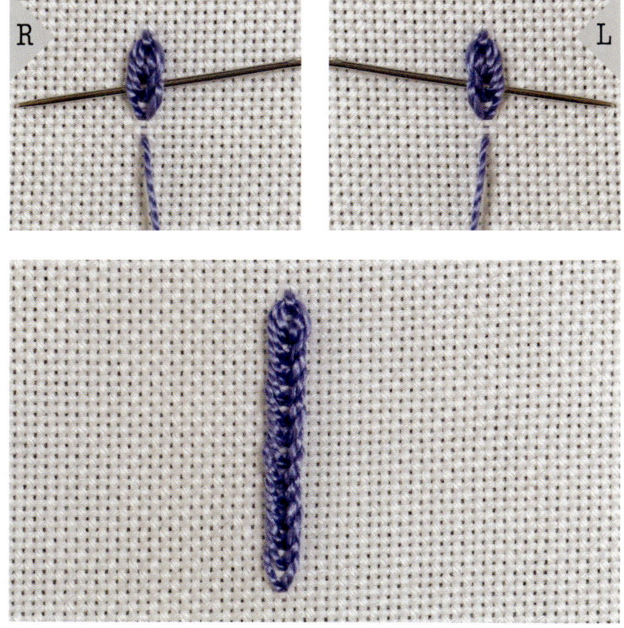

◊ Completed line of broad or heavy chain

Chain Stitch (Buttonholed Double)

Buttonholed double chain stitch is a decorative stitch that is wonderful to use as a surface embroidery stitch or for an edging. It can be used anywhere you would use buttonhole or blanket stitch and looks great around appliqué pieces. It is fun to work in circles, too! This composite stitch has a foundation of double chain that is then buttonholed. When you start buttonholing, it can feel messy, but once you're past the first few stitches, it behaves.

1. Start with a working a line of double chain stitch (page 63).

2. Bring your needle up from the back of the fabric and pass it under the outer loop of your first chain stitch. With the thread wrapped under the needle, pull it through to create a buttonhole stitch. Note that you are passing the needle under the thread of the chain stitch, not through the fabric.

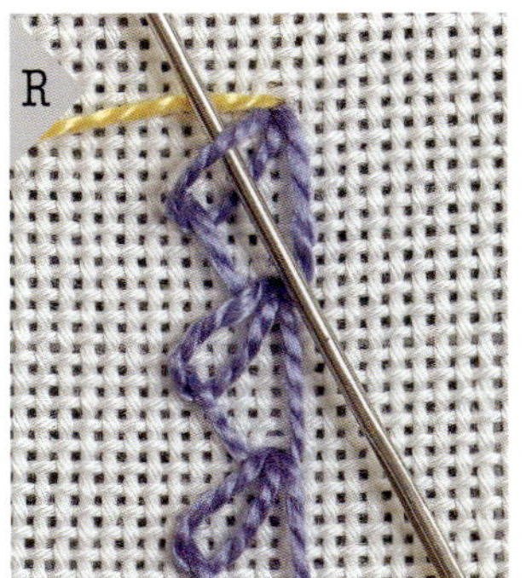

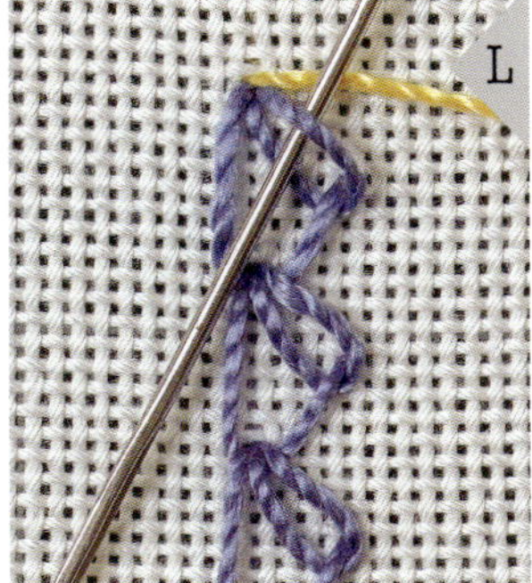

3. Repeat this to make the second buttonhole stitch.

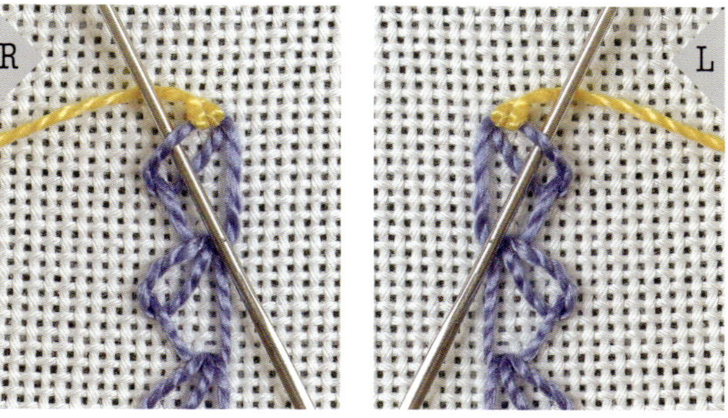

4. Repeat this along the chain stitch, nudging the stitches along the thread with your needle. Take your thread to the back of the fabric at the end of the chain stitch.

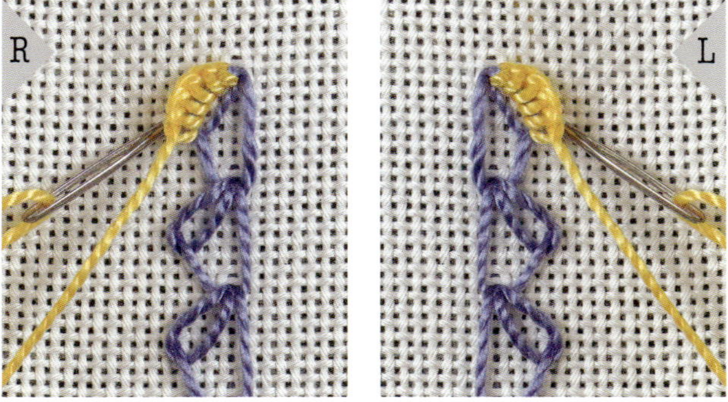

5. Bring your needle out at the start of the next set of chain stitches and start to work the next set of buttonhole stitches.

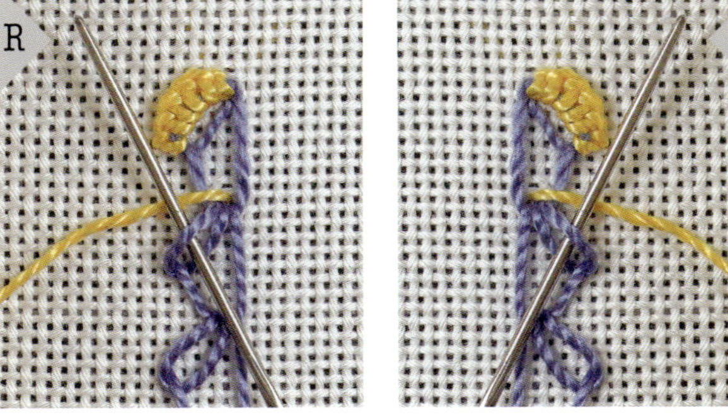

6. Repeat this along the line until you have finished.

◊ Buttonholed double chain stitch used in contemporary embroidery project

Chain Stitch (Chained Triple)

Chained triple chain is made up of a cluster of three detached chain stitches that are chained together in a line.

1. Bring the needle up through the fabric and take a bite of the fabric with your needle pointed upward. Wrap the thread under the needle.

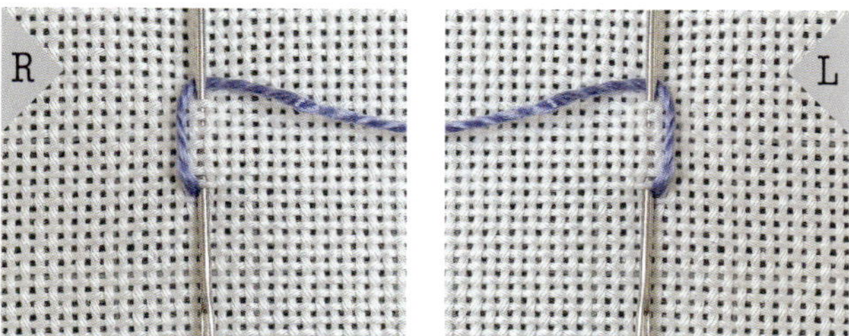

2. Pull your thread through and secure the loop with a small straight stitch.

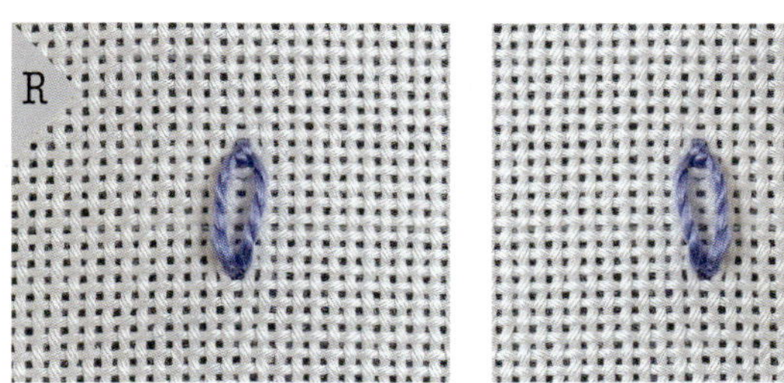

3. Bring your needle up at the base of the chain stitch you just created and make a second detached chain stitch on the angle illustrated.

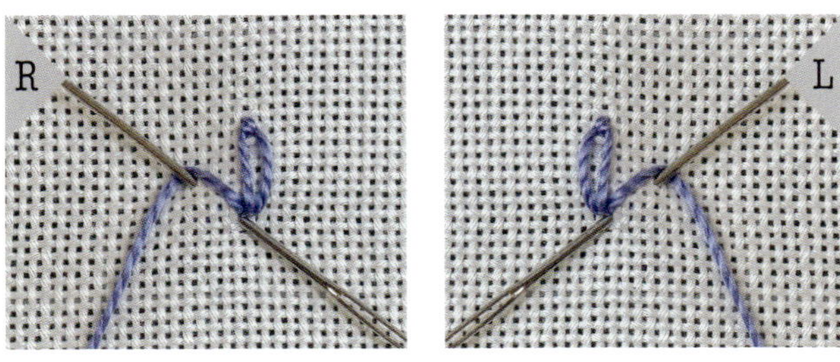

4. Repeat this to create a third detached chain stitch on the angle illustrated.

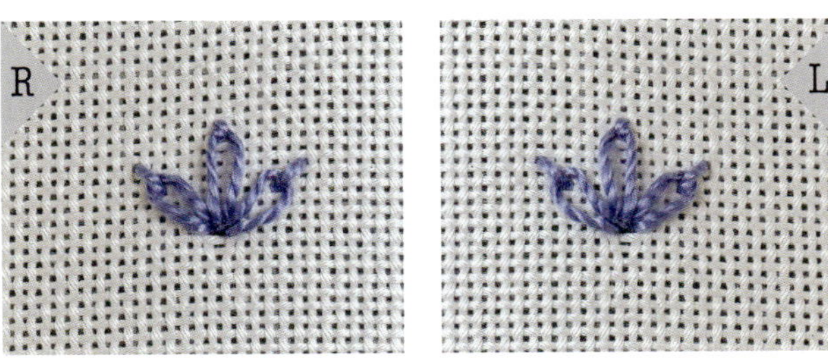

5. Bring your needle out below the 3 detached chain stitches you have just created. Pass the needle under all 3 detached chain stitches. Pull the thread through. Note that you are passing the thread under the stitches not through the fabric.

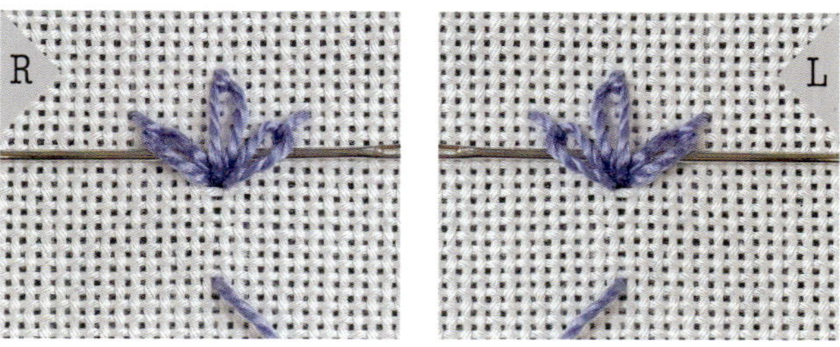

6. Take the needle back into the fabric where the thread emerges to complete a reverse chain. Bring the thread out close to the base of the chain to start the next motif.

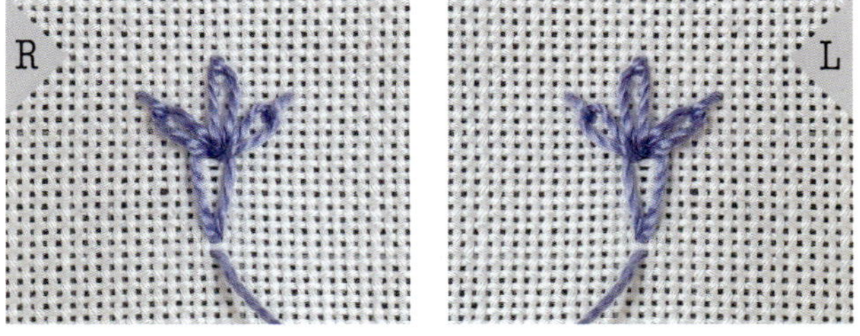

7. Work a detached chain at an angle.

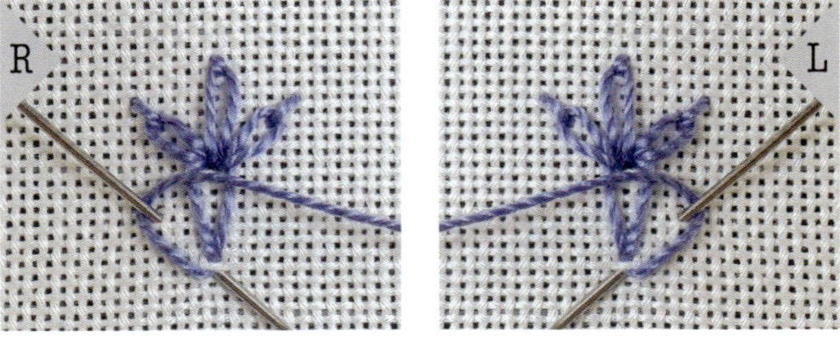

8. Work a second detached chain stitch to complete the motif.

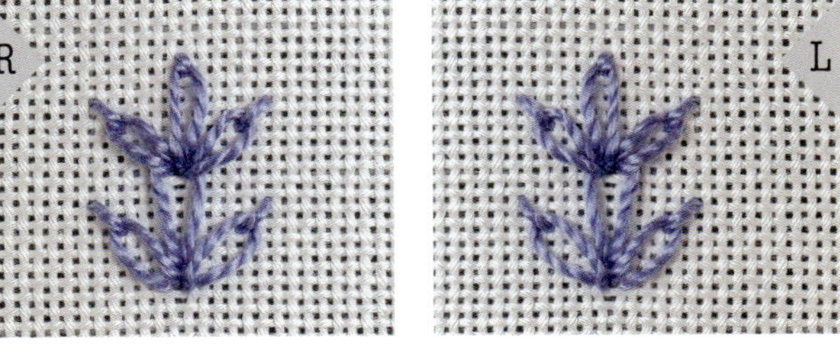

9. Continue in this manner along the line.

I added beads to the central chain stitches on a section of chained triple chain stitch worked on a contemporary embroidery stitch roll.

Chain Stitch (Double)

Double chain stitch creates an interesting decorative line that you can use around the edges of items, collars, necklines, and more.

1. Start with an angled regular chain stitch (page 185). Bring the needle from the back of the fabric and reinsert the needle so that the point emerges at an angle to the line to be stitched. With the thread wrapped under the point of the needle, pull the needle through the fabric to make the first chain stitch.

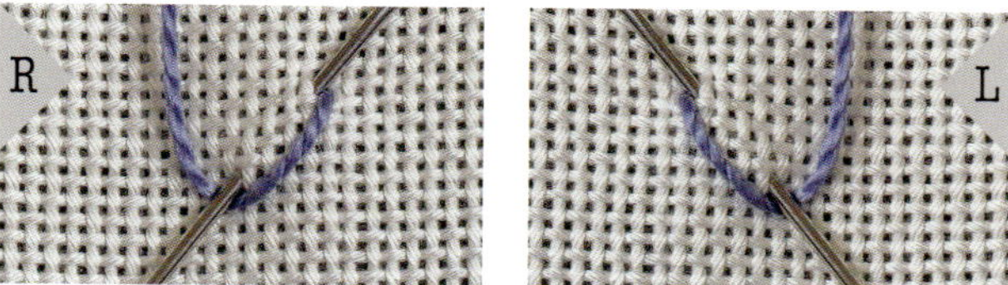

2. Insert your needle where you started the first chain stitch and take a larger bite of the fabric. Whatever chain length you choose, the bite of the fabric should be approximately 2 chain stitch lengths. With the thread wrapped under the point of the needle, pull the needle through.

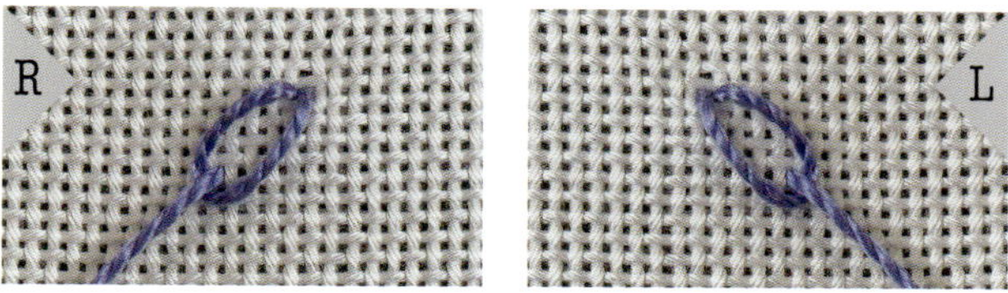

3. Make the angled chain stitch.

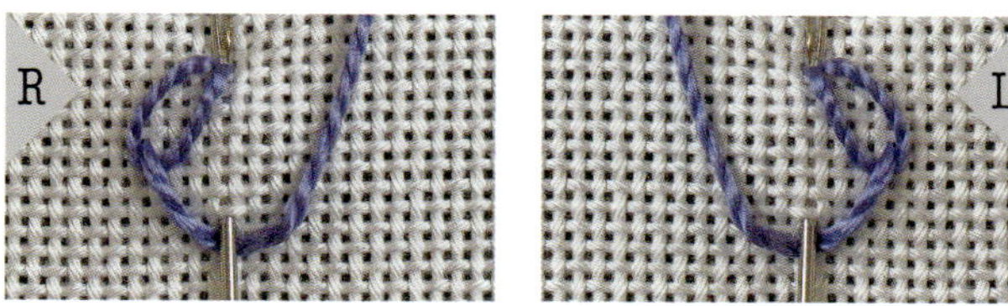

4. With the thread wrapped under the point of the needle, pull the needle through.

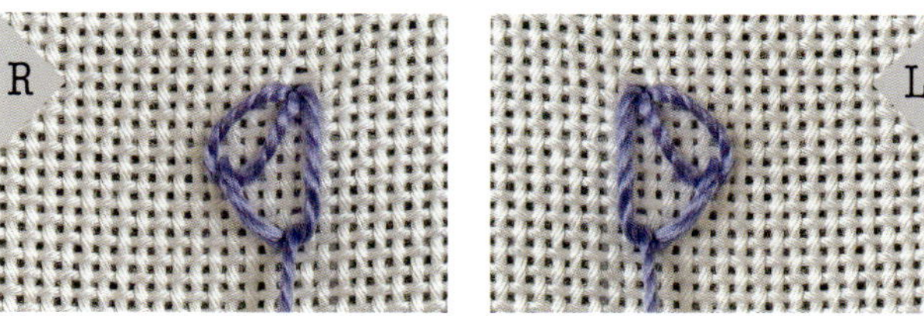

5. Continue down the line, making an angled chain stitch and then a larger chain stitch.

Completed line of double chain stitches

Double chain used to outline appliqué piece in slow-stitch project

Chain Stitch (Crossed Double)

This variety of chain stitch is made up of a chain stitch (page 185) and then a twisted chain stitch, which repeats along the line. It creates a textured line that swings from side to side. This stitch looks complex but is not difficult to work. By changing your spacing, you can create a series of scallops; worked in a slightly irregular manner, it makes a great organic line for use in flower sprays and the like.

1. Start with a regular chain stitch by bringing your needle from the back; take a bite of the fabric and wrap the thread under the needle.

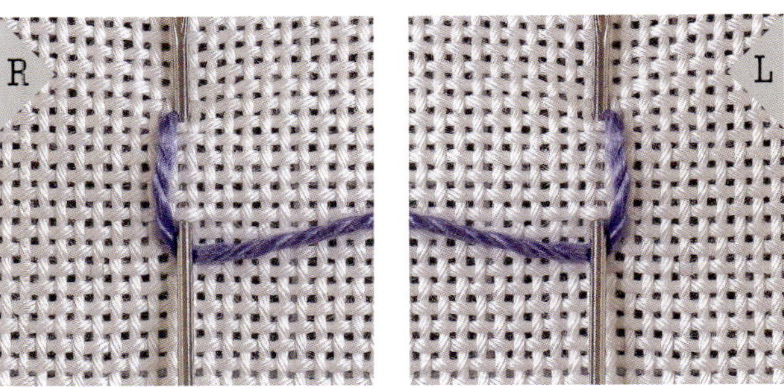

2. Pull the needle through to create a single chain stitch.

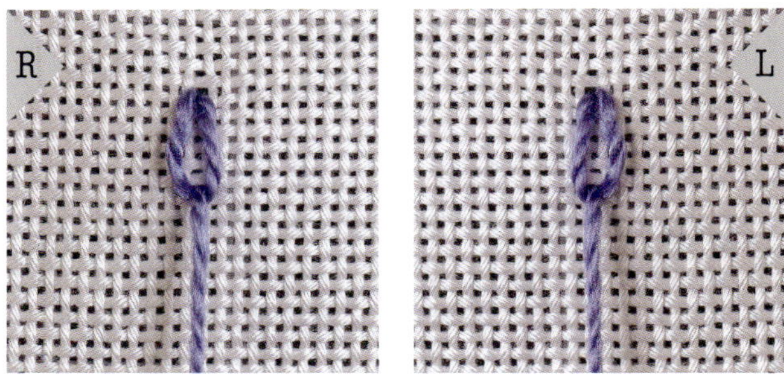

3. Angle your needle to the side and take a bite of the fabric. Insert your needle to the side of the single chain stitch. Wrap the thread under, then over, the needle.

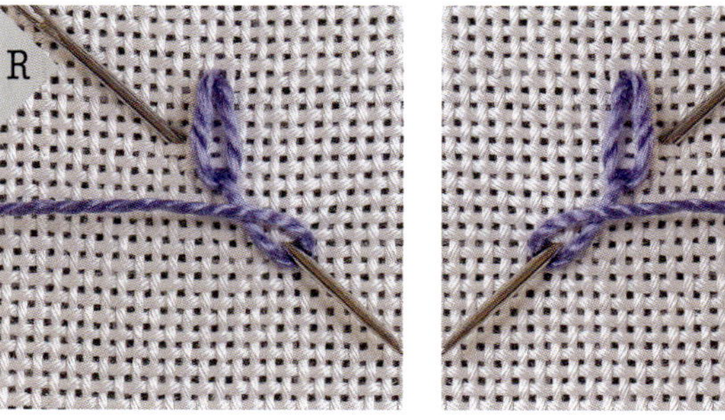

4. Pull the needle through to create a single twisted chain stitch that points to one side of the line.

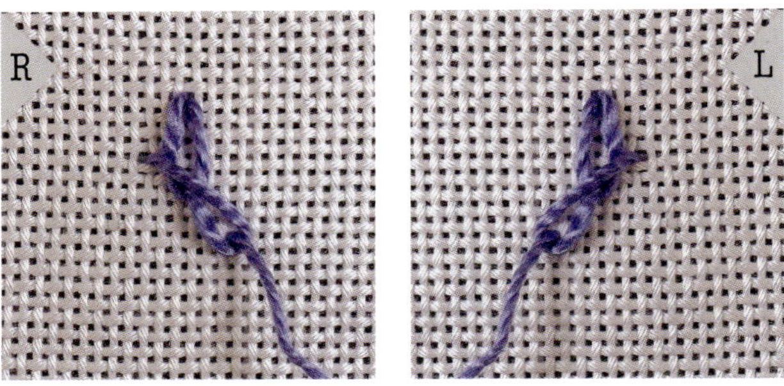

5. Create a single chain stitch.

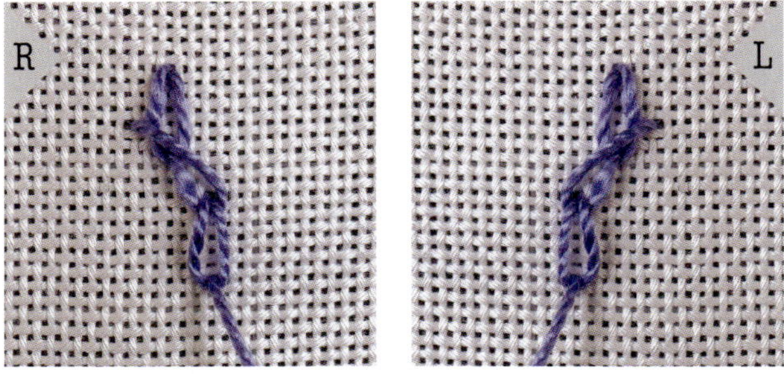

6. Create a twisted chain stitch.

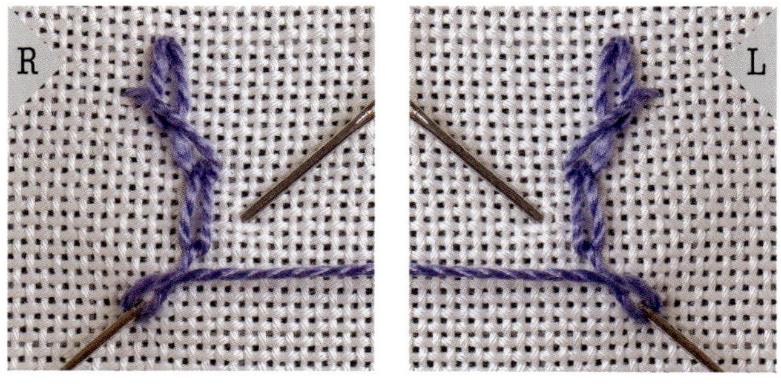

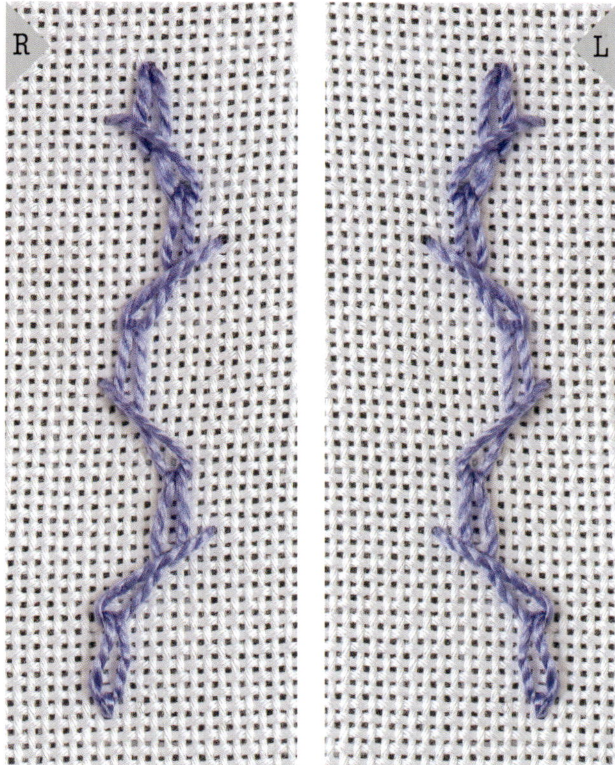

As you can see, crossed double chain creates an interesting textured wavy line.

Crossed double chain stitch worked along the edge of a seam. I used hand-dyed perle cotton #5.

Chain Stitch (Double Twisted)

Double twisted chain makes a nice border that is quickly and easily worked. The second part of the stitch mirrors the first. Once your hands understand the motion of the twist, or the wrap over the needle, the stitch becomes simple, and you quickly fall into a rhythm.

1. This stitch is worked vertically. Bring your thread up through the fabric and insert the needle at a diagonal angle with the point emerging a short space along the line to be stitched. Cross the thread over the needle and then wrap it under the point of the needle.

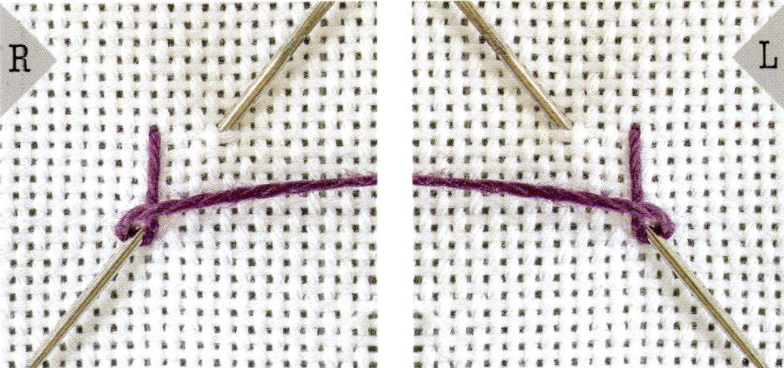

2. Pull the needle through the fabric. The angled part of the stitch will form the central pattern, so keep the width of each stitch uniform.

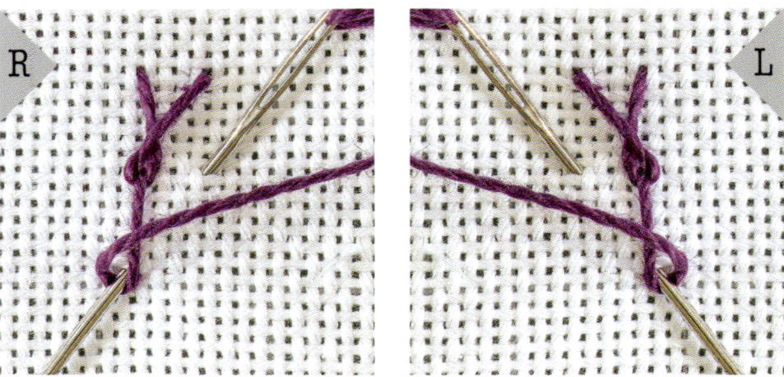

3. Continue working this stitch as evenly spaced as possible until you reach the bottom of the line. Take your thread to the back of the fabric and tie it off.

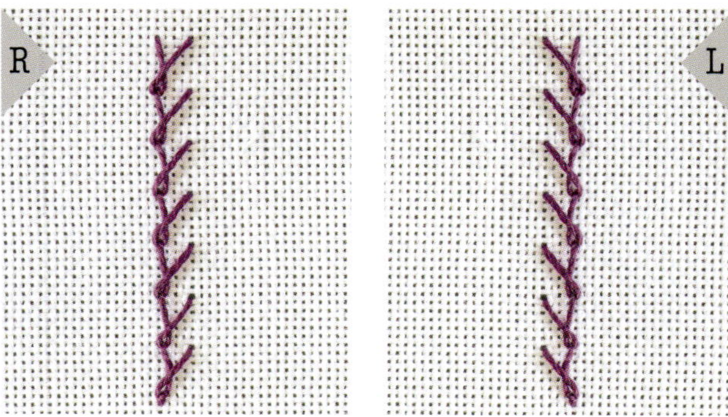

4. Bring your thread out at the top of the line to start the second part of the stitch. Work so that the angled part of the stitch meets and mirrors the first row.

◊ Completed line of double twisted chain stitch

Double twisted chain worked in variegated perle cotton #8 thread

Chain Stitch (Interlaced)

Interlaced chain stitch is an easy and attractive stitch. I have used a contrasting color thread to lace the stitches so you can easily see what I am doing. If you use the same color thread, the line of stitching produced is wide and like a braid.

1. Work a line of slightly larger chain stitches (page 185) with a loose tension; the row will tighten slightly as you lace it.

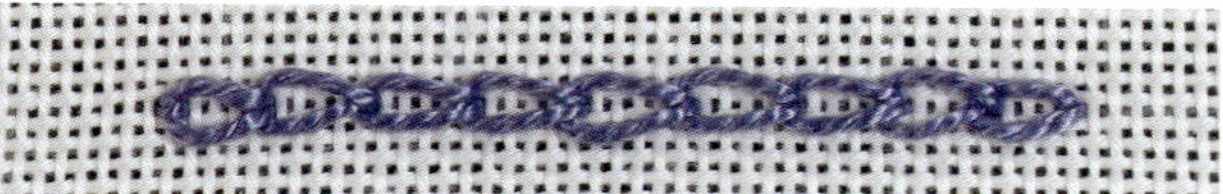

2. During this lacing phase, use a blunt tapestry needle to avoid splitting the foundation stitches. Bring your needle out in the middle of the first chain stitch, at the start of the line. Slide the needle underneath the loop on the second chain with your needle pointing toward the center. Pull the new thread through.

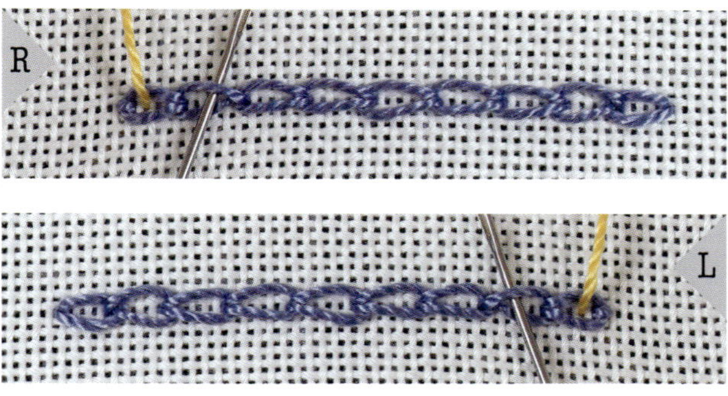

3. Move back to the first chain, and with your needle pointed up, pass the needle under the first chain again. Pull the thread through.

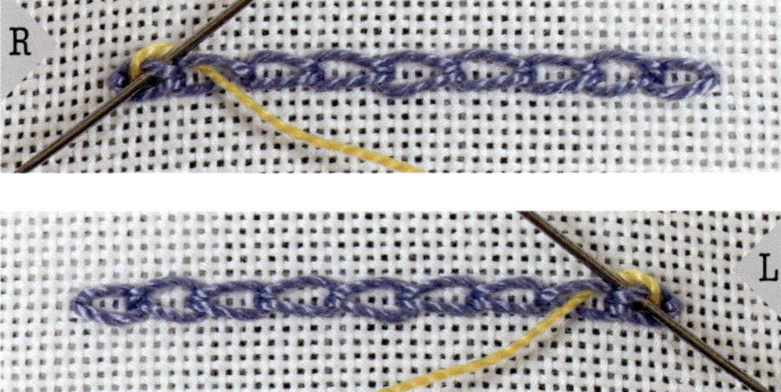

4. Pass the needle under the middle of the third chain stitch.

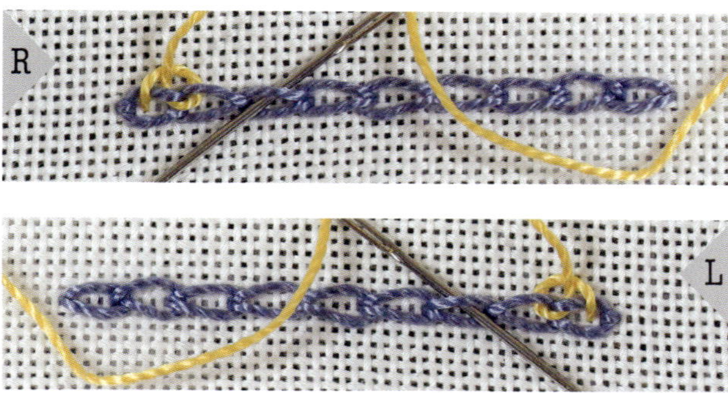

5. Move back 1 stitch and pass the needle under the loop.

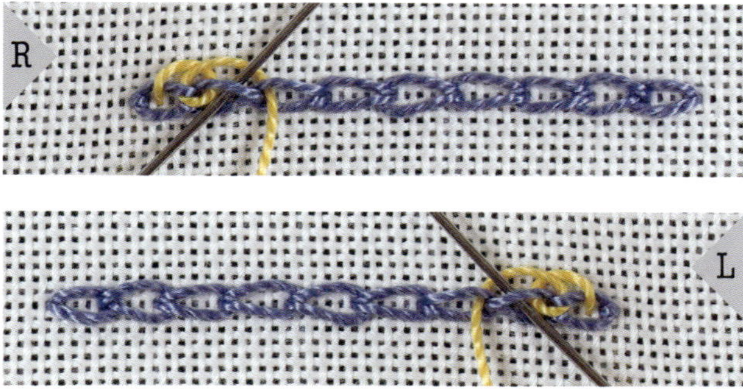

6. Continue along the line looping the lacing thread as you go. Take care not to pull the lacing stitches too tight. Allow them to relax into position. Take the needle to the back of the work next to the last chain stitch.

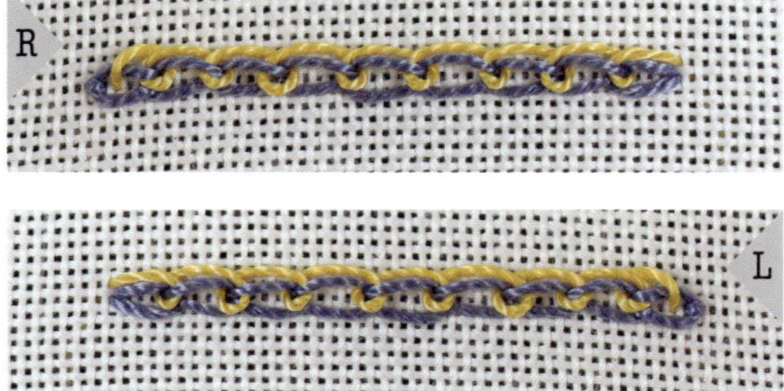

7. Turn your work. Bring your needle out on the other side of the chain stitches and lace the other side.

8. To couch down the loops, bring your needle up at the first laced loop. Normally, you would use a matching color thread to the lacing thread, but for purposes of demonstration, I have used a third color.

9. Catch the loop down with a small straight stitch.

10. Catch the loops along the line.

11. Catch the loops along the other side.

Chain Stitch (Linked)

Work linked chain stitch from top to bottom.

1. Begin by making a slightly long chain stitch (page 185). Insert your needle at the top of the line and have it emerge from the fabric pointing down. Wrap your thread under the needle and pull it through.

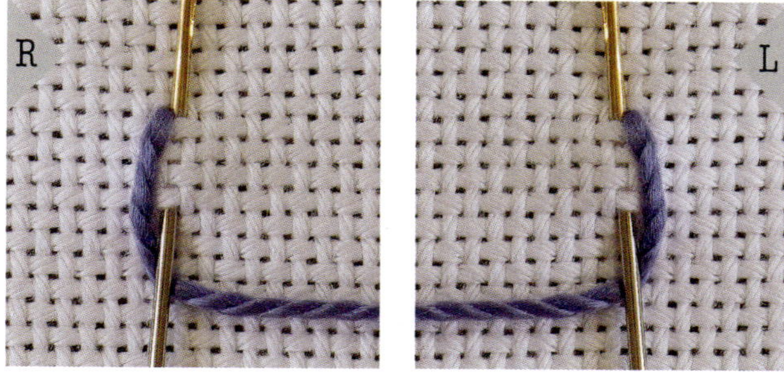

This creates the first chain stitch.

2. Insert your needle at the base of the chain, turn your needle and, pointing upward, make a backstitch so that the needle tip emerges from the middle of the first chain.

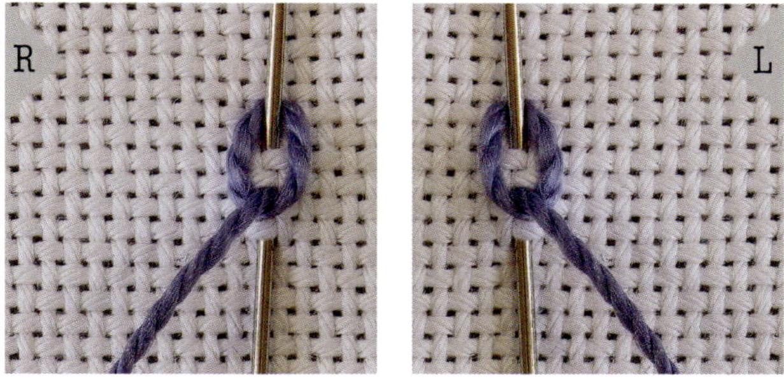

3. Pull your thread through so that it is now emerging from the middle of the first chain stitch.

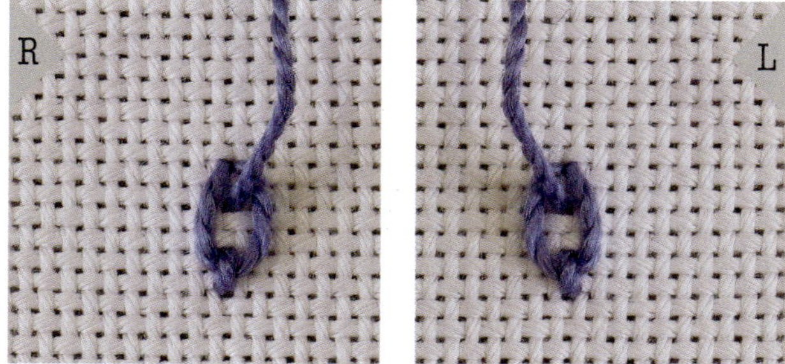

4.Turn your needle and insert it where the thread emerges; with the needle emerging farther down the line, make another chain stitch.

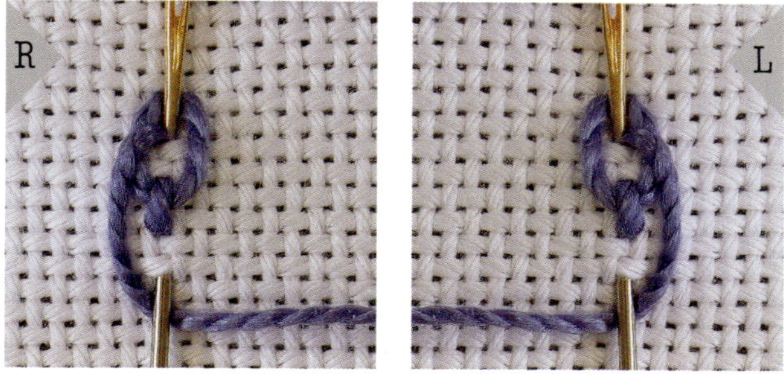

5. Continue making stitches in this forward-and-backward motion down the line. When you reach the end, you will need to make a small, additional stitch to finish the line neatly.

Chain Stitch (Linked Double)

Linked double chain stitch consists of two chain stitches worked side by side, which are then linked with a single chain to form a line. This stitch will follow a curve well and lends itself to experimentation—you can widen the chain stitches and play with spacing. It looks particularly effective if you use a thread with a firm twist such as a perle cotton.

1. Start with a chain stitch (page 185). Take a vertical bite of the fabric. Have the point of your needle emerge a short space along the line to be stitched. Wrap your thread under the needle. Pull the thread through to create the first chain stitch.

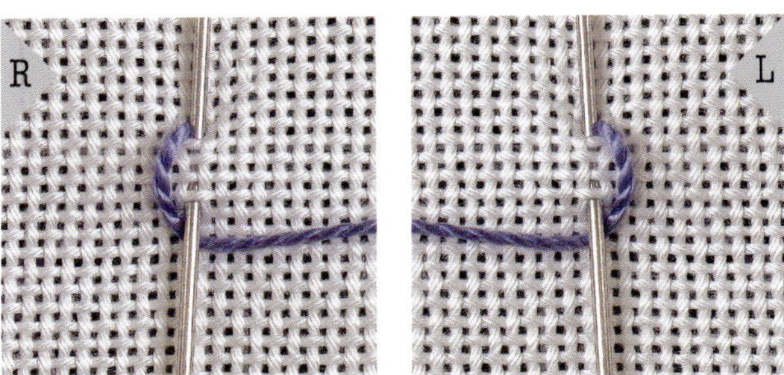

2. Make a second chain stitch at a slight angle to the main line you want to stitch.

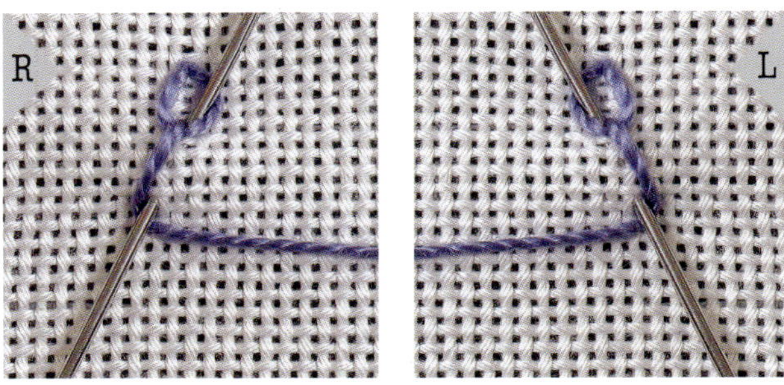

3. Pull the thread through.

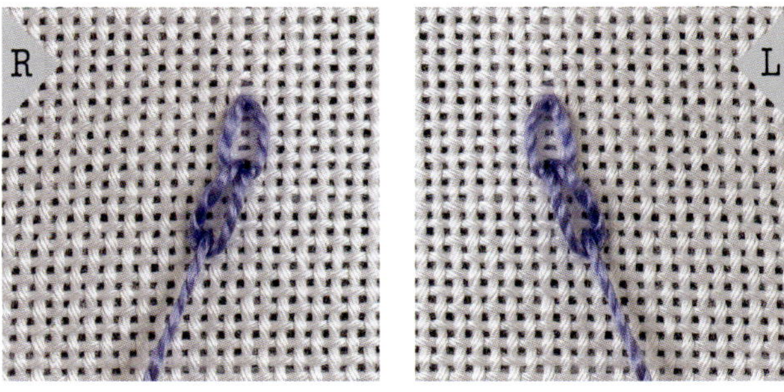

4. Make a second chain stitch pointing in a diagonal manner.

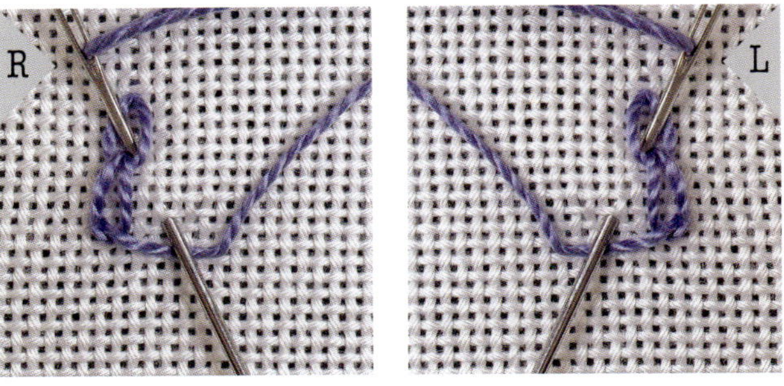

5. Pull your thread through.

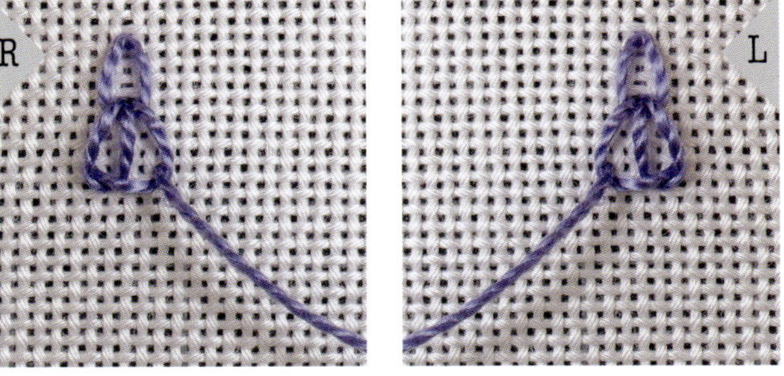

6. Work a chain stitch below the 2 stitches you have just created. Place your needle in the middle of the first chain stitch to center the stitch on the line you want to work.

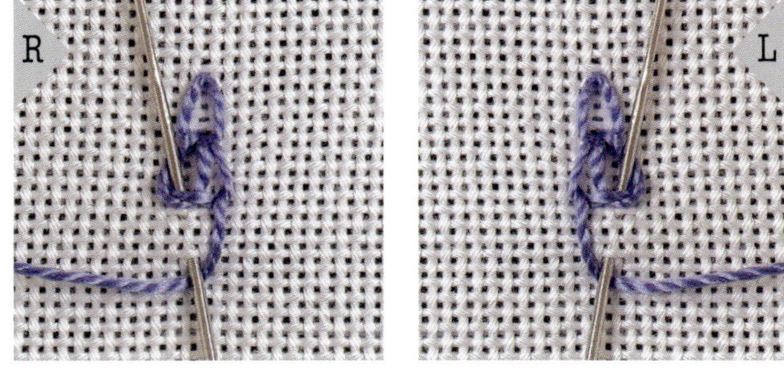

7. Continue along the line in this manner working a unit of 2 stitches and then a single chain stitch.

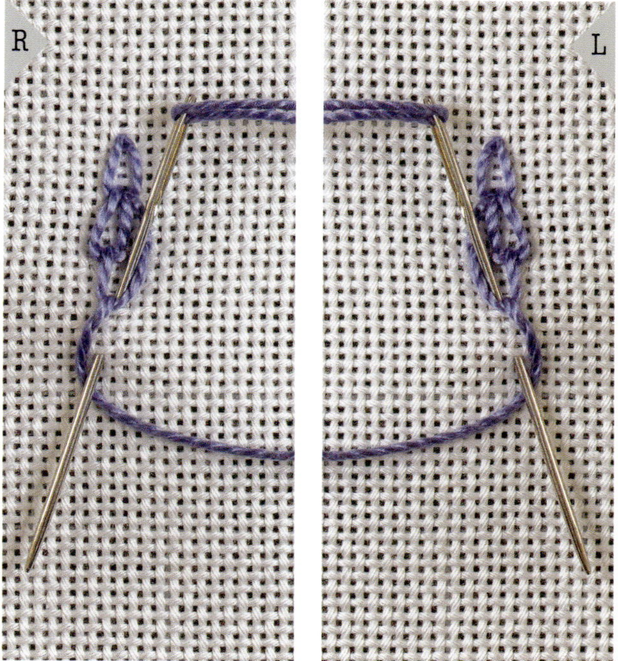

8. Continue in this manner until you complete the line. Tie off with a small straight stitch.

◊ Linked double chain stitch worked in hand-dyed perle cotton #5

Chain Stitch (Open Chained Bar)

Open chained bar is a versatile form of couching that can be used for borders and outlines. It is created by working open chain stitch (page 73) over larger threads. For the couched yarn, you can use a large variety of threads, including textured novelty yarns and metallics.

1. Lay down 2 or 3 strands of thread or 1 thick thread or ribbon. You can use most threads, as they will be couched down using open chain stitch (page 73). The width of your couching thread will determine the width of the open chained bar.

2. Bring your thread out next to where you started your couched thread. Reinsert your needle on the diagonal and wrap your thread under the needle pull it through the fabric.

3. Move along the line and insert the needle on the diagonal. Wrap the thread under the needle and pull it through the fabric.

4. Continue in this manner along the line.

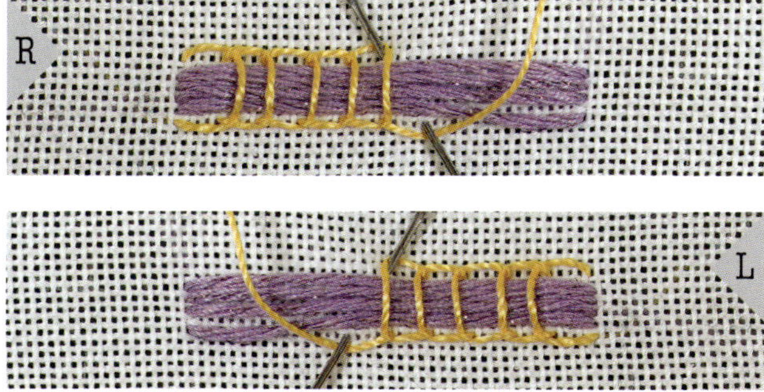

5. Tie off your last stitch with a small straight stitch.

◊ Open chained bar worked using variegated thread over 4 strands of yellow novelty thread

Chain Stitch (Open Chain)

Open chain stitch is also known as *Roman chain, square chain,* and *ladder stitch.* By adjusting the spacing between the stitches, you can stretch it out to create a lacy open texture or close it up to create a weighty line.

Work this stitch over two imaginary lines. If you need to mark the fabric, mark two parallel guidelines using a water-soluble or air-erasable marker.

1. Bring the needle up through the fabric and reinsert it on the diagonal. With the thread wrapped under the needle, pull the needle through the fabric and leave a loose loop.

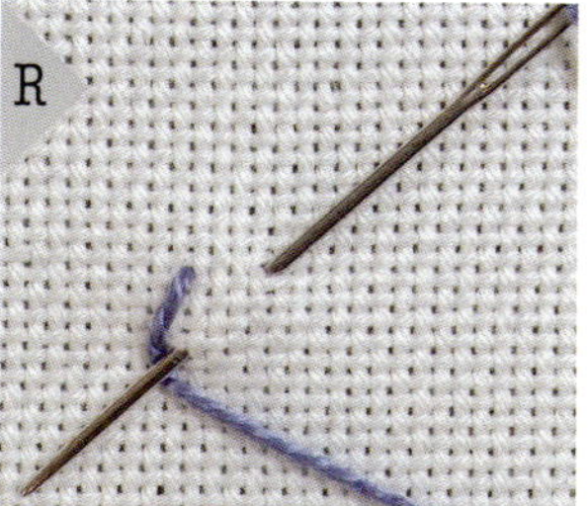

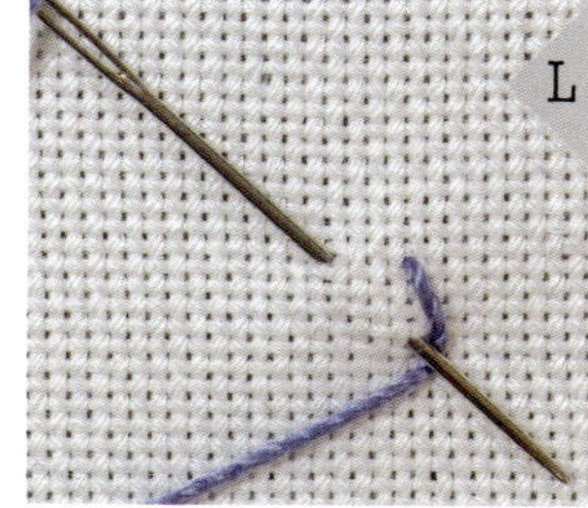

2. Move down the line and insert the needle inside the loop on a diagonal angle. With the thread wrapped under the needle, pull the needle through the fabric to create a second loop.

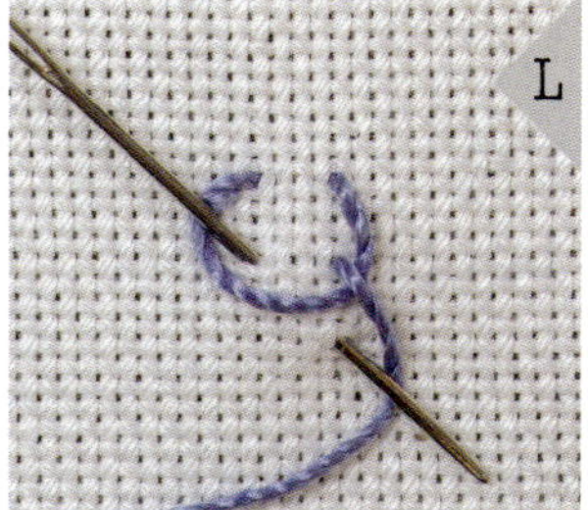

3. Repeat these steps and continue down the line.

4. Tie your last stitch off with two small straight stitches.

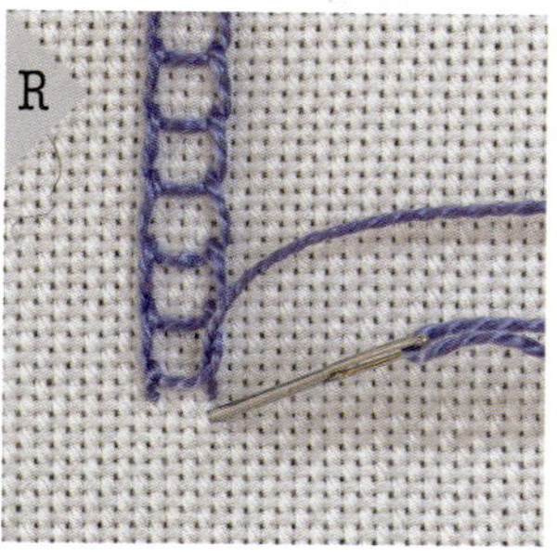

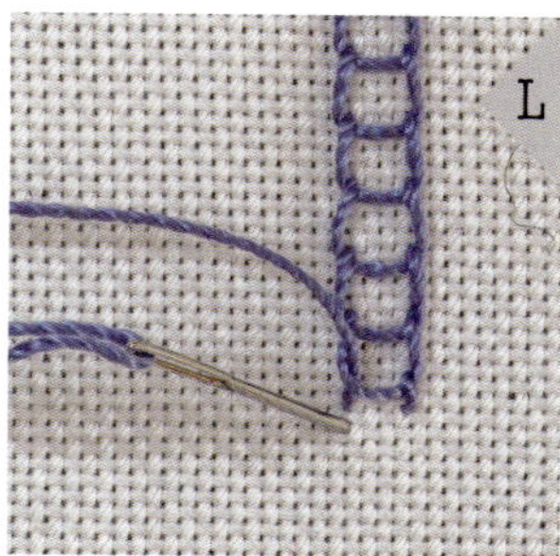

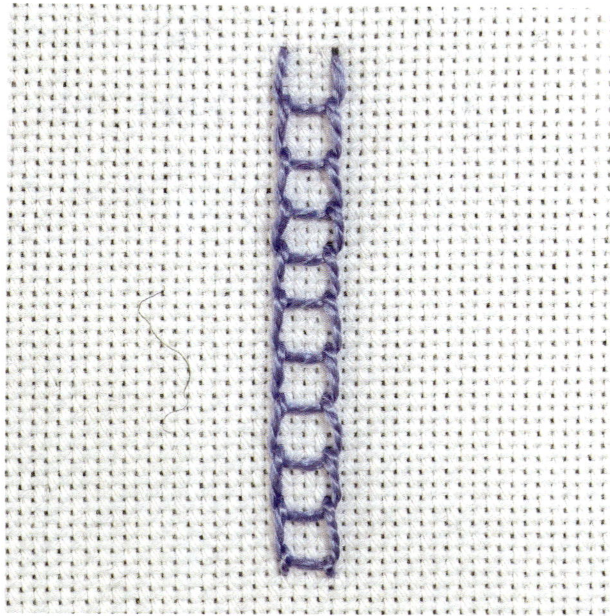

◊ Completed line of open chain stitch

Chain Stitch (Raised)

Raised chain produces a textured raised line. The width and the spacing of the foundation stitches will influence the look and texture of this stitch. As you work the second journey of this stitch, take care that you are not passing the needle through the fabric.

1. Start with a ladder of straight stitches as your foundation.

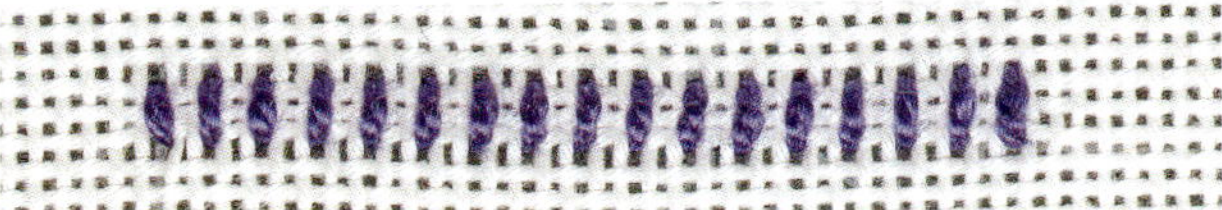

2. Bring your needle to the front of the fabric at the end of the ladder. Take your needle over the top of the first bar and slide your needle under. Point your needle upward and to one side.

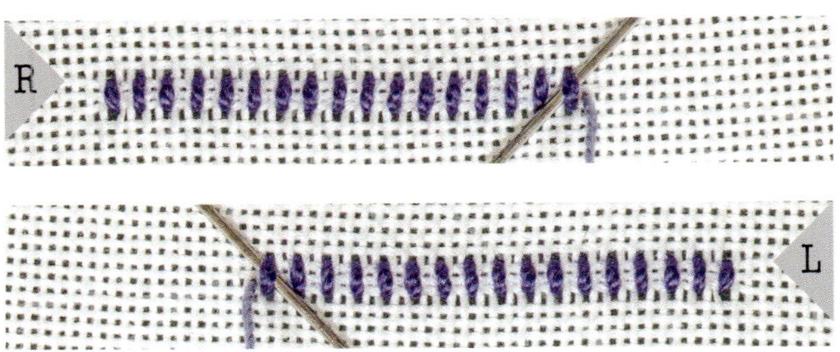

3. Pull your needle back through by sliding it under the same bar and wrapping your thread under your needle.

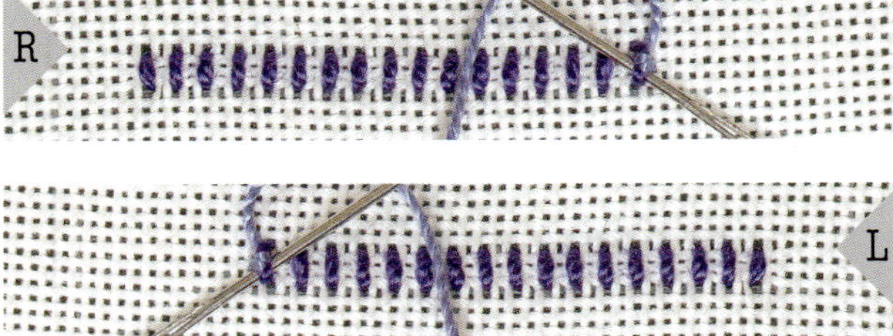

4. Pull the thread through. This loop creates the first chain.

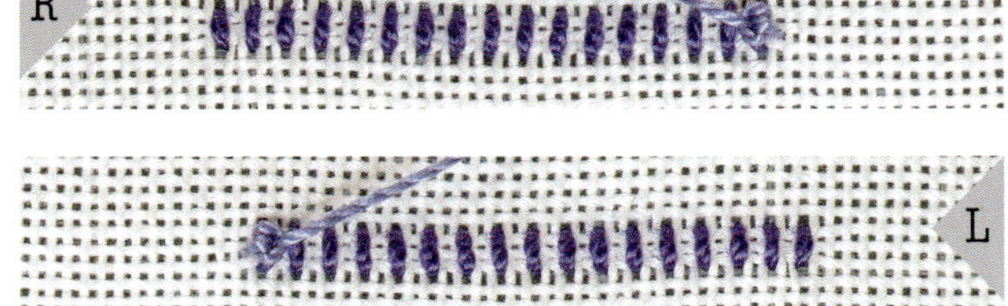

5. Slide your needle under the second bar and wrap your thread under the needle. Pull your needle through to make the next loop. Move along the ladder of stitches repeating these actions.

6. Move along the ladder, repeating this action to make a loop on each bar.

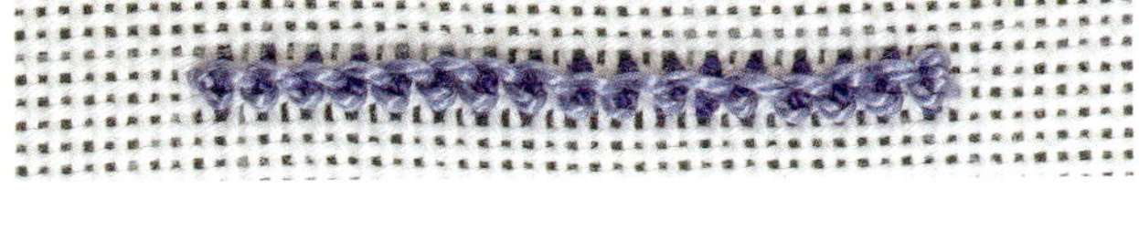

◇ Raised chain stitch worked in perle cotton #5

Chain Stitch (Raised Open)

Open raised chain is quickly worked, producing a textured line that will follow a curve well. The width of the open chain stitches and the spacing will affect the look and texture of this stitch, which lends itself to experimentation.

In this demonstration, I have used different color threads so you can clearly see how the stitch is worked. Normally, you would use matching threads.

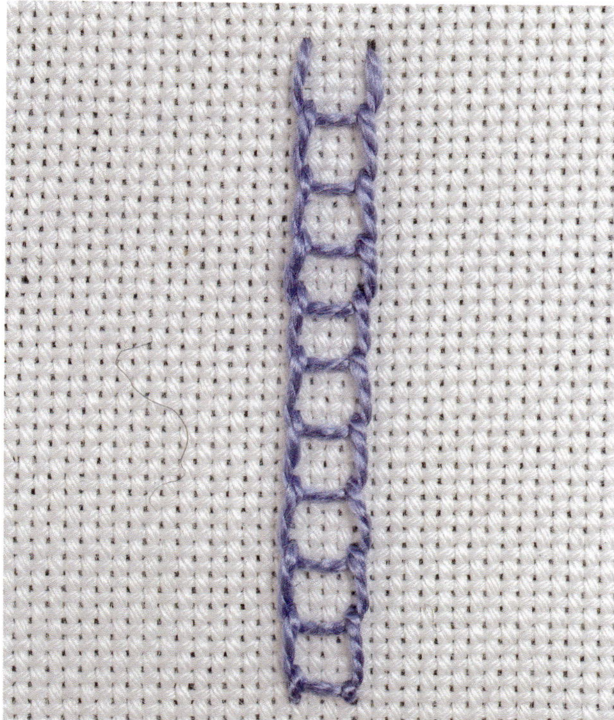

Start with a foundation of open chain stitch (page 73) ready to work a secondary thread on the bars of the open chain stitch.

Tip Use a blunt tapestry needle to avoid splitting the foundation stitches.

1. Hold your work in a vertical position and bring your thread to the front of the fabric at the top of the line.

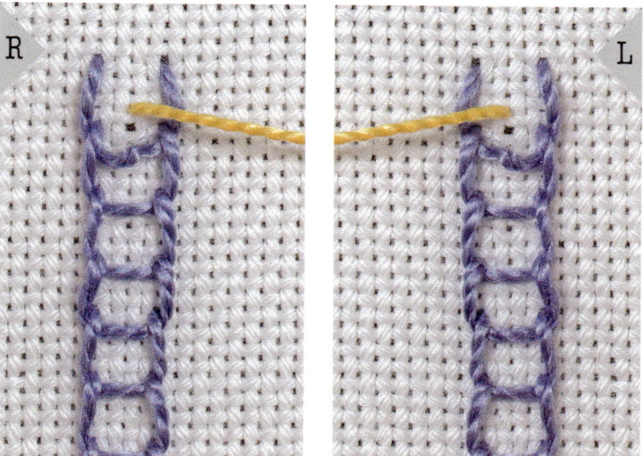

2. Take your needle over the top of the first bar of the open chain and slide your needle under the first bar. Point your needle upward and to one side.

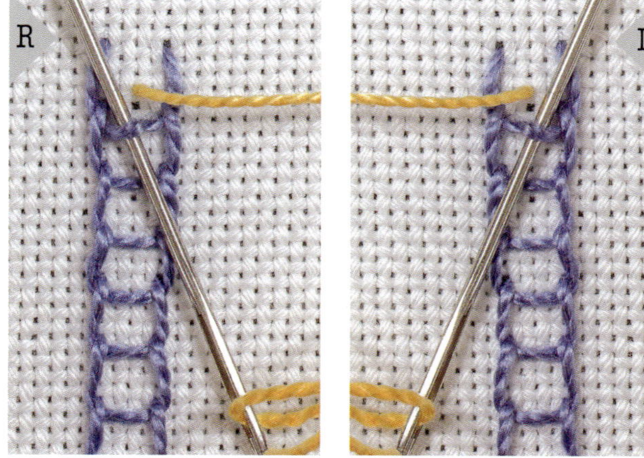

3. Pull your needle through. Take care that you are not passing the needle through the fabric. With your needle pointed down, slide it under the same bar on the other side of the working thread. Wrap your thread under your needle and pull through. This loop creates the first chain.

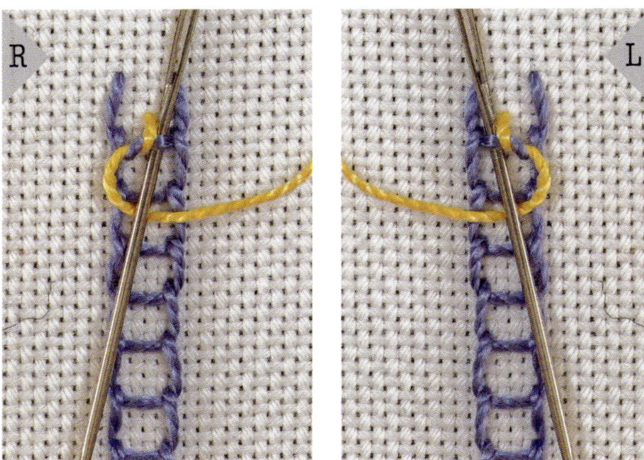

4. Move down the open chain foundation stitches to the next bar. Take your needle over the top of the second bar and slide your needle under. Angle and point your needle upward.

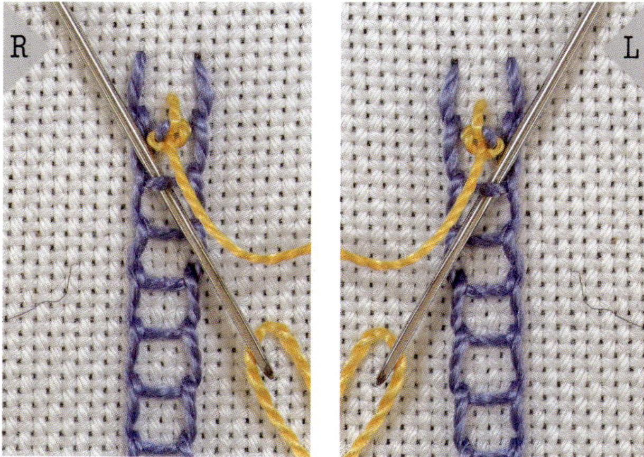

5. Slide your needle downward under the same bar but on the other side of the working thread. With your thread wrapped under your needle, pull through to create a loop on the bar'.

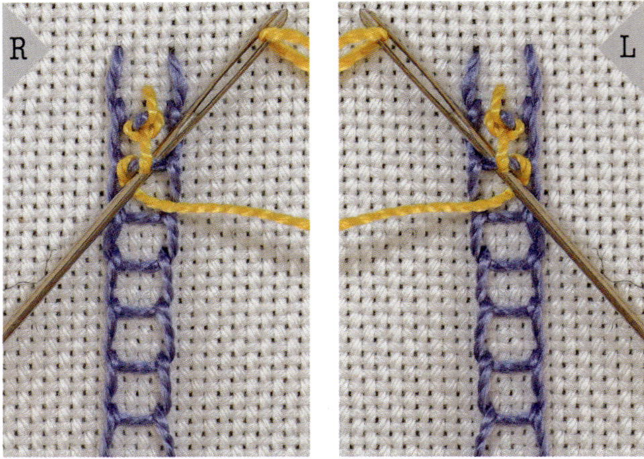

6. Repeat Steps 4–5 down the line of open chain stitch.

Chain Stitch (Reverse)

Also known as *broad chain stitch,* reverse chain creates a line that is slightly wider than a regular chain stitch (page 185). The advantage of this stitch is that you can often produce a neater looking stitch using this technique. A thread that has a firm twist, such as perle cotton, works well.

Work this stitch in a downward direction.

1. Start by working a detached chain stitch (page 187) upside down. Bring the needle out a little further below the line. Leave enough space for 1 chain stitch.

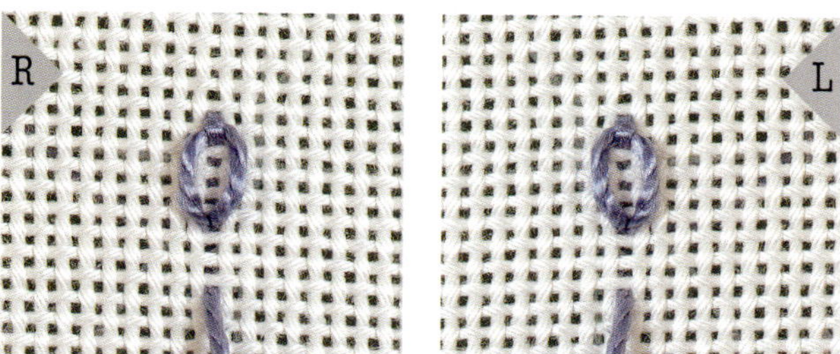

2. Slide the needle under the chain stitch, but not through the fabric. Take the needle back down through the fabric where it emerged.

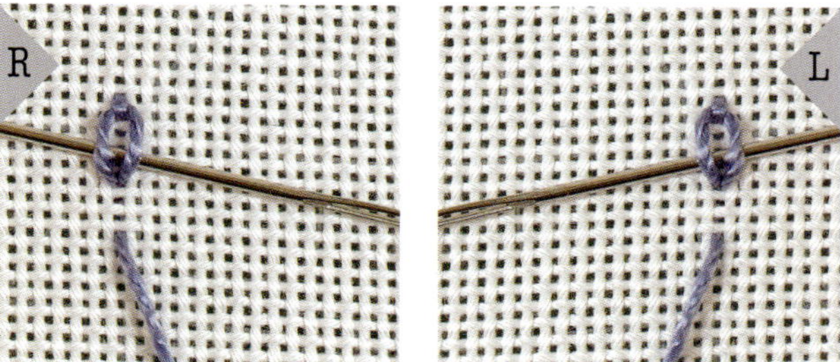

3. Repeat this along the line. When stitching, don't pull too tight, and you will get a good shape to each chained loop.

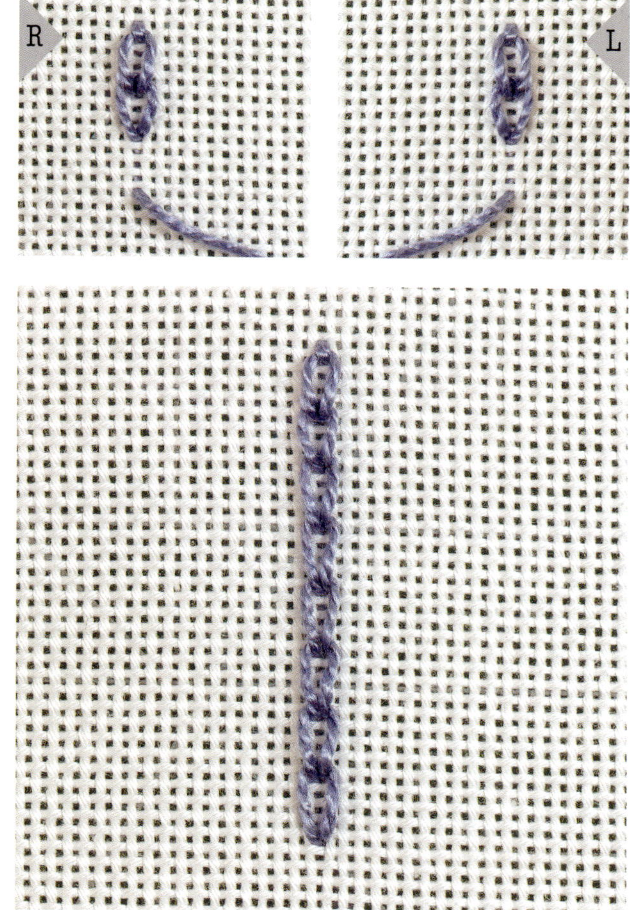

◊ Completed line of reverse chain stitch

Chain Stitch (Stacked Triple)

Stacked triple chain stitch produces a wide decorative line. You can work it using the same thread throughout the process, or use a different color thread for the last line of chain stitches.

1. Work 2 parallel rows of chain stitch (page 185) with the stitches aligned.

2. In the next step, you will chain stitch both rows of stitches together. Bring your thread out in between the rows.

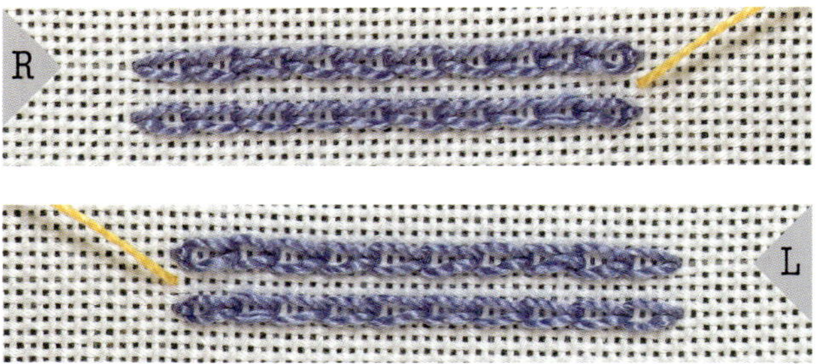

3. Pass your needle under the inner sides of the chain stitches. Pull your needle through.

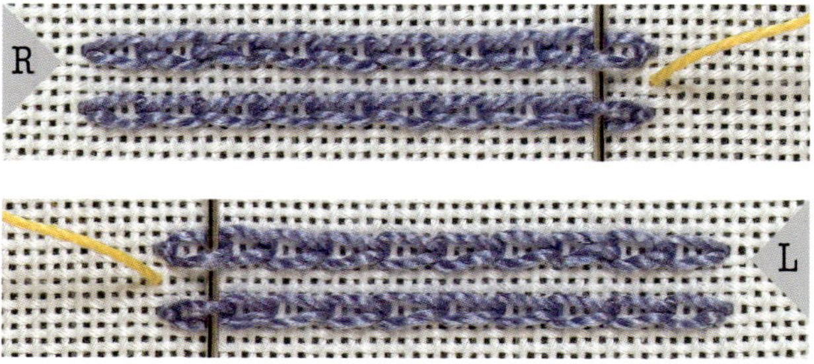

4. Take your needle back through the fabric where the thread emerged to make a chain stitch. Take a small bite of the fabric and have your needle emerge before the top of your stacked chain stitch.

5. Make a second stacked chain stitch.

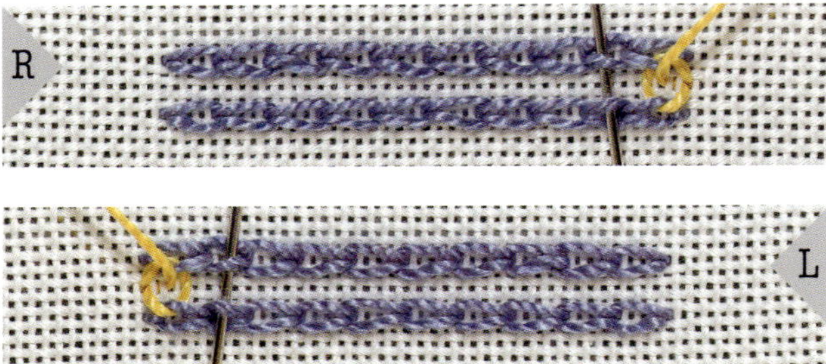

6. Work this way until you have finished the line.

Stacked triple chain stitch worked with a foundation row of turquoise perle cotton #5. The top journey was worked in different threads. The top row is perle cotton #5. The middle row is a novelty thread with a metallic fleck. The bottom row is a rayon thread.

The horizontal lines in this sample are stacked triple chain stitch with the foundation rows worked in white perle cotton #5 and the top journey worked in light tan perle cotton #5.

Chain Stitch (Tied Double)

Tied double chain stitch is made up of two chain stitches that are tied with a fly stitch. Units can be used as singles sprinkled over the surface of an area, or arranged either in a horizontal or a vertical line.

1. Start with a chain stitch (page 185). Insert your needle and have the point of the needle emerge from the fabric at a 45° angle. Wrap your thread under the needle. Pull the thread through and anchor the loop with a small straight stitch to tie it off.

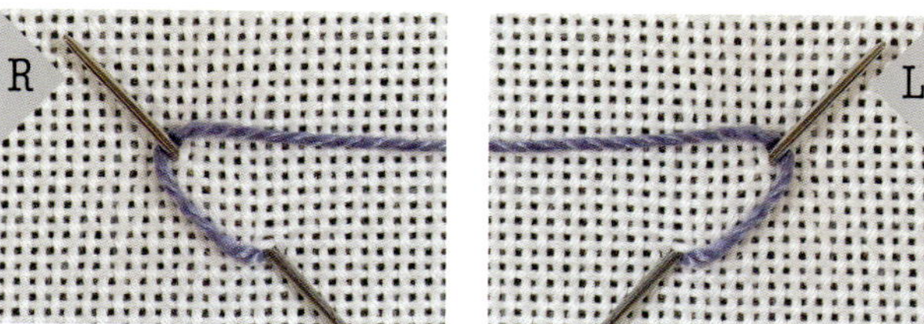

2. Make a second chain stitch at a 45° angle. Do not tie off the loop.

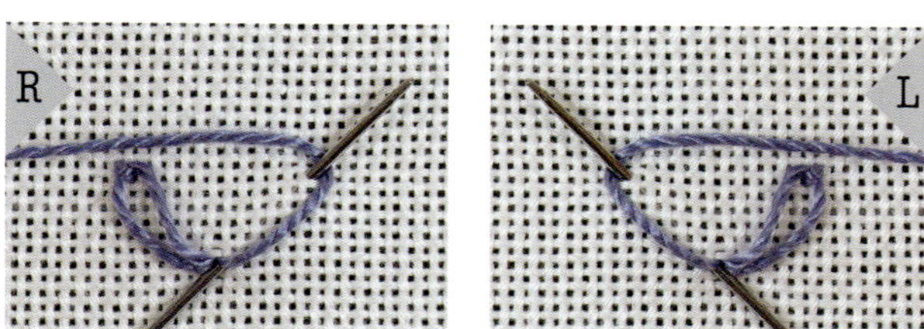

3. To anchor the stitch with a fly stitch, insert your needle at the top of the first chain stitch at an angle. Position the needle so that the point emerges above the center point of the 2 chain stitches.

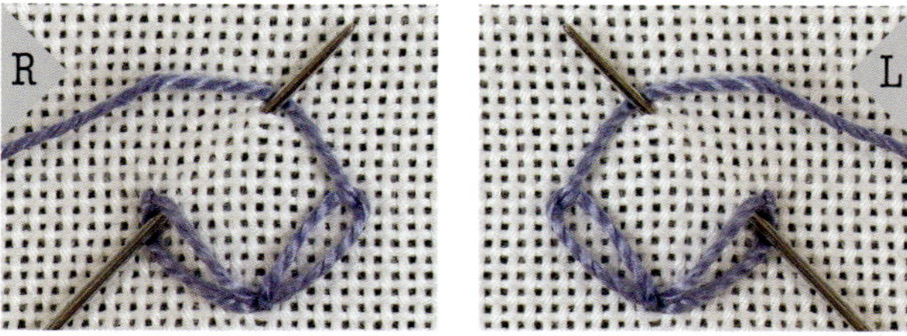

4. Anchor the fly stitch with a small straight stitch. This is a single tied double chain stitch. These units can be arranged in patterns.

5. To work the stitch in a horizontal line, start your chain stitches in line with the first unit.

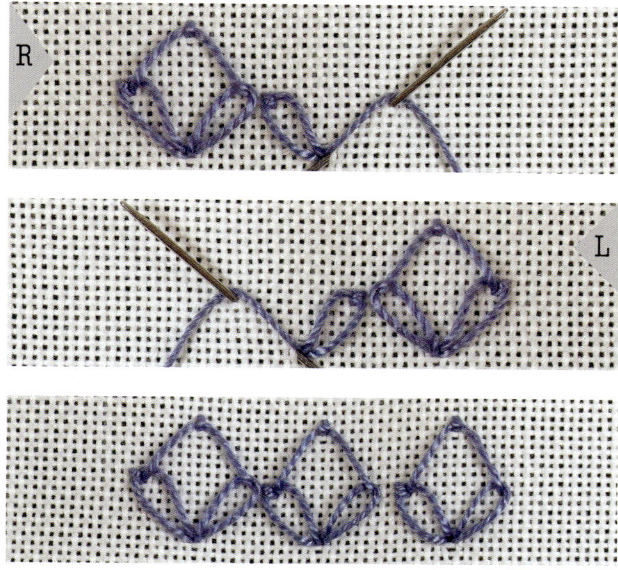

◊ Horizontal tied double chain stitches

6. To work the stitch in a vertical line, do not tie off the fly stitch. Instead, anchor the fly stitch with the first chain stitch of the next unit.

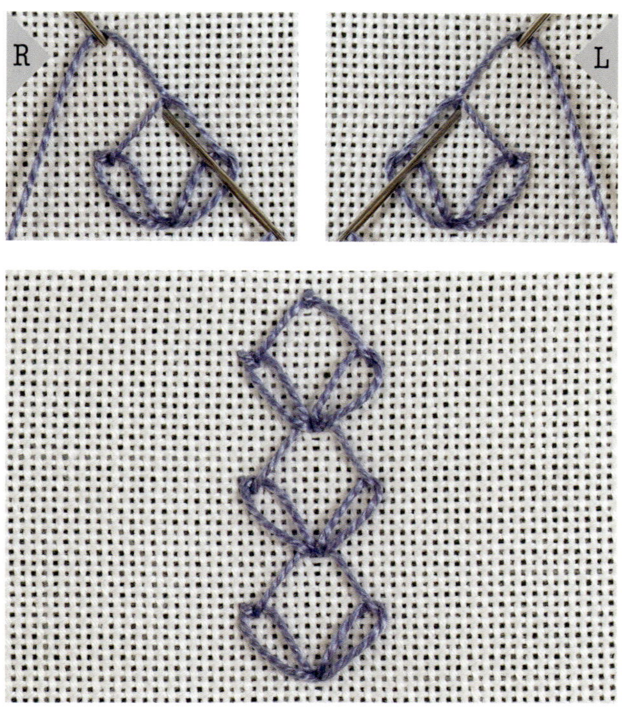

◊ Line of tied double chain stitch

Chain Stitch (Whipped Double)

Whipped double chain stitch is useful if you want a very dramatic, strong, hard-wearing line that is still capable of following a curve easily. In the illustrations, I have used two colors so that you can see what is happening, but you can work this stitch in the same color. During the whipping phase, use a blunt tapestry needle to avoid splitting the foundation stitches.

1. Work 2 parallel rows of chain stitch (page 185) with your stitches the same size and sitting side by side. Make your stitches a little loose; the row will tighten slightly as you whip it. If the foundation rows are too tight, the work will pucker.

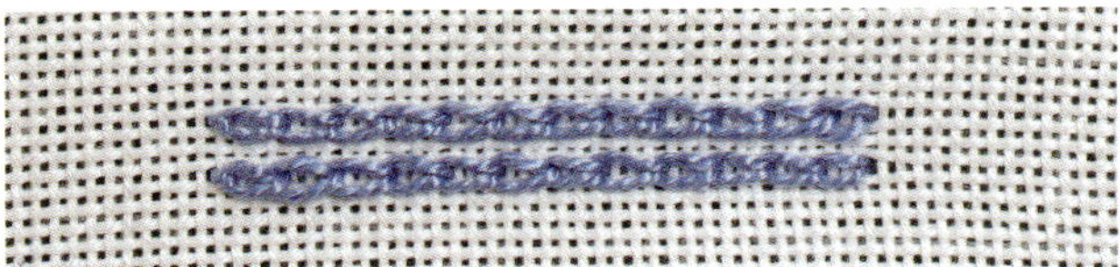

2. Bring your whipping thread out in the middle of both rows. Pass your needle under the first 2 loops and pull through.

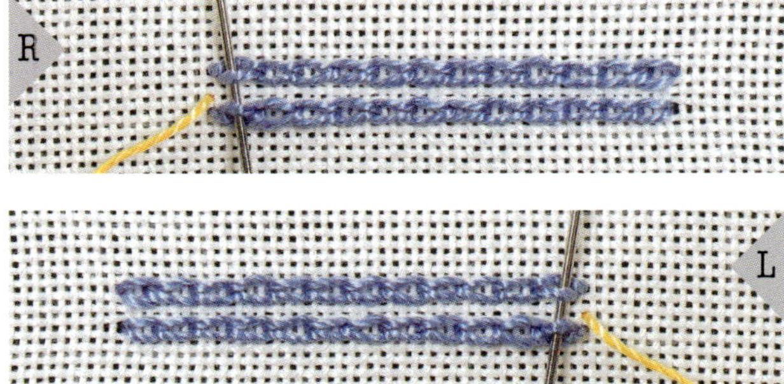

3. Continue whipping the center stitches along the line.

4. For the best results, make sure not to pick up any of the fabric, and keep the whipping even.

Whipped double chain stitch worked in orange/pink perle cotton #5 and whipped with blue thread, used in slow-stitch project

Whipped double chain stitch worked in blue perle cotton #5 and whipped with yellow perle cotton #5 thread

Chain Stitch (Whipped Open)

Whipped open chain stitch produces a wide decorative band. The width and spacing of the open chain stitches will influence the look and texture of this stitch.

Tip Use a blunt tapestry needle to avoid splitting the foundation stitches.

1. Start by working 2 lines of open chain stitches (page 73) side by side. Make sure the stitches sit next to each other. Bring your whipping thread out at the base in the center of the 2 lines of open chain stitches. Take your needle under the first stitch on the central side of the open chain stitches.

2. Pull your thread through to create the first whipped stitch. Whip the second stitch.

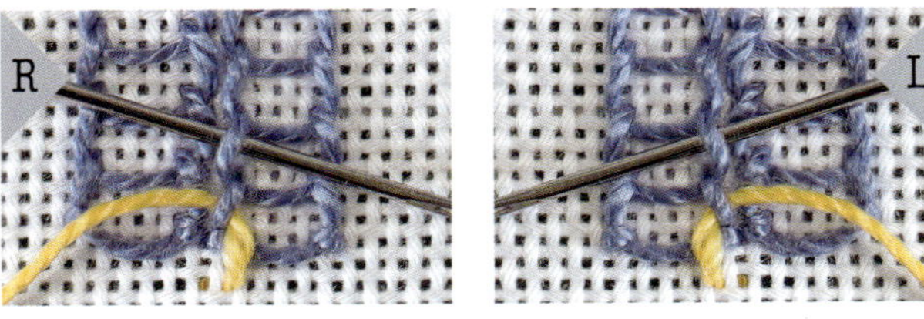

Whipped open chain stitch worked and whipped in variegated perle cotton #8 thread

3. Continue up the line. At the top, take the whipping to the back of the fabric. Bring your whipping thread out at the base to start again.

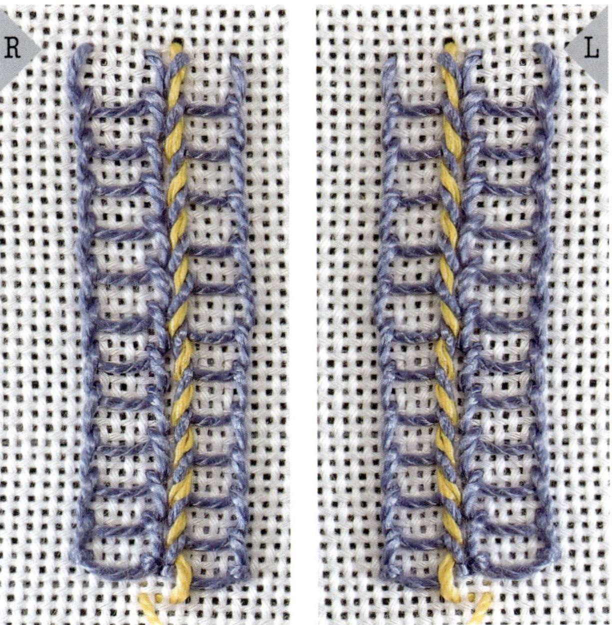

4. Whip the other side of the open chain stitch in the same way and take the thread to the back.

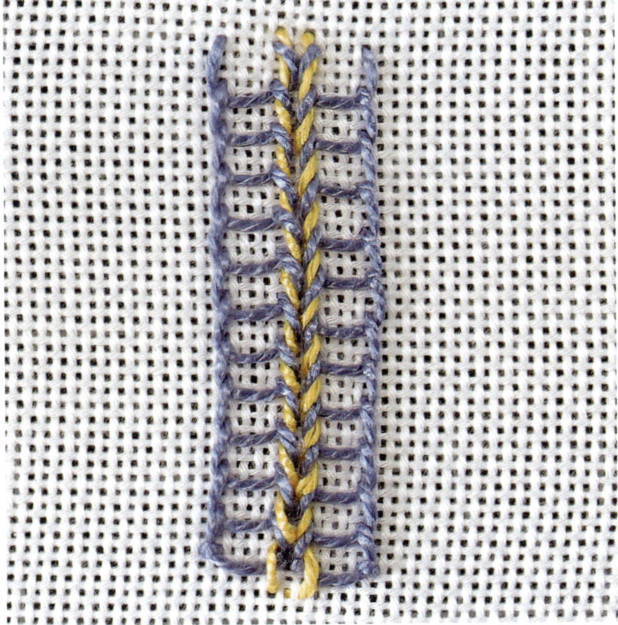

Chain Stitch (Wrapped Reverse)

Wrapped reverse chain is a textured stitch, ideal for leaves and flower petals, but it can also be used to speckle over an area as a fill. It is an easy and quick stitch to work as it is made up of two or three reverse chain stitches (page 77) that are "wrapped" using a larger detached chain stitch.

1. Work in a downward direction. Start with a single detached chain stitch (page 187) worked upside down in the direction you want the line of stitches to go.

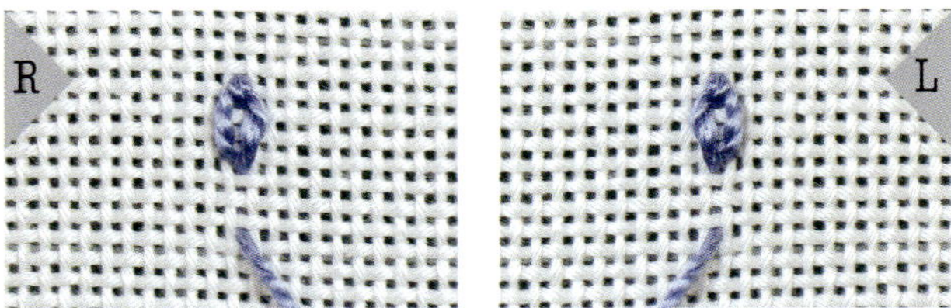

2. Bring the needle out at the base of the detached chain and a little farther down the line, making sure you leave space for 1 chain stitch. Slide the needle under the chain stitch. Take the needle back down through the fabric where it emerged.

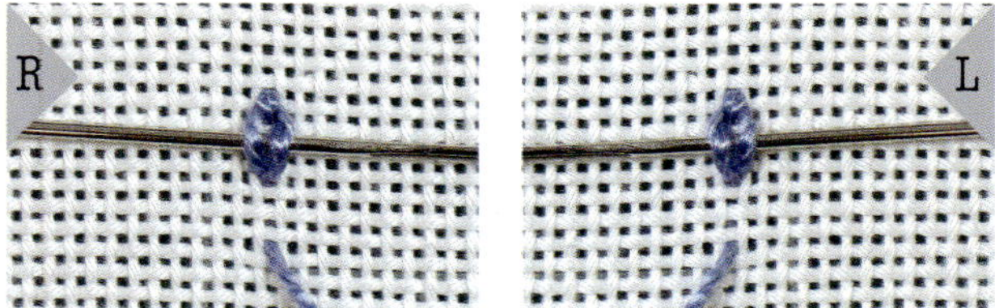

3. Work 3 reverse chain stitches.

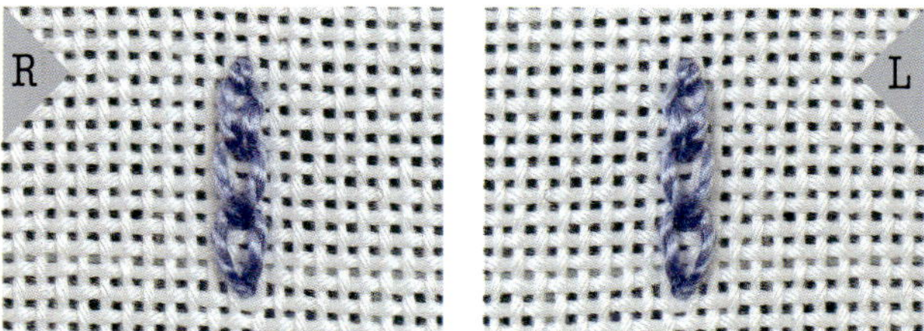

4. To wrap the reverse chain stitches, insert your needle at the top of the first stitch and have your needle emerge at the bottom of the last stitch. Wrap your thread under the needle and pull it through the fabric.

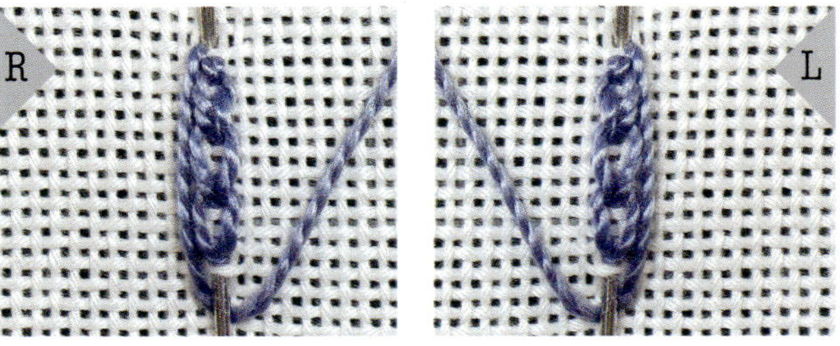

5. Secure this final chain stitch with a small tie stitch.

◊ Wrapped reverse chain stitch worked using perle cotton #8

Chained Bullion Knot

Chained bullion knot consists of a bullion knot with a surrounding detached chain stitch. The combination of these two stitches produces a knobbly, plump stitch that is ideal to use where you want a highly textured stitch. You can use it anywhere that you may have used a detached chain or lazy daisy stitch.

Tips

- Start with a four- or five-wrap bullion; then, as you master those, add more wraps.
- Use a hoop or frame so that you have both hands free to work the knot.
- Use a straw or milliners needle because they have the same width for both the eye and the shaft, which makes it easier to slide the wrapped bullion knot along the needle.
- If stranded cotton threads get tangled in your hands, try a twisted thread, like perle cotton #8 or #5.
- Wrap your thread clockwise, following the natural twist in which it was spun. If it untwists as you wrap, your thread was spun in the opposite direction to most threads, so wrap your bullion counterclockwise. Simply put, wrap clockwise most of the time, but if for some reason this untwists your thread, wrap counterclockwise.

1. Start with a bullion knot.. Bring the thread from the back, turn your needle, and take a bite of the fabric. Emerge near the place that the thread comes out of the fabric. The distance between these 2 points determines the length of the knot.

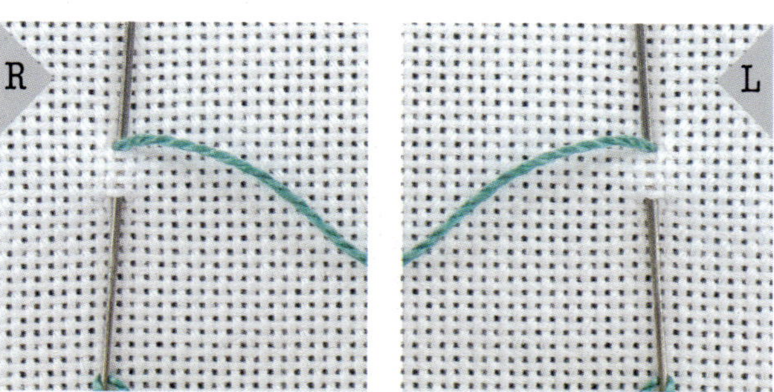

2. Wrap the thread around the needle 5 or 6 times, making sure the thread coils up the needle the same length as the stitch just taken. Do not cross the wraps on the needle.

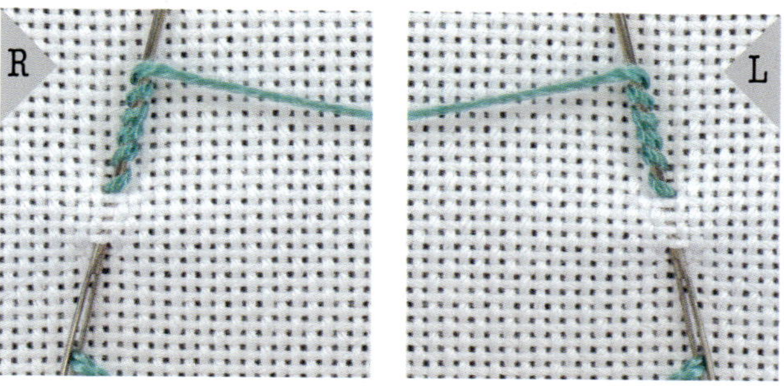

3. Grab the needle between your thumb and first finger.

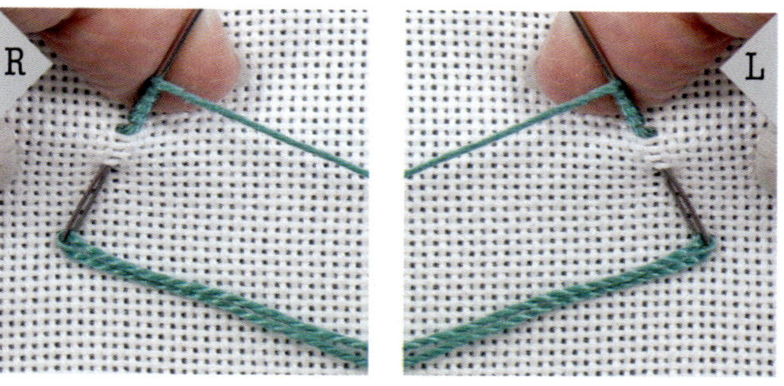

4. Grip the bullion and gently start to pull the thread through the coil while holding it between your first finger and thumb, preventing it from knotting in on itself. Pull the working thread up and away from you.
As the coil tightens, change the direction and pull it toward you.

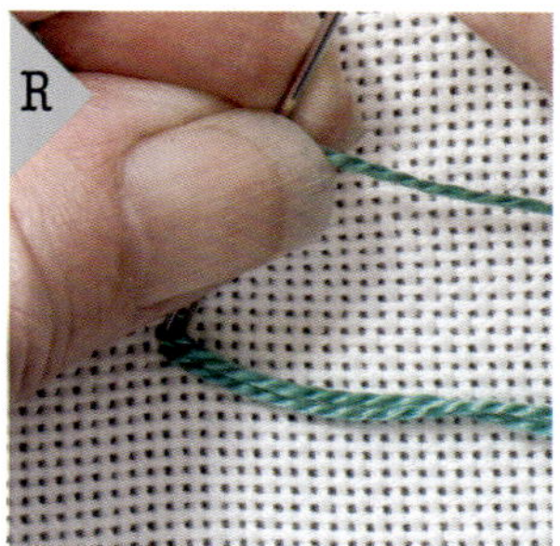

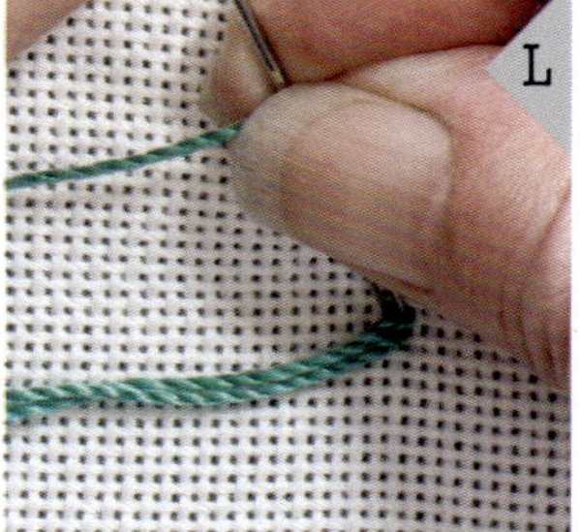

5. If the bullion bunches or looks untidy, pass the needle under the bullion and rub it up and down the length of the bullion to smooth out the coils. Stitchers call this "rubbing the belly" of the bullion.

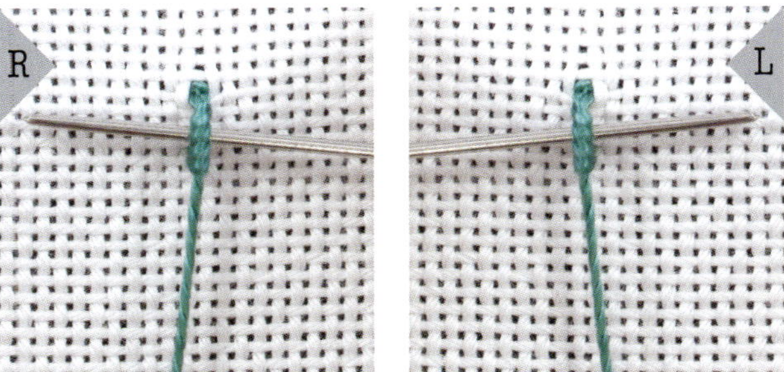

6. When smooth, take the needle through the fabric at the point where the thread first emerged.

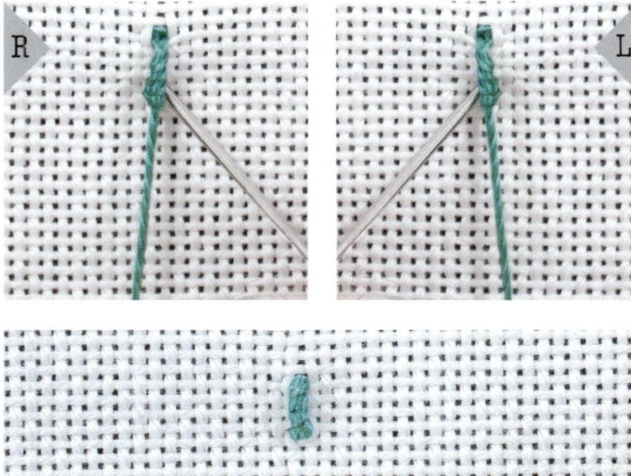

◊ The coil of thread should now lie neatly on the surface.

7. Bring your thread up at the top of the bullion knot.

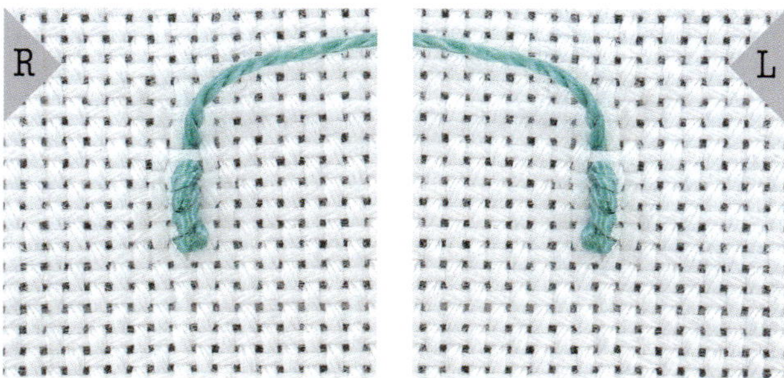

8. Insert the needle so that the point emerges at the base of the bullion knot. Wrap your thread under the needle and pull the thread through to make a chain stitch that wraps around the bullion knot.

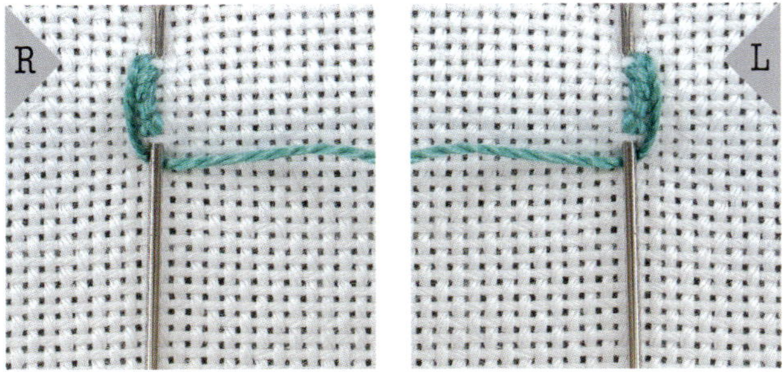

9. Tie off the chain stitch with a small straight stitch, and you have completed a chained bullion.

Chained bullion knot used around a Suffolk puff (yo-yo) in slow-stitch project

Chevron Stitch (Closed)

1. Work this stitch between 2 imaginary parallel lines. If you need to mark the fabric, mark 2 parallel guidelines using a water-soluble or air-erasable marker. Bring the thread up on the top line. On the same line, move back and insert the needle with the tip pointing toward the middle of the stitch.

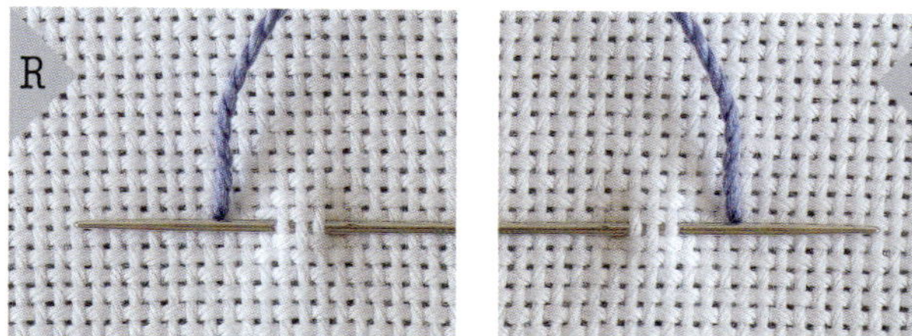

2. Pull the needle through to make the stitch.

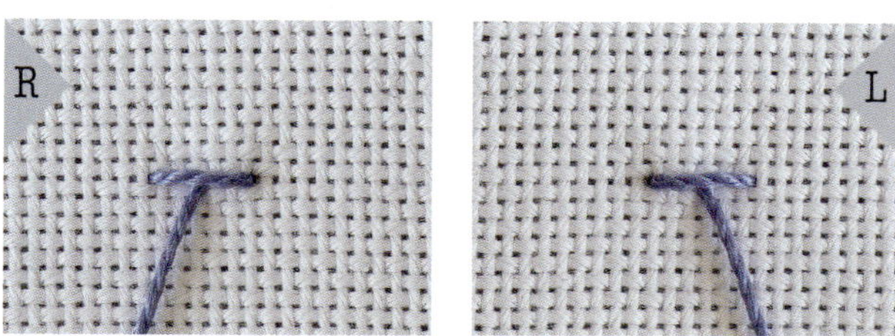

3. Move diagonally down to the bottom line and insert the needle. Pull your needle through.

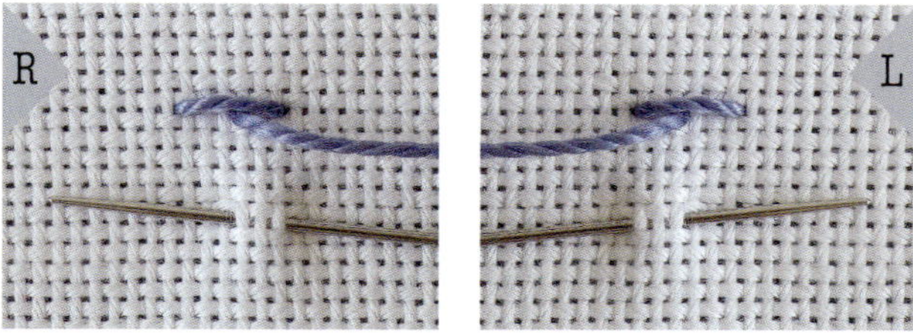

4. Pull the thread through.

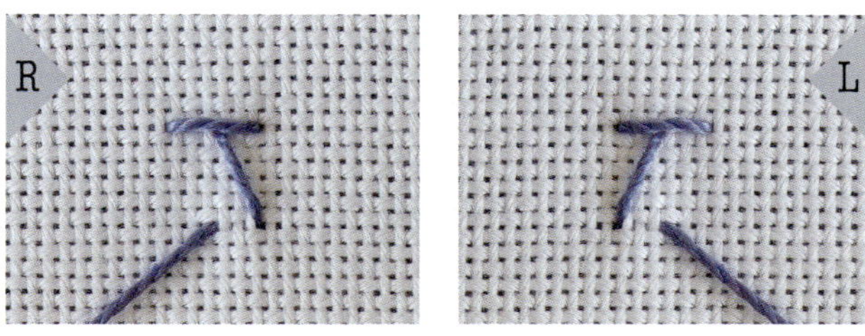

5. Move back and insert the needle with the tip pointing toward the middle to make the foot of the stitch.

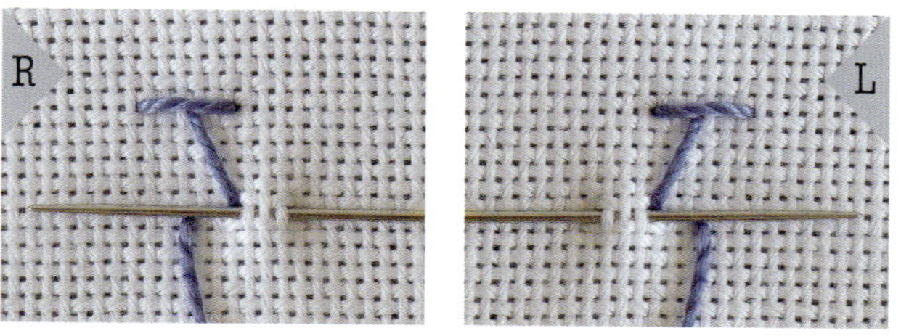

6. Take your needle to the top line and insert your needle. Note that the tip of the needle is emerging next to the last stitch.

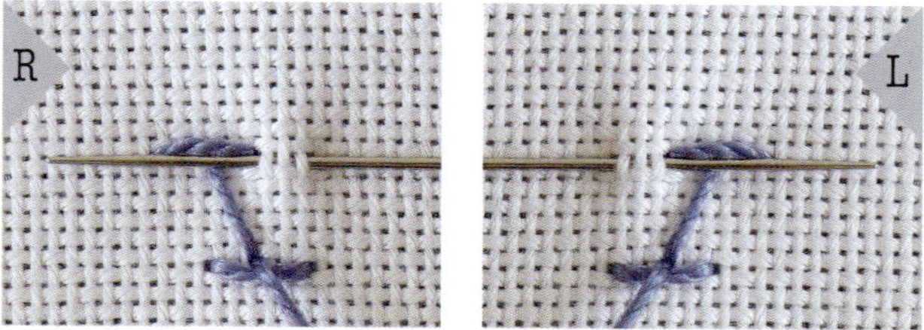

7. Pull your needle through and move back and insert the needle with the tip pointing toward the middle of the stitch.

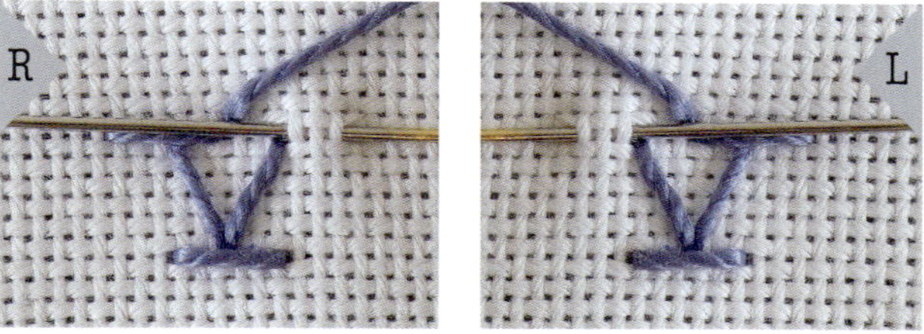

8. Work along the row, alternating a stitch up and down, with each stitch touching the previous stitch.

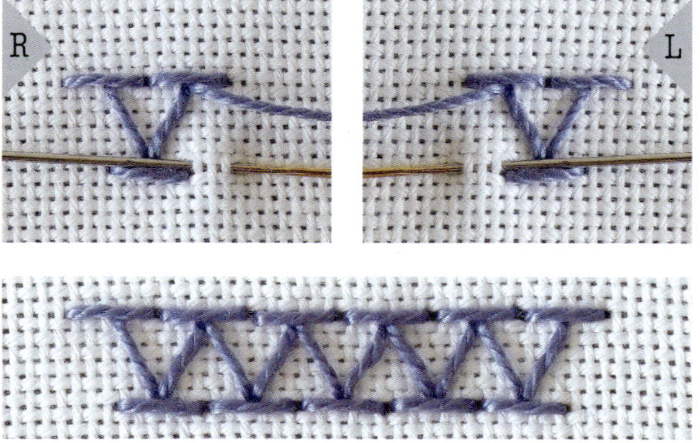

◊ This stitch can be very effective worked row upon row.

◊ Closed chevron stitch worked row upon row

◊ Closed chevron stitch is a closed variety of chevron stitch that can produce a dense filling.

Chevron Stitch (Closed Laced)

Laced closed chevron stitch creates a quick and easy decorative filling stitch. The stitch is worked over a foundation of closed chevron stitches. You can change the height of the closed chevron stitches to create very different looking fills. While lacing the stitch, take care not to take your needle through the fabric. You can use novelty and metallic threads to lace, which means this stitch can be used in numerous creative ways.

1. Work a row of closed chevron stitches (page 85). Bring your needle out at the top of the row.

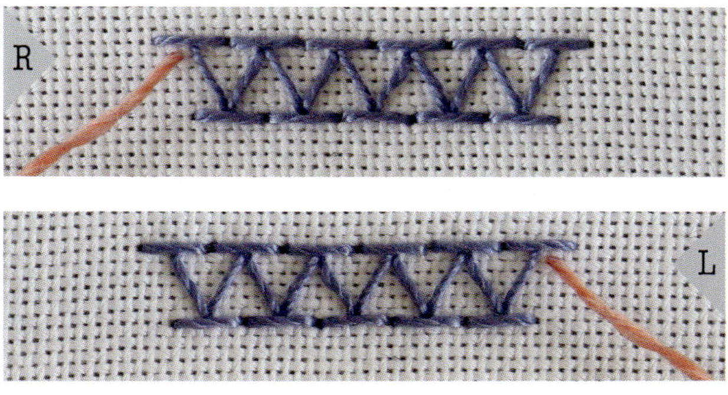

2. Pass your needle under the first bar of the chevron stitch.

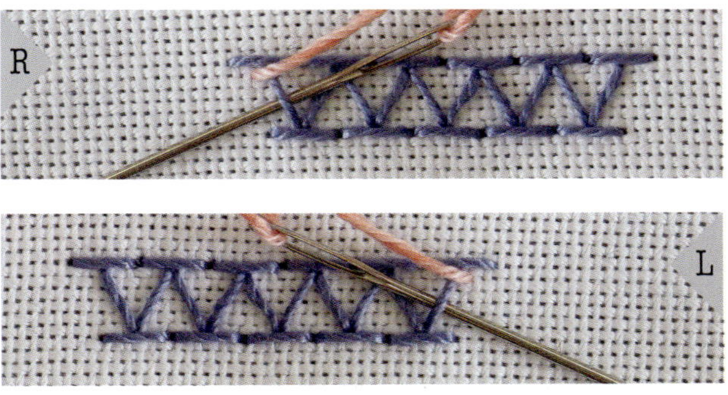

3. Pull your needle through. At this stage, the thread should wrap around the bar.

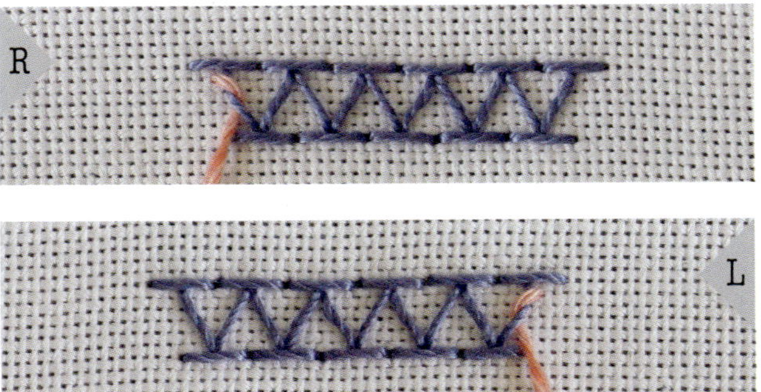

4. Pass your needle under the second bar of the chevron stitch.

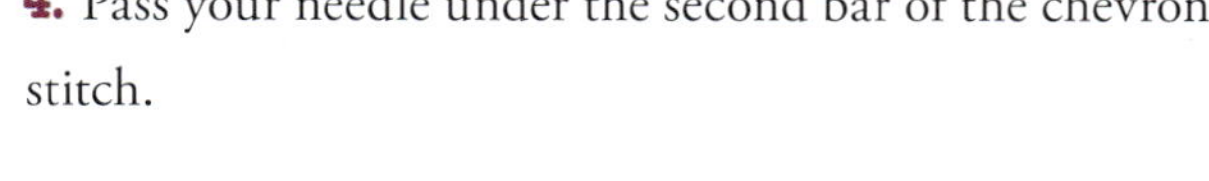

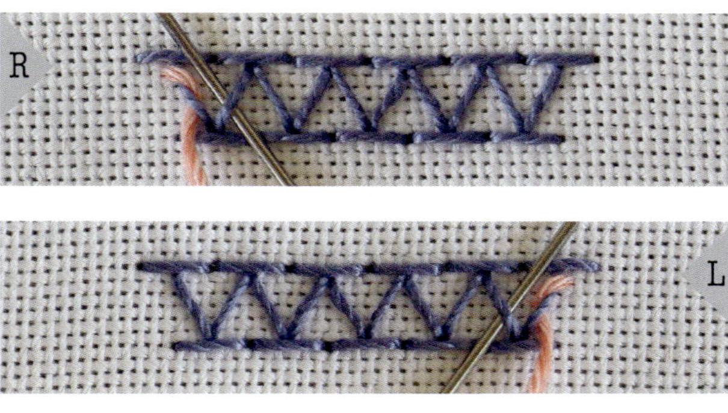

5. Pull your needle through. Pass your needle under the third bar of the chevron stitch.

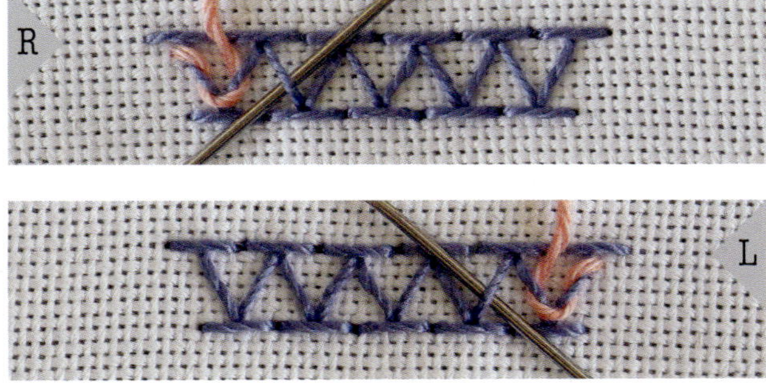

6. Continue along the line.

◊ Laced closed chevron stitch used in a more free-form manner with beads and sequins

◊ Laced closed chevron stitch laced with metallic thread

Chevron Stitch (Closed Whipped)

Whipped closed chevron is worked over a foundation of closed chevron stitches (page 85), producing a braid-like line. As with all lacing and threaded stitches, you can use novelty and metallic threads, which means this stitch can be used in numerous creative ways. While lacing the stitch, be careful not take your needle through the fabric.

1. Work a row of closed chevron stitches (page 85). To start the lacing, bring your needle out at the bottom of the row.

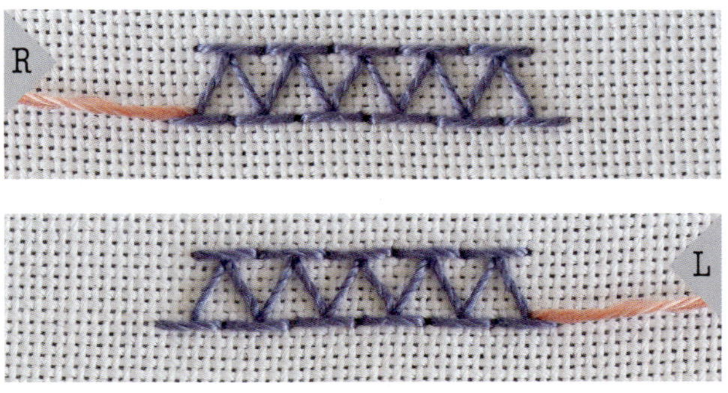

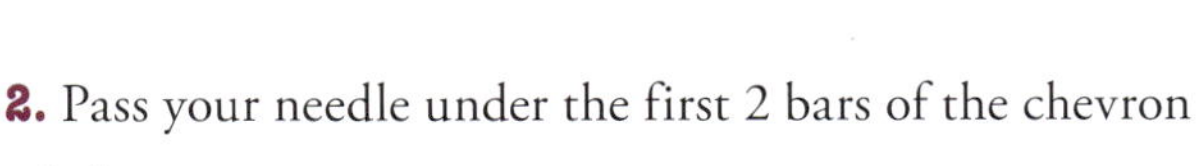

2. Pass your needle under the first 2 bars of the chevron stitch.

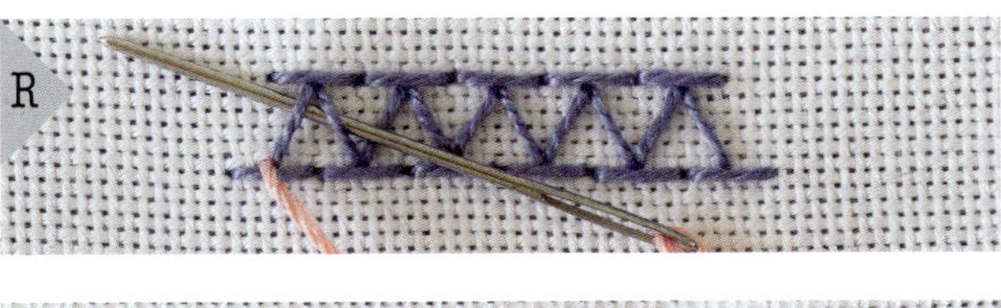

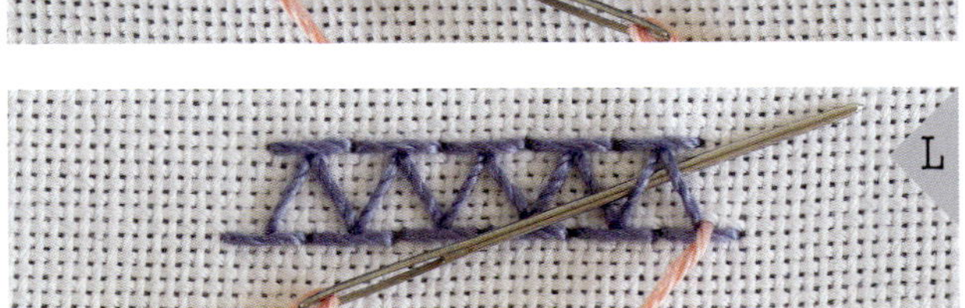

3. Pull your needle through. Move to the base of the stitch and pass your needle under the next 2 bars of the chevron stitch.

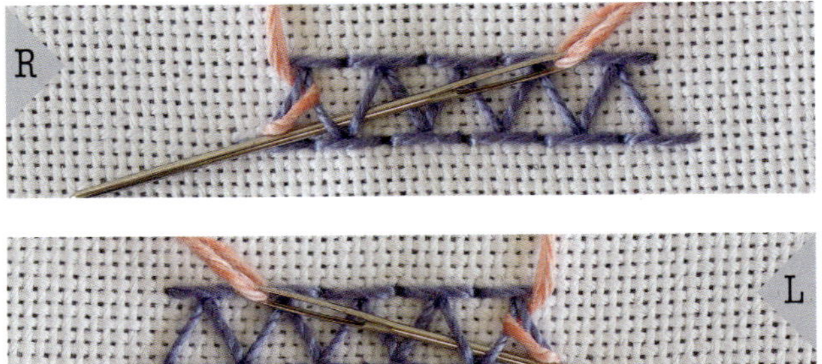

4. Pull your needle through. Move to the top of the foundation stitches and pass your needle under the next 2 bars of the chevron stitch.

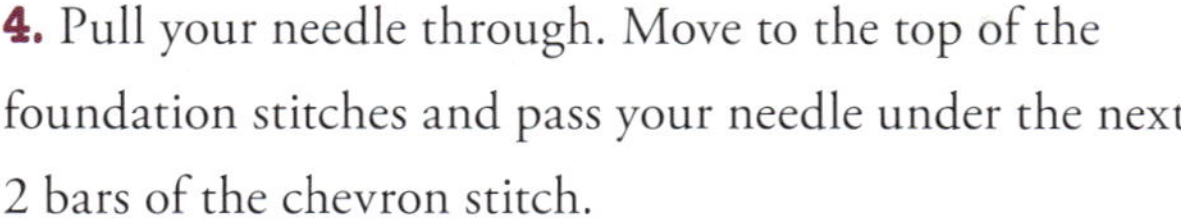

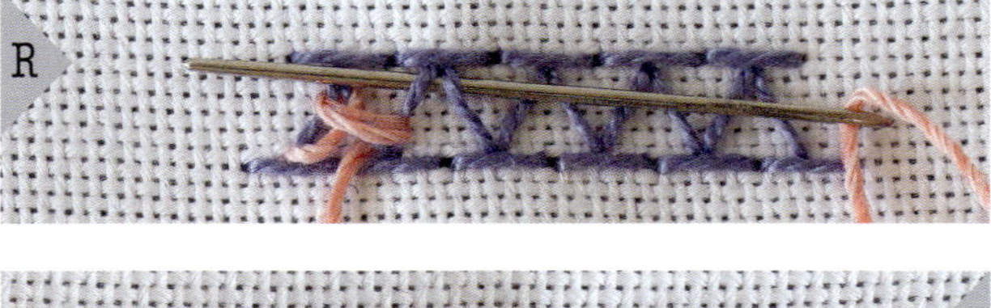

5. Continue in this manner along the line.

Chevron Stitch (Laced Version 1)

Laced chevron stitch creates a decorative filling. You can change the spacing and height of the foundation stitches for a different appearance.

1. Create 2 offset lines of arrow-shaped stitches.

2. Bring your thread out on the bottom row. Note that the second part of the stitch is lacing, and you do not take your needle through the fabric.

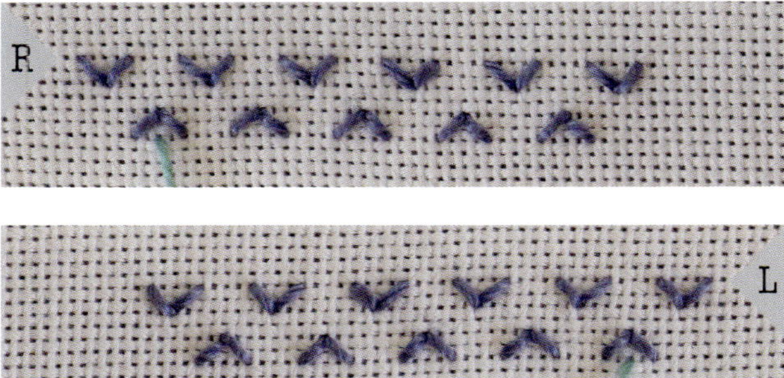

3. Pass the needle under the arrow stitches. Pull your thread through.

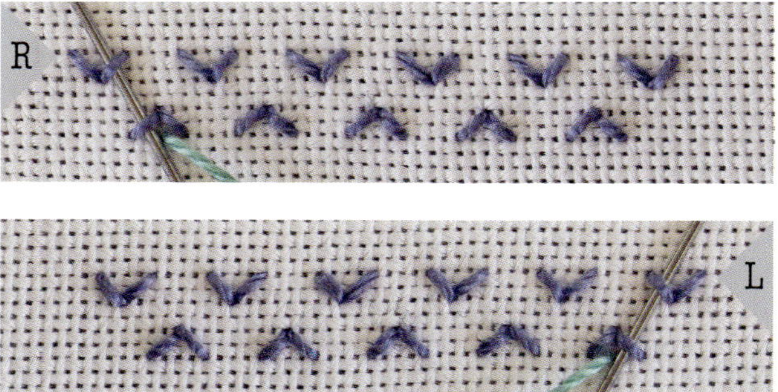

4. On the top line, pass the needle under the arrow stitches. Pull your thread through.

5. Continue up and down along the line until completed.

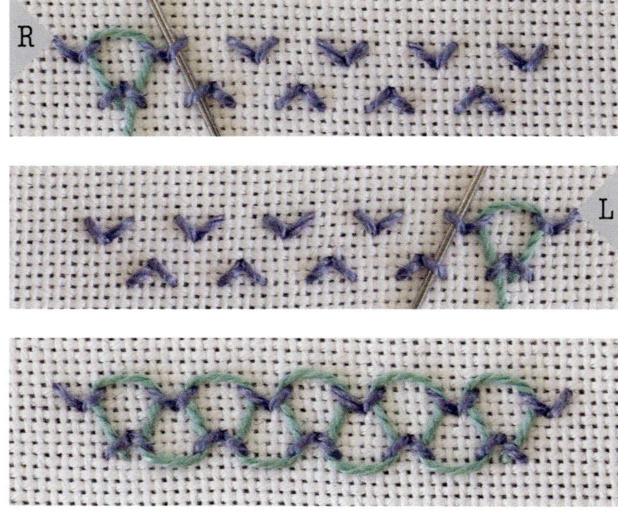

◇ Completed line of laced chevron stitch version 1

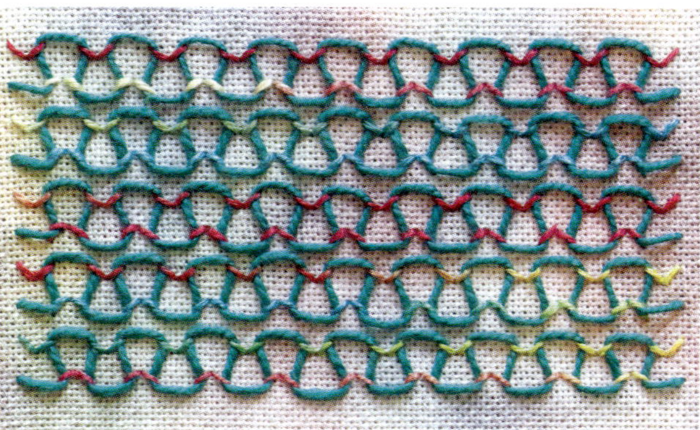

Chevron stitch laced on foundation stitches that have been worked in variegated thread

Chevron Stitch (Laced Version 2)

You can use laced chevron stitch as a single decorative line or work it row upon row to create a decorative filling. You can change the spacing of the rows and the height of the foundation stitches to develop numerous variations. You can use novelty threads to lace the chevron-shaped stitches. The second part of this stitch is lacing, so take care not to take your needle through the fabric.

1. Work a line of evenly spaced arrow-shaped stitches.

2. Create a second offset lines of arrow-shaped stitches.

3. Bring your lacing thread out at the top of the row. Pass the needle under the arrow stitch. Pull your thread through.

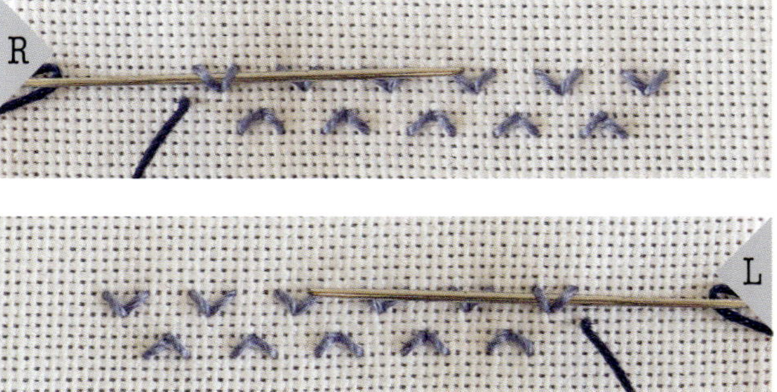

4. On the bottom row, pass the needle under the arrow stitches. Pull your thread through.

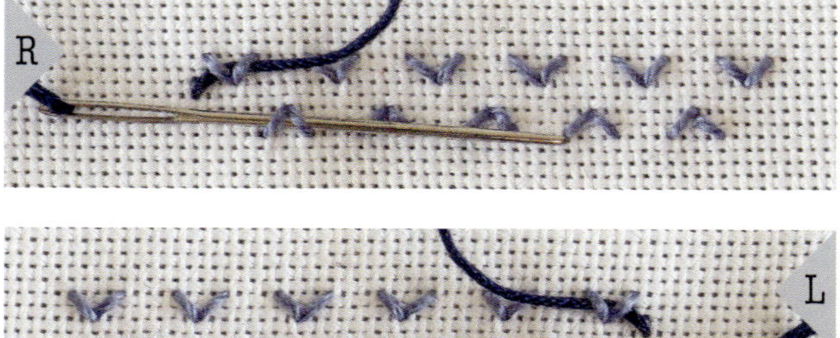

5. Continue up and down along the line until completed.

◊ Chevron stitch laced with metallic thread

Chevron Stitch (Raised)

Raised chevron stitch can be worked with a regular chevron stitch or as closed chevron (page 85). You can play around with the chevron stitches, changing the space between and the height of the stitches to create endless possibilities. It creates a solid fill, which is ideal for items such as bags and purses that may need to take a little wear.

1. Work a line of straight stitches sitting snugly next to one another as the foundation.

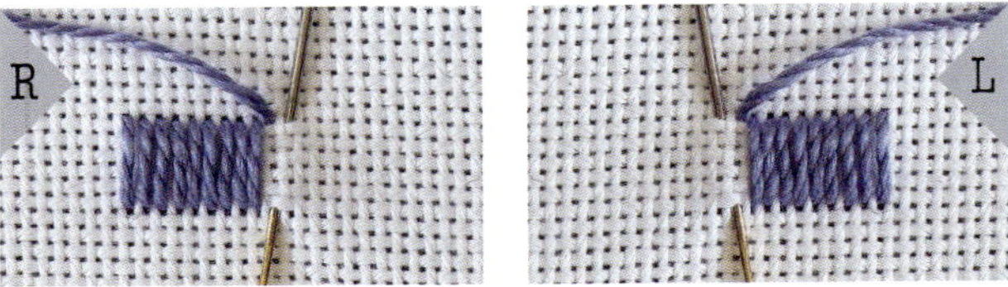

2. Bring your thread out on the top line. Move along the line and take a bite of the fabric.

3. Pull the needle through to make a small stitch. Take the needle diagonally down to the bottom line and insert it. Point the needle back. Pull your needle through.

4. With your needle pointing back, take a second bite of the fabric to make the foot of the stitch. Have your needle emerge at the base of the next diagonal stitch.

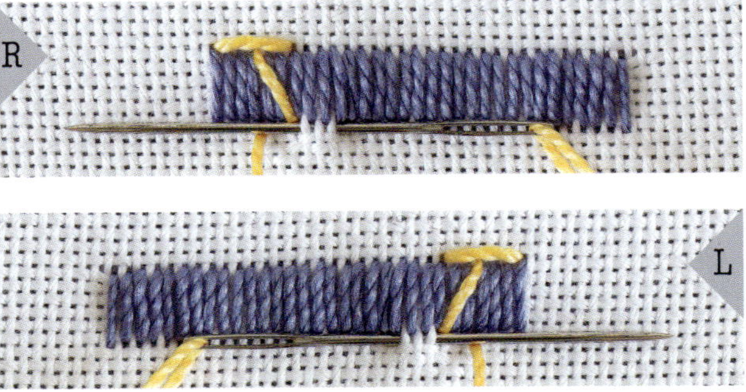

5. Take your needle to the top line and repeat the process again.

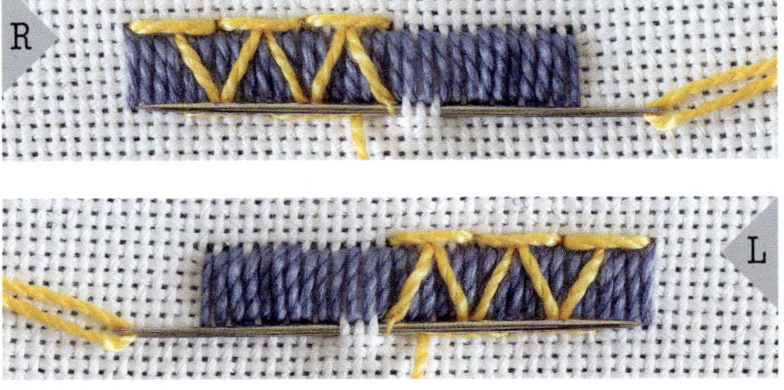

6. Work closed chevron stitches, alternating up and down until you have completed the row.

◊ Bar of worked on a foundation of regular chevron stitches

◊ Raised chevron stitch worked row upon row

Chinese Cross-Stitch

Chinese cross-stitch is a great little stitch that works up into a very useful filling or border stitch. It looks great on even-weave fabrics, or it can be scattered across an area in a free-form manner.

Chinese cross-stitch is constructed over six vertical and four horizontal threads.

1. Make a horizontal straight stitch over 6 threads of your fabric.

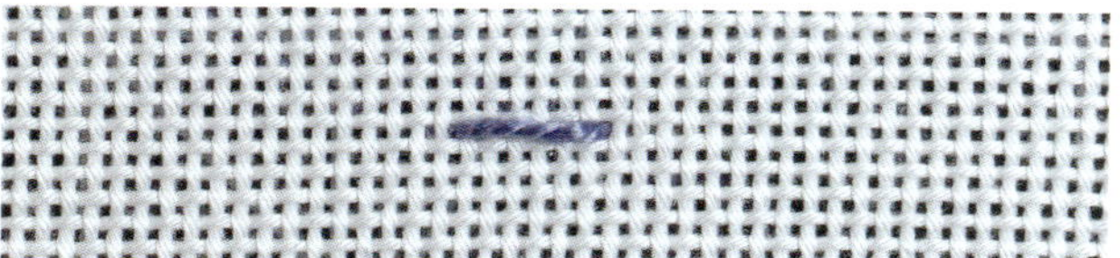

2. Work a vertical stitch over 4 threads.

3. Complete the block by working a second vertical stitch over 4 threads.

4. The next block is a half drop. From the base of the last vertical stitch, work a horizontal straight stitch over 6 threads. This is the start of your next block.

5. Complete the block by working 2 vertical stitches.

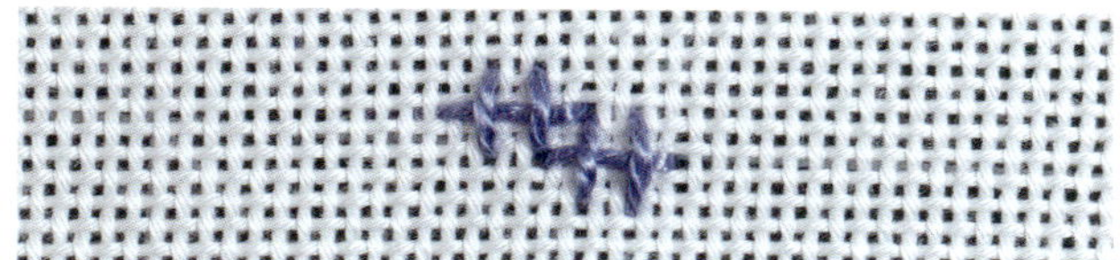

6. After completing the second block, move up so that your next block is in line with your first block and continue the pattern of stitching.

◊ Chinese cross-stitch worked row upon row as filling

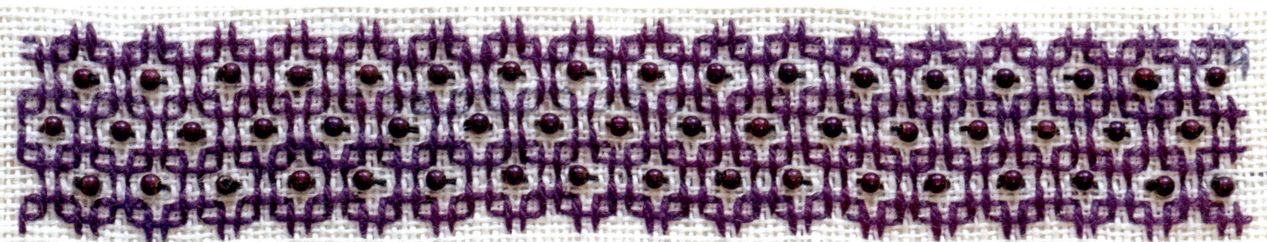

◊ Chinese cross-stitch worked row upon row with seed beads added

Cloud Filling Stitch

Cloud filling stitch, also known as *Mexican stitch,* is usually worked on even-weave fabric. For this stitch, when you lace, you can use the same thread or a thread of a different color or thickness.

Tip For a neat finish, count the threads of your fabric to keep the foundation stitches evenly spaced.

1. Work a grid of small vertical straight stitches, with every alternate row offset as shown. Do not work these stitches too tightly, as you will be threading another thread under them.

2. Thread your second thread in a blunt needle as you do not want to split the foundation threads as you lace. Bring your needle up on the top row. Pass the needle under the first stitch and pull it through; then pass the needle under the first stitch on the row below and pull it through.

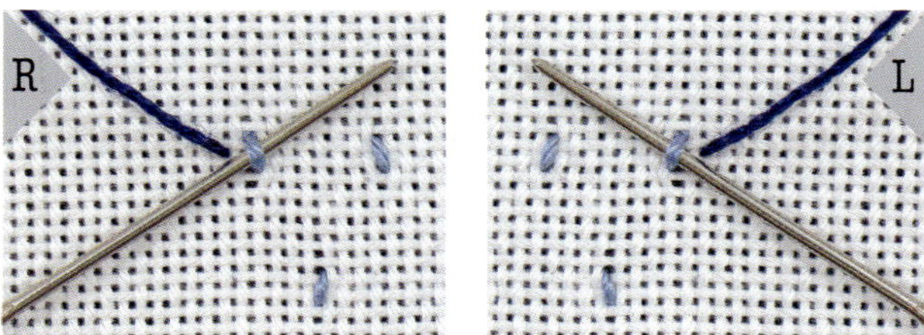

3. Continue threading in this up and down manner until the row is laced.

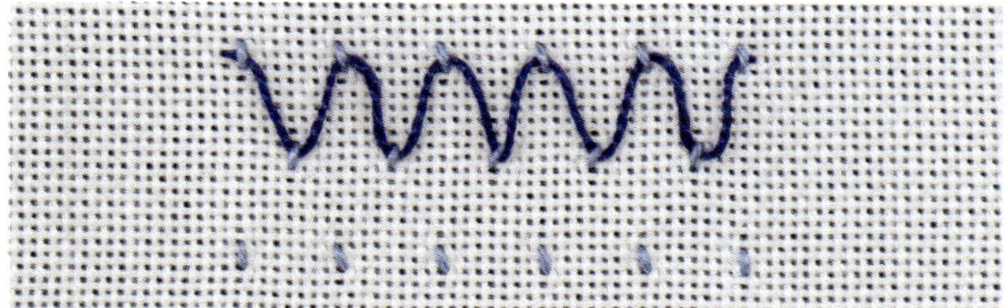

The second row of lacing is the mirror image of the first.

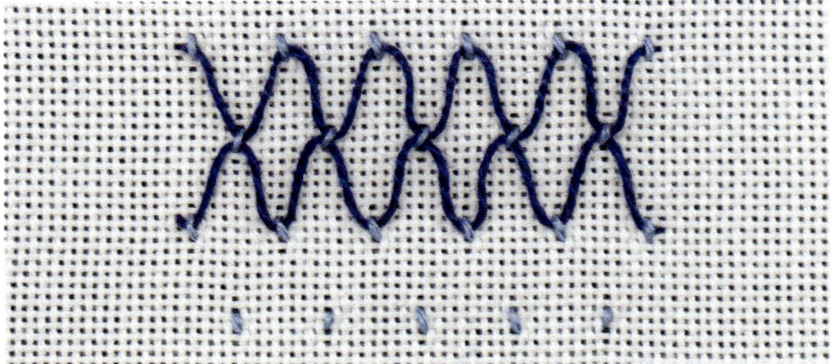

4. Continue this lacing row upon row until the area is done.

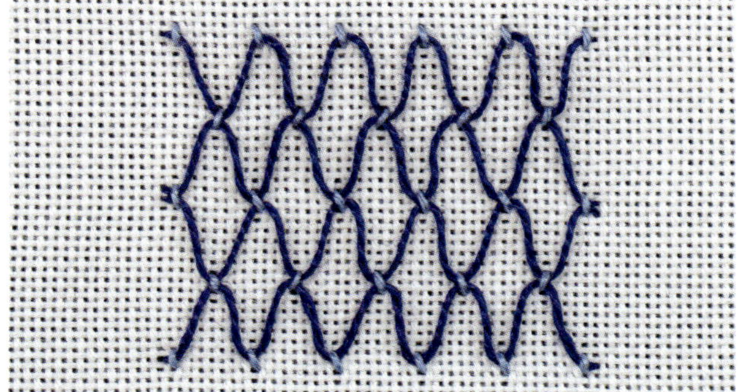

Cloud filling stitch worked in variegated thread on hand-dyed background

Coral Stitch (Double Zigzag)

Double zigzag coral stitch is simply a development on zigzag coral stitch (page 100). The mechanics of the stitch are the same.

Work this stitch between two parallel lines. Follow the line of the weave in the fabric as your guide, or mark the lines using a water-soluble or air-erasable marker because the lines will not be covered with stitching.

1. Make a line of zigzag coral stitch (page 100).

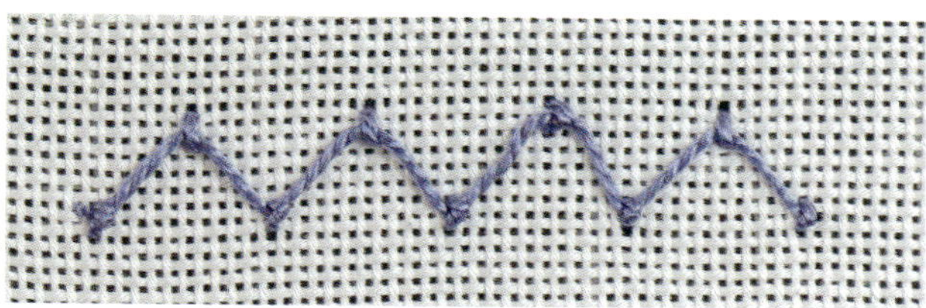

2. For the second journey, I have used a different color thread so you can clearly see what is going on. The second line of zigzag coral stitch is worked offset to the first. Make a second line of zigzag coral stitch by starting at the top of the line.

3. The first stitch of the row is placed at the top of the line if the previous line started at the bottom. If you started the first line at the top, start the second line at the bottom. It does not matter which way around it is. The placement of stitches just has to be the opposite of the first row.

4. Continue in this manner zigzagging down the line. At this stage, you have created a line of double zigzag coral stitch. Tie off your work at the back.

Coral Stitch (Interlaced)

Interlaced coral stitch is an interesting variation of coral stitch (page 186) that creates a decorative line of small disks. It follows a curved line well.

1. Bring the thread up from the back of the fabric. Insert the needle at a slight angle above your working line. Bring the needle tip out just below the line, and wrap the thread over and under the needle.

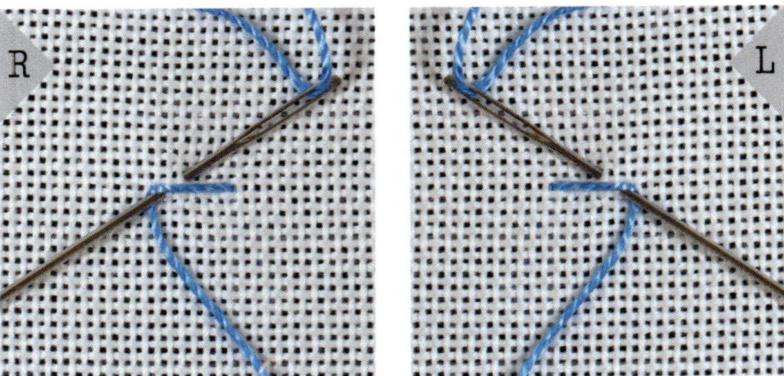

2. Pull the needle through the fabric to form the first knot.

3. Continue in this manner along the line.

4. On the second journey, use a tapestry needle when lacing so you do not split the foundation stitches. Bring your thread out at the end of the line and pass the needle from top to bottom under the first stitch.

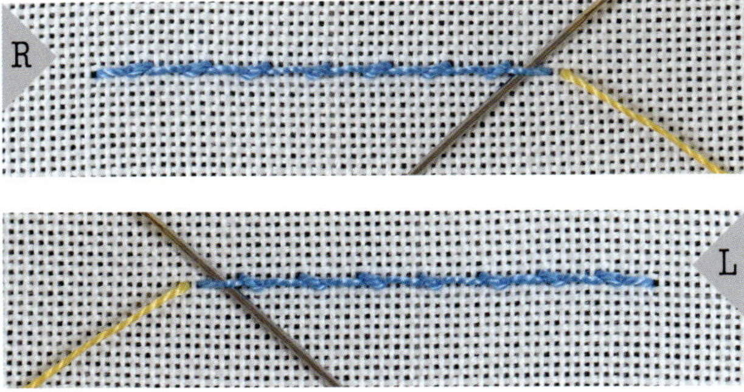

5. Start to lace the stitches by passing the needle under the next stitch from the bottom to the top of the line.

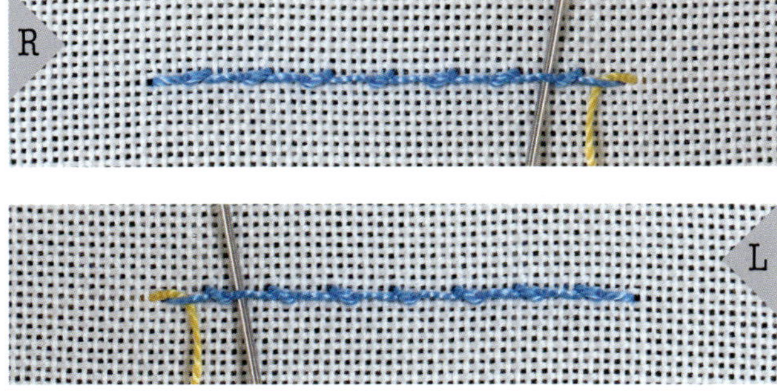

6. Take your needle back and over the top of the line. Pass your needle from the top to the bottom of the line.

7. Pull the thread through gently. Do not pull tight. Let the thread wrap itself around the stitch.

8. Move along the line, passing the needle under the next stitch from the bottom to the top.

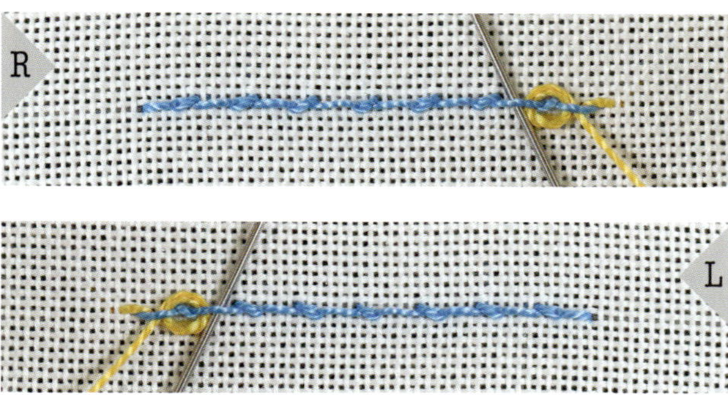

9. Take your needle to the next stitch along, and pass the needle from the top to the bottom of the line.

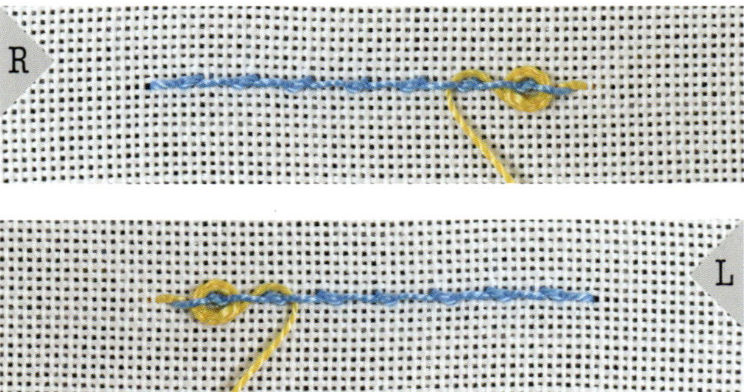

10. Move back a stitch to pass the needle under from the bottom to the top.

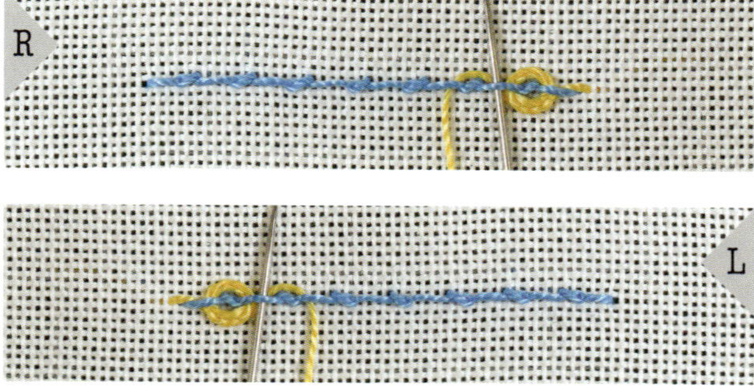

11. Repeat this lacing movement until the end of the line.

◊ Detail of interlaced coral stitch used in wall piece

Coral Stitch (Wrapped)

Wrapped coral stitch is also known as a *coral knot with an extra wrap*. That is actually a good description. This stitch produces a thick bobbly line that is quick to work and follows a curve well.

Use a twisted thread such a perle cotton #5 and work the stitches fairly close together for the best effect.

1. Bring your thread out and make a small coral knot by inserting the needle and taking a bite of the fabric at a slight angle above your working line. Bring your needle out just below the line, and wrap the thread over and under the needle.

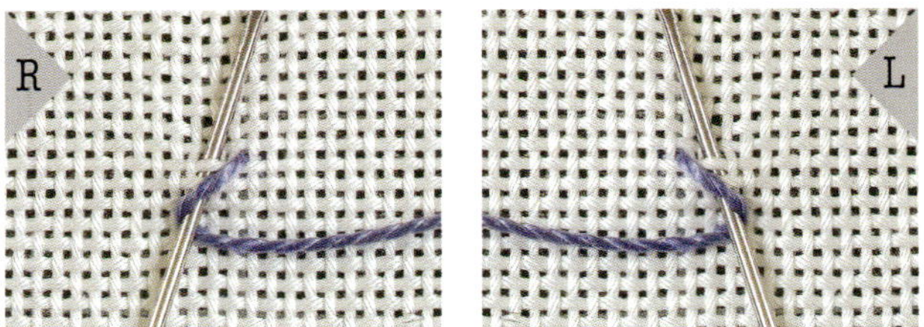

2. Pull your thread through to make your first coral stitch.

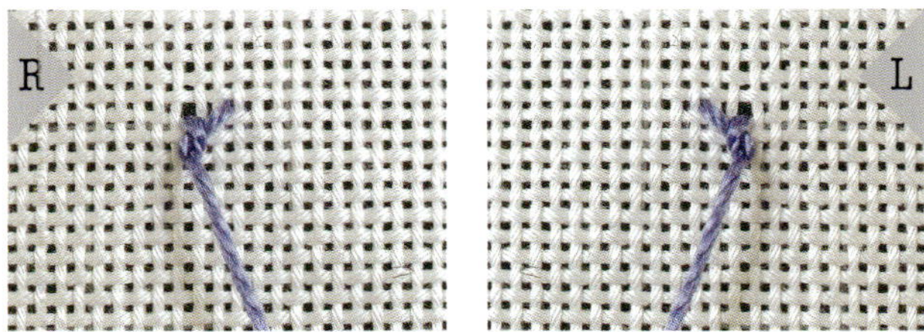

3. Once you have made the first coral stitch, slide the needle under the bar of thread that sits above the knot. This action will wrap the coral stitch.

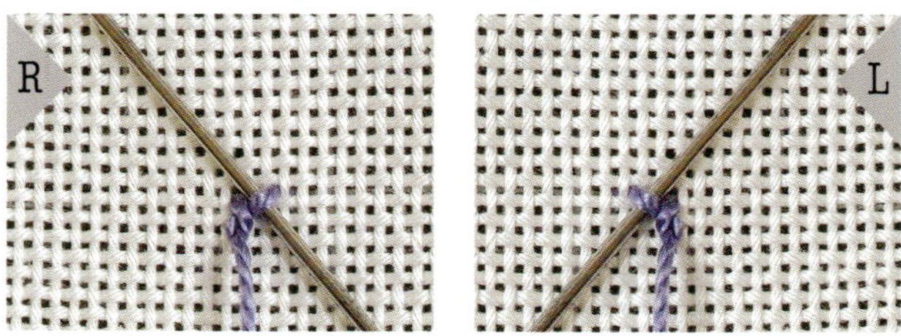

4. Pull your thread through.

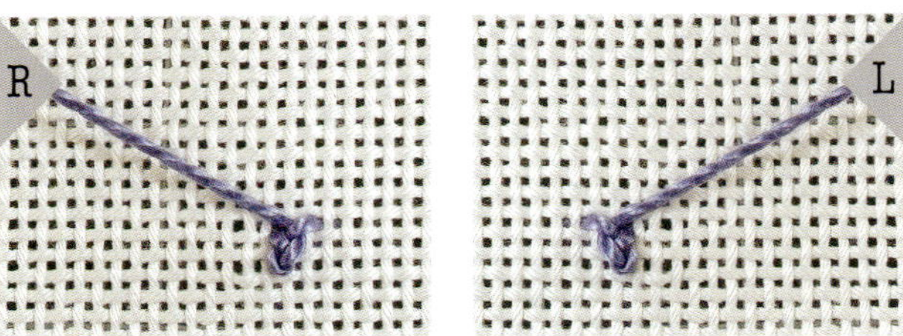

5. Make another coral stitch.

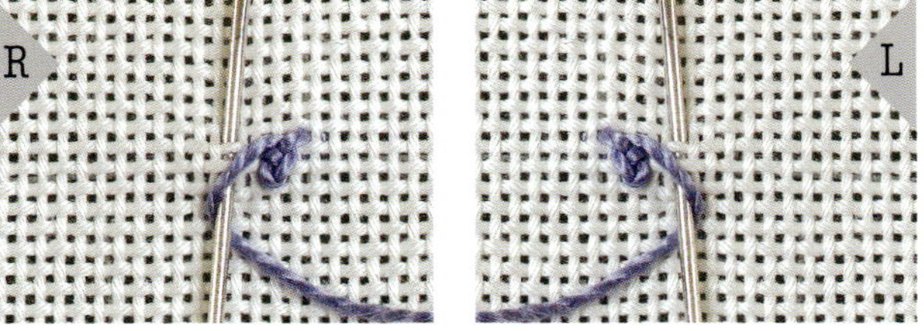

6. Pass your needle under the top loop formed between the 2 stitches, and take your thread around the knot before making the next coral stitch.

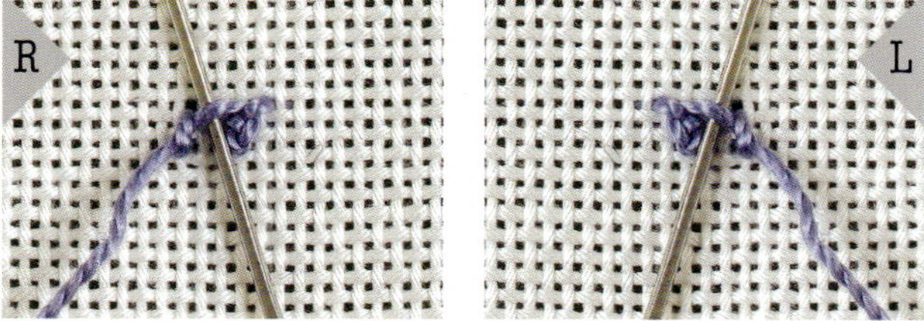

The finished line looks like an interesting line of knots.

◊ Wrapped coral stitch worked using variegated hand-dyed perle cotton #5, used in slow-stitch project

Coral Stitch (Zigzag)

Zigzag coral stitch is a variety of coral stitch (page 186, which, in turn, is based on twisted chain stitch. Zigzag coral stitch is fun, and once you get in the rhythm, it is quick to do. You can also use thicker threads to create a border on your work.

Work this stitch between two parallel lines. If you need to mark the lines, use a water-soluble or air-erasable marker because the lines will not be covered with stitching. With stitches like this, I use the threads in the weave of the cloth as my guide.

1. Bring the needle up from the back of the work and make a small twisted chain stitch by taking a small bite of the fabric with the point of the needle emerging below the line. Wrap the thread over the needle and under the point. Pull the needle through the fabric.

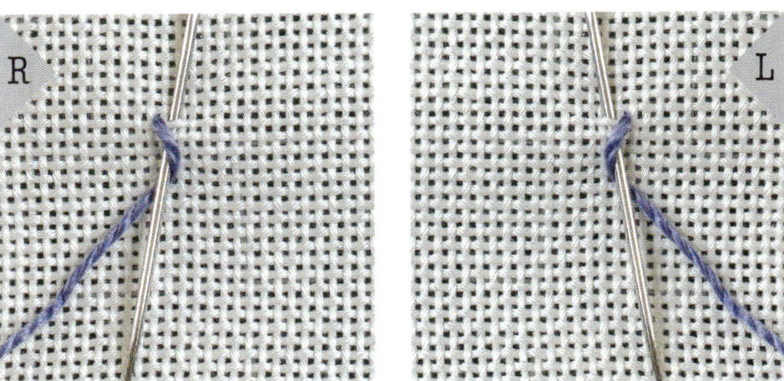

2. Move diagonally to the top of the line and make the next twisted chain stitch.

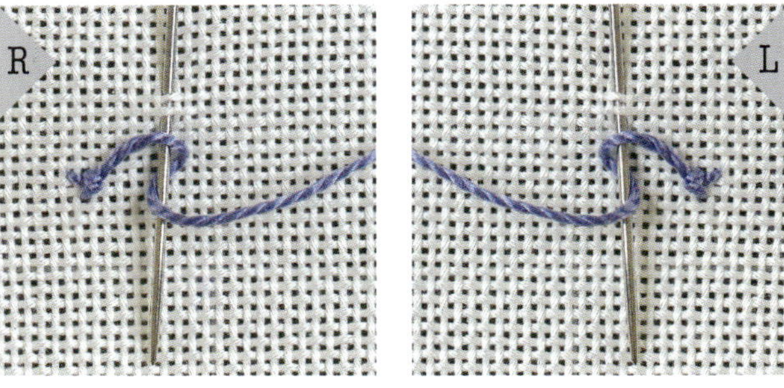

3. Take your thread diagonally to the bottom line and make a twisted chain stitch.

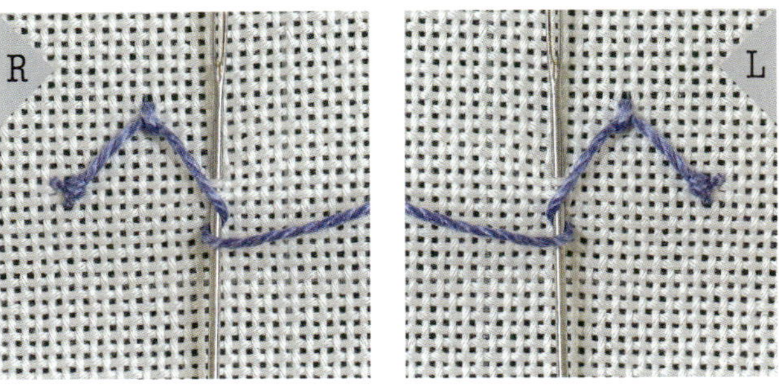

4. Continue in this manner, zigzagging along the line, which is, of course, how the stitch got its name!

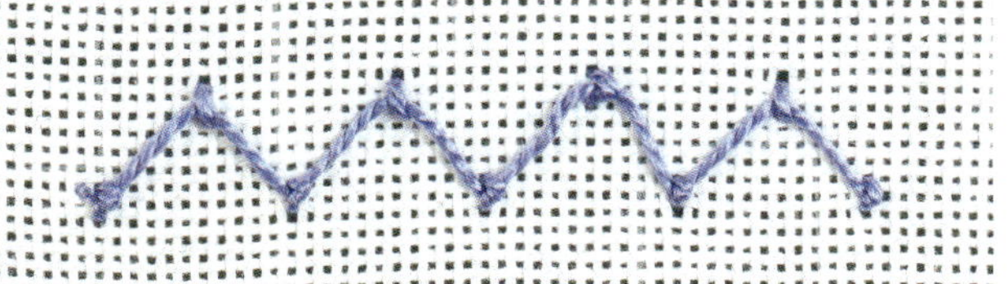

Cretan Stitch (Chained Triangle)

Chained Cretan triangle is a variety of both Cretan stitch and buttonhole stitch (page 183).

1. Bring your thread out on the bottom of the line. Move diagonally to the top line and insert your needle. The point of insertion will be the apex of the triangle. Pull your thread through.

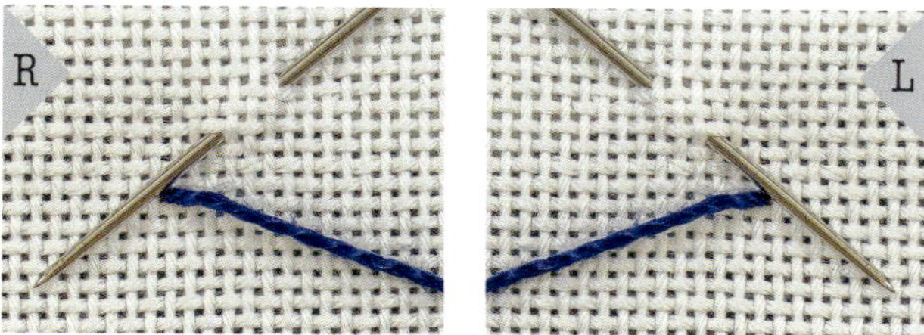

2. Make a small diagonal stitch by inserting the needle at the base of the diagonal stitch. Have the needle emerge in line with the apex of the triangle. Keeping the thread under the needle, pull it through your fabric.

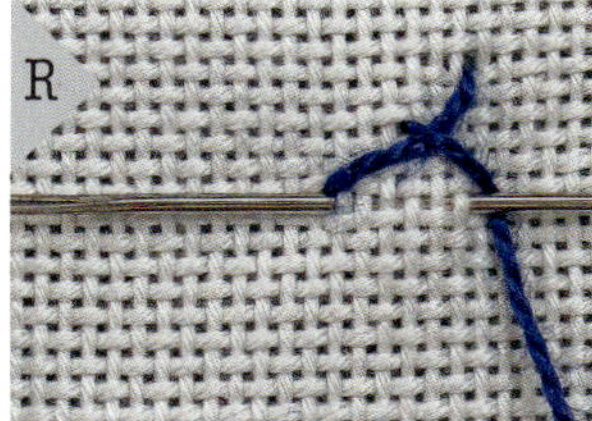

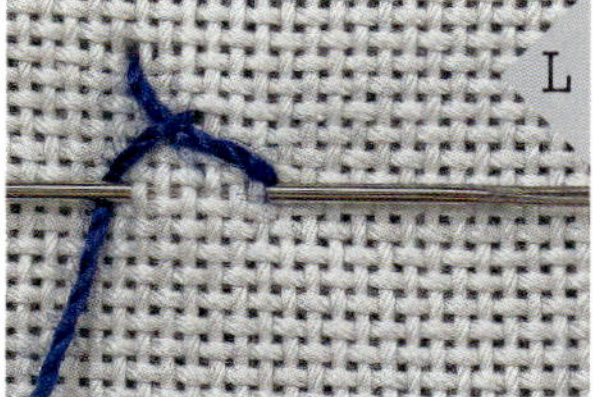

3. Insert your needle at the apex of the triangle. Make a small diagonal stitch. Keeping the thread under the needle, pull it through your fabric.

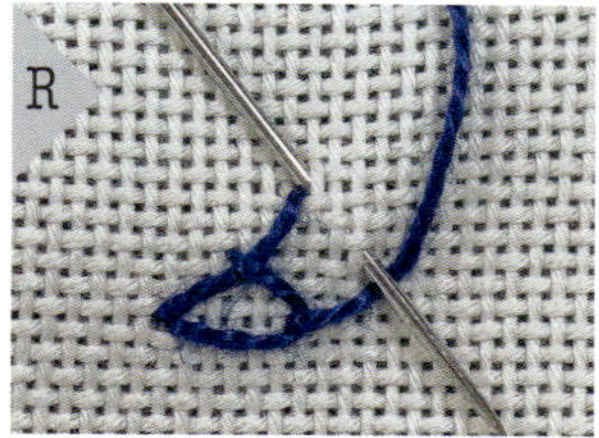

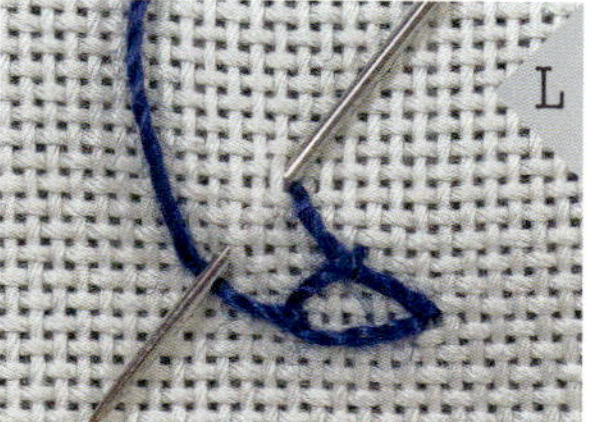

4. Insert your needle on the bottom line inside the stitch. Have your needle emerge on the bottom line, at a point that will complete the triangle. Keeping the thread under the needle, pull it through your fabric.

5. Continue these steps along the line.

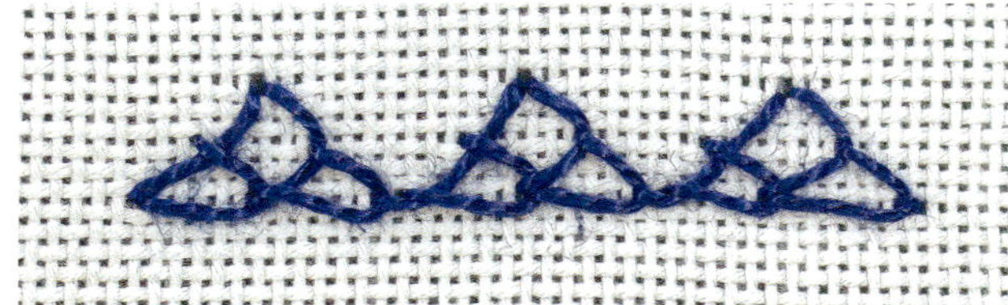

◊ Chained Cretan triangle used on crazy quilt seam

◊ Chained Cretan triangle worked back-to-back and laced with metallic thread

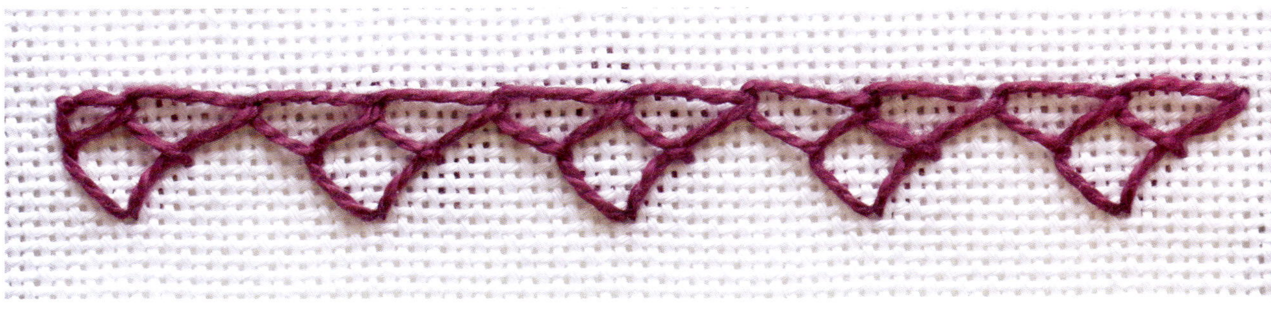

◊ Chained Cretan triangle worked in perle cotton #5

◊ Chained Cretan triangle used on crazy quilt seam

Cretan Stitch (Raised)

Raised Cretan stitch is also known as *interlaced band, double Pekinese stitch, herringbone ladder filling,* and *figure of 8 stitch.* No matter its name, it is an interesting composite stitch worked in two parts. The foundation stitches are two parallel offset lines of backstitch, which are then laced. The second thread can be a different type or color of thread, and you can use novelty threads and yarns to great effect.

Tip For this stitch to look its best, don't pull the lacing thread too tight. Keep your laced loops relaxed.

Changing the length of your foundation backstitches will influence the appearance. If you lengthen them, the laced band will be more open; if you shorten the backstitches, the band will be more braid-like and dense.

1. Work 2 lines of offset backstitches. The key to this stitch is to remember to offset the lines of backstitches. If you use novelty yarns and thread to lace, make your backstitches a little larger and work them slightly looser to accommodate the thicker threads.

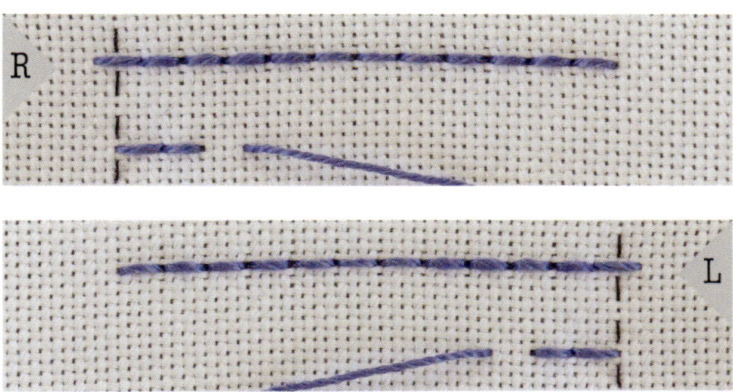

2. When working the second row, pay attention to where each stitch starts and how it lines up against the row above or below. I have marked the starting point of the second row with basting stitches to show how the stitches are offset.

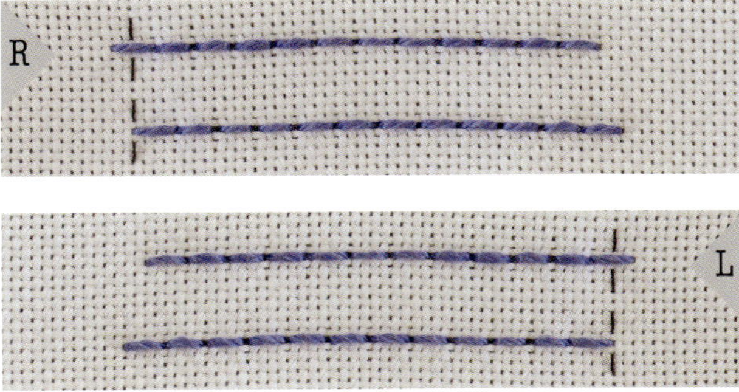

3. Choose a second thread for lacing. Bring the thread out between the rows of backstitch. With your needle pointing toward the middle of the 2 lines, pass your needle diagonally under the first stitch on the top line. With the thread under the needle, pull it through. As you lace, always point your needle to the center of the 2 foundation rows.

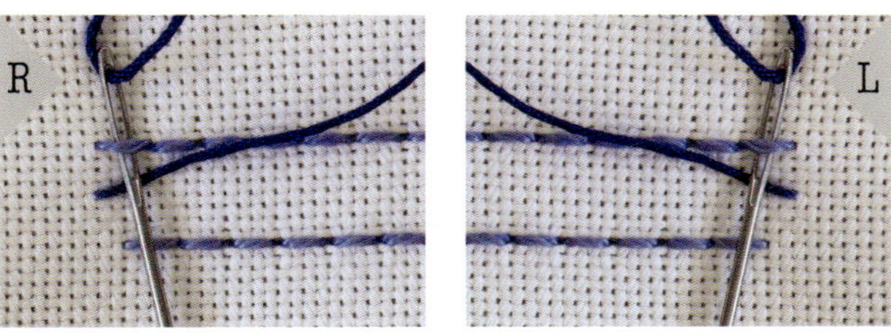

4. Turn your needle, take it over the first backstitch on the bottom line, and slide your needle under the stitch. With your needle pointed to the middle of the foundation lines and with the thread under the needle, pull it through.

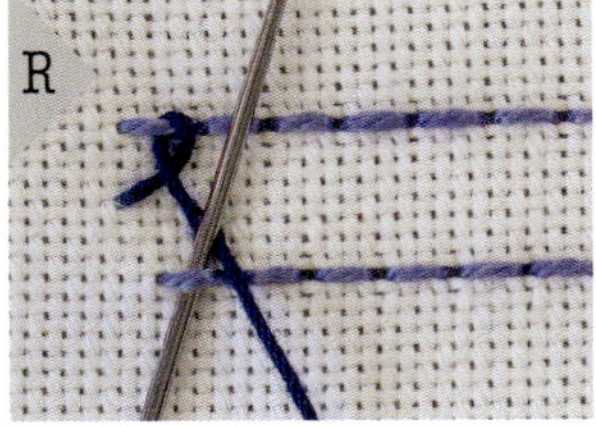

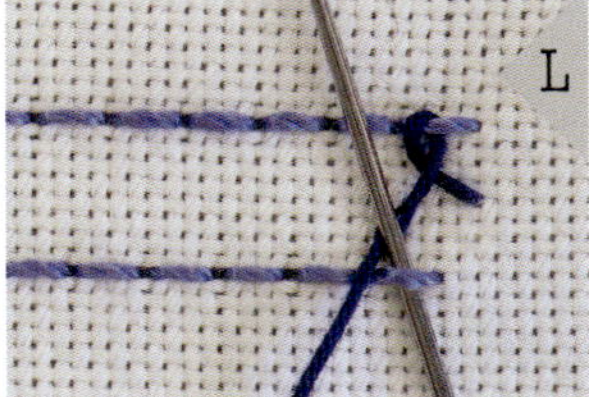

5. Moving from top to bottom and back, continue lacing your thread along the line.

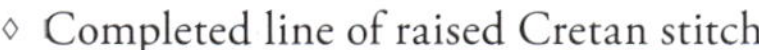

◊ Completed line of raised Cretan stitch

◊ Raised Cretan stitch worked in perle cotton #8

◊ Raised Cretan stitch worked on small contemporary embroidery piece

Cretan Stitch (Scottish)

Scottish Cretan stitch is so called because it resembles thistle heads. It makes a great border, or it can be added to organic sprays as an interesting texture for spiky twigs.

1. The stitch starts with 3 Cretan stitches worked fairly close together. Work vertically between 2 imaginary lines. Bring the needle through the fabric at the start of the line. Move across and slightly down the line and insert your needle on the outside edge to make a small stitch by pointing the needle to the center. Keeping the thread under the needle, pull it through your fabric.

2. Move to the other side of the line and repeat the action.

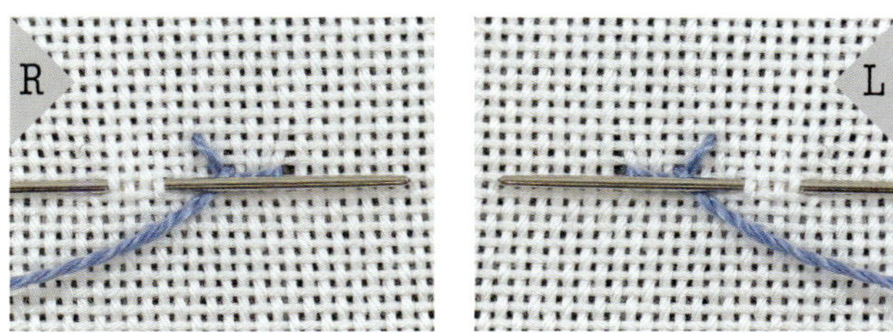

3. Make sure that, with each small stitch, the thread is under the needle.

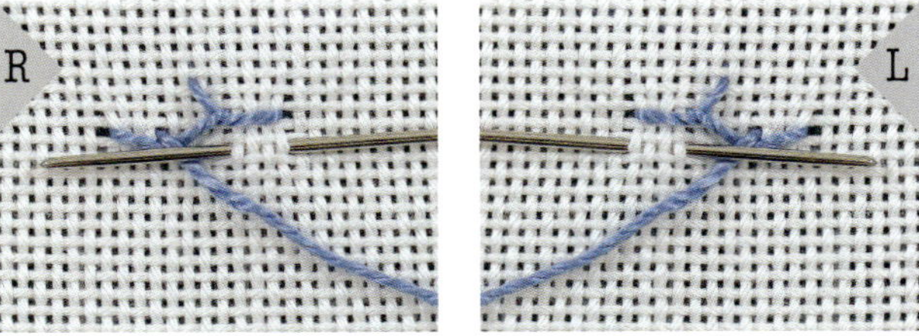

4. Continue working until you have 3 Cretan stitches.

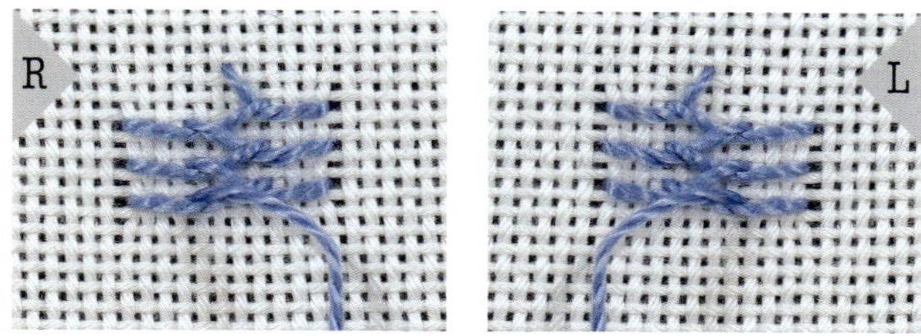

5. Pass the needle up one side under the stitches. Do not go through the fabric.

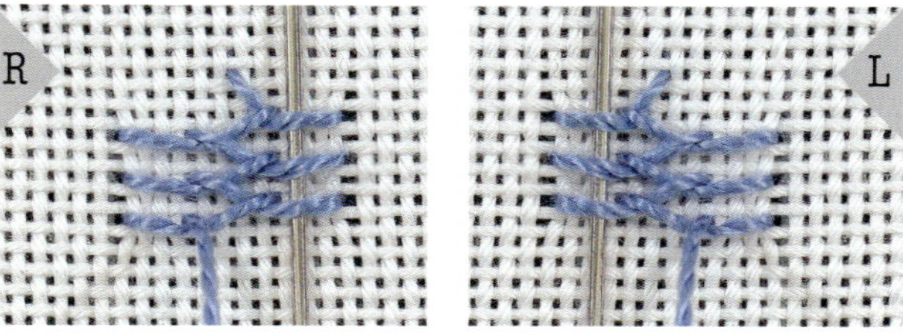

6. Pass the needle down the other side under the stitches. Do not go through the fabric.

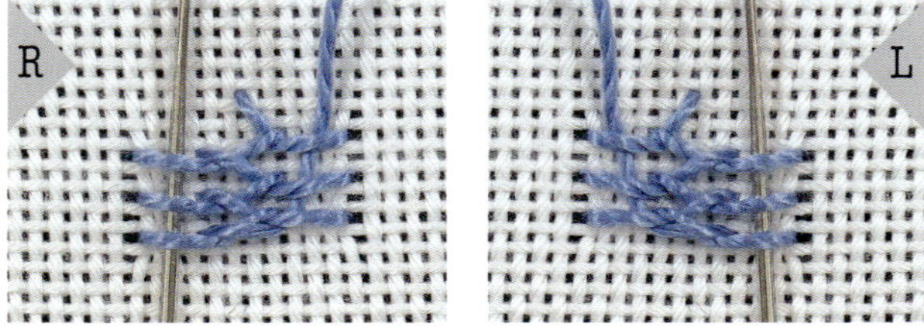

7. Pull your thread gently through, making it snug but not too tight. This creates the first set of Scottish Cretan stitches.

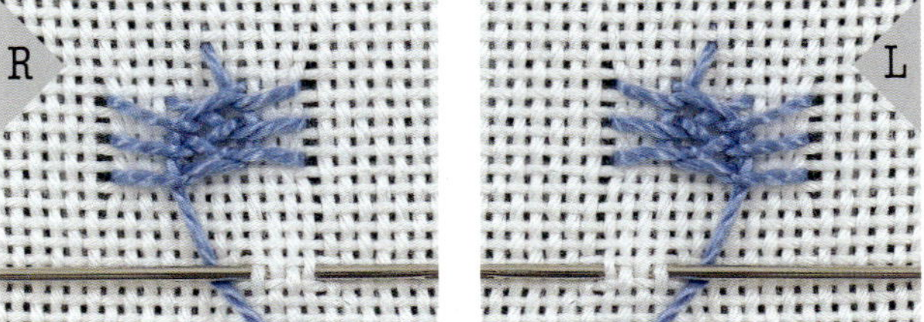

8. Continue down the line until you have the number of stitches you require.

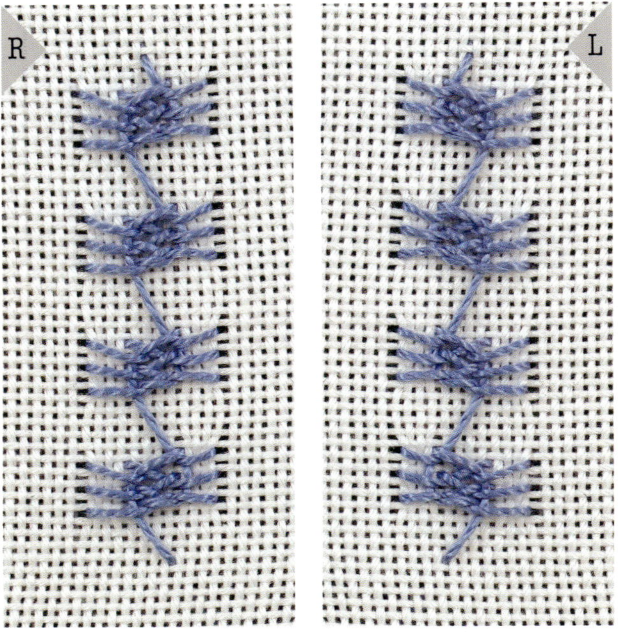

◊ You can vary the look of Scottish Cretan stitch by spacing the Cretan stitches either closer together or farther apart.

◊ Scottish Cretan stitch worked in perle cotton #5

Danish Knot

Danish knot is also known as a *double knot.* It is worked as an isolated stitch and can be used on plain- and even-weave fabrics. It is a quick and hard-wearing knot that looks good in a thread with a firm twist, such as perle cotton #5 or #8.

1. Start with a small diagonal stitch. This forms a bar onto which the stitch is made. Bring your needle up again at the side of the diagonal stitch. Slide your needle under the diagonal stitch. Take care that you are passing the needle under the stitch and not through the fabric.

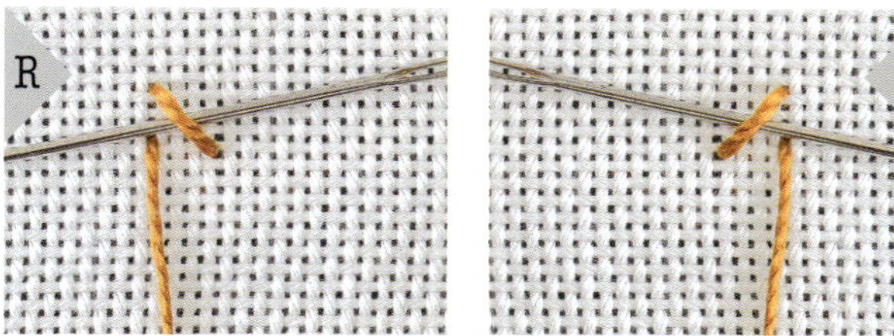

2. Pull your thread through to produce the first loop over the diagonal bar. Pull snug but not too tight.

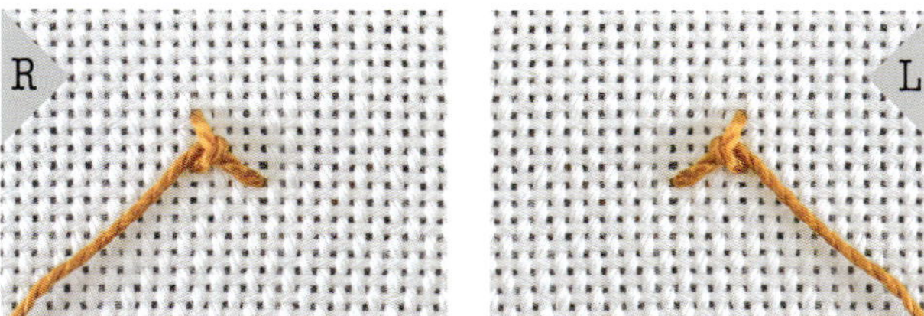

3. Move along the diagonal stitch and pass the needle under the bar. Loop the thread under the needle.

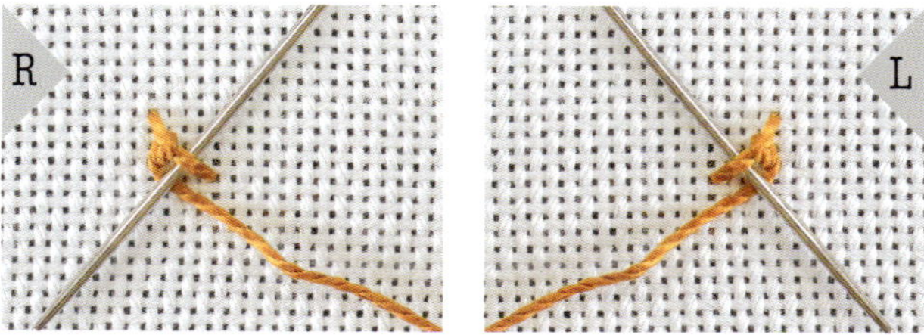

4. Pull the needle through. Pull the thread snug to form a knot. Take the needle to the back of the fabric under the knot.

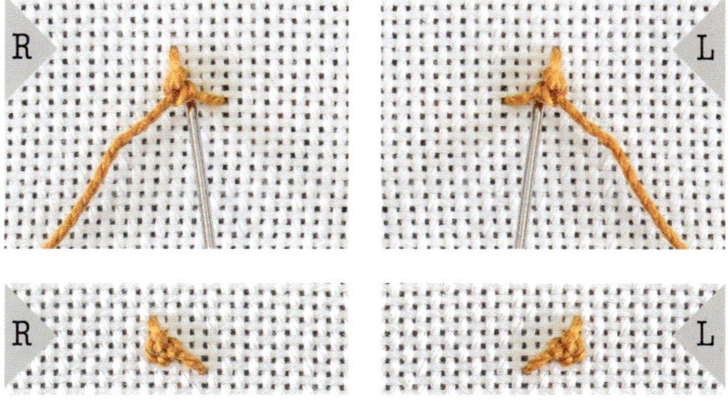

◊ Finished Danish knot

◊ Danish knot sprinkled over area to create filling

Diagonal Barred Cross-Stitch

Diagonal barred cross-stitch is best worked on even-weave fabrics. It creates a lovely filling stitch worked diagonally across an area.

Work over four or eight horizontal and four or eight vertical threads.

1. Work a vertical straight stitch.

2. Work a horizontal straight stitch to cross that stitch.

3. Make a diagonal stitch from the bottom of the vertical stitch to the side of the horizontal stitch.

4. Start the next unit of the stitch with a vertical stitch and repeat Steps 2–3 to finish the line.

5. Continue along the diagonal line.

6. Continue to fill the area. To finish off, add backstitches around the edge.

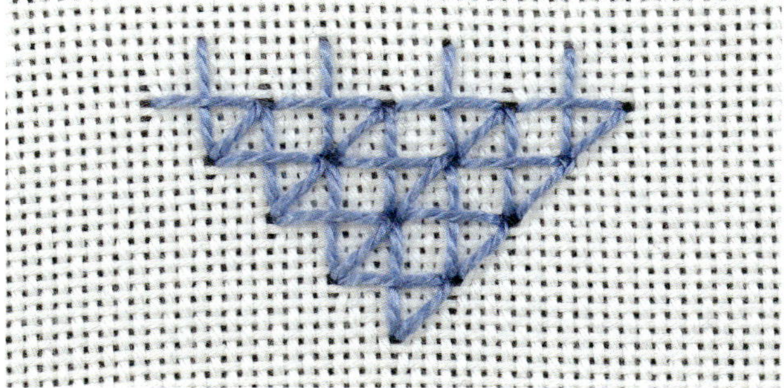

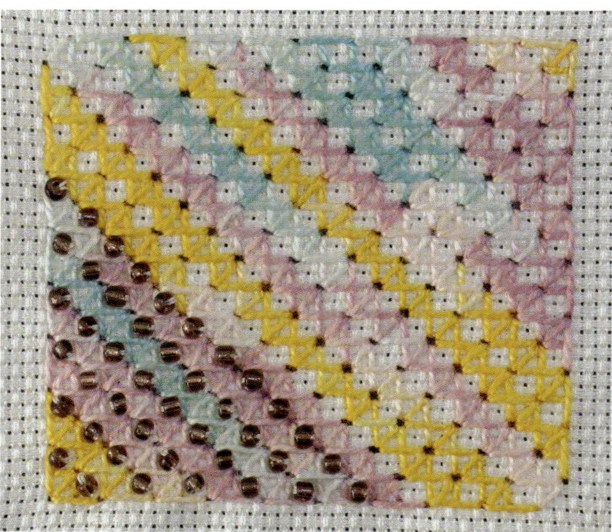

Diagonal barred cross-stitch worked in variegated perle cotton #5 thread

Double Pekinese Stitch

Double Pekinese stitch is also known as *interlaced band*. It is an interesting stitch worked in two parts where you can use novelty threads and yarns to great effect. The foundation stitches are two parallel offset lines of backstitch. The lines of backstitches are then laced. The lacing thread can be a different type or color.

If you want to use thicker novelty yarns and threads, start with foundation rows of longer backstitches to accommodate them.

1. Work 2 lines of offset backstitches.

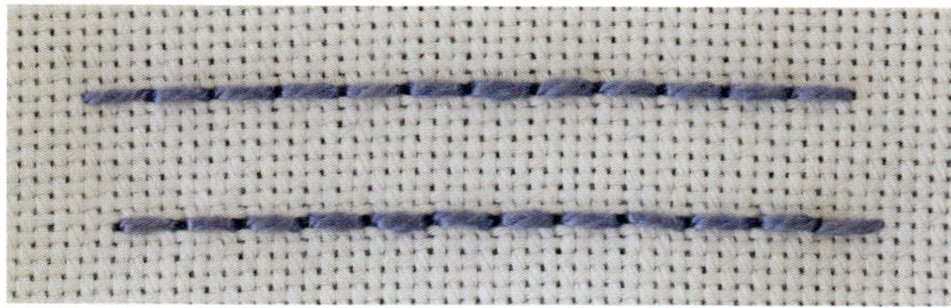

2. To begin lacing, bring the thread out in between the rows of backstitch and take the needle under the second backstitch on the top line. Pull your needle through.

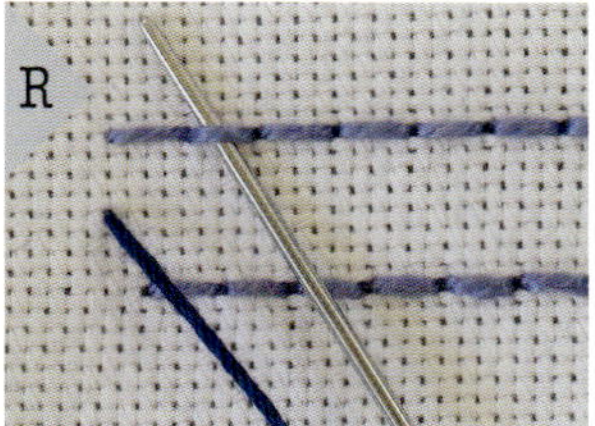

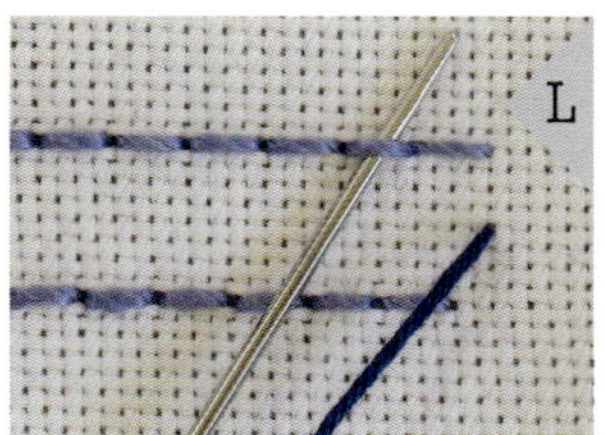

3. Turn your needle, take it under the first backstitch on the top line, and pass it under the stitch. In the same motion with the thread under the needle, pass your needle under the second stitch on the bottom line. Pull your needle through.

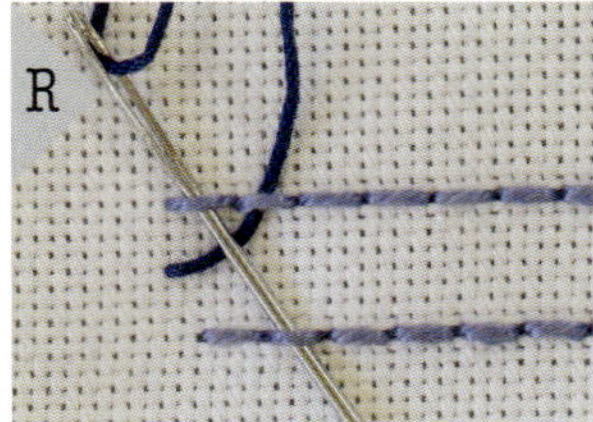

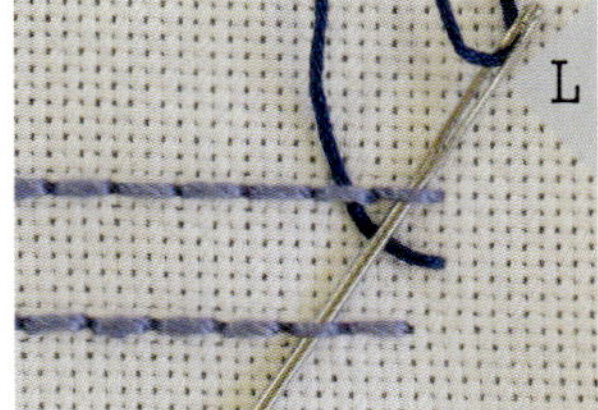

4. Pass your needle under the first stitch on the bottom line, and with the thread under the needle, pass your needle under the third stitch on the top line. Pull your needle through.

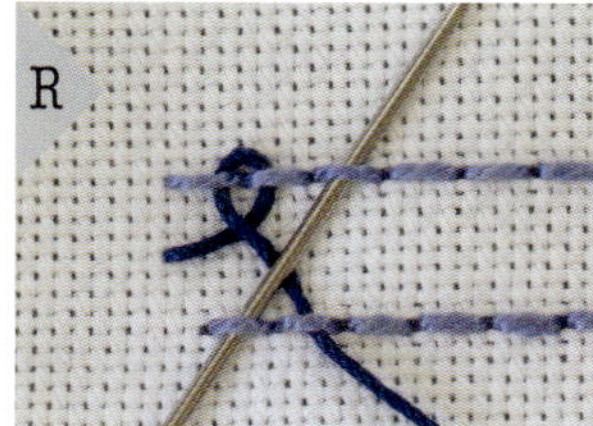

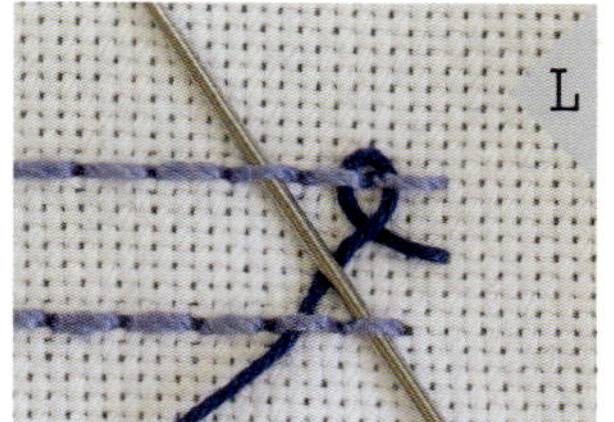

5. Pass your needle under the second stitch on the top line, and with the thread under the needle, pass your needle under the third stitch on the bottom line. Pull your needle through.

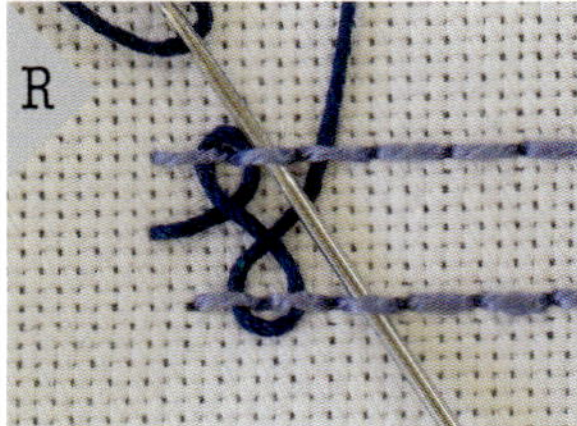

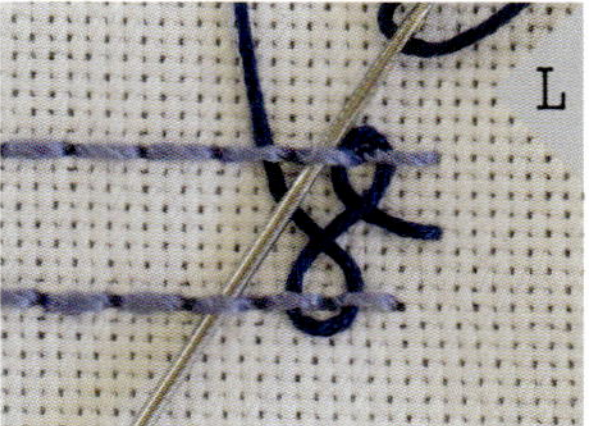

6. Moving back and forth, from top to bottom, continue lacing your thread along the line. Keep your laced loops relaxed and don't pull the lacing thread too tight.

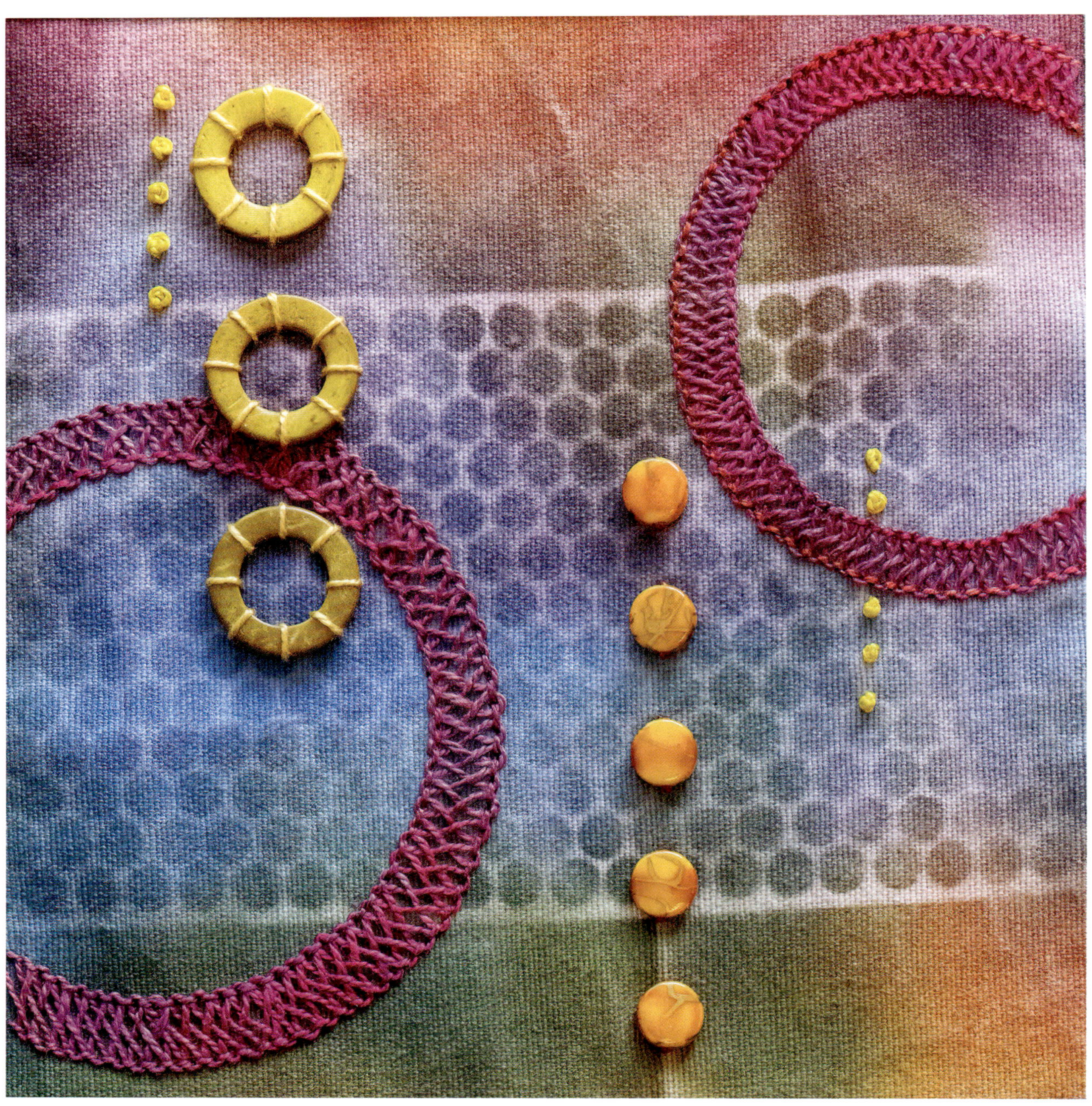

◊ Sample of double Pekinese stitch worked in a bright pink perle cotton #5 thread on a sun-dyed background

Eastern Stitch

Eastern stitch is also known as *Egyptian buttonhole.* Many people think of this stitch as an even-weave stitch that has to be worked on a grid, but it will follow a softly curved line, too.

When working this stitch, maintain a slightly loose tension.

1. Make a vertical straight stitch at the left side of an imaginary square.

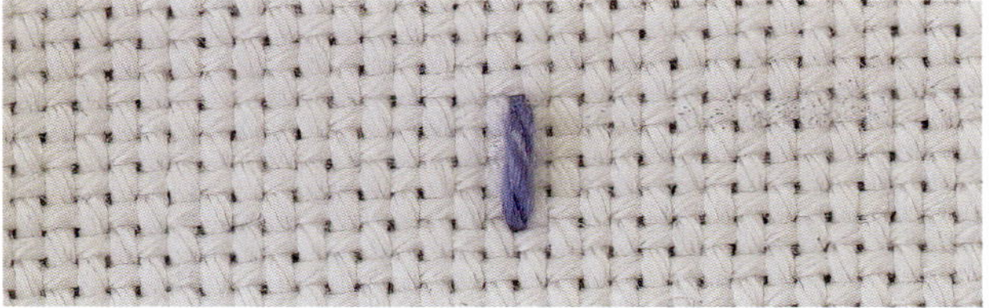

2. Add a horizontal straight stitch at the top of an imaginary square. These 2 stitches form the foundation bars of each unit.

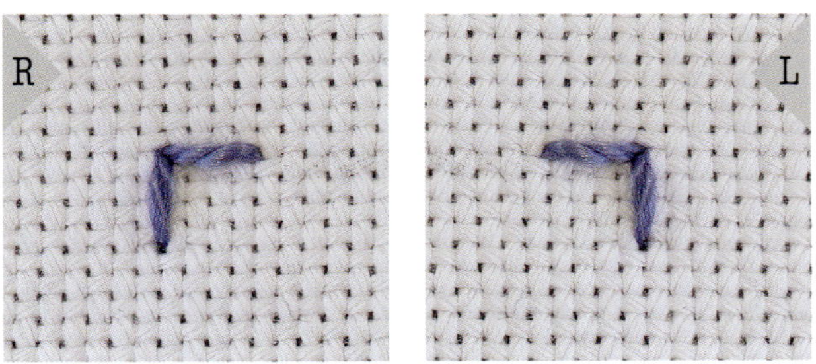

3. Taking the needle diagonally across the back of the fabric, bring the thread up through the fabric, at the bottom right-hand corner.

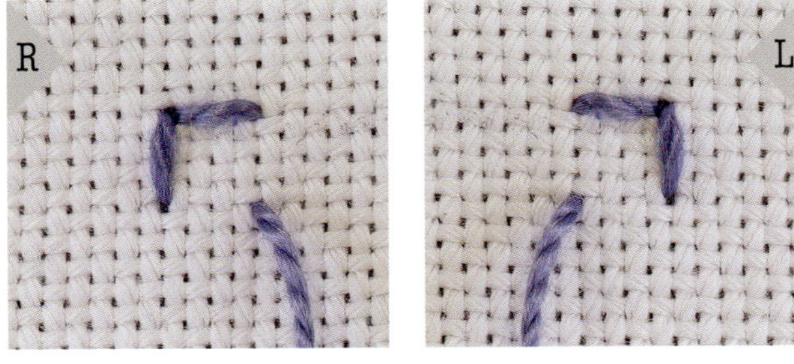

4. Take the needle over the top and pass it under the vertical stitch, making sure the thread is kept to the top of the needle.

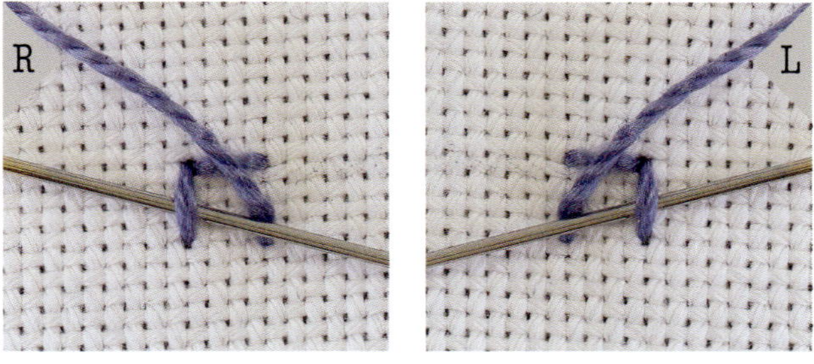

5. When you pull the thread through, it should form a loop over the vertical bar stitch.

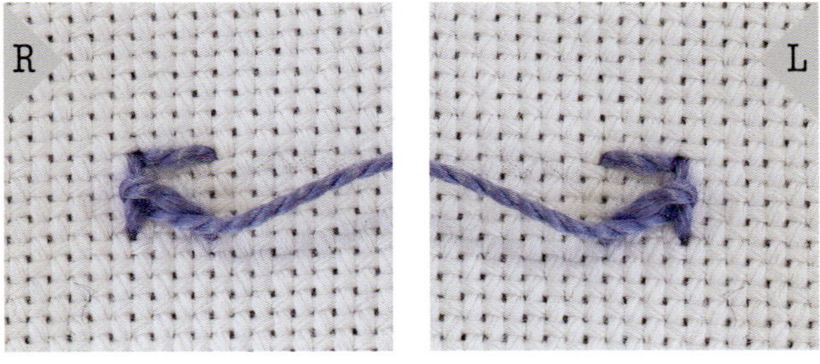

6. Take the needle over the top of the horizontal bar and pass the needle under the stitch making sure the thread is kept to the right of the needle so that when you pull it through, it forms a loop over the horizontal stitch.

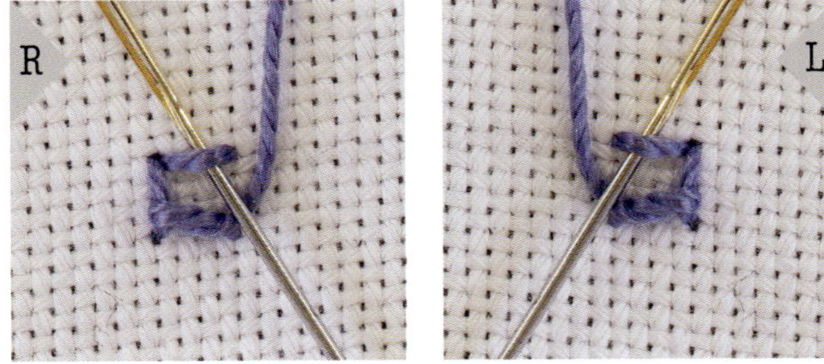

7. Pull your thread through. Don't pull too tight. The cross loop should sit snug on the fabric, not a tight knot.

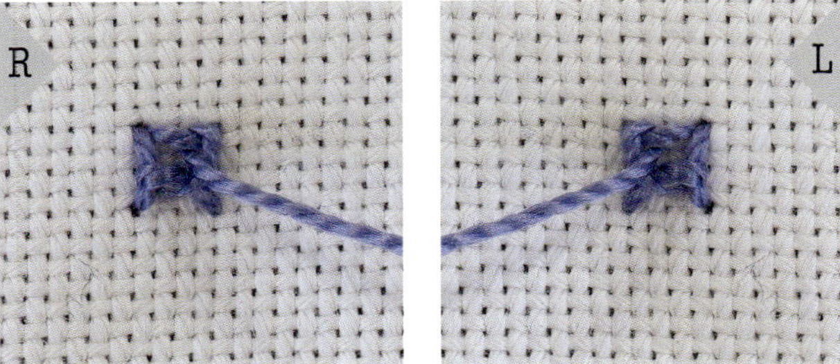

8. Take the thread through the fabric at the bottom right-hand corner, bringing it out at the top-left corner of the next stitch and repeat the process. You can work along a line or a curve.

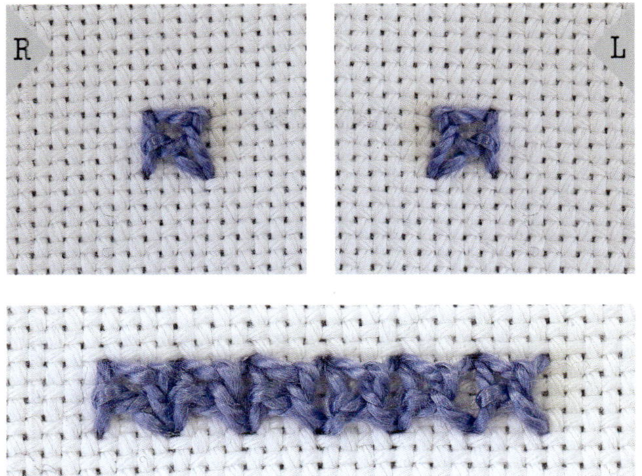

◊ Line of completed Eastern stitch

◊ Eastern stitch used in abstract flower motif

Ermine Stitch

Ermine stitch is made up of three straight stitches—one vertical, and two diagonal—which cross in the lower half of the vertical stitch. You can change this stitch by changing the height of the vertical stitch, or you can space the units in different formations to form patterns. The top of this stitch should be wider than the bottom.

1. Start with a straight vertical stitch.

2. Cross the stitch below the midpoint of the vertical stitch.

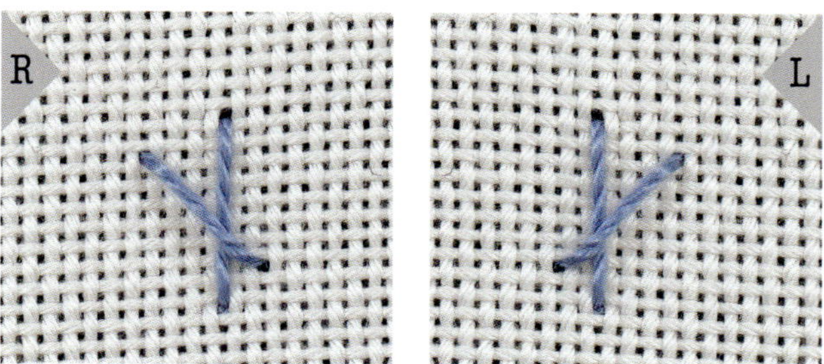

3. Cross the stitch from the other direction but still below the midpoint of the vertical stitch.

◊ Ermine stitch worked on lightly dyed Aida cloth

Eskimo Stitch

Eskimo stitch is a quick, easy, decorative line that can be used for borders or built up row upon row to create patterns and fills. This stitch is worked on imaginary parallel lines.

1. Lay a foundation line of evenly spaced running stitches.

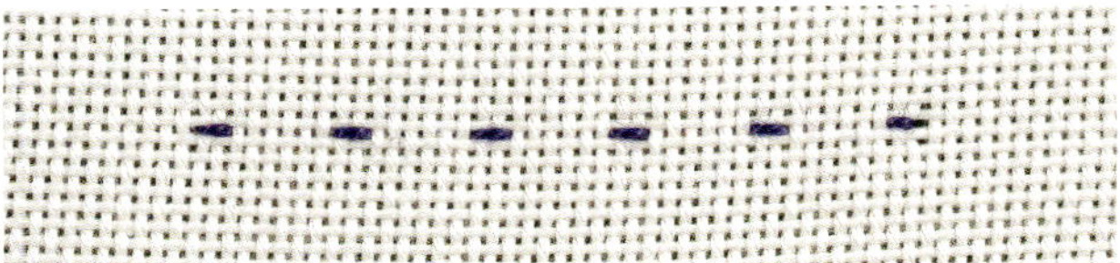

2. Have your needle emerge on the line below the running stitches at the point where, if you drew an imaginary line downward, it would lie in between the running stitches.

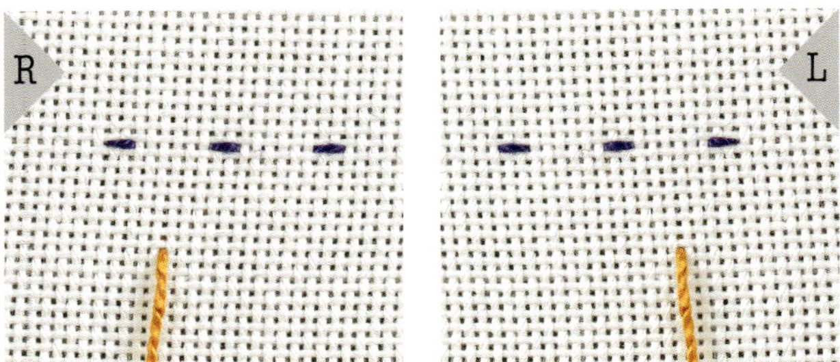

3. Pass your needle under the first running stitch and take it over and then through the next running stitch.

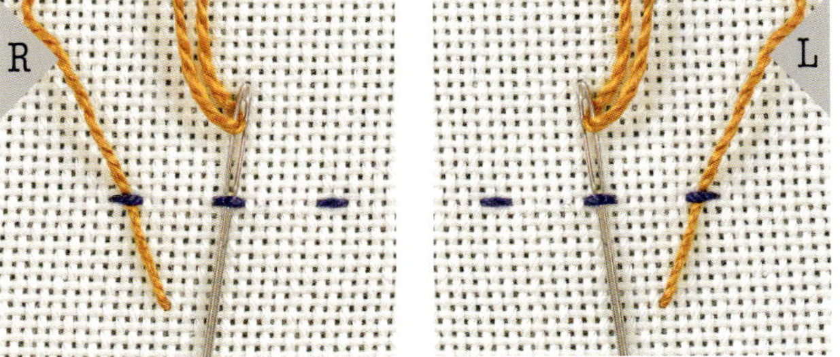

4. Take your needle back into the fabric at the point where you began the stitch. Bring your needle out at the point shown, ready to create the next stitch.

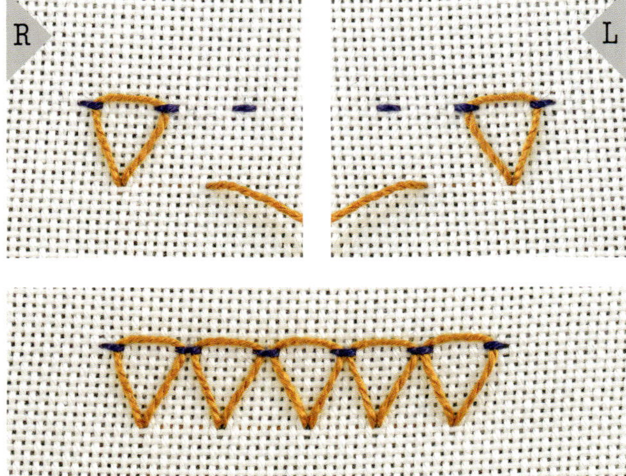

Line of completed Eskimo stitch

◊ Eskimo stitch worked face-to-face using variegated thread on hand-painted background

Eskimo Stitch (Crossed)

Crossed Eskimo stitch is a simple variation of Eskimo stitch (page 114). This stitch is worked on imaginary parallel lines.

1. Work a foundation line of evenly spaced running stitches.

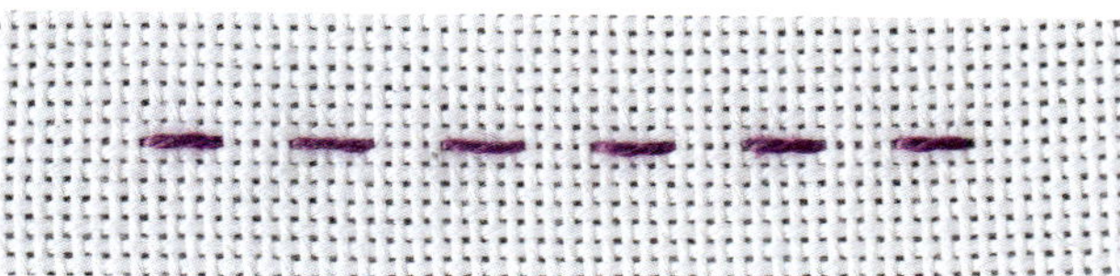

2. Bring your needle from the back, on the line below the running stitches. If you drew an imaginary line downward, it would lie in line with the end of the first running stitch. Pass your needle under the second running stitch.

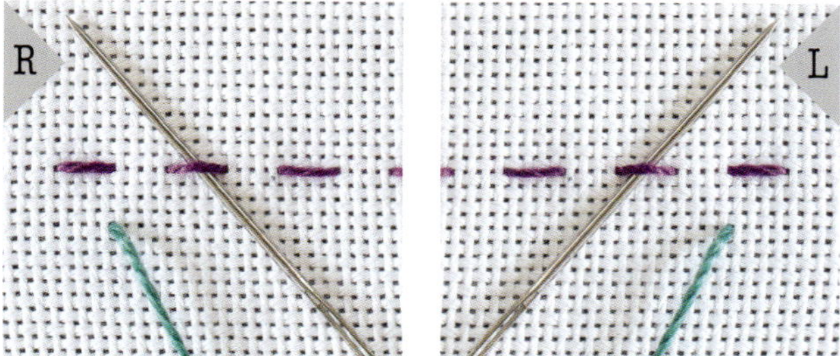

3. Move back a stitch and pass your needle under the stitch. Insert your needle in-line with the start of the second running stitch.

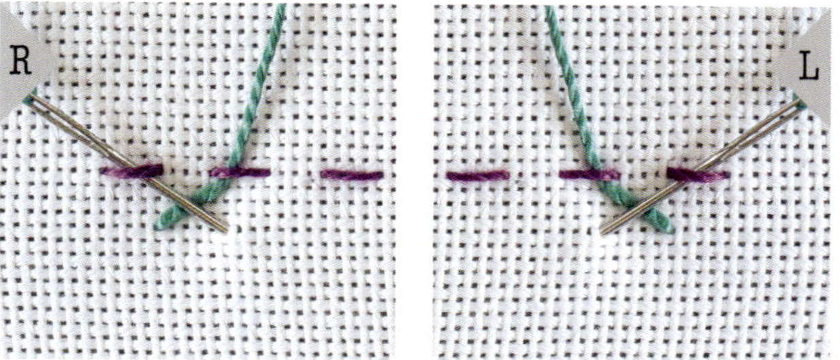

4. Pull your thread through to create a crossed Eskimo stitch.

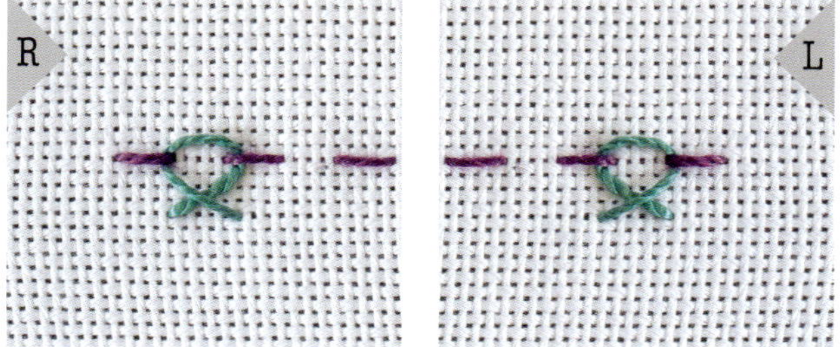

5. Work in this manner along the line.

◇ Rows of crossed Eskimo stitch worked in variegated thread face-to-face to form pattern

Feather Stitch Filling

When straight single feather stitch is worked in rows back-to-back, it becomes a stitch called feather stitch filling.

This filling stitch lends itself to numerous simple additions, such as adding a simple cross-stitch between two rows, but a seed bead, bugle bead, French knot, chain stitch, oyster stitch, or fly stitch could also be added easily to create more interest.

To start this stitch, imagine two parallel vertical lines or mark the lines using a water-soluble or air-erasable pen.

Work this stitch from top to bottom in lines.

1. Bring the needle out at the top of the line to be worked, insert the needle on the other line, and make a small diagonal stitch downward. Keep the thread under the point of the needle, and pull the thread through the fabric to make the stitch.

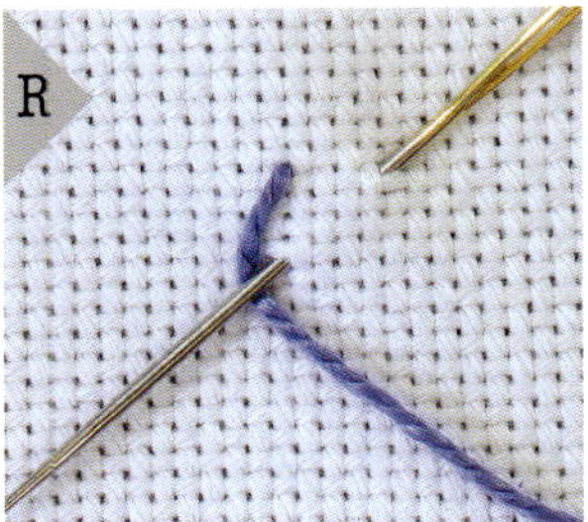

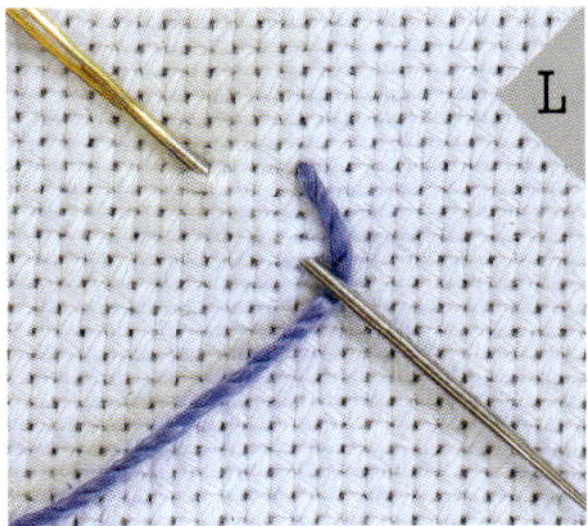

2. On the opposite side of the line, insert the needle and make a small stitch in a downward direction and, keeping the thread under the point of the needle, pull the thread through the fabric to make the stitch.

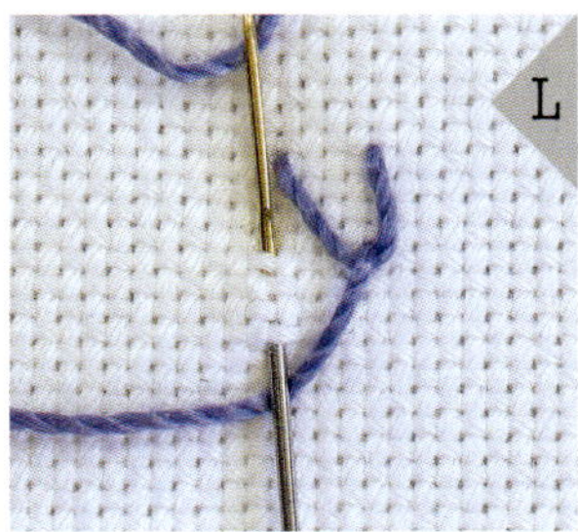

3. Repeat Steps 1–2, alternating until you have a line of single feather stitches.

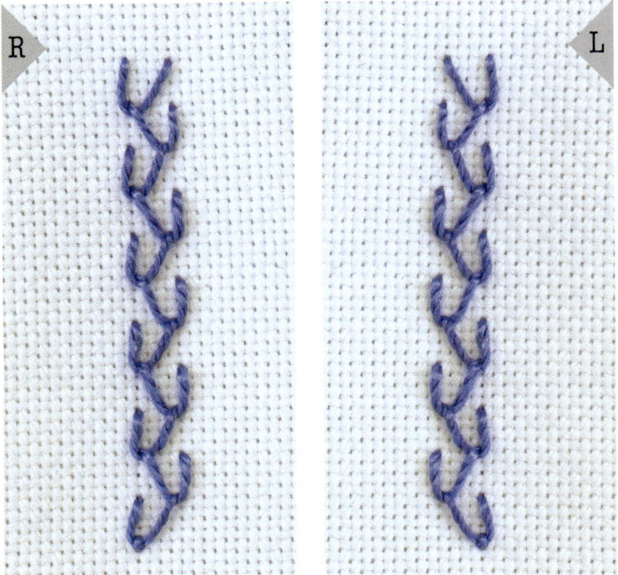

4. Bring your needle out at the top of your next line and begin working a line of single feather.

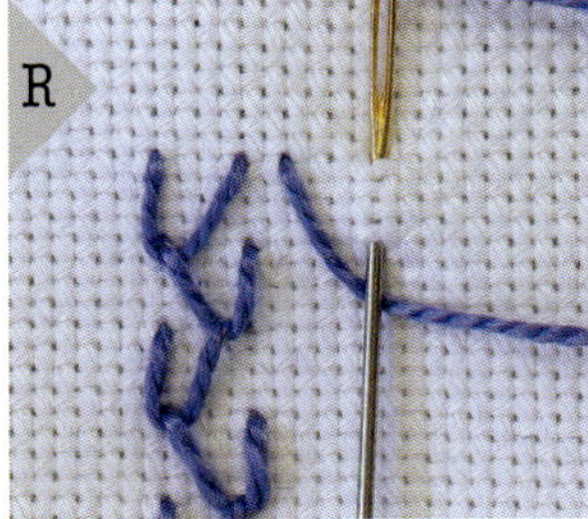

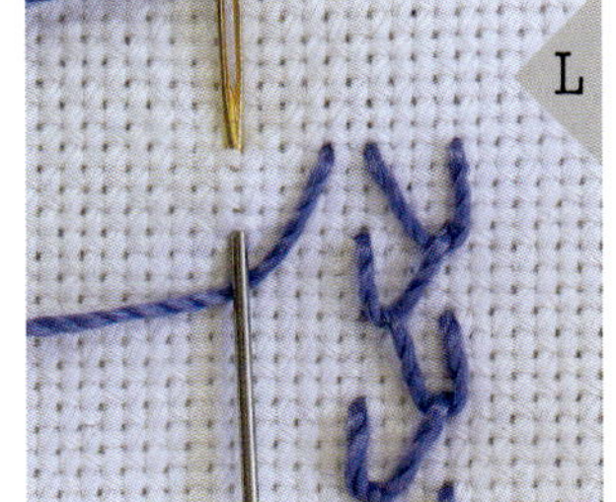

5. Work your next line in a mirror image of the first.

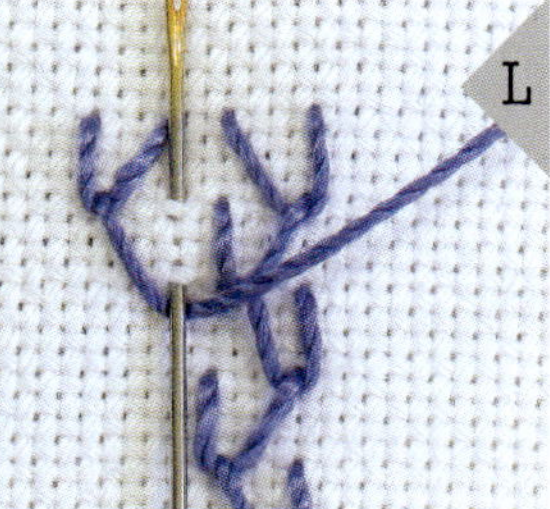

6. Work in this manner, adding lines until you have filled the area you want to cover.

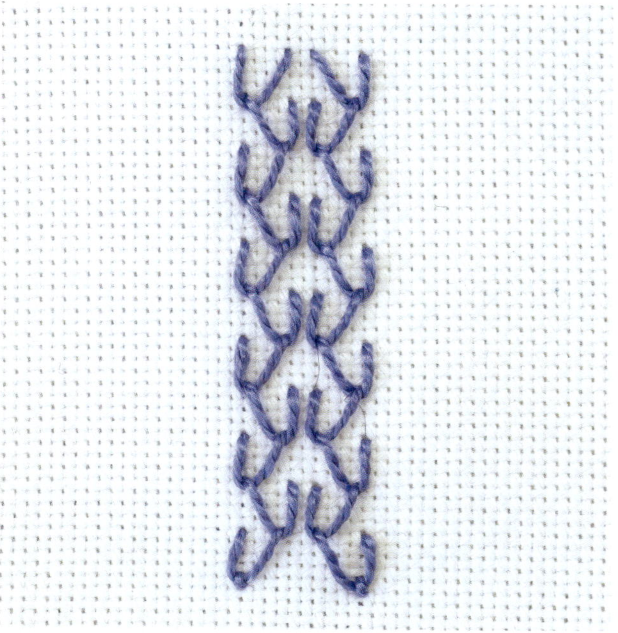

◇ Sample of feather stitch filling, worked using hand-dyed thread on hand-painted background

Fern Stitch

Fern stitch is quick, easy, and very useful, particularly in floral designs. You can also work this stitch as a single unit to make a bird footprint. It is perfect for creating a trail of prints across a sandy beach scene. The stitch holds a curve well, and you can vary the length of the side spines to create a very organic line.

1. Bring the thread from the back of the fabric and work a vertical straight stitch.

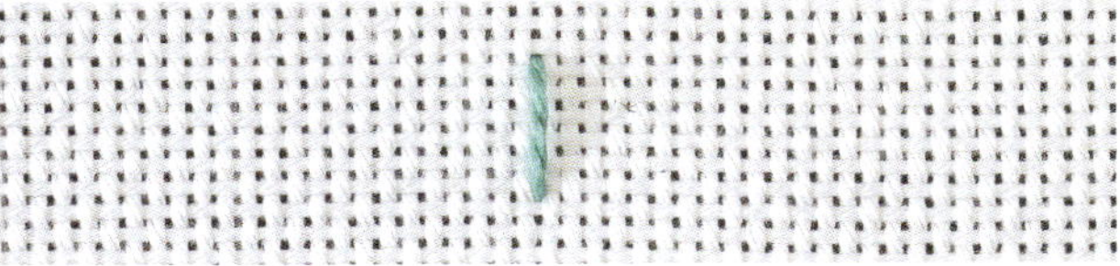

2. Work a diagonal straight stitch on one side of the first stitch.

3. Work a diagonal straight stitch on the other side to finish the first unit.

4. Continue repeating these units along the line.

◊ Fern stitch used in slow-stitch project using perle cotton #8

Fern Stitch (Whipped)

Whipped fern stitch consists of a foundation of fern stitch (page 118), which is then whipped. The whipping thread can be a different color, a novelty yarn, a metallic thread, or even a ribbon.

1. Start with a foundation of fern stitch (page 118).

2. Bring your needle out at the bottom of the line and pass it under the first vertical straight stitch. Take care not to pass your needle through the fabric. Pull the thread through.

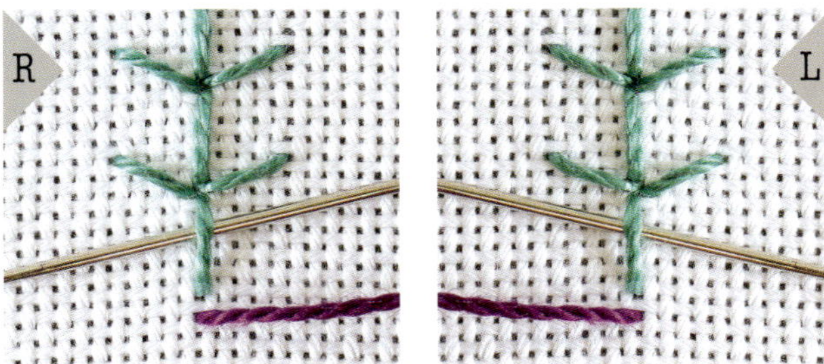

3. Move to the second vertical straight stitch and pass the needle under to continue whipping. Pull your thread through.

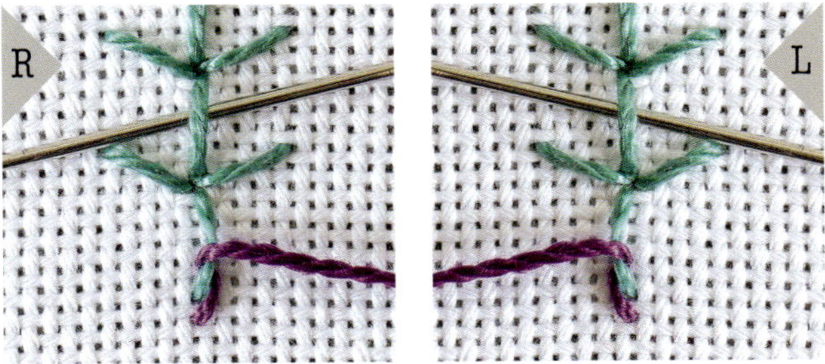

4. Continue whipping along the line.

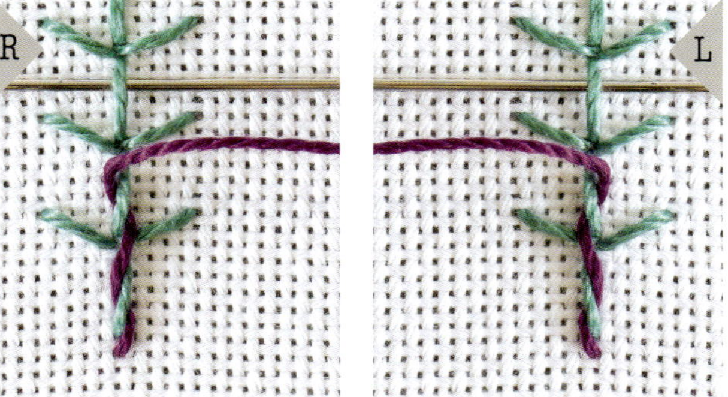

5. When you reach the end of the line, take your needle to the back and tie off.

◊ Small motif worked using whipped fern stitch

Fern Stitch (Woven)

Woven fern stitch has a foundation of fern stitch (page 118). It can be worked as a decorative band and looks particularly good when worked in variegated hand-dyed thread.

In this example, I have shaped the top to be more like a leaf shape.

1. Start with a foundation of fern stitch (page 118).

2. To weave, bring your needle out at the base of the leaf, and pass your needle under the central bar.

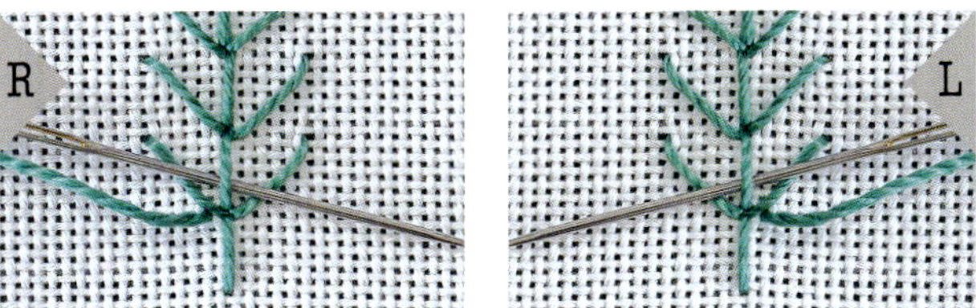

3. Turn your needle, and weave your needle under the first bar, over the central bar, and under the last bar.

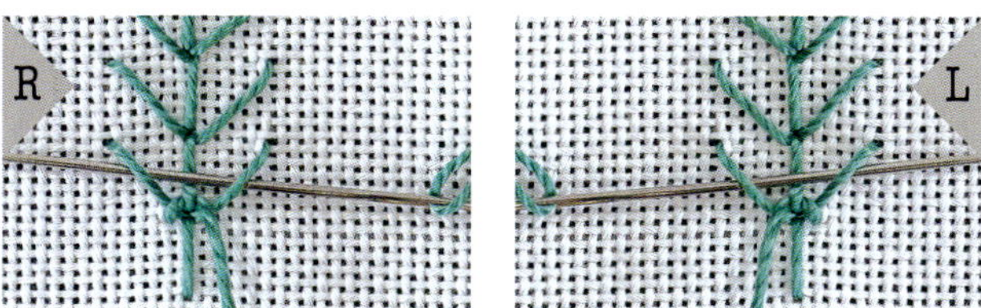

4. Weave up to the base of the next unit of fern stitch, and take your needle to the back of the fabric just under the weaving so that it is hidden.

5. Bring your needle from the back of the fabric very close to the next fern stitch, ready to start weaving.

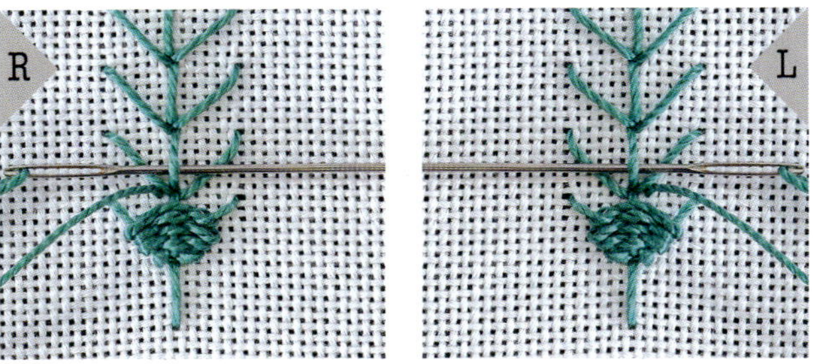

6. Work, weaving in this manner, up the line until all units are woven. Take your needle to the back and tie off.

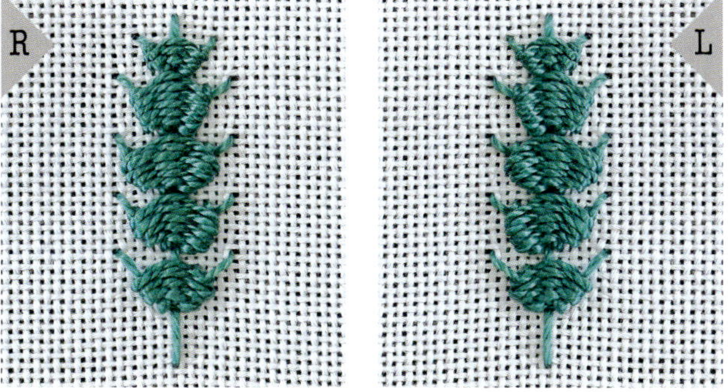

◊ Woven fern stitch worked in variegated perle cotton #5

Fly Stitch (Arrowhead)

Arrowhead fly stitch creates a border pattern, or you can work it row upon row as a fill. Most often, you see it worked on even-weave fabric but you can work this stitch in a free-form manner for interesting patterning. It is quick, easy, and fun to work.

This stitch consists of a series of fly stitches that are worked close together, gradually expanding and lengthening their arms so that the stitches sit snugly inside one another.

1. To create the first small fly stitch, bring the thread up from the back and take a small bite of the fabric by inserting the needle level with where the thread emerged. Angle your needle at a downward angle so that the needle emerges between the 2 points.

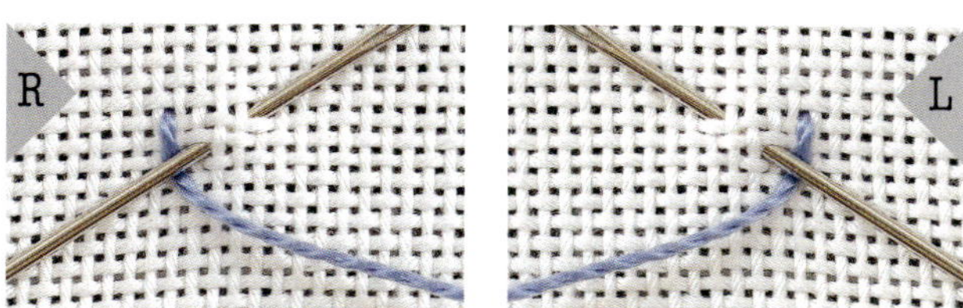

2. With the thread wrapped under the needle, pull it through the fabric. Secure the V in position with a small vertical straight stitch.

3. Have your needle emerge next to where you started the first fly stitch. Make a fly stitch a little wider and with the base of the V a little below the first stitch.

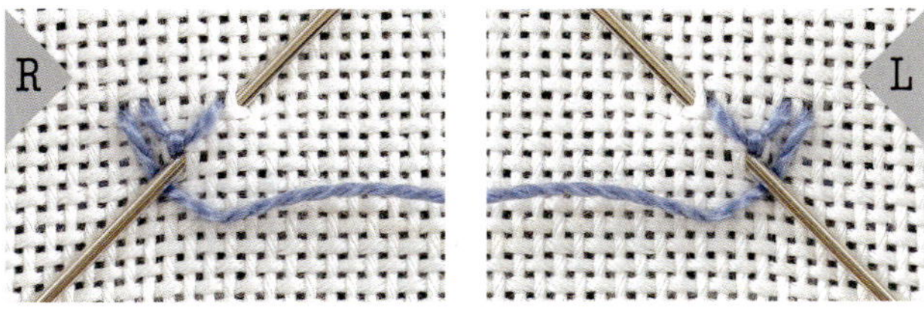

4. Tie off the fly stitch with a small straight stitch before continuing to the next fly stitch.

5. Make a third fly stitch a little wider and with the base of the V a little below the last stitch.

6. You can repeat making fly stitches 3 to 8 times.

7. Continue making fly stitch units down the line.

Arrowhead fly stitch worked using variegated perle cotton #8 thread

Arrowhead fly stitch worked close together using variegated perle cotton #8 thread

Fly Stitch (Closed)

Closed fly stitch is most often used to form a leaf shape. The stitch is made of a series of fly stitches that are stacked close together, and it is quick, easy, and satisfying. You can shape this stitch by expanding the arms of each stitch in a stepped manner.

1. Start by making a fly stitch with a sharp V (page 188). Take a small bite of the fabric and angle your needle downward. With the thread under the needle, pull it through the fabric.

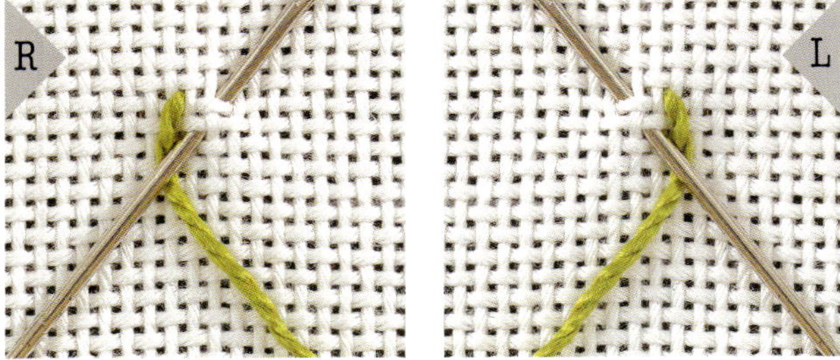

2. Tie off the fly stitch with a small straight stitch.

3. Make your second fly stitch a little wider, farther down the line. In this instance, I used the weave of the fabric as my guide, going 1 thread down and making the stitch 1 thread wider. It does not matter if you are not quite so precise, but make sure the next stitch is close to the last.

4. Tie off with a small straight stitch.

5. Make a third fly stitch a little farther down the line and a little bit wider.

6. At this point, you can continue down the line, filling the shape with straight sides, or if you want a wider leaf, keep working the fly stitches wider, dropping down the line with each stitch as you go.

7. When your leaf is the length you want, make 1 or 2 narrower stitches.

8. When you have your leaf, take the thread to the back and work a single straight stitch in the middle of the V stitch.

9. You can use the leaf as is.

10. You can also add a stem using backstitch or stem stitch.

Fly Stitch (Whipped)

Whipped fly stitch is a quick way to create a branch-like stitch with a central ridged line. Whipped fly stitch is also known as *whipped attached fly stitch.* This stitch has many creative possibilities as the thread that you use to whip it with can be of a heavier weight to the foundation stitches. You can use a contrasting color or have fun with novelty yarns and metallic threads.

Tip Be careful not to pick up the background fabric or split the fly stitches. Use a blunt tapestry needle while you are whipping to avoid this problem.

1. Begin working a vertical line of fly stitches (page 188). Take a small bite of the fabric and angle your needle downward. With the thread under the needle, pull it through the fabric.

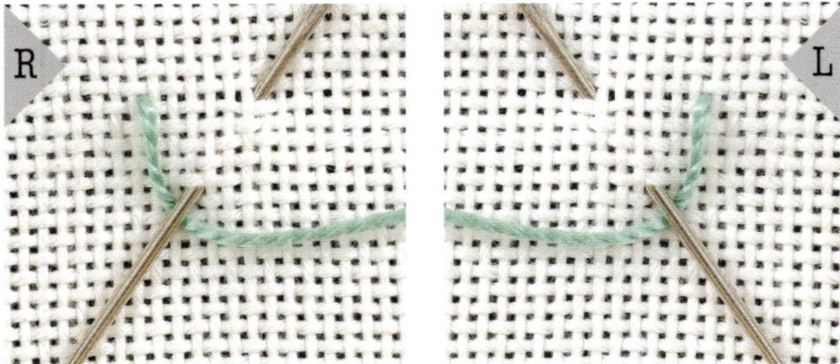

2. Pull the needle through and secure the V with a small straight stitch.

3. Repeat these steps to work a line of fly stitches.

4. To whip the row of fly stitch in a second thread, bring your needle out at the base of the line of stitches. Pass your needle under the straight stitch at the base of the V in the first fly stitch. Take your whipping thread through.

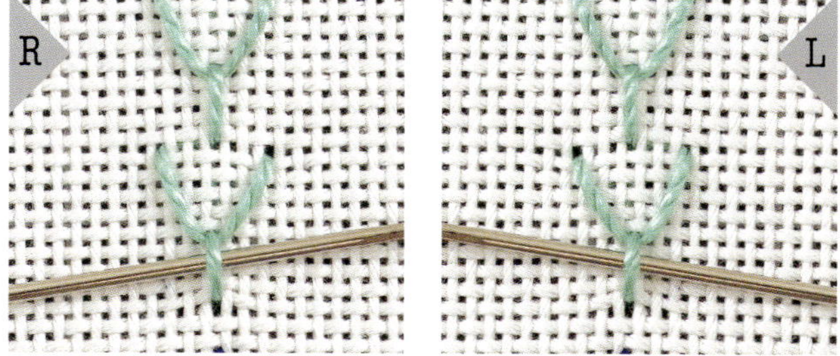

5. Move to the next fly stitch, whipping each stitch as you move up the line.

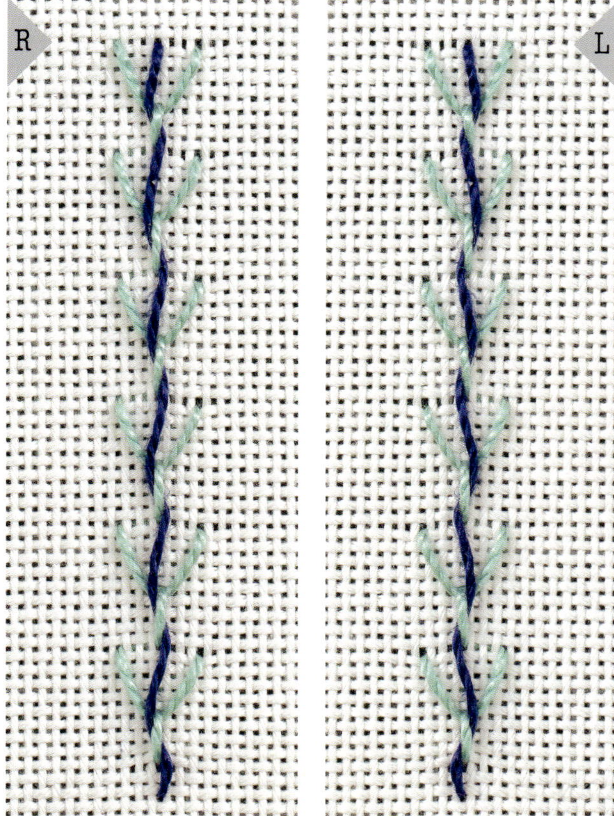

◊ Whipped fly stitch worked in perle cotton #8

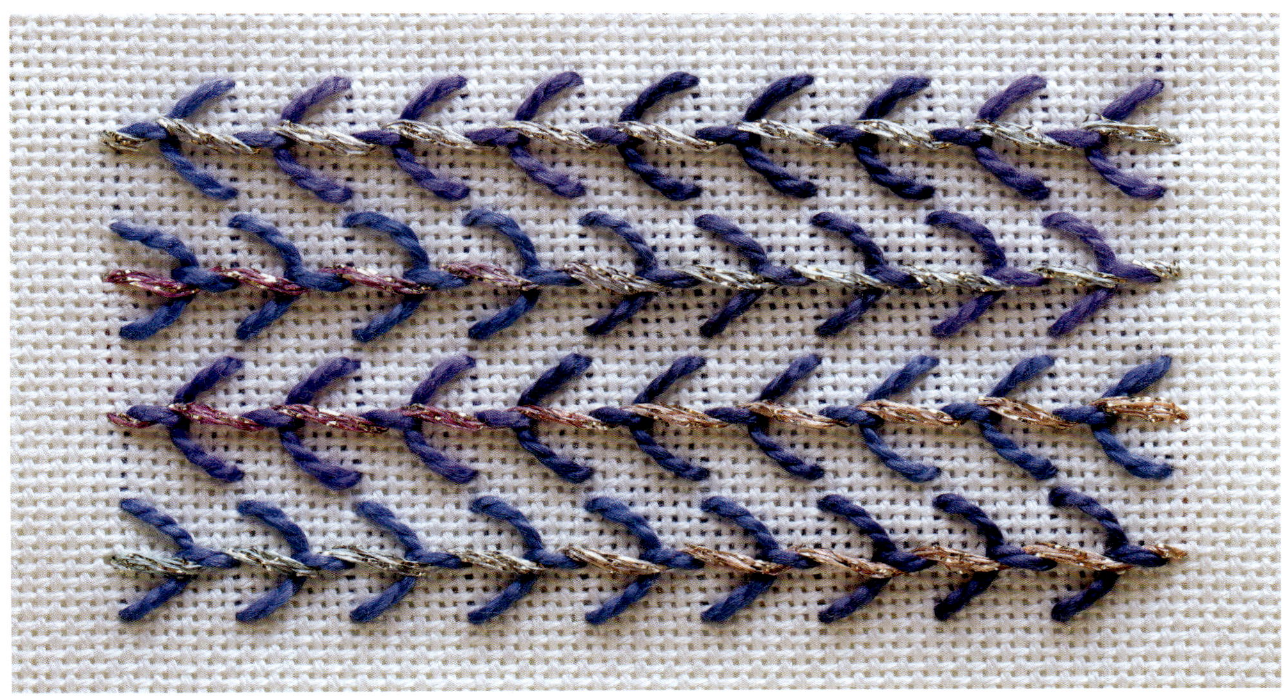

◊ Whipped fly stitch worked row upon row to form regular pattern

Free-form Cross-Stitch

Normally, cross-stitch is worked on even-weave fabric to create neat rows and patterns. Free-form cross-stitch is loose and informal, and it breaks the rules.

Free-form cross-stitch is simply crossed stitches worked in a free-form manner. You can work free-form cross-stitch close together, or sprinkle them across an area to create a sparse fill. And you can vary the stitches to provide gradients and varied texture, as in the fabric postcard above.

Free-form cross-stitch can add energy to a piece. Free-form cross-stitch used in the background adds a sense of energy to the design on a fabric postcard I made titled *Duelling Fiddlers.*

Ghiordes Knot

Ghiordes knot is known by many names, to list a few *Turkey knot stitch, Turkey rug knot, single Turkey knot, knot tufting, quilt knot stitch, tufted knot stitch, rya stitch, Damascus edge,* and *single knotted Smyrna rug stitch.*

Ghiordes knot creates a texture that is like the plush pile of a rug. It is a stitch that has traditionally been used in canvas work or needlepoint but is enjoying a revival as one of the textured embroidery stitches. You can use this stitch to represent things like the middle of flowers, thistle tops, dandelion puffs, grass, moss, animal fur, fur coats, animals, wreaths, garlands, or even Santa's beard! This stitch works anywhere you need a bit of fluffy texture.

Tip For an even tension, stretch the fabric in an embroidery hoop or frame.

I have used stranded cotton to illustrate how to work this stitch. Ghiordes knot can be described as tightly packed backstitches with a loop hanging between each stitch. Each row is worked above the other; the rows are then cut to form the fluffy pile.

1. Leave the tail of your thread at the front of the fabric. Move your needle along the line and pick up 1 or 2 threads to make a small backstitch.

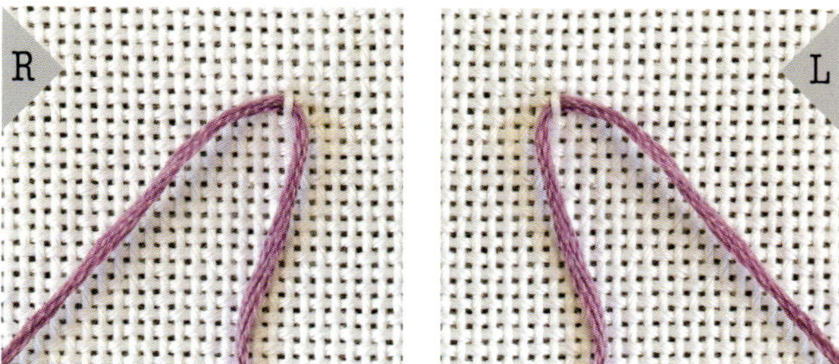

2. Make another small backstitch. As you pull the needle through, leave a loop of thread on the front of the fabric.

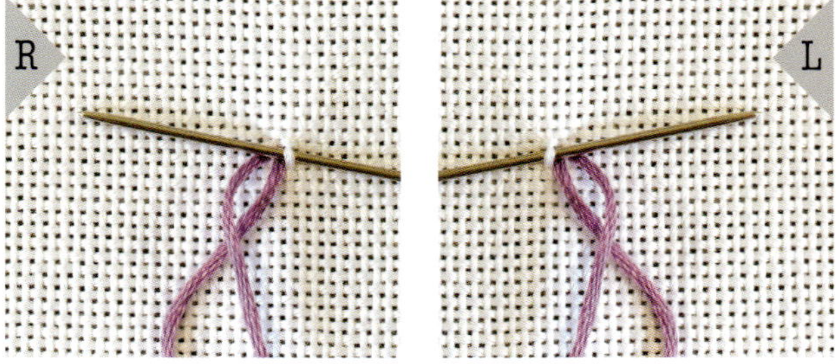

3. Pull the thread all the way through, ready to make the next backstitch.

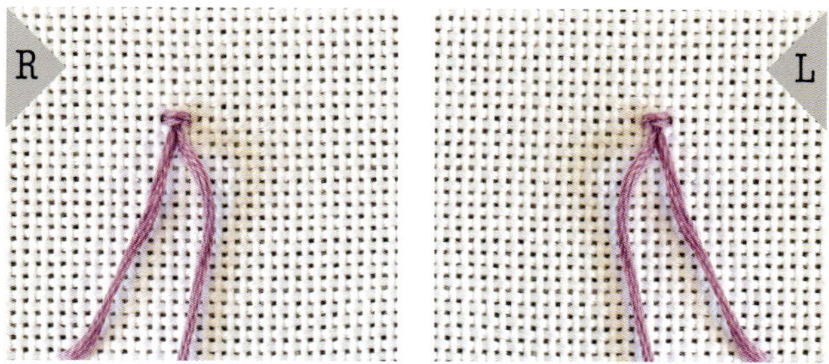

4. Continue creating loops along the line.

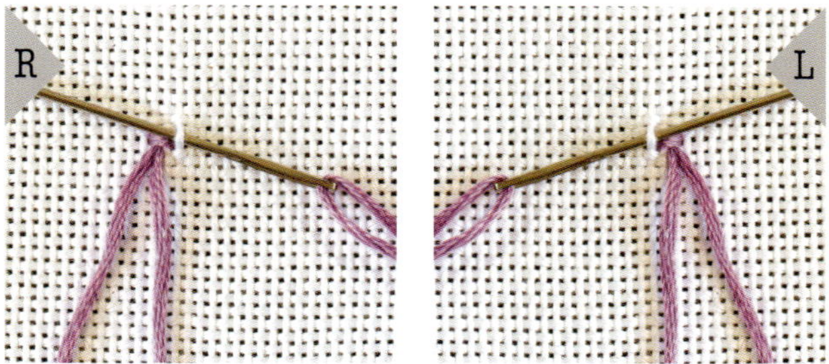

5. As you work, if the loops are getting in your way, hold them aside with your thumb.

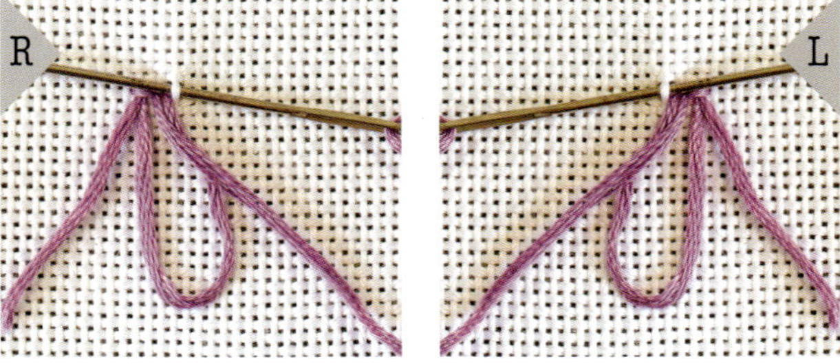

6. Move to the next row, leaving little or no space between the rows. They have to be packed tight to hold the stitches in the fabric.

7. Work row upon row, leaving little space between the rows.

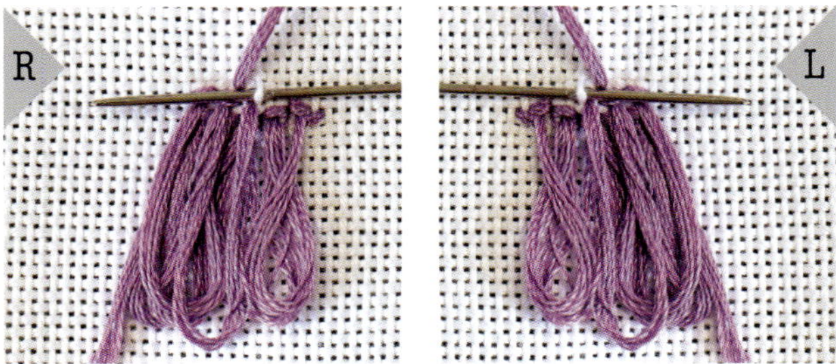

8. Continue to fill the area with packed stitches.

9. Once you have covered the area and completely packed it tight with many loops of thread, snip and trim the loops with scissors.

10. If you have worked the loops closely enough, the stitches won't come out. At first they will look like just a bunch of threads. Tease them a bit with your needle, rub them a bit, and then trim them to shape.

◇ Ghiordes knot worked on fabric book page

Herringbone Stitch (Backstitched)

Backstitched herringbone is a composite stitch that combines herringbone (page 189) and backstitch (page 184). It is quick and easy to work, yet the structure lends itself to many adaptations. Variations in spacing change the look considerably.

Work backstitched herringbone along two parallel lines. If you need to mark the lines, make sure to use a water-soluble or air-erasable marker because backstitched herringbone will hide only parts of the line that you mark.

1. Start by bringing the needle out on the top line to be worked. Move your needle to the bottom line and take a bite of the fabric.

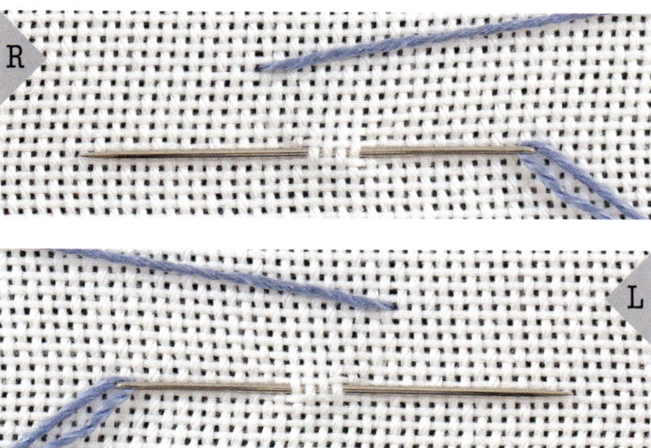

2. Pull your needle through and make a small backstitch.

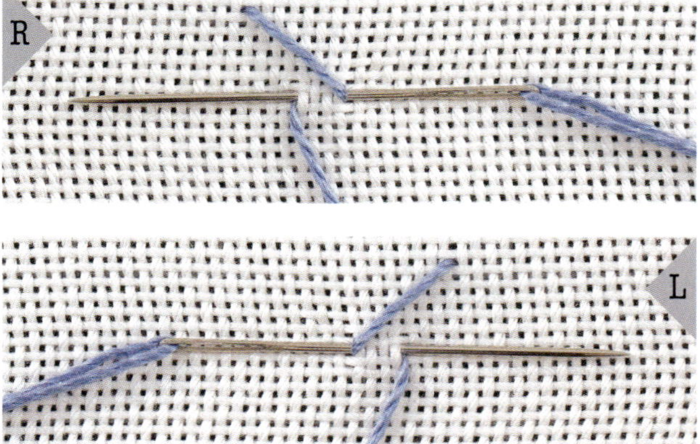

3. Pull your thread through to complete the backstitch.

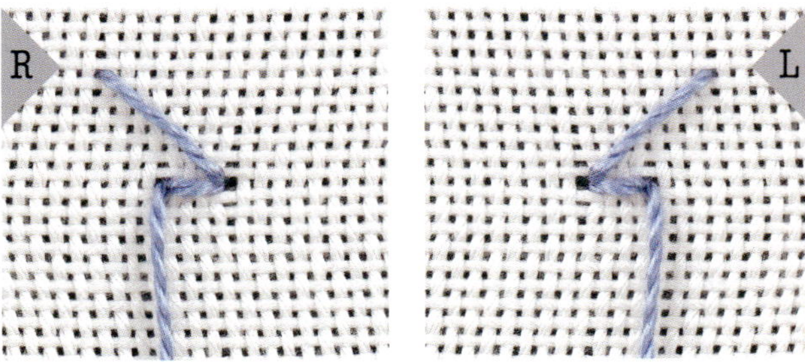

4. Move to the top line and take a bite of the fabric.

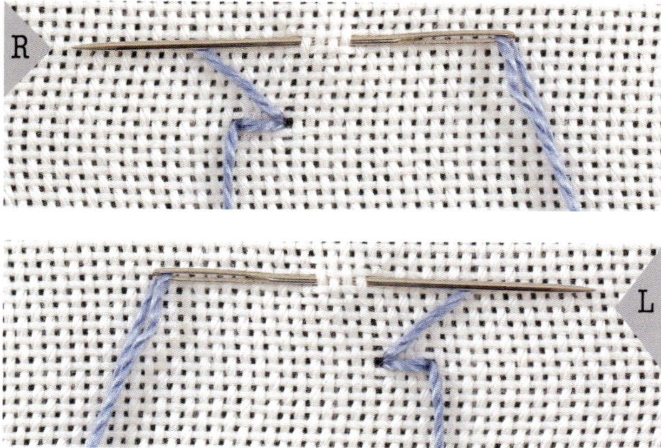

5. Make a backstitch on the top line.

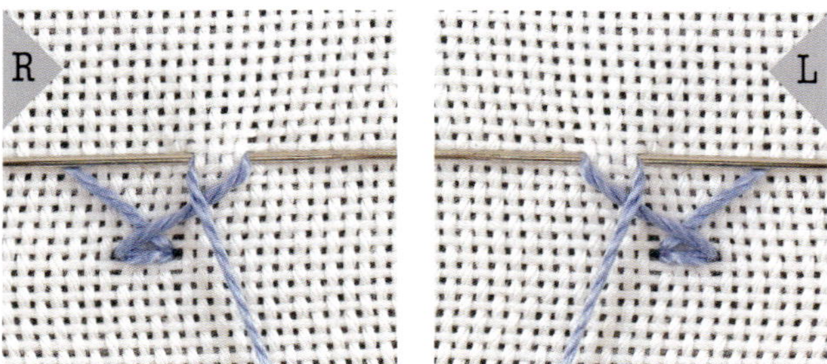

6. Take your needle to the lower line, repeating the steps until you have finished the line.

◊ Backstitched herringbone worked in variegated perle cotton #8

◊ Backstitched herringbone worked in variegated perle cotton #8, row upon row

Backstitched herringbone worked offset in perle cotton #5. These are also worked slightly narrower and closer together than the previous examples.

Herringbone Stitch (Backstitched Laced)

Laced backstitched herringbone stitch is a simple and quick technique. For the lacing journey, you can use embroidery threads to lace this stitch, but it can also be very effective if you explore novelty threads, threads such as silk ribbon, or metallic threads. When you lace this stitch, use a blunt tapestry needle so you don't accidentally split your foundation stitches.

1. Work a foundation line of backstitched herringbone (page 129). Bring your lacing thread out at the top of the line. Pass your needle under the first crossbar. Make sure to lace between the stitch and the fabric, and take care not to take your needle through the fabric.

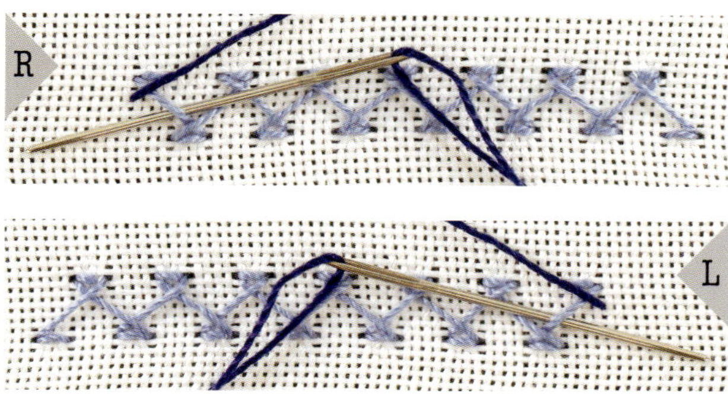

2. Turn your needle and take the lacing thread under the second crossbar.

3. Once again, turn your needle and take it under the crossbar of the backstitched herringbone.

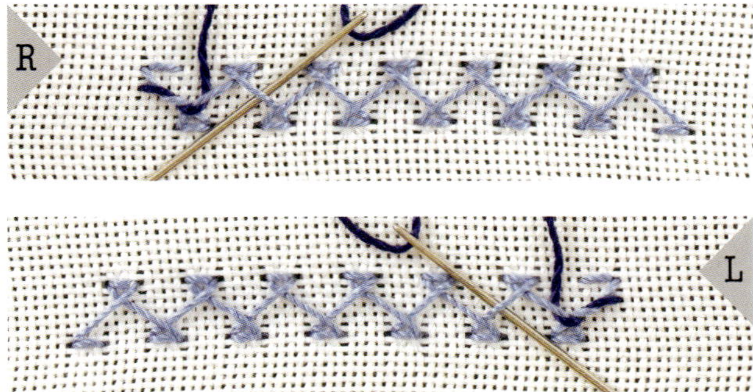

4. Continue along the line with the up and down lacing movement until the end of the line.

◊ Single line of laced backstitched herringbone stitch

◊ Three rows of laced backstitched herringbone stitch

Two rows of laced backstitched herringbone stitch laced with novelty metallic thread. I also worked three straight stitches between the units.

Herringbone Stitch (Backstitched Tied)

Tied backstitched herringbone is an interesting variation of backstitched herringbone (page 129) that can be used as a border or worked row upon row as a fill.

1. Work a line of backstitched herringbone (page 129).

2. Bring your needle out on the top row, just below the first backstitch. Make a small straight stitch.

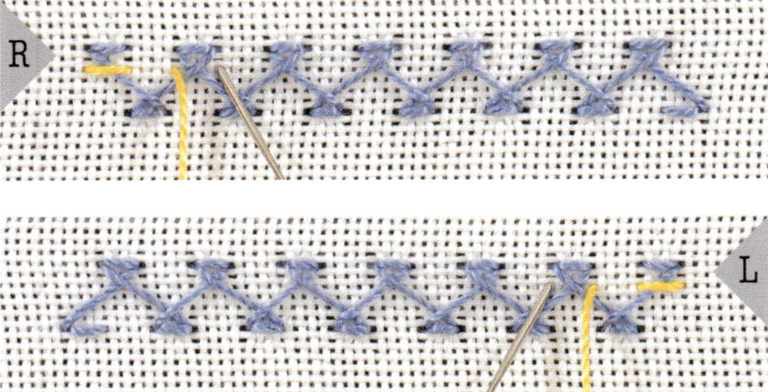

3. Continue to the end of the row.

4. Turn your work and repeat along the bottom line.

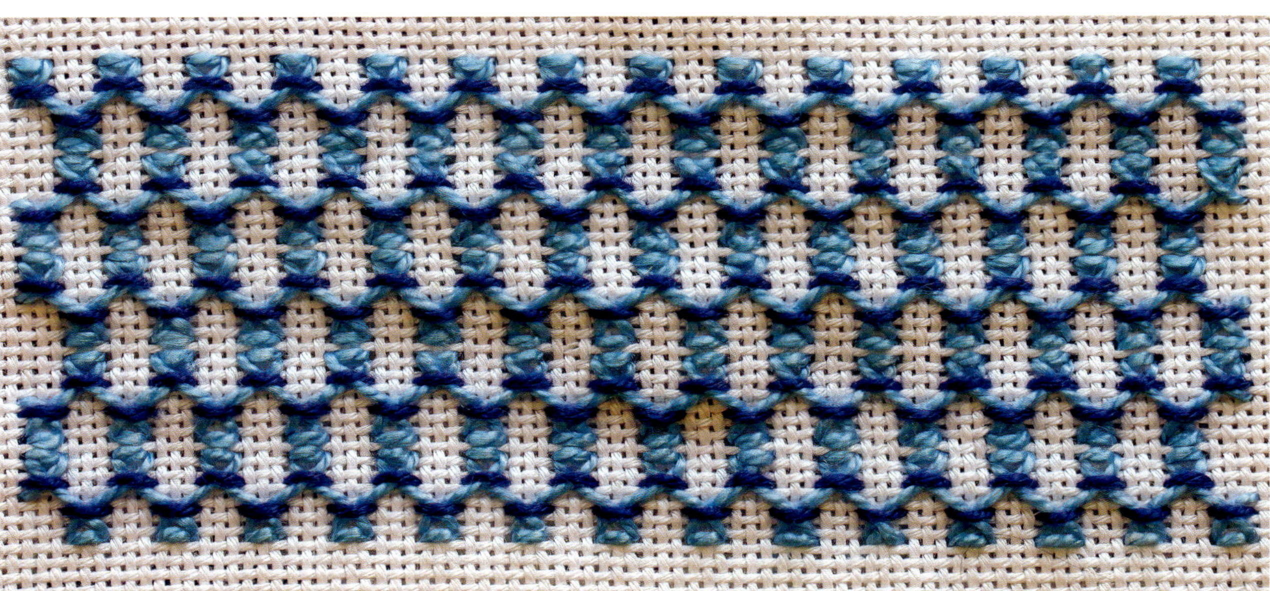

◇ Tied backstitched herringbone worked row upon row as fill

Herringbone Stitch (Backstitched Threaded)

Threaded backstitched herringbone has a lacing technique that is simple and quick to work. You can use embroidery threads or thicker novelty threads, such as yarn, silk ribbon, or metallic threads. For the lacing journey, use a blunt tapestry needle so you don't accidentally split your foundation stitches.

1. Start with a line of backstitched herringbone (page 129).

2. Bring your thread out on the top line of your backstitched herringbone. Pass your needle under the backstitch pointing downward. Pull your thread through.

3. With your needle pointing upward, pass it under the second foot bar of your foundation stitches. Make sure to lace, and take care not to take your needle through the fabric. Pull your thread through.

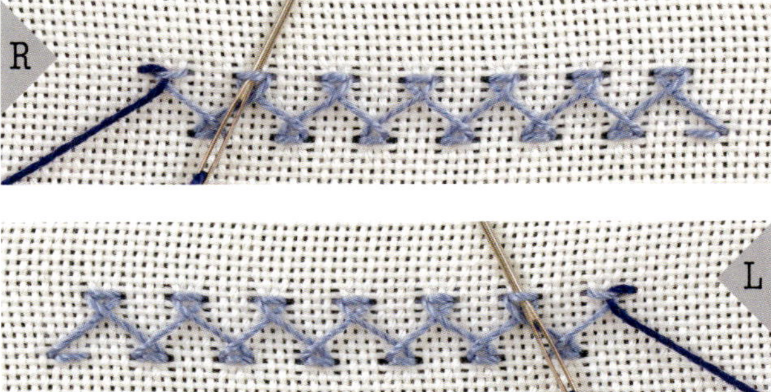

4. Turn your needle so that it faces downward and take the lacing thread under the third foot bar. Pull your thread through.

5. Continue lacing the backstitched foundation stitches up and down until the end of the line. Take your thread to the back.

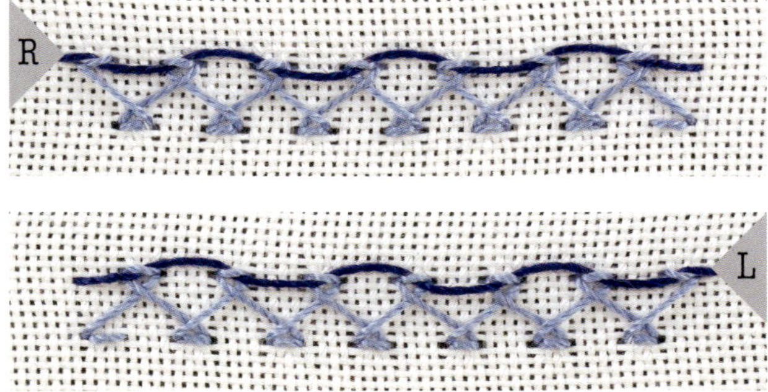

6. Bring your thread up near where you took it to the back of the fabric and move back along the line lacing in the same manner.

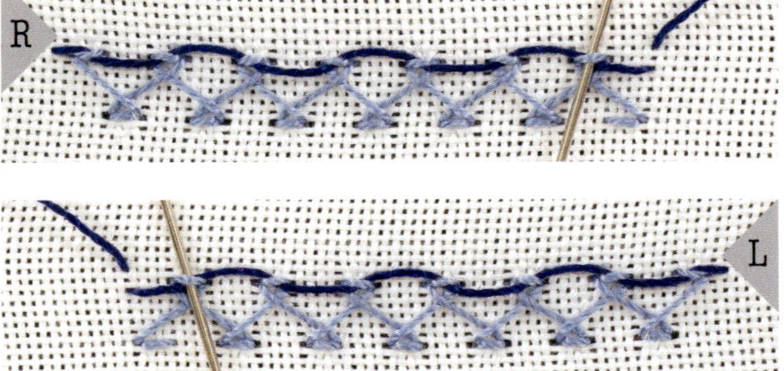

7. Continue along the line.

8. When you have completed lacing the top line, repeat Steps 2–7 to complete the bottom line.

◊ Single line of threaded backstitched herringbone

◊ Threaded backstitched herringbone worked row upon row as fill.

Herringbone Stitch (Backstitched Whipped)

Whipped backstitched herringbone can be used as a border or worked row upon row as a fill. You can be creative with the threads you choose to whip with. Try thicker novelty threads, such as yarn, silk ribbon, or metallic threads, to discover some interesting effects. For the whipping journey, use a blunt tapestry needle so you don't accidentally split your foundation stitches.

1. Work a line of backstitched herringbone (page 129). Bring your needle out on the top line. With your needle pointing down, pass your needle under the first backstitch. Pull your thread through.

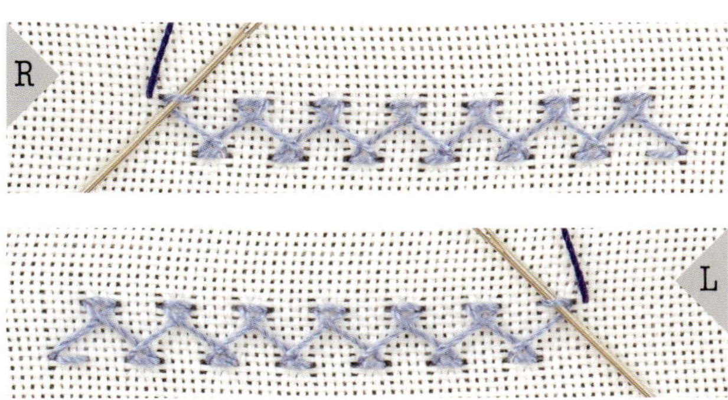

2. Move along the line, and pointing your needle downward, pass your needle under the second backstitch. Pull your thread through.

3. Continue along the line. Take your needle to the back of the fabric.

4. Repeat the same process to whip the bottom line.

◇ Whipped backstitched herringbone worked row upon row. This is whipped with a metallic flecked thread.

Herringbone Stitch (Closed)

Closed herringbone stitch is also known as *shadow stitch, double backstitch,* and *crossed backstitch.*

This variety of herringbone produces a textured line of crossed stitches. It consists of herringbone stitches that are worked so closely together that you see little of the background fabric. On the back of the fabric, it will show two lines of backstitches, which is known as *double backstitch.* This is used in a type of embroidery called *shadow work.* For this type of embroidery, you work closed herringbone stitch on the back of sheer or semi-sheer fabric, so you can see the stitches through the fabric. The shadow of the work is seen (hence, the name). When worked in shadow work, closed herringbone is also known as *shadow stitch.*

Closed herringbone stitch is, of course, a surface embroidery stitch, too. It is very useful to define a good strong line on a border or as part of an edging. This stitch is worked between two imaginary lines. If you need to mark the lines, use a water-soluble or air-erasable marker.

1. Start by bringing the needle out on the bottom of the line to be worked. Take the needle up and make a small stitch on the upper line, pointing your needle toward the start of the line. Pull the thread through.

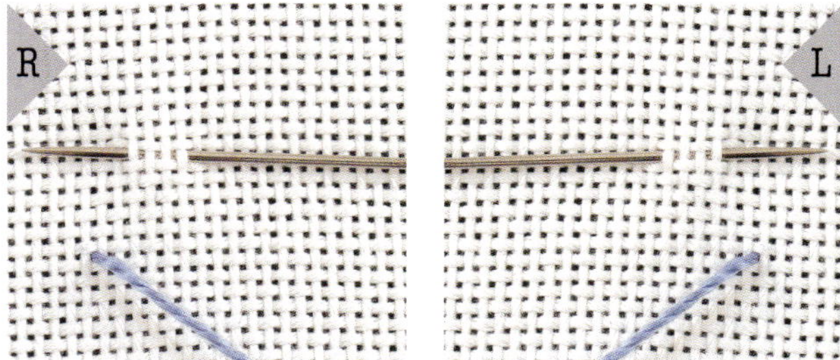

2. Insert the needle on the lower line, but have the needle tip emerge in line with the upper stitch, and make a small stitch that points toward the start of the line.

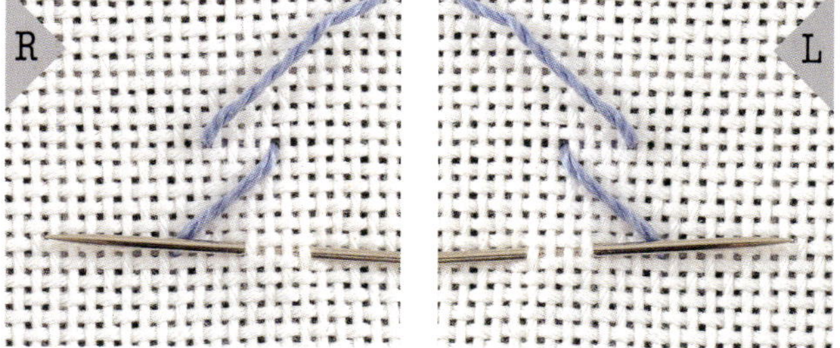

3. Insert the needle on the upper line and take a small bite of the fabric. Have the needle emerge next to the previous stitch.

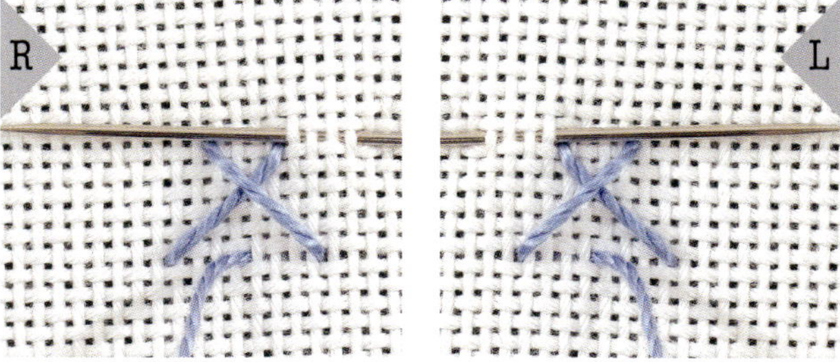

4. Continue in this manner along the line, working each herringbone stitch close to the previous stitch.

Closed herringbone stitch worked row upon row in perle cotton #5

Herringbone Stitch (Closed Raised)

Raised closed herringbone is a stitch that is usually worked in the shape of a leaf and incorporated in floral sprays. It is a quick, easy, self-padding stitch that adds texture and interest to a spray. I have demonstrated using a leaf shape, but this stitch works well with any shape that has a central spine such as an insect body or geometric shapes such as diamonds and triangles.

Mark a leaf shape on your fabric. Use a pen that is easily removed, such as a water-soluble or air-erasable marker. The stitch will cover the outline, but sometimes you can still see the pen marks so it is best to be able to remove them.

1. Make a straight stitch from the base of the stitch to the middle on the centerline, bringing the needle out a little further along.

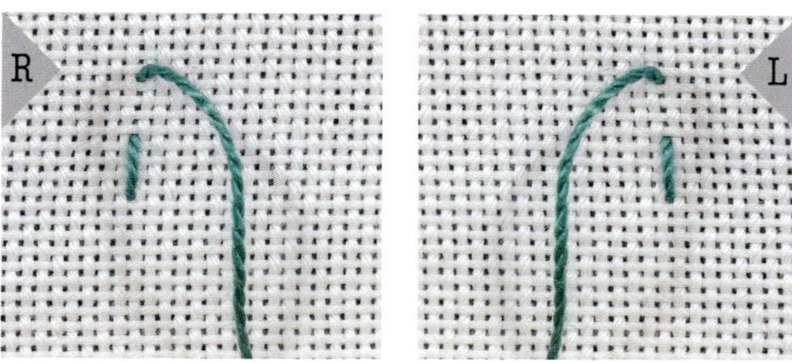

2. Slide the needle under the straight stitch and pull your thread through.

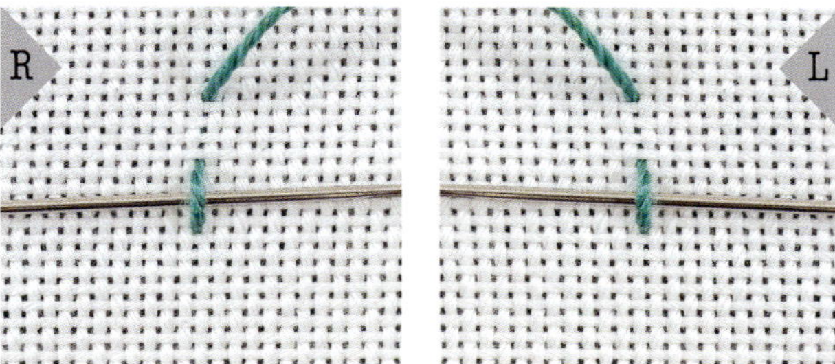

3. Take your needle across the stitch and insert it near the point where the thread emerged in Step 1. When you take the needle to the back, the working thread should be crossed.

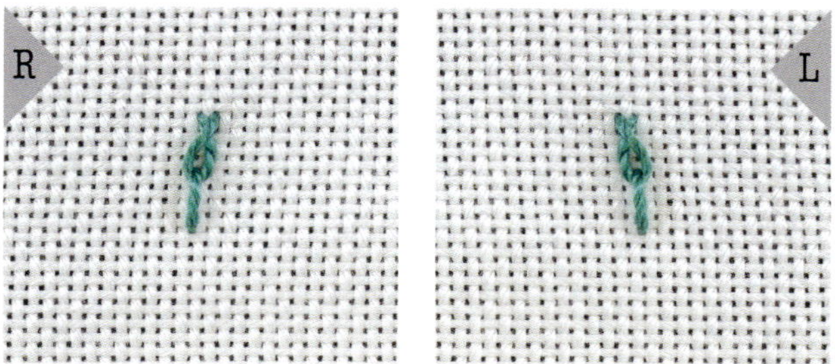

4. Start to shape the leaf. Bring your needle out and a little down the side of what will become a leaf shape.

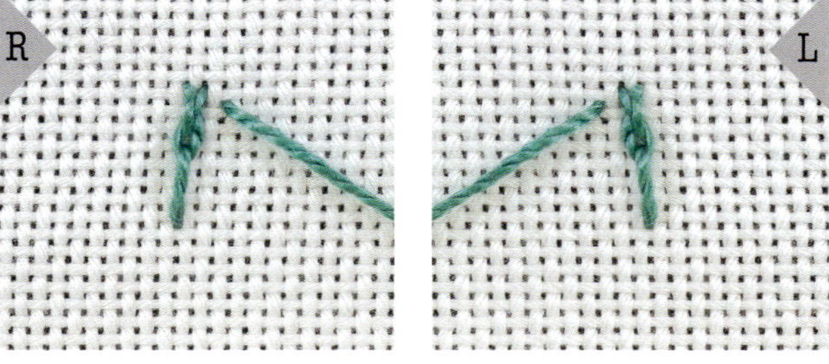

5. Pass the needle under the straight bar stitch. Pull the thread through.

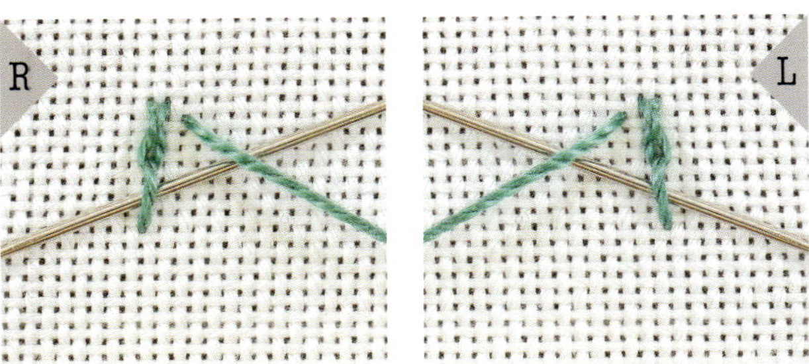

6. A little down the side of the leaf, take the needle to the back of the fabric so the working thread is crossed.

7. Continue in this manner, working down the leaf. Widen your stitches as you work to follow the shape. As you come toward the base of the leaf, make your stitches slightly narrower to follow the leaf shape.

Herringbone Stitch (Fancy)

Fancy herringbone stitch is a fun and easy stitch to work. It is useful as a border as it works up like a braid.

Tip When lacing this stitch, use a tapestry needle to avoid splitting the thread on the foundation row.

1. Work a line of herringbone stitch (page 189).

2. Tie the top crossed part of the herringbone stitch with a cross. Start with the bottom of the cross and work a vertical straight stitch; then add a horizontal straight stitch.

3. Tie each part of the thread intersections top and bottom with small upright cross-stitches. Make sure you work the bottom of the cross vertically and the top of the cross horizontally.

Tip Keep your cross-stitches slightly loose as you will be lacing through these stitches and you need to leave a little slack to be able to do this.

4. Bring your lacing thread from the back of the fabric, and with your needle pointing downward, take it under the top horizontal bar of the first cross-stitch.

5. Move to the next cross, and with your needle pointing upward, pass it under the horizontal bar of the cross-stitch.

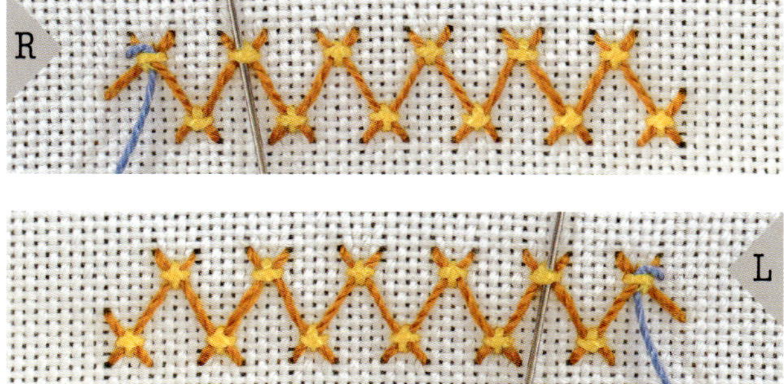

6. Take your needle back to the first cross and pass it under the cross-stitch again so that you have a complete loop.

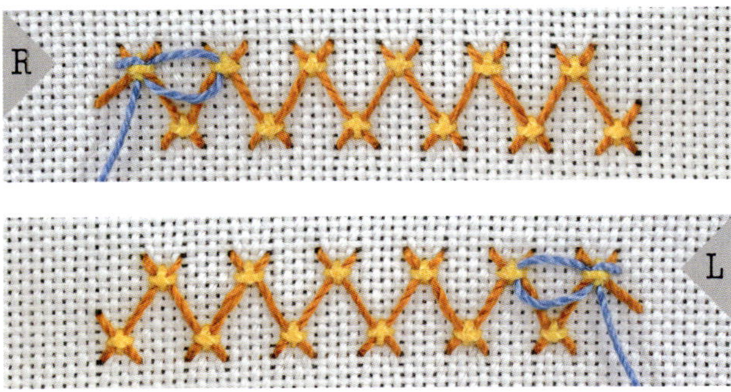

7. Move to the bottom line, and with your needle pointing down, pass your needle under the bar of the next cross, and pull your thread through.

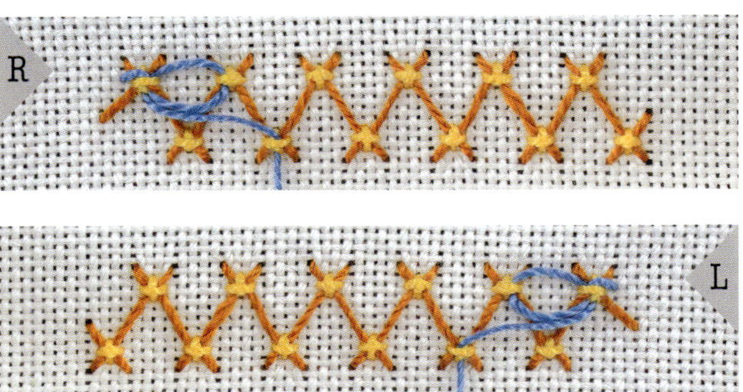

8. Move back and pass your needle under the first crossbar on the bottom line, and pull the thread through.

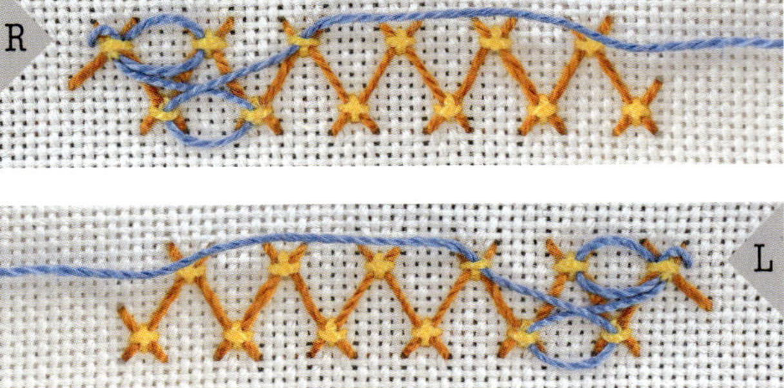

9. Move the top line and repeat this lacing pattern. Continue to the end of the line.

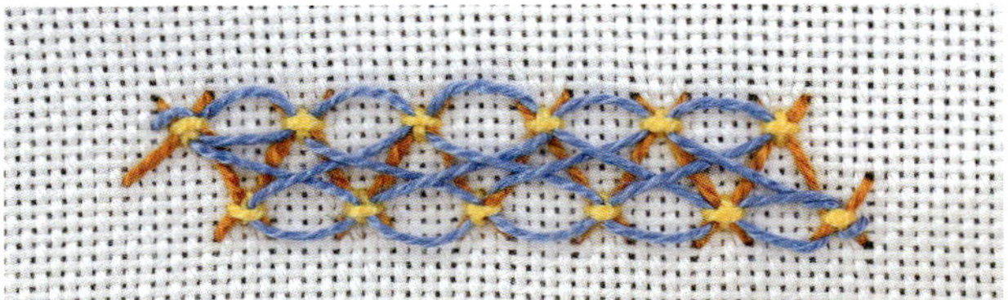

Herringbone Stitch (Twisted)

Twisted herringbone is a stitch that creates a decorative line for borders and edges or can be worked row upon row to create a fill.

Work twisted herringbone along two imaginary parallel lines. If you need to mark these lines on your fabrics, use a water-soluble or air-erasable marker.

1. Start by bringing the needle out on the lower line. Take your needle to the top line and, with your needle pointing toward the start of the line, make a small stitch and pull the thread through.

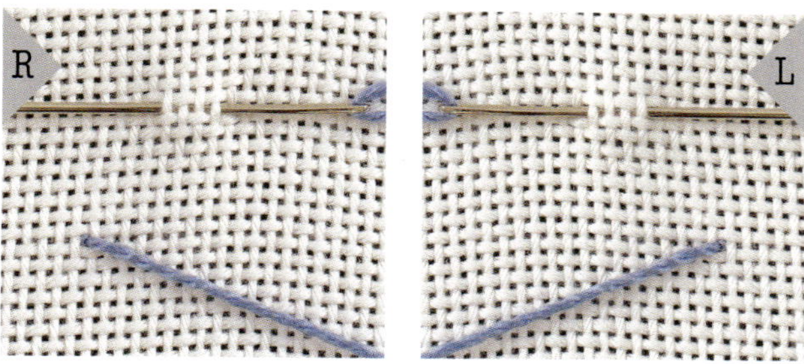

2. Pass your needle under the diagonal stitch that you have just created and pull your thread through.

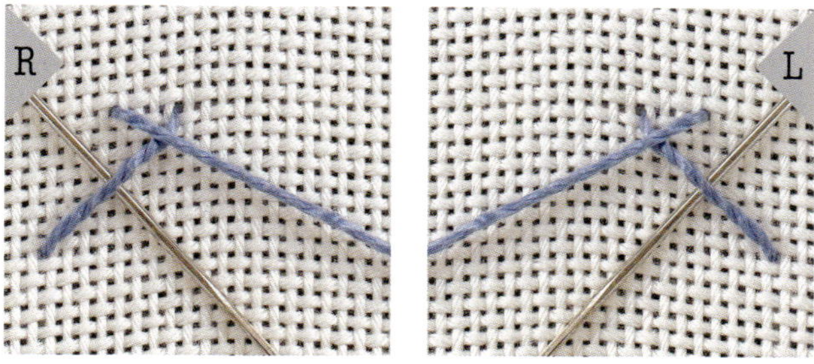

3. Insert your needle on the lower line with your needle pointing toward the start of the line and make a small stitch. Pull the thread through.

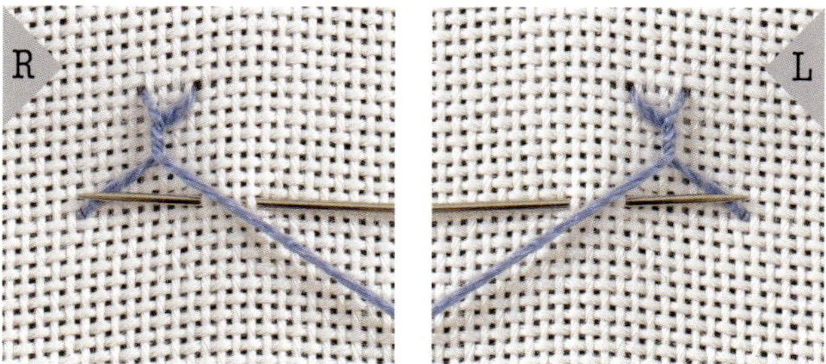

4. Pass your needle under the diagonal stitch and pull your thread through to create the second twist.

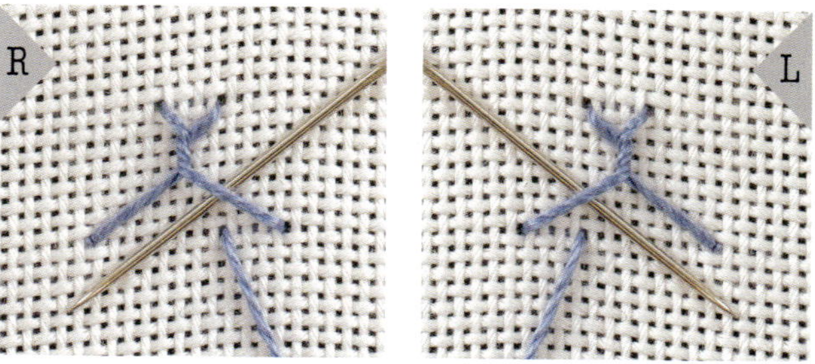

5. Move to the top of the line and continue in this manner along the line.

Twisted herringbone worked in variegated perle cotton #8 on hand-painted Aida cloth

Herringbone Stitch (Twisted Backstitched)

Backstitched twisted herringbone is a stitch that works well row upon row as a filling stitch, or you can use it for borders and edges.

Work backstitched twisted herringbone along two imaginary parallel lines. If you need to mark these lines, use a water-soluble or air-erasable marker.

1. Start by bringing the needle out on the lower line. Take your needle to the top line and with your needle pointing toward the start of the line, pull the thread through.

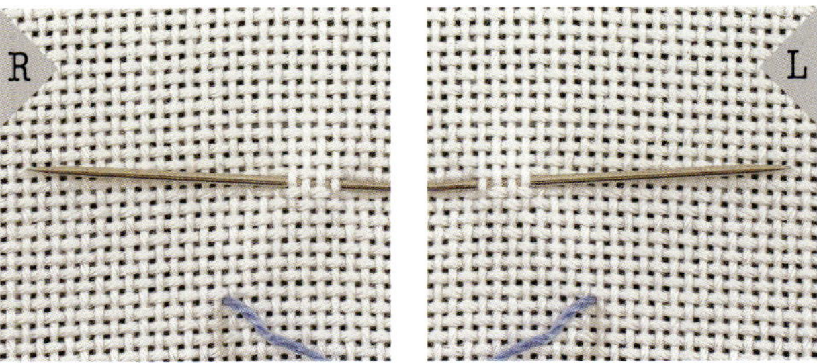

2. Make a backstitch and pull your thread through.

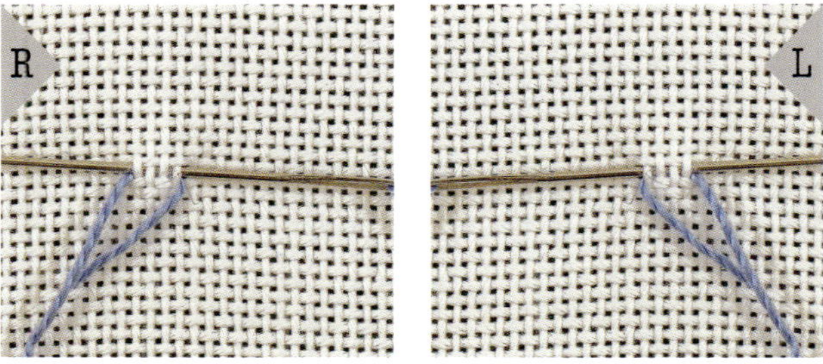

3. Pass your needle under the diagonal stitch and pull your thread through.

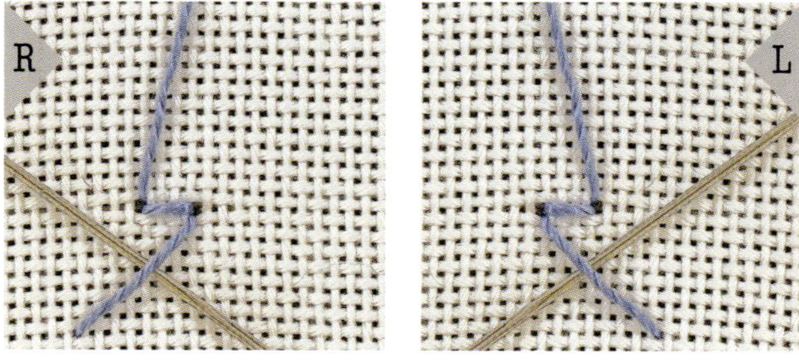

4. Insert your needle on the lower line and make a small stitch. With your needle pointing back toward the beginning of the line, pull the thread through.

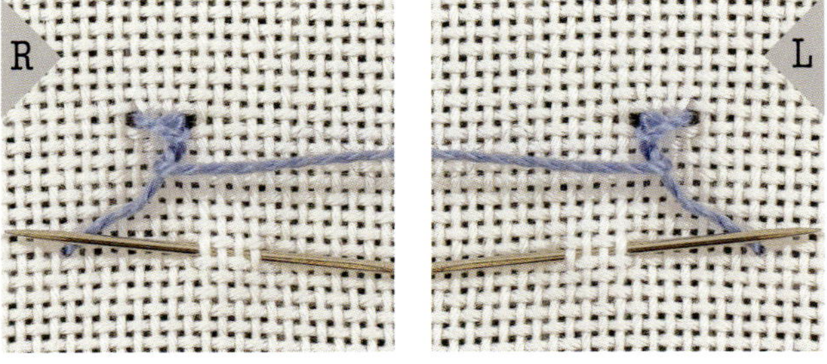

5. Make a backstitch and pull your thread through.

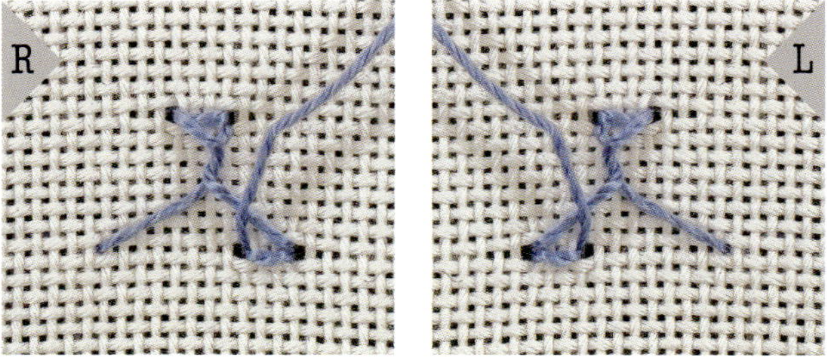

6. Pass your needle under the diagonal stitch and pull your thread through to create the second twist.

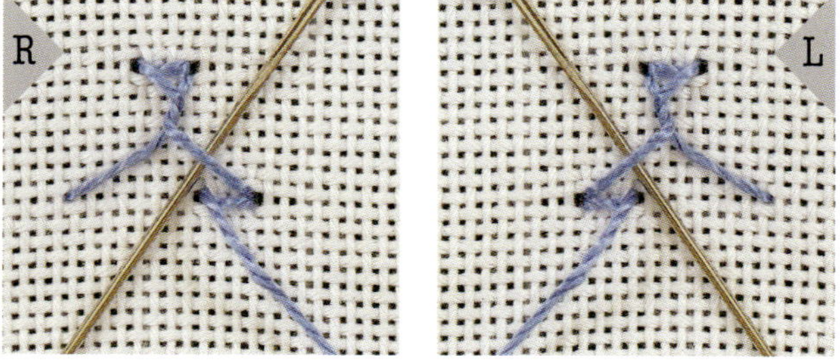

7. Continue in this manner along the line.

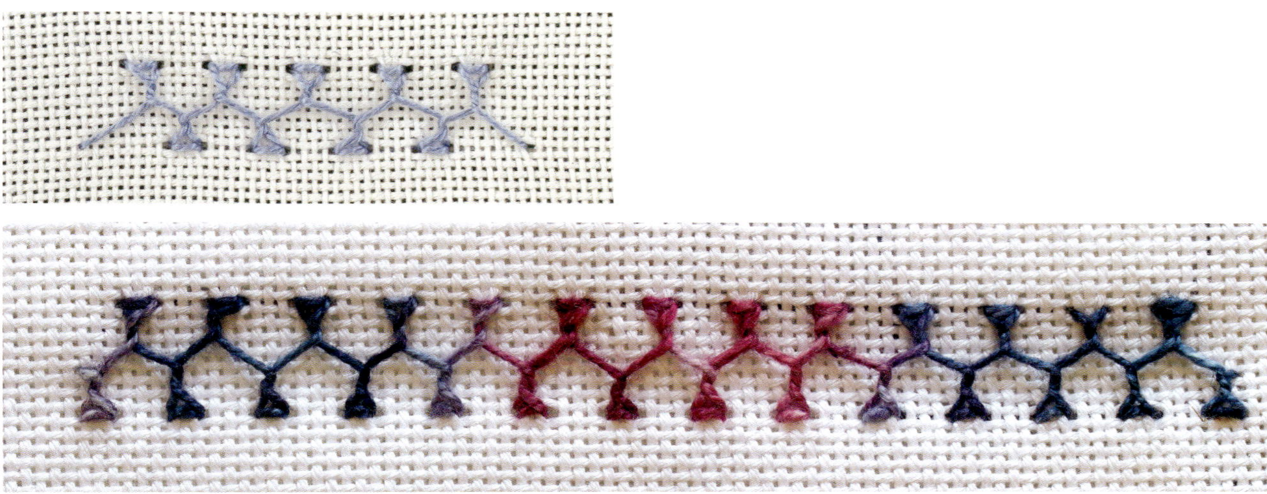

◊ A single row of backstitched twisted herringbone worked ivariegated perle cotton #8

◊ Backstitched twisted herringbone worked row upon row to form a pattern using variegated perle cotton #8

Italian Knotted Border Stitch

Italian knotted border stitch is useful for borders and edges, as you can work this stitch where you would normally use buttonhole stitch to finish an edge. Worked in a compact manner, it forms a neat line, with the knot reinforcing the edge. Italian border stitch can be arranged in patterns or worked as a disk in a circle to create flowers.

1. Italian knotted border stitch is a variety of fly stitch (page 188) and you begin the stitch in the same way. Take a bite of the fabric with your needle inserted at a slight angle. With the thread wrapped under the needle, pull it through the fabric.

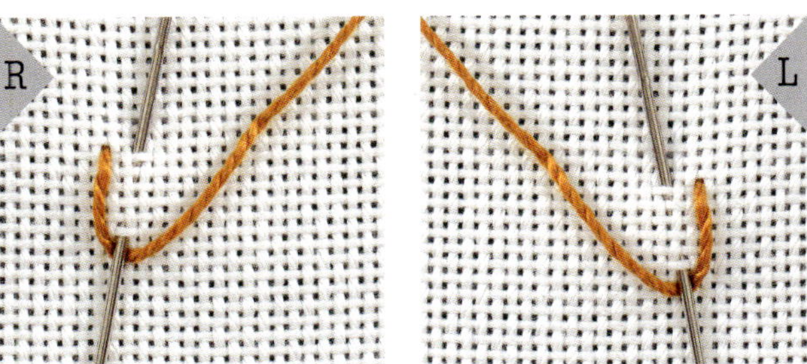

2. Wrap your working thread once around the needle and insert the needle at the base of the V to tie down the stitch and secure the stitch with a knot.

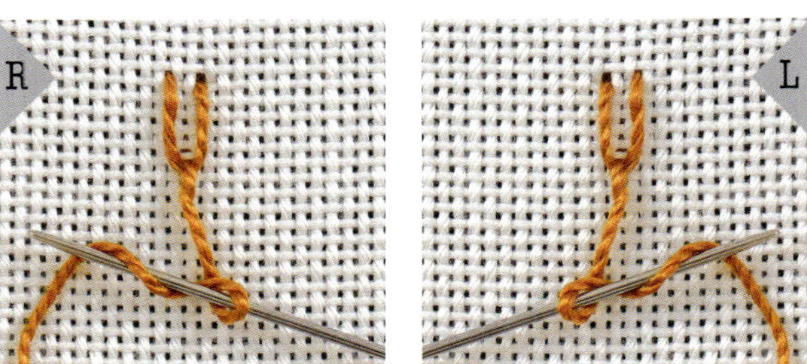

3. As you pull the needle to the back, keep the tension of the working thread even by guiding the thread under your thumb. Gently place your thumb over the stitch and pull the thread through evenly and gently.

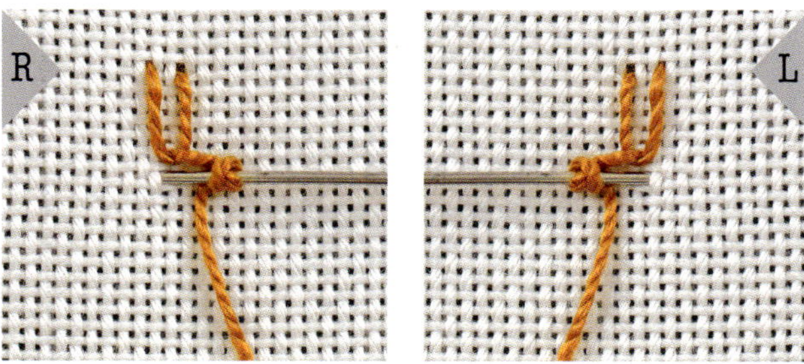

Completed Italian knotted border stitch

◊ Italian knotted border stitch worked in circle to form a flower

Laced Cross-Stitch

Laced cross-stitch can be used to fill areas or as a simple patterned band. You can lace with a contrasting color or thread to create interesting effects. Novelty yarns are great fun to use with this stitch.

1. Start with a grid of cross-stitches (page 186).

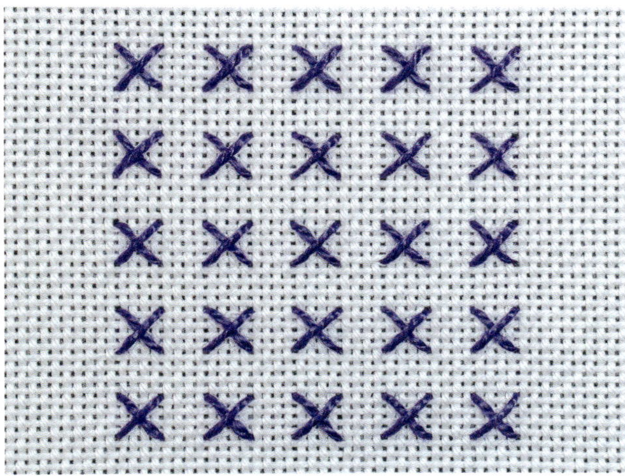

2. Bring your thread out just under the first cross. Pass your needle under the cross that sits diagonally lower on the grid.

3. Pull your needle through and continue to lace across the horizontal row, taking your needle to the back of the fabric just under the last cross. Bring your needle back to the front of the fabric just under the cross below.

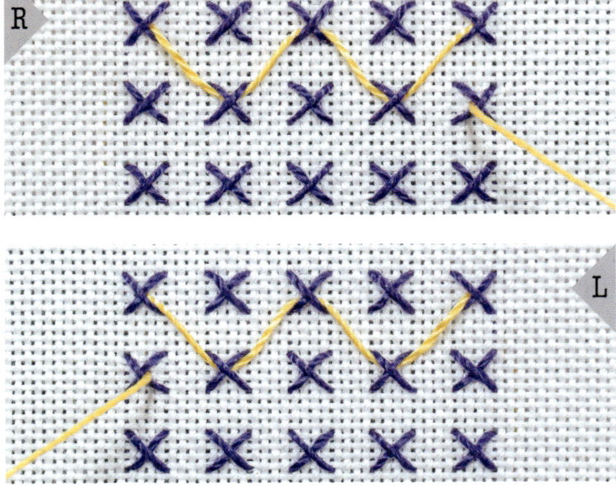

4. Turn and lace back the other way.

5. Work each row in the same manner until the grid is covered.

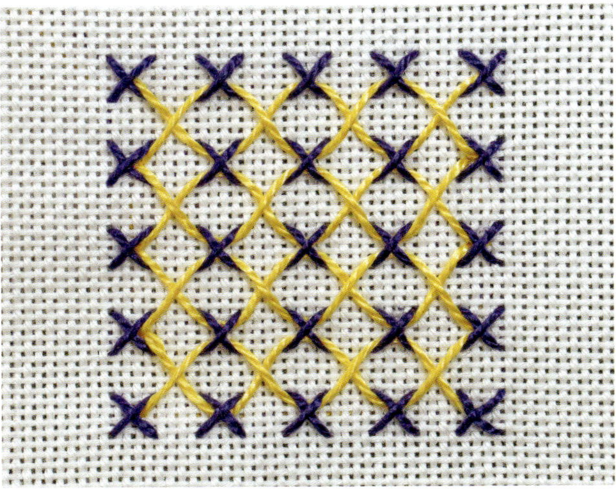

Laced cross-stitch worked with foundation of perle cotton #8 laced with metallic thread. Sequins and beads were added last.

Leviathan Stitch

Leviathan stitch is also known as *Smyrna cross-stitch.* It is a form of double cross-stitch and is usually worked on evenweave fabric, but you can also use it to sprinkle across an area if you want some stitching that is not too dense.

There are many variations and adaptations to leviathan stitch, some worked on the point like these instructions, while others are worked square. Some are worked in lines side by side or spaced out and interspersed with other stitches. In other examples, you can find this stitch worked side by side and row upon row, to create a dense, textured area. The main thing to remember is to work this stitch over an even number of threads, usually four, six, or eight threads.

This stitch is ideal to use for geometric spot motifs or borders, or worked small and sprinkled across an area.

1. Start with a straight vertical stitch.

2. Cross the first stitch with a horizontal straight stitch.

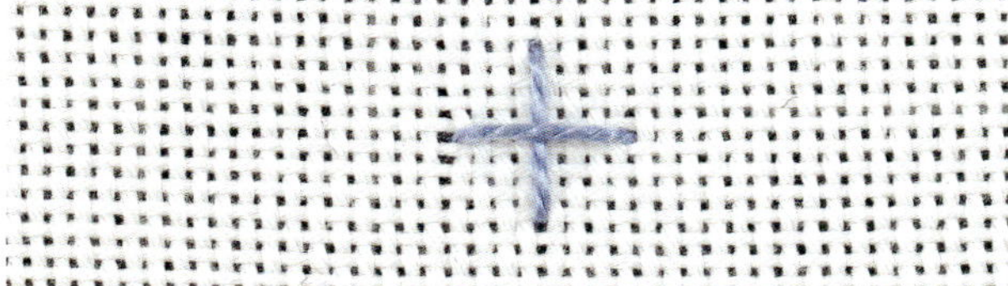

3. Make a diagonal stitch.

4. Cross with a second diagonal stitch in the other direction.

◊ Leviathan stitch worked square in variegated thread on hand-dyed background

Lock Stitch

Lock stitch is also known as *lock stitch band.*

There is a single and double version of this stitch. Lock stitch consists of a row of laced vertical straight stitches. The single version is laced along the bottom, and the double is laced top and bottom.

You can experiment with different threads. The lacing is not complex, so novelty yarns and thicker threads can be used.

Tip Use a blunt tapestry needle to avoid splitting the foundation stitches.

1. Work a row of straight stitches of equal length.

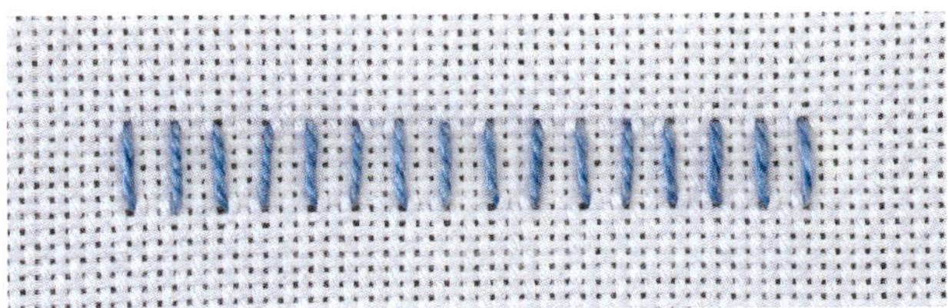

2. Pass the needle under the first stitch with the tip pointing toward the start of the line. Pull the thread through.

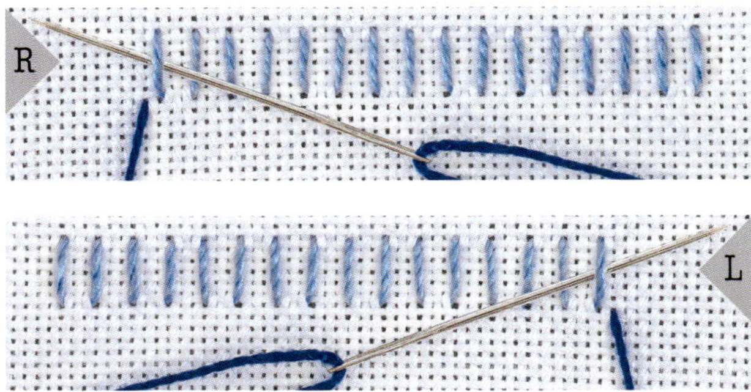

3. Pass the needle under the next straight stitch with your needle pointing toward the start of the line. Pull the thread through. Take care to lace and not to pick up any of the fabric as you work along the line.

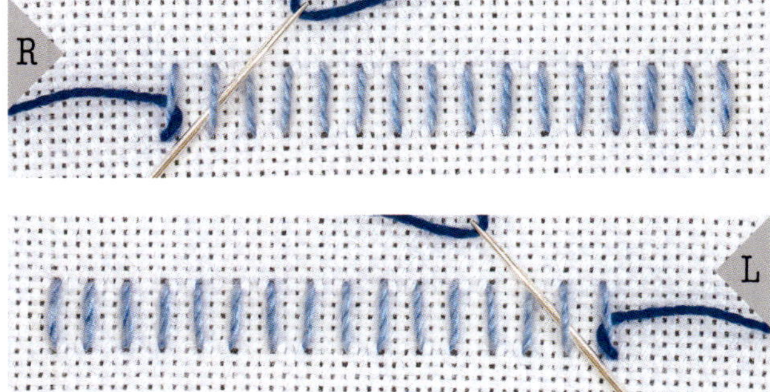

4. Work the next 2 stitches in the same way. The lacing thread will naturally fall in 1 direction and then the other.

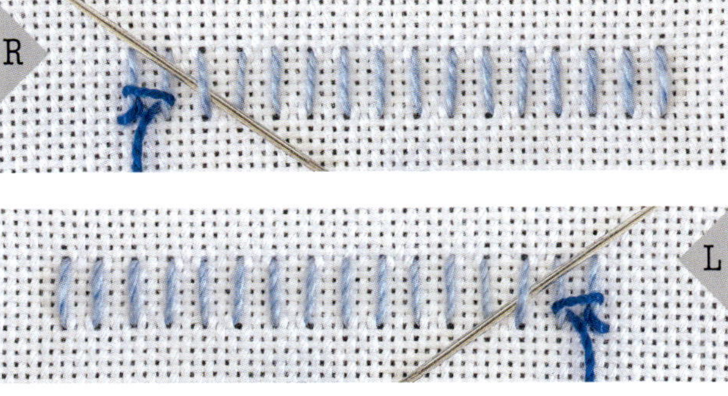

5. Continue in this manner along the line of foundation stitches. This is the single version of the stitch.

6. For the double version of lock stitch, turn your work and lace the straight stitches in the same manner.

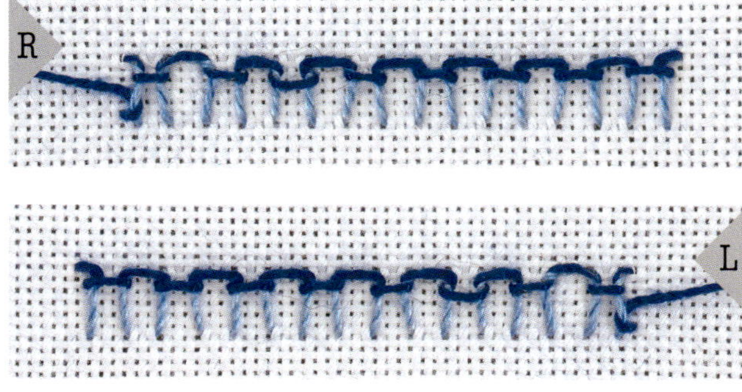

7. Continue in this manner along the line until complete.

◊ Lock stitch worked as a single band in variegated perle cotton #8 on hand-painted background

◊ Lock stitch worked row upon row as filling, using variegated perle cotton #8 on hand-painted background

Looped Bullion Knots

Tips

- Before you try this stitch, practice a few normal-length bullion knots to establish the feel of the tension you need to use for a successful knot.
- Stretch the fabric in a needlework hoop or frame so that you have both hands free to work the knot.
- Use a straw or milliners needle. Straw or milliners needles have the same width for both the eye and the shaft, which makes it easier to slide the wrapped bullion knot along the needle.
- Use a twisted thread, like perle cotton #8 or #5.
- Wrap your thread clockwise, following the natural twist in which it was spun. If it untwists as you wrap, your thread was spun in the opposite direction to most threads, so wrap your bullion counterclockwise. Simply put, wrap clockwise most of the time but if for some reason this untwists your thread, wrap counterclockwise.

Looped bullion knots are worked the same way as bullion knots but with 10 to 50 more wraps. Controlling this many wraps takes a little practice. I strongly recommend that you use a straw or milliners needle for this stitch.

1. Bring the thread from the back, turn your needle, and take a small bite of the fabric with the needle emerging at the start of the stitch. In the demonstration, I have picked up only 2 threads of the fabric.

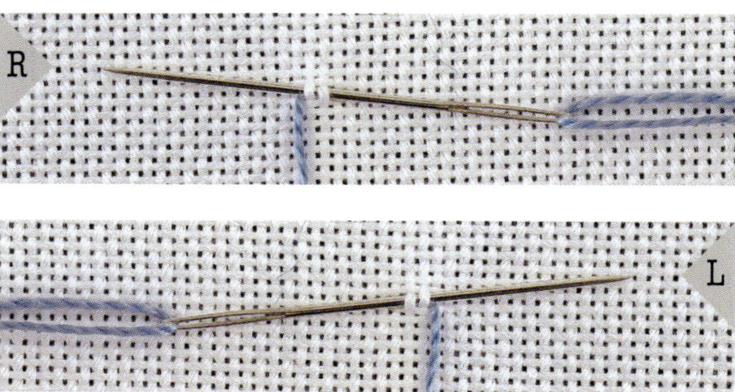

2. Wrap the thread round the needle 10 to 50 times. The more times you wrap, the larger your loop will be. Make sure the thread coils up the needle. Do not cross the wraps on the needle.

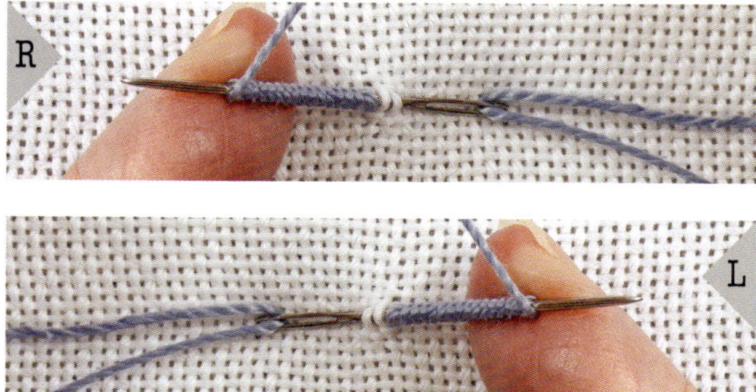

3. Hold the needle between your thumb and first finger.

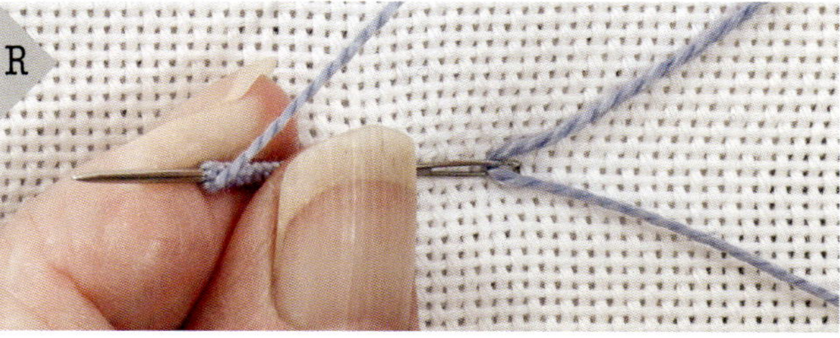

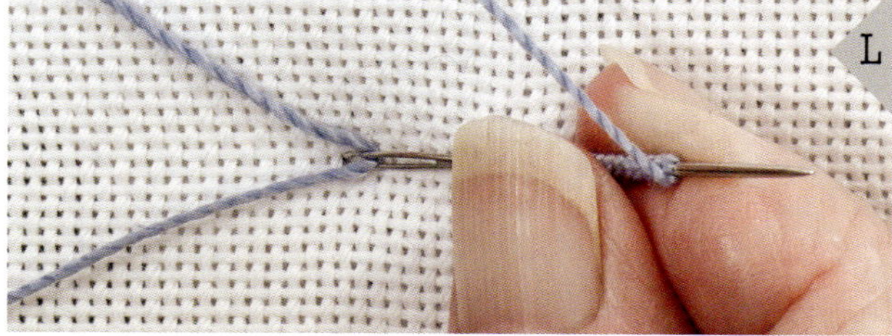

4. Grip the bullion and gently start to pull the thread through. Pull the needle through the coil, while holding the coil between your first finger and thumb. Gripping the coil will keep the bullion knot smooth and prevent it from knotting in on itself. Pull the working thread up and away from you. As the coil tightens, change the direction so that you are pulling the thread toward yourself.

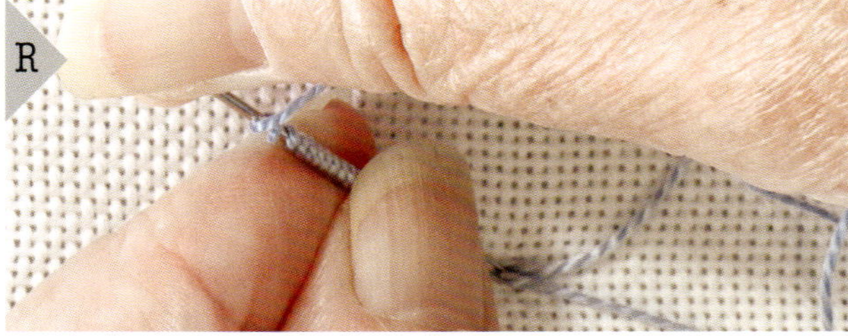

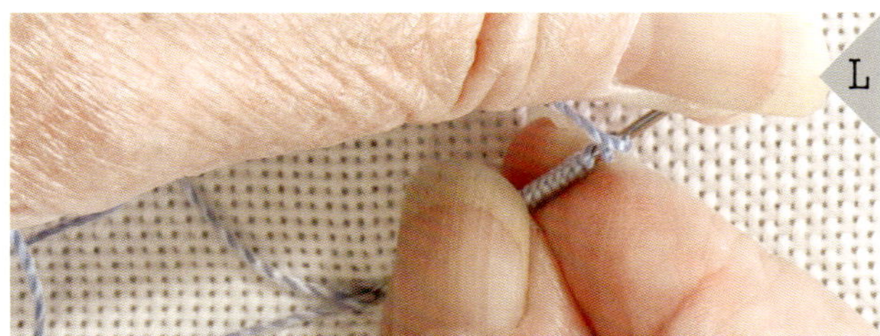

5. If the bullion bunches with the needle under the bullion, rub the needle up and down the inside length of the bullion to smooth it out. Take the needle through the fabric at the point where the thread first emerged.

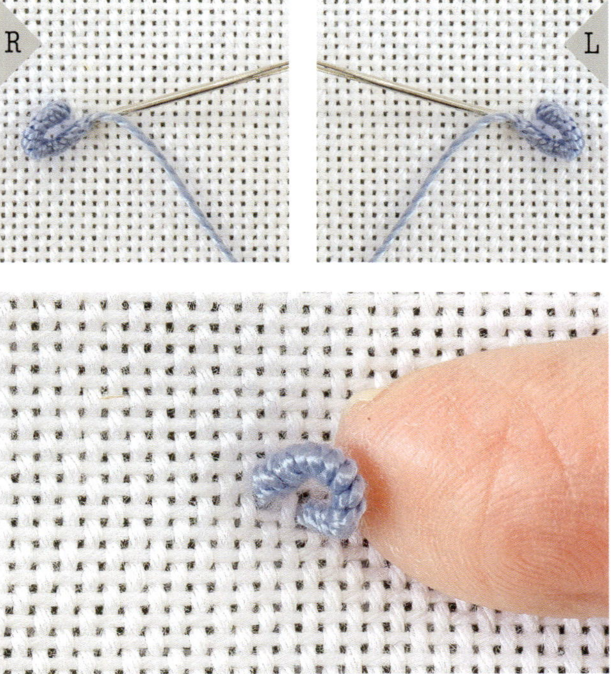

◊ The bullion loop stands proud of the surface.

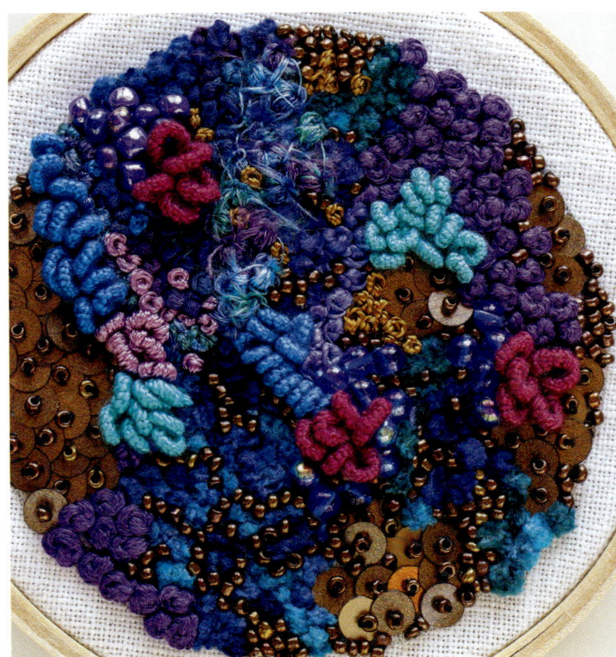

Looped bullion knots worked in perle cotton #5 thread stand proud against French knots, sequins, and beads.

◊ Detail of looped bullion knots used in small hoop piece

Maidenhair Stitch

Maidenhair stitch is a highly decorative variety of feather stitch (page 187) that follows curves well and has many uses in contemporary embroidery. It consists of three branches of stitches that sit on alternate sides of a central line.

1. Create a single V stitch by bringing your needle out at what will be the top line of the stitch. Move your needle along that line and insert the needle at the same level. Make a stitch on a downward angle so that the needle emerges between the 2 points to create a centerline of the stitch.

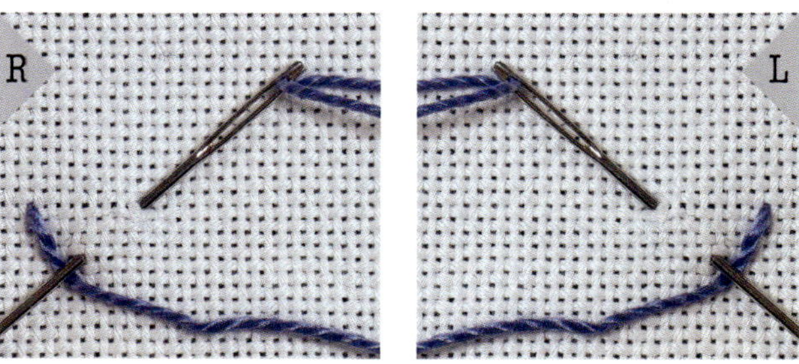

2. With the thread under the needle so that it creates a V shape, pull your needle through.

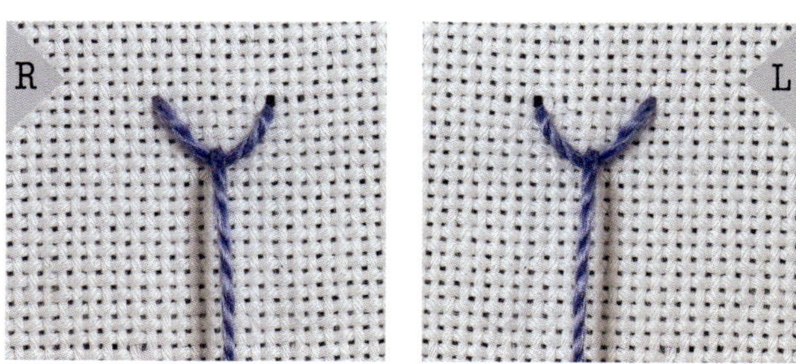

3. Move your needle along and insert it on the top line again. Have your needle emerge on the centerline, below the first stitch. Pull your needle through.

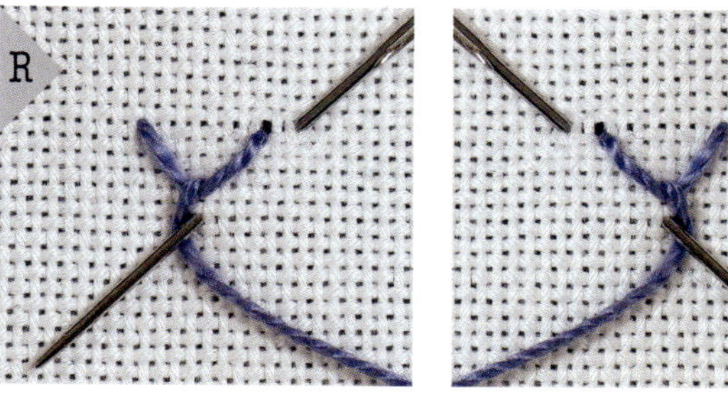

4. Move your needle along and create the third branch of this stitch by inserting your needle on the top line again. Once again, have your needle emerge on the centerline, below the first stitch. Pull your needle through. This creates the third branch of the stitch.

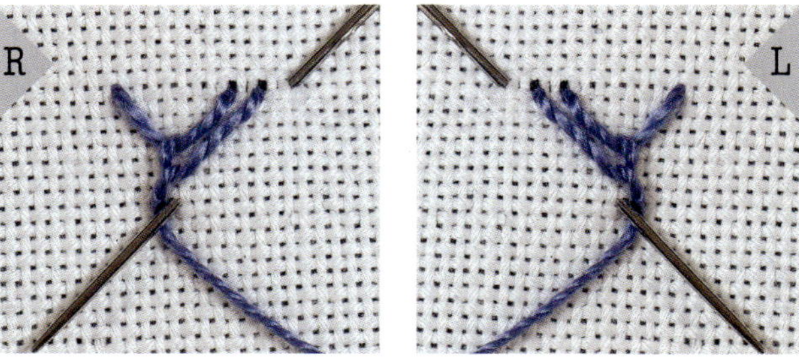

5. Move to the opposite side of the centerline and insert your needle.

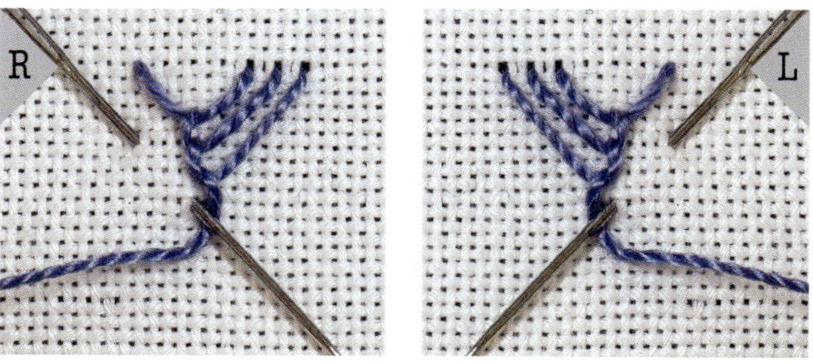

6. Make your second branch.

7. Make a third branch.

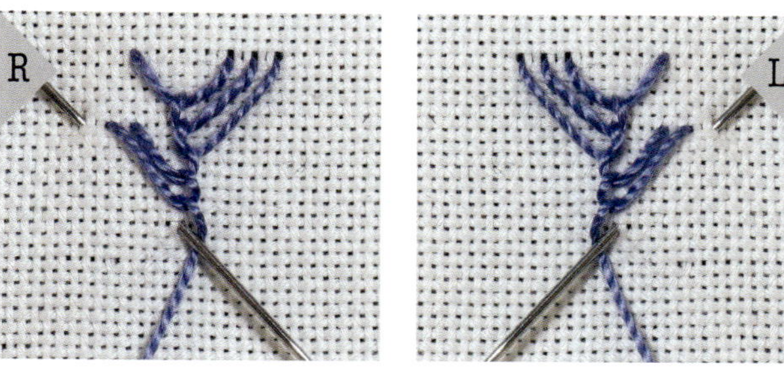

8. Continue down the line alternating your branches from side to side.

Maidenhair stitch worked in perle cotton #5 in slow-stitch project

Maidenhair stitch worked in slow-stitch project

Moss Stitch

Moss stitch is also known as *cross and twist stitch.* If it is worked as a needlepoint stitch, it is known as *knotted cross.* This is an isolated stitch that can be used on plain- and even-weave fabrics. It is effective when worked on a small scale sprinkled over an area, and it's often found in crewel work as a powdering to decorate a shape. An interesting modern variation is to work the top stitch in a contrasting color or different weight of thread.

1. Start with a cross-stitch (page 186).

2. Bring the thread out at the top of the stitch. Slide the needle under the cross. Wrap the thread under the needle as you would a chain stitch. Pull the thread through.

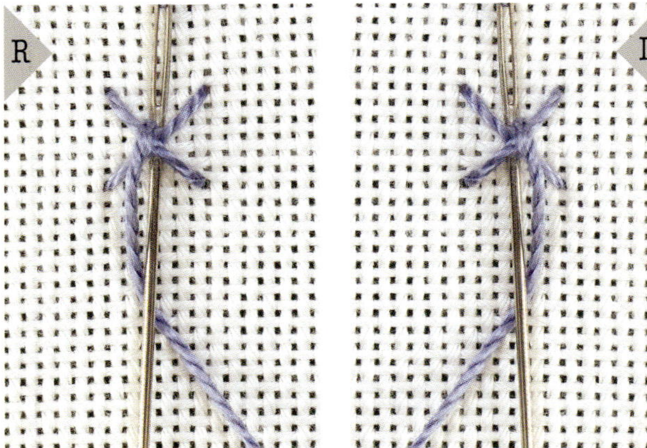

3. A the base of the chain, take it through the fabric.

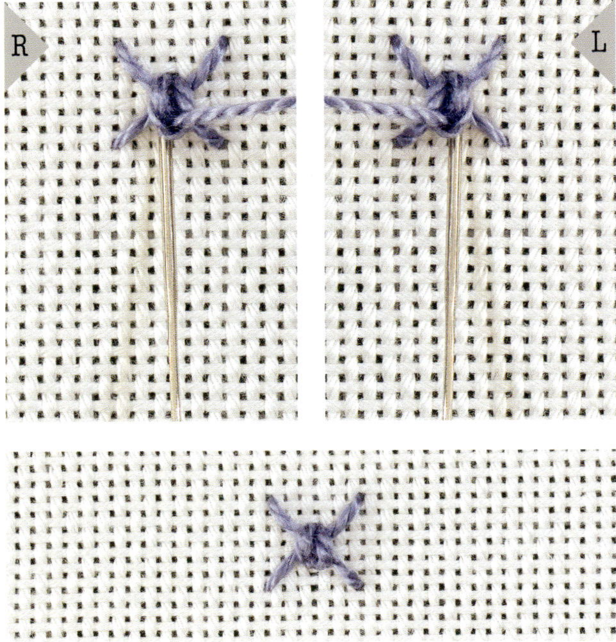

Completed moss stitch

◊ Moss stitch used over lace in slow-stitch project

Needle Woven Bar

Needle woven bars are great fun to make, and they add texture to your embroidery. You mainly see woven bars in traditional drawn thread work, where the horizontal threads are withdrawn from the foundation fabric. Woven bars are then worked on the vertical threads.

Contemporary needle weaving embroidery makes use of this stitch, too. You can work them in a freestyle manner to great effect. The examples here are woven bars worked on the surface of the fabric, which means they become raised stitches. You can work them much longer to create depth and interest.

1. Work 2, 4, or 6 straight stitches. Don't work them too tightly as these are the foundation stitches that will be woven. The foundation stitches must be an even number. I have used 2, but you need to be able to divide them into balanced groups. So, if you wanted to work 4 stitches, 2 foundation stitches would be on one side and 2 foundation stitches would be on the other side.

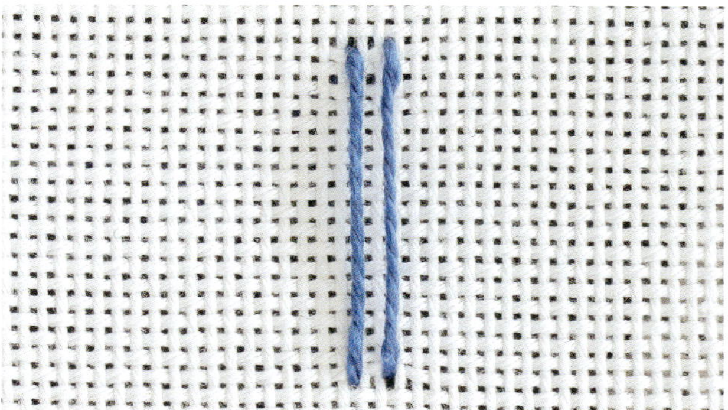

2. To weave, use a blunt needle such as a tapestry needle to avoid splitting any of the foundation threads. Bring your thread out from the back of the fabric and, with your needle pointing toward the middle of the stitch, pass your needle under the first straight stitch or the first group of stitches.

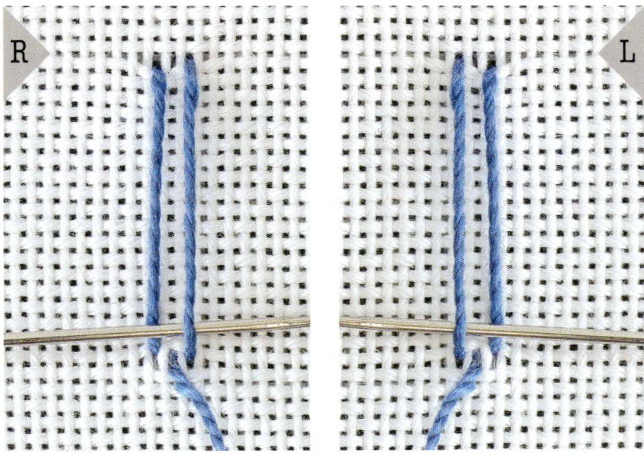

3. Take the thread over the foundation stitch, turn your needle, and pass it under the stitch on the other side. You aren't taking the needle through the fabric but weaving the foundation stitches. Always keep your needle pointing toward the middle of the stitch.

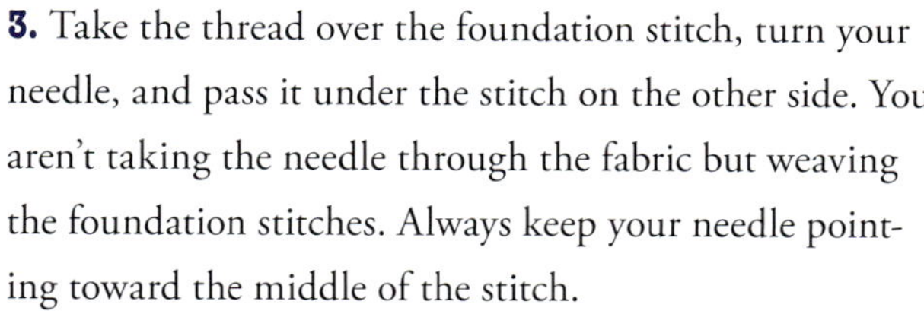

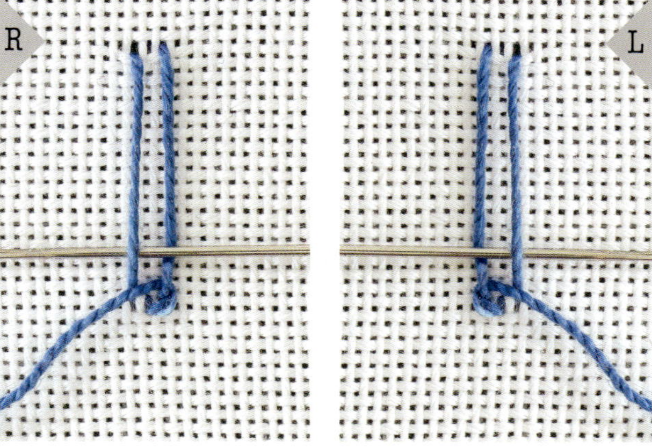

4. Turn your needle and take the thread over a foundation stitch and then under a foundation stitch. Repeat this back-and-forth weaving action.

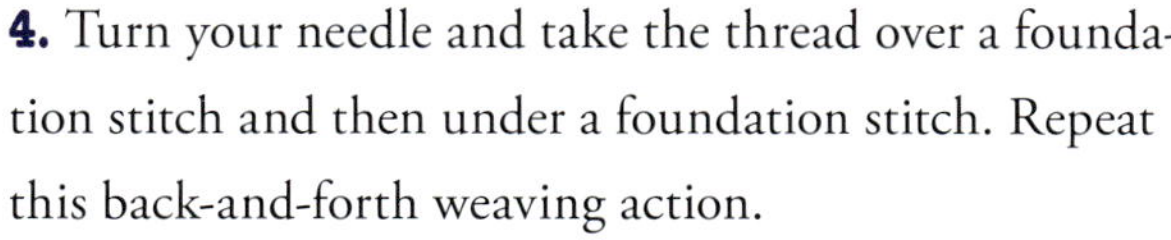

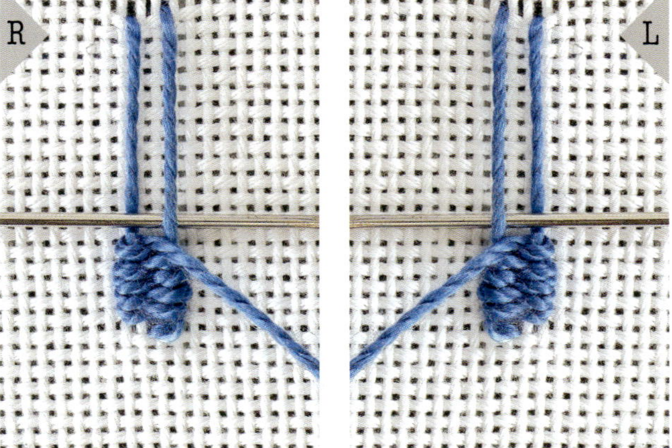

5. Pack your stitches by gently nudging them down the bar with your needle. They should be snug but not so tight that they stretch or distort the foundation bars. When you have worked the bar, take your weaving thread to the back, and tie off the thread.

◊ Needle woven bars used in contemporary embroidery panel

Oyster Stitch Tied with a Bullion Knot

Oyster stitch is normally tied with a small straight stitch, but in this variety, a bullion knot is used to tie it off. The bullion can be as long or as short as you wish and makes for an interesting variation.

Tips

- Use a straw or milliners needle. Straw or milliners needles have an eye the same width as the shaft, which makes sliding the wrapped bullion knot along the needle easy.
- Stretch the fabric in a needlework hoop.
- If stranded threads get tangled, try a twisted thread like perle cotton #8 or #5.
- Wrap your thread in a clockwise direction. If clockwise untwists your thread, wrap counterclockwise.

1. Start by bringing the thread to the front of the fabric and with your needle pointing downward, insert the needle and take a bite of the fabric. Wrap the needle by crossing the working thread over and then under the needle.

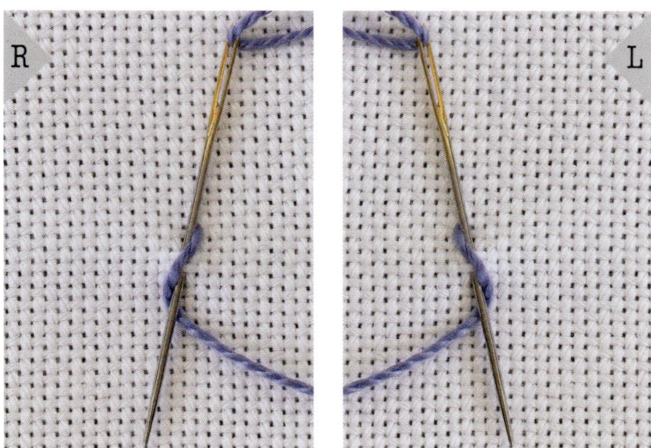

2. Pull the needle through the fabric. Make the working thread a little snug, until the loop lies flat.

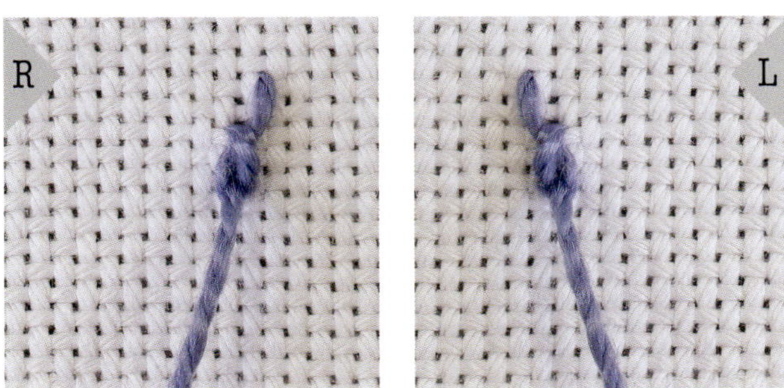

3. Pass the needle under the thread above the loop that has formed. Slide the needle through without picking up the foundation fabric.

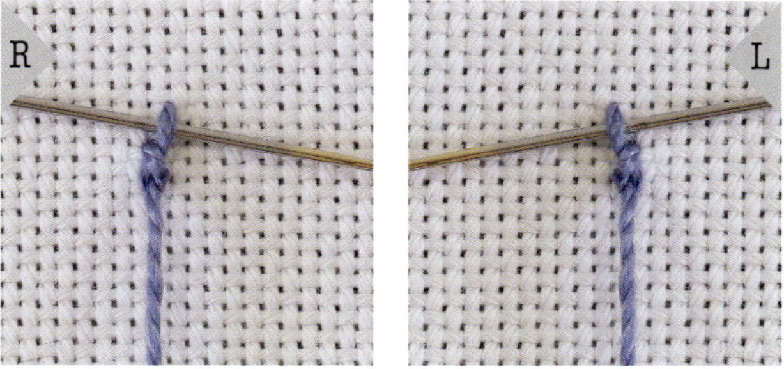

4. Pull the thread through.

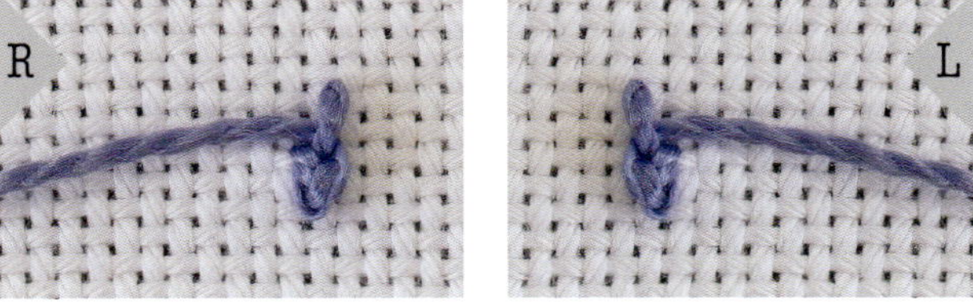

5. Insert the needle through the fabric at the top of the stitch. Point your needle downward, and slide it behind the knot so that the needle exits the cloth at the base. Wrap the thread under the needle.

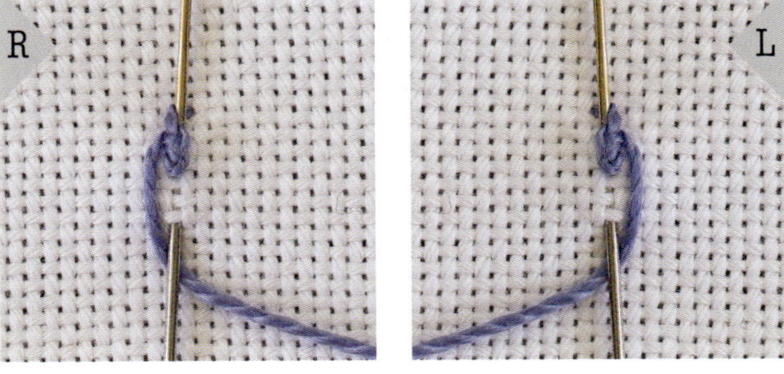

6. Pull the needle through.

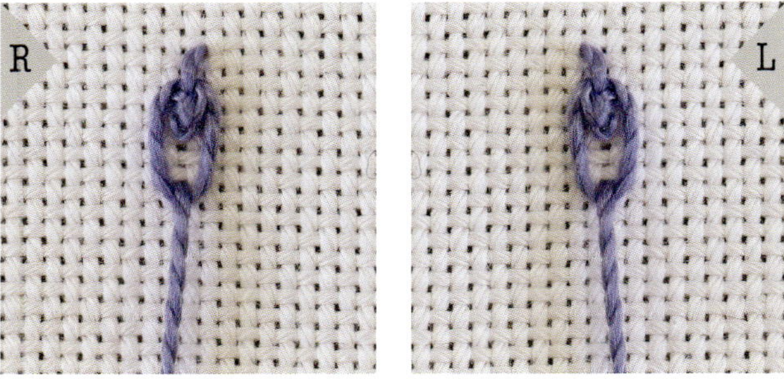

7. Turn your work to tie off with a bullion knot. Insert the needle a small space away from where it emerged from the fabric. The distance between these 2 points determines the length of the knot.

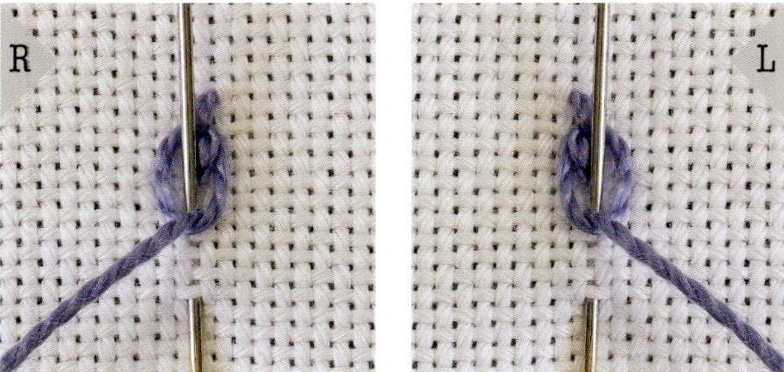

8. Wrap the thread around the needle 5 or 6 times. Do not cross the wraps on the needle; instead, make sure the thread coils up the needle. The coil of thread on the needle should be the same length as the distance between where the needle enters and exits the fabric.

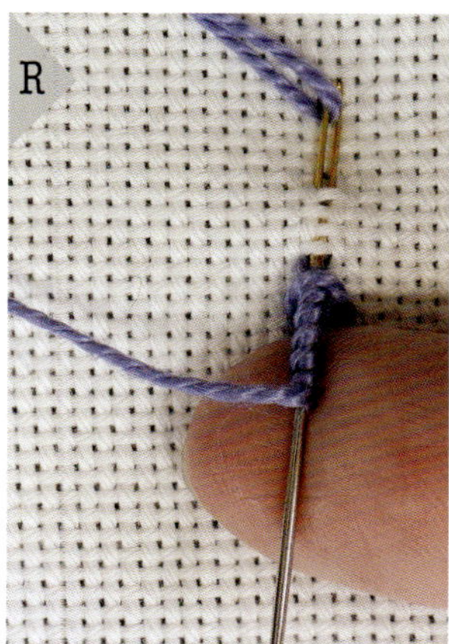

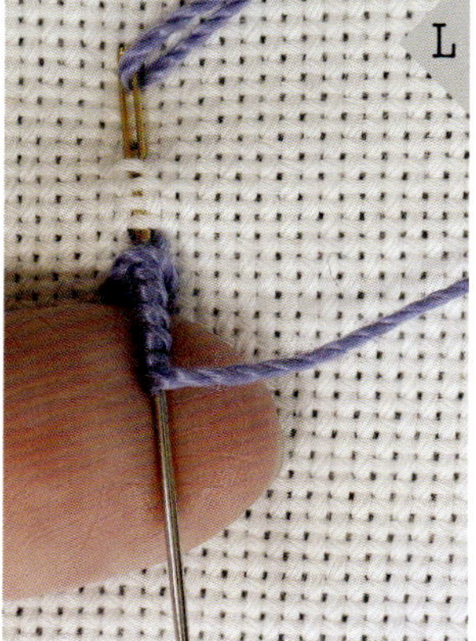

9. Pull the needle through the coil, while holding the coil between your first finger and thumb. Gripping the coil will keep the bullion knot smooth and prevent it from knotting in on itself.

Tip: To Tidy Up a Messy Knot If the bullion bunches or looks untidy, pass the needle under the bullion and rub it up and down the length of the bullion to smooth out the coils. Stitchers call this "rubbing the belly" of the bullion.

Oyster stitch tied with bullion used to decorate Suffolk puff in slow-stitch project

Oyster stitch tied with bullion used to decorate doily in slow-stitch project

Persian Border Couching (Version 1)

Persian border couching can be used as a border on the edges of items. For a contemporary twist, you can use novelty threads or incorporate beads to add extra zest.

For this stitch you use 3 different threads: a foundation thread, a couching thread, and a working thread that secures the couched thread. In my example, I have used a gold foundation thread, a blue couched thread, and a blue cotton sewing thread to secure the couched thread to the fabric.

Tip With this stitch, it helps to use a hoop and keep your piece under tension. If securing the couching thread with sewing thread feels awkward, simply hold the couching thread flat to the fabric with your thumb while stitching it into place.

1. First, lay 4 to 6 lines of straight stitches that you will couch over.

2. Bring the thread you are going to couch up from the back of the fabric. On the other side, bring your sewing thread from the back of the fabric, ready to secure the couching thread.

3. Take the couching thread across the top of the foundation stitches. With a little straight stitch, secure the couched thread to the fabric with your sewing thread. Pass the sewing thread needle under the fabric to have it emerge on the opposite edge of the foundation stitches.

4. Continue along the line of the foundation stitches, couching the thread in a zigzag motion.

◊ Persian border couching worked using variegated perle cotton #5 to hold some metallic threads to the fabric

Persian Border Couching (Version 2)

This version of Persian border couching is worked with two groups of foundation stitches. In my sample, I have used a yellow-gold thread and worked with two units of four foundation stitches.

1. Make 2 sets of foundation stitches. Bring your couching thread from the back and begin couching as you would in Persian border couching version 1 (page 159).

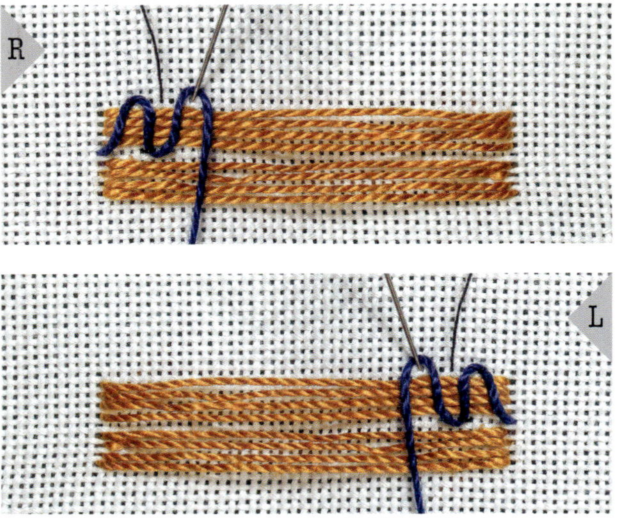

2. Work 4 or 5 couched stitches; then take your couching thread across both sets of foundation stitches to the bottom of the second group.

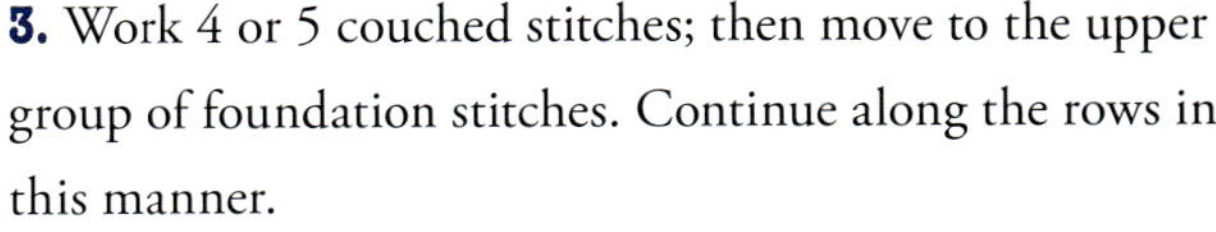

3. Work 4 or 5 couched stitches; then move to the upper group of foundation stitches. Continue along the rows in this manner.

Portuguese Border

Portuguese border stitch forms a highly textured braid-like stitch. On the second journey, you can change threads—which means you can produce interesting effects by varying the top thread and experimenting with hand-dyed variegated threads, novelty yarns, silk ribbon, and metallic threads. The stitch forms a good braid-like ridge that is ideal to use for strong lines. You can work it on a curve by changing the angle of the foundation stitches. Tension is important with this stitch. Keep the whipping loose enough that the foundation stitches do not distort.

1. The stitch is worked from bottom to top. Work a vertical line of straight stitches. Don't work them too tightly as these stitches will be laced with a second thread.

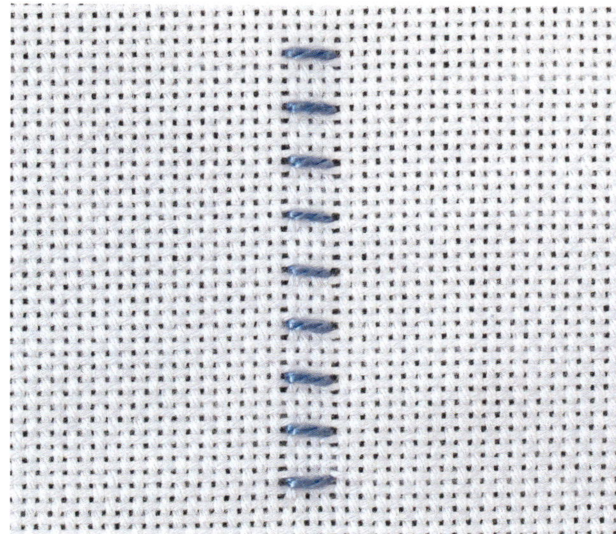

2. Bring your needle out at the base of the foundation stitches and pass it under the first 2 rungs. Ensure you have your needle pointing slightly outward with the thread inside of the line of the needle. Pull your thread through and repeat so that 2 stitches are wrapped on the first 2 rungs.

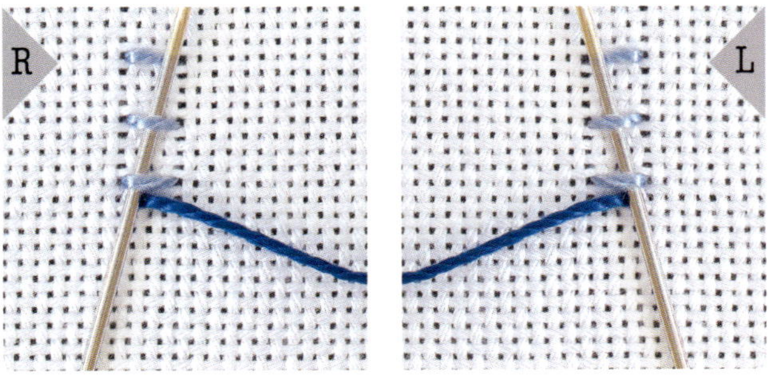

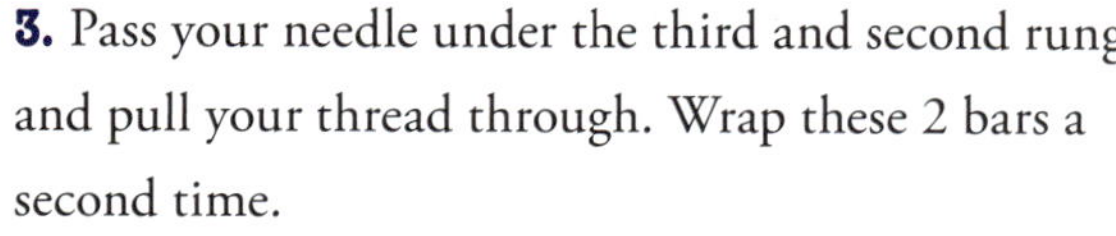

3. Pass your needle under the third and second rung and pull your thread through. Wrap these 2 bars a second time.

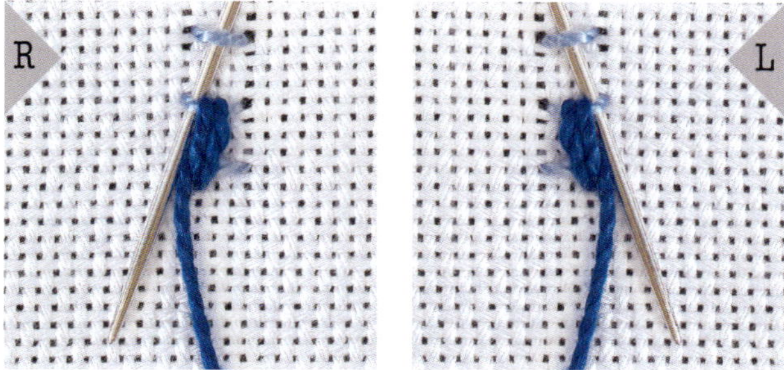

4. Continue wrapping each bar twice until you reach the end of the line.

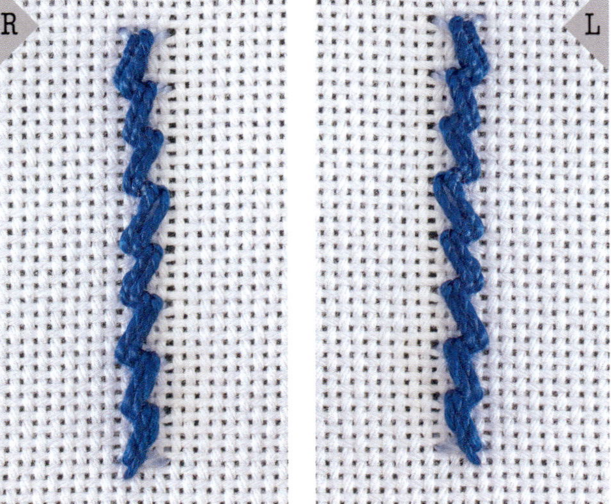

5. Return to the base of the line, and wrap the other side using the same technique.

6. Continue up the line until the other side of the stitch is worked.

◊ Portuguese border stitch used in little flower motif

Rhodes Stitch

Rhodes stitch is a very useful canvas work stitch that is very effective when combined with surface embroidery. It is made up of straight stitches that rotate 360° within a shape, which builds up a mound of thread in the center where all the threads cross. Rhodes stitch is usually worked on an even-weave fabric. This distinctive stitch can be worked within a number of geometric shapes, including a square, rectangle, circle, oval, diamond, and heart. You can create endless patterns of these shapes, with numerous designs and patterns to be discovered. Since the stitch can be varied so much, it makes it fun to work.

Rhodes stitch is also known as *Berlin star.*

This stitch can be worked in a clockwise or counterclockwise direction. The main thing is to keep working in the same direction once you have decided to move in one or the other.

1. Work this stitch within an imaginary square. Start with a diagonal straight stitch.

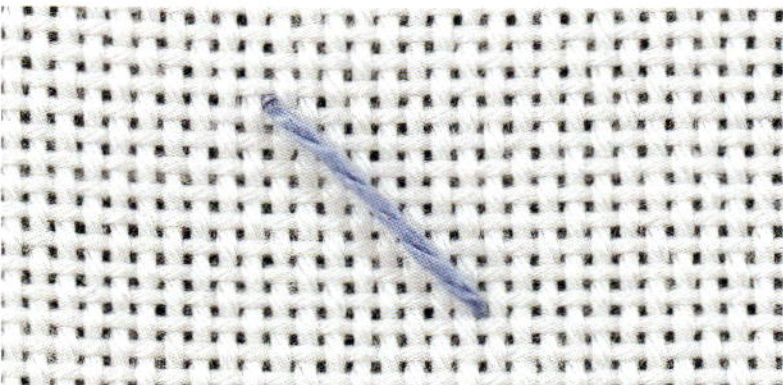

2. Make a second stitch, crossed and positioned 1 thread over from the first.

3. Make a third stitch 2 threads over from the first, crossing and fanning the stitches.

4. Create a fourth straight stitch 3 threads over from the first.

5. Continue to fan the stitch with a fifth stitch 4 threads over from the first.

6. On the sixth stitch, drop 1 thread to turn the corner of the square and to start forming the side of the square.

7. Take the seventh stitch.

8. Continue in a clockwise direction to complete the square.

Rhodes stitch used in abstract piece on hand-painted linen background

Rice Stitch

Rice stitch is also known as *William and Mary* and *crossed corners.* This is a stitch that has many varieties as it is tremendously versatile. It is easy to work and covers the background quickly.

1. Start with a foundation of a single crossed stitch.

2. Create a diagonal straight stitch.

3. On 1 corner, work a small diagonal stitch over the leg of the cross.

4. Work small diagonal cross-stitches on all points of the cross. Build this up into units that create a filling.

◊ Rice stitch worked in mix of threads. I changed threads constantly, often mid-row, to create a fill that was interesting and vibrant.

◊ Rice stitch used as border worked in mix of threads. I randomly switched threads to create interest.

Russian Stitch

This stitch can be sprinkled all over an area in a free-form manner or used in a more controlled pattern.

Russian stitch is made up of three detached chain stitches (page 187) grouped in a triangular formation.

1. Start with a detached chain stitch (page 187). Bring the needle up through the fabric and take a bite of the fabric.

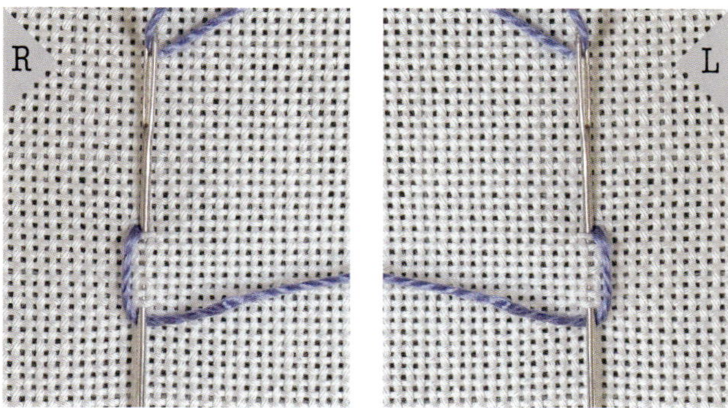

2. With the thread wrapped under the point of the needle, pull the needle through the fabric to make the first stitch.

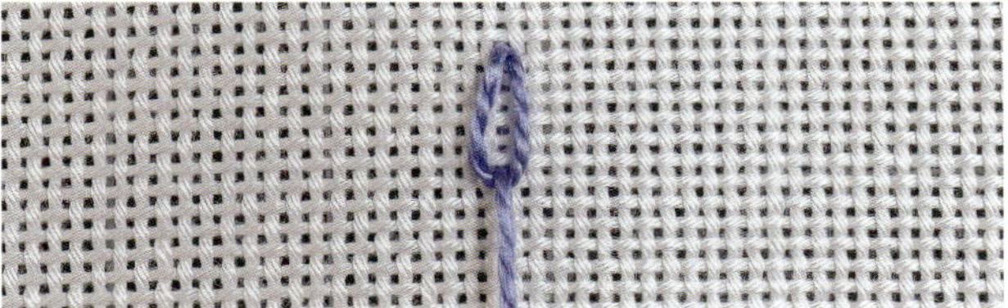

3. From the base of the chain stitch, work a second detached chain stitch at an angle.

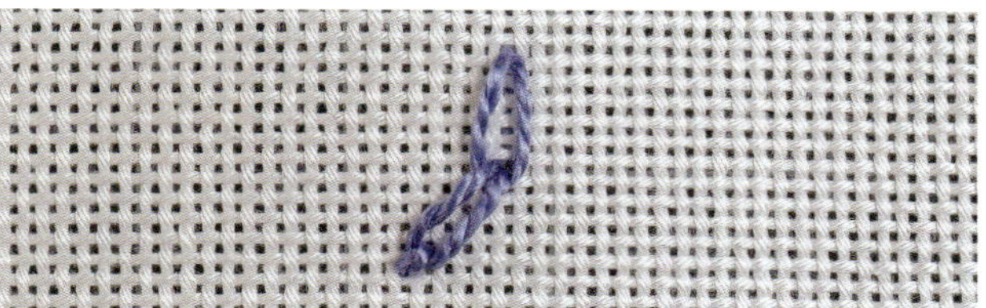

4. Take your needle to the back, bring it up at the base again, and work a third detached chain stitch.

◊ Russian stitch worked in a hand-dyed variegated #8 perle cotton thread on stitch roll.

Sailor Stitch

This stitch is also known as *sailor edge stitch.*

Sailor stitch is a buttonhole stitch with a chained base that can be used for decorative purposes or, because the chain forms a hard-wearing ridge, makes it a useful finish for project edges.

Work sailor stitch from top to bottom.

1. Bring your needle out at the top of the line, move it down the line, and take a small bite of the fabric.

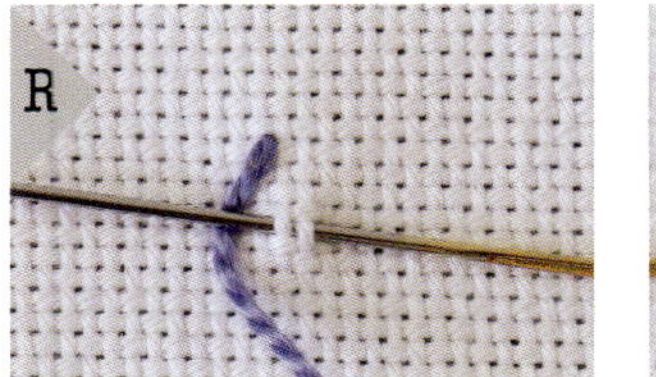

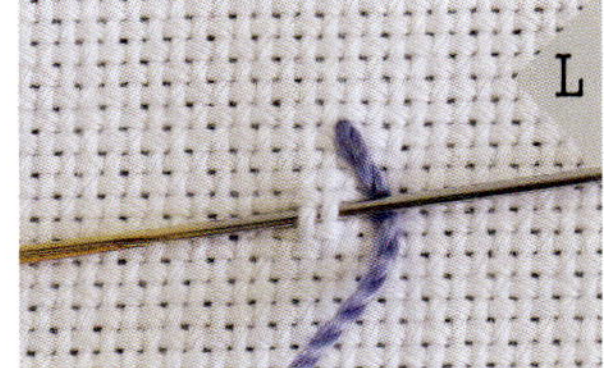

2. Keeping the thread under the needle tip, pull the needle through so you have a small buttonhole stitch.

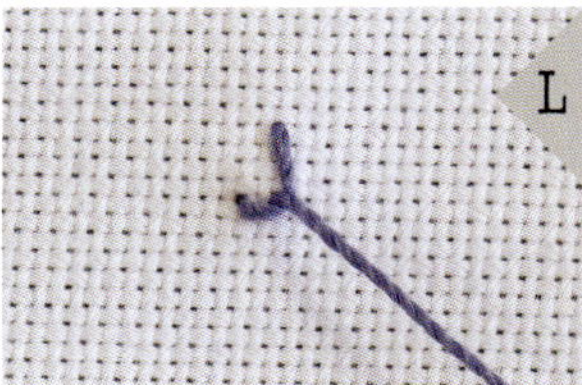

3. Insert your needle at the base of the buttonhole stitch with the needle tip emerging further down the line. Wrap your thread under the needle as you would a chain stitch and pull the needle through.

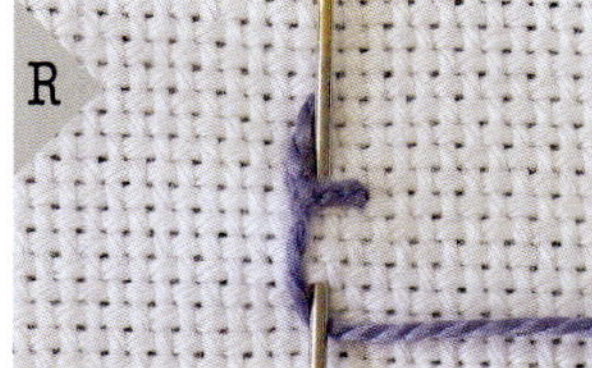

4. To secure the chain stitch, tie it off with a small buttonhole stitch by taking a small bite of the fabric.

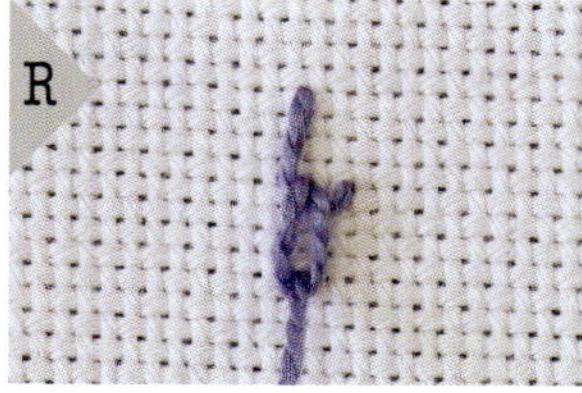

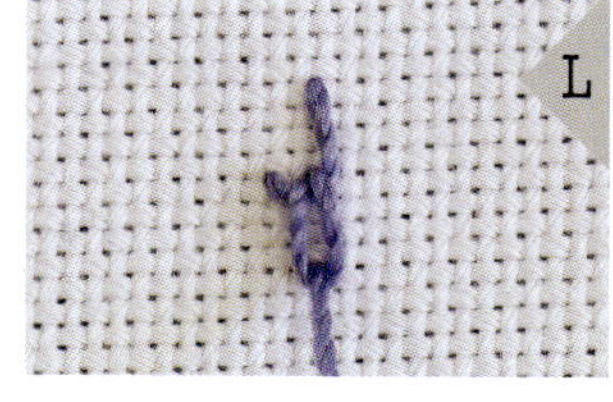

5. Continue down the line. I think of the rhythm as being buttonhole, chain, buttonhole, chain, and so on.

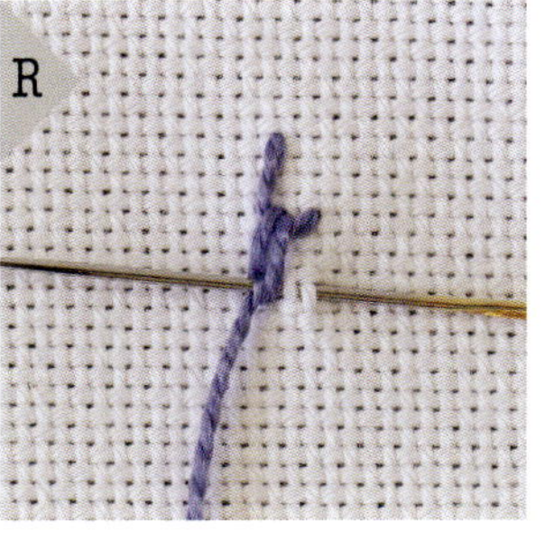

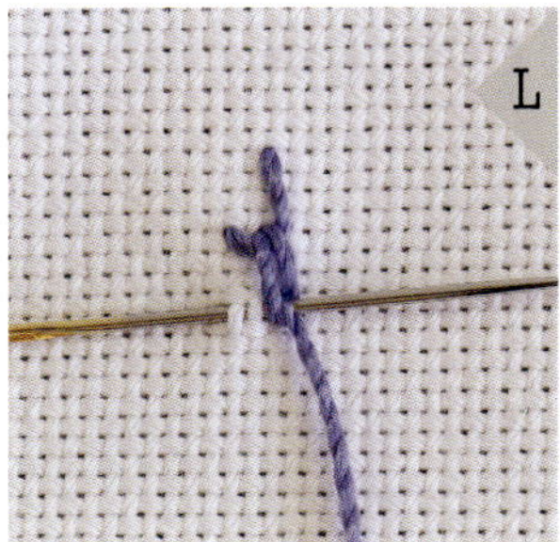

◊ Line of sailor stitch

Sailor stitch used to outline appliqué piece in slow-stitch project

Seed Stitch

Seed stitch is one of the simplest stitches to work and is also known as *seed filling, speckling, isolated backstitch, seeding, dot stitch,* and *rice stitch.* This stitch is created by scattering tiny straight stitches randomly over the surface of your fabric.

In contemporary embroidery, you can vary the weight of the thread with thick and thin threads used over the same area. Seed stitch can be worked in a more free-form manner. You can change not only the direction but also the stitch length and spacing. You can work dense areas with stitches piled up against each other. Or work seed stitch sprinkled sparsely across a surface for a little light touch.

Start in the middle of a shape and add random straight stitches. Each stitch is placed at a different angle. Traditionally, the stitches are quite evenly spaced, with the length of each stitch the same. The randomness is created by pointing the stitches in different directions. Build up the area until it is filled. If you want a light, airy feel, space the stitches farther apart. A close dense spacing of stitches over an area creates quite a visually strong filling.

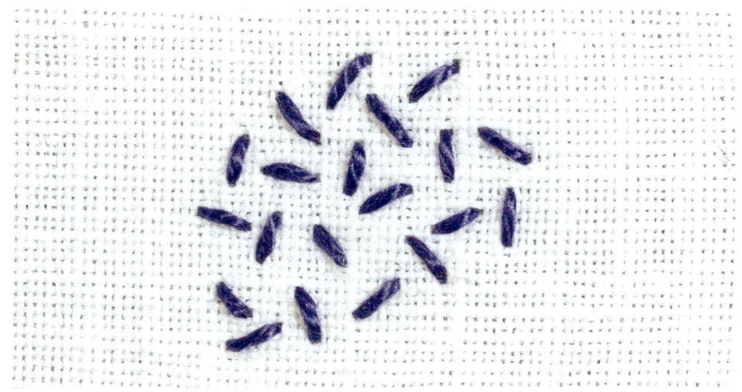

◊ Seed stitch is very useful in slow-stitch projects.

Seed Stitch (Double)

Double seed stitch is a variety of seed stitch (page 167) and is often called by the same name. It is arranged on the fabric and spaced in a similar manner to seed stitch. You can work double seed stitch on plain- or even-weave fabric. To vary the look, use different color threads or threads with different thicknesses. If you use a metallic thread and sprinkle beads in among the stitches, you can add more life and a contemporary feel to your work. In contemporary embroidery, the "rule" of keeping the two stitches side by side can be bent, and you can leave small gaps between the two stitches or angle one stitch and not the other, creating a little V shape.

This stitch consists of two backstitches worked side by side close together with no space between the stitches, or worked in the same hole. Sprinkle pairs across an area.

◊ Double seed stitch used as filling worked in perle cotton #5

Sorbello Stitch

Sorbello stitch, or *Sorbello knot,* originated in the village of Sorbello, Italy. It is a very simple yet effective stitch, and once you get into the rhythm, it works up quickly. It looks like a cross-stitch with a knot in the middle.

When working this stitch, keep it at a fairly loose tension.

1. Start with a horizontal straight stitch. Imagine this stitch is the top of a square. Bring your thread out on the bottom corner.

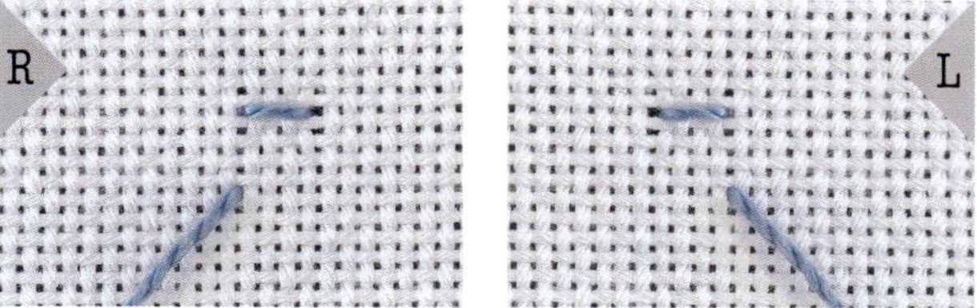

2. Pass the needle under the horizontal straight stitch, being sure the thread is under the needle. Pull your needle through.

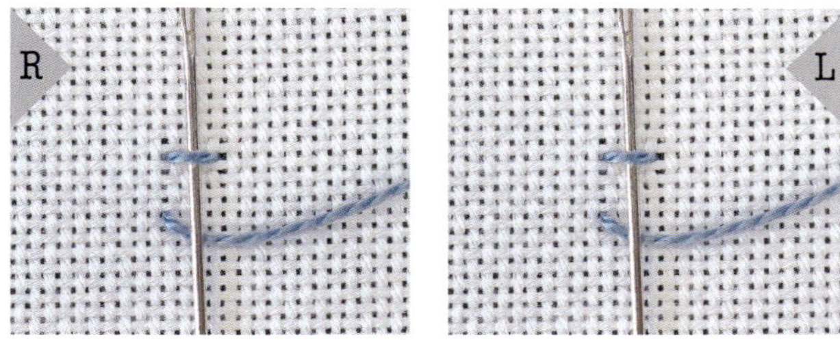

3. When you pull the thread through, it should form a loop over the straight stitch.

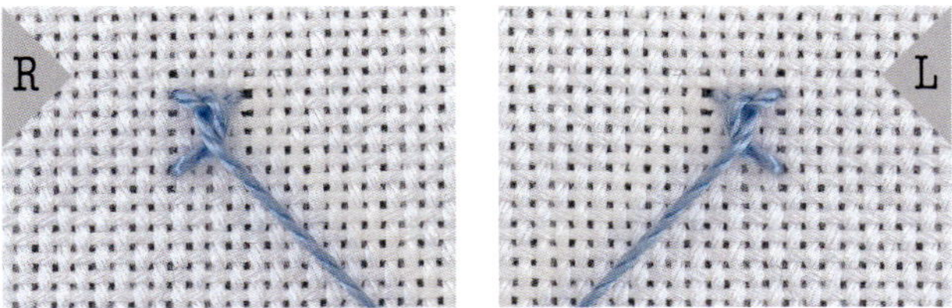

4. Pass the needle under the horizontal straight stitch again, keeping the working thread under the needle. Pull your needle through.

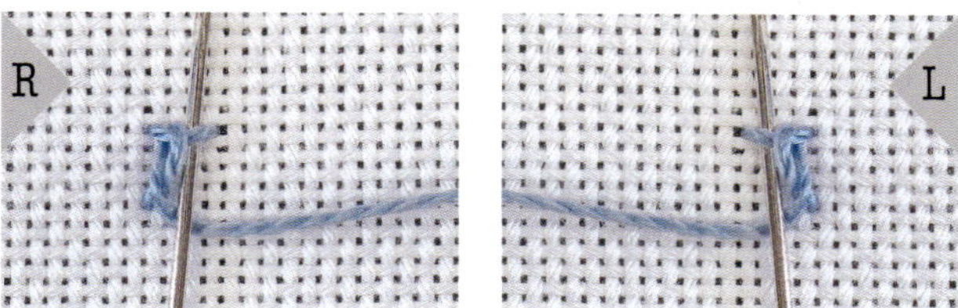

5. To complete the stitch, take your needle to the back at the opposite corner of your imaginary square.

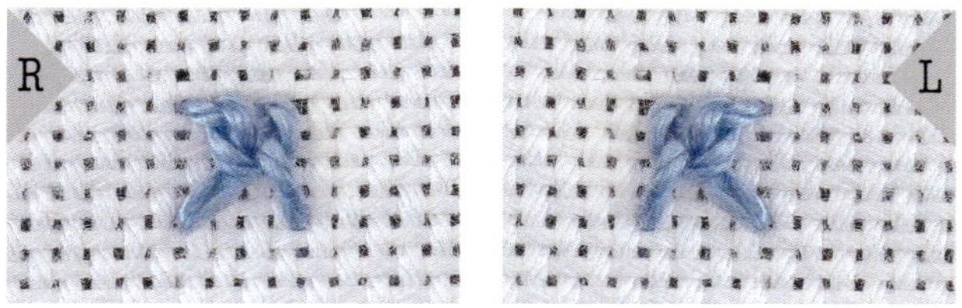

◊ Sorbello stitch elongated and arranged in square

Sprat's Head

Sprat's head is a great stitch to use if ever you have a geometric design that requires a triangle shape.

1. Work within an imaginary triangle. Bring your needle up at the base of the triangle. Insert your needle at the top of the triangle and take a very small bite of the fabric. Pull the thread through.

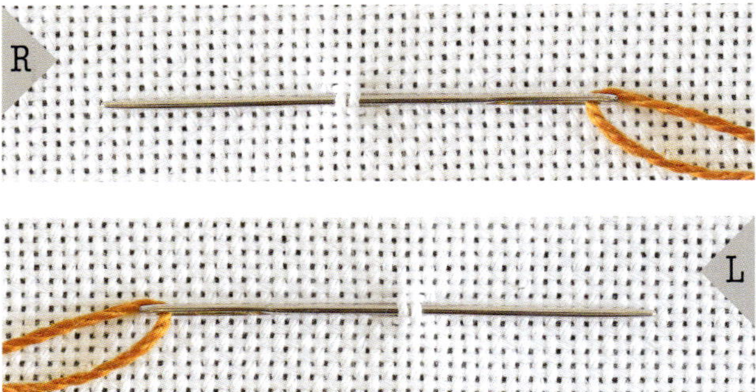

2. Insert your needle at the base of the triangle. Have your needle emerge next to where you started the stitch. Pull your thread through.

3. Move to the top of the triangle again, but make a stitch that is diagonally stepped down 1 thread. Pull your thread through.

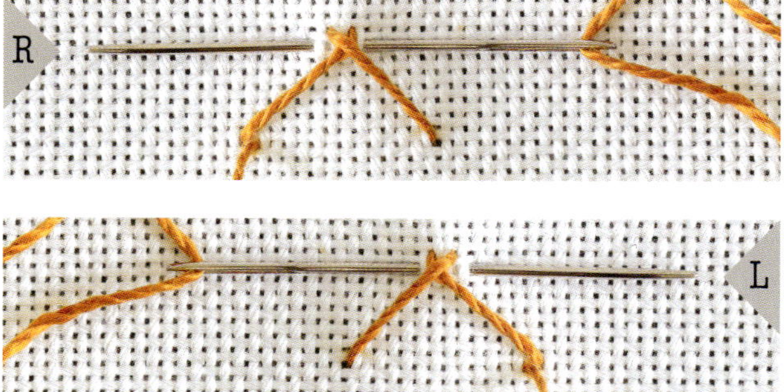

4. Move to the base and insert your needle 1 thread in from the previous stitch and have the needle emerge 1 thread in from the previous stitch. Pull your thread through.

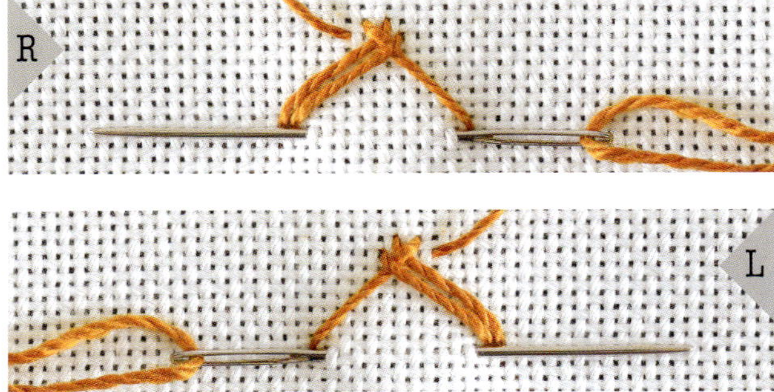

5. Repeat Steps 3–4 until the triangle is completed.

Small abstract design using sprat's head stitches sprinkled over the area.

Tête de Boeuf Stitch

Tête de boeuf is also known as *bull's head stitch, head of the bull,* and *ox head stitch,* because the two protruding stitches can look like horns. Tête de boeuf stitch is easy and quick to work. You can scatter stitches over an area to create patterns or arrange them in circles with the horns pointing outward and then inward.

1. Start as you would a fly stitch (page 188). With the thread wrapped under the needle, pull it through the fabric.

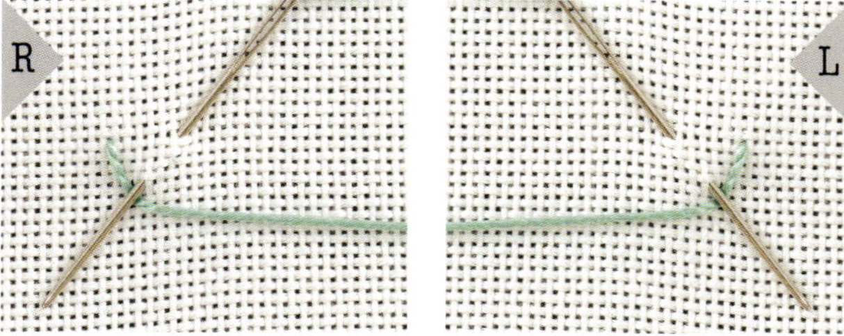

2. Secure the V in position with a detached chain stitch (page 187). To do this, insert the needle so that the point emerges below.

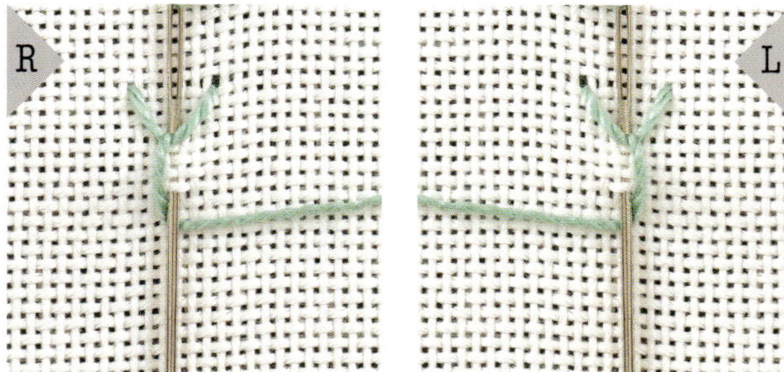

3. With the thread wrapped under the needle, pull the needle through to make the stitch. Take your thread to the back of the fabric, securing the loop with a small straight stitch.

◊ Tête de boeuf worked in perle cotton #5 thread

Trailing Stitch

Trailing stitch is also known as *overcast stitch.* This stitch is a type of couching stitch that resembles a fine cord and is good for outlining shapes with a strong line. Use a hoop to maintain a neat tension.

1. Lay down 3 or 4 straight stitches that will be the core of this stitch. Try to make the core the same color as the trailing stitches. I have used different colors so you can see what is happening. If you want to work this stitch on a curve or around a complex shape, use some small straight stitches worked in cotton sewing thread to keep things under control. These stitches will be covered with the trailing stitches.

2. Start in the middle or partway along the line. Bring your needle up on one side of the core. Take your needle over the core thread and take the needle down on the other side.

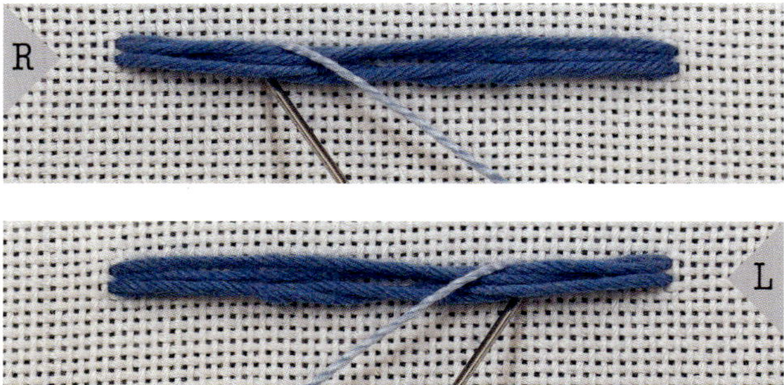

3. Make sure your stitch is straight across the core thread. Each stitch should sit at a right angle to the core. Continue working stitches side by side.

4. Move along the line to the end. Return to pick up where you started and work in the opposite direction to complete the line.

◊ Trailing stitch used in detail of book cover

Ukrainian Square Knot Stitch

Ukrainian square knot creates a textured, square-shaped knotted stitch that is worked in a square over 2 × 2, 3 × 3, or 4 × 4 threads. The stitch can be placed as an individual unit and used as a speckling scattered across an area or built up in patterns.

1. Start with 2 straight stitches. These will form the top and bottom of the square. Have your thread exit the fabric at the corner.

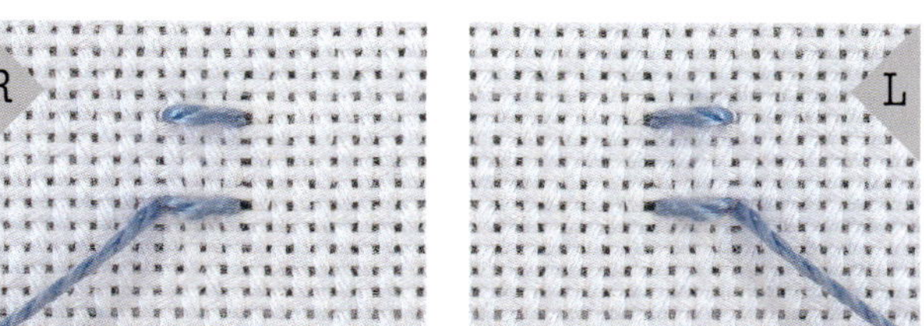

2. Take your needle over the top and pass it under the top bar.

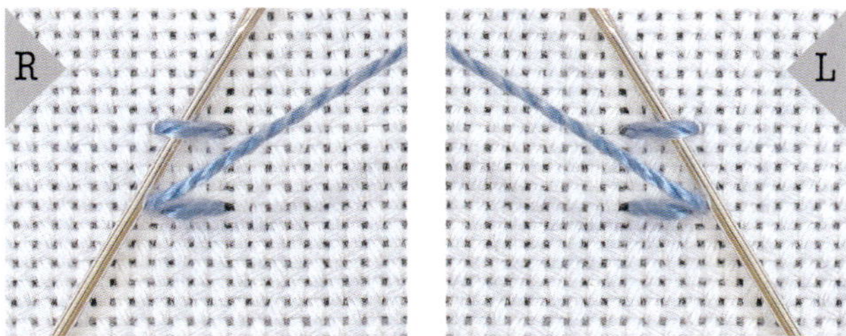

3. Pull your thread partly through, leaving a loose loop.

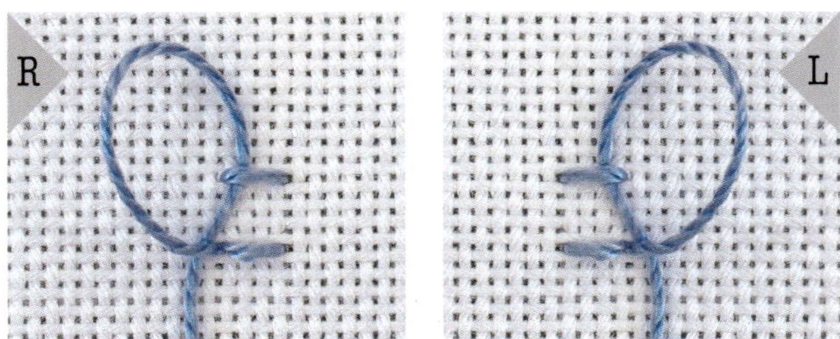

4. Pointing your needle upward, pass it through the loop. This will help secure the knot in the next part of the stitch.

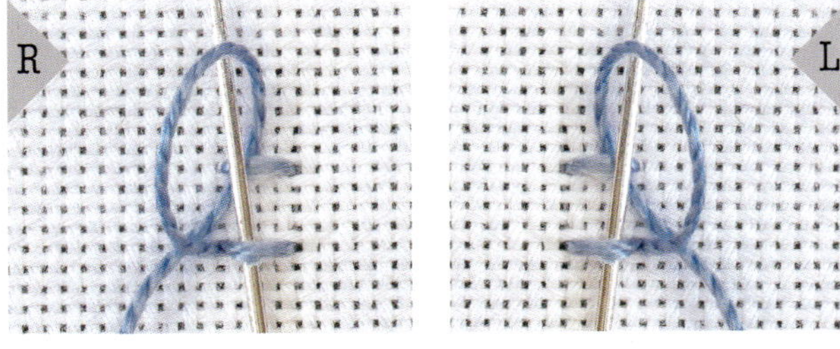

5. Insert your needle in the top corner of the straight stitch. Pull the thread through, easing the loop into a knot so that it is snug but not tight.

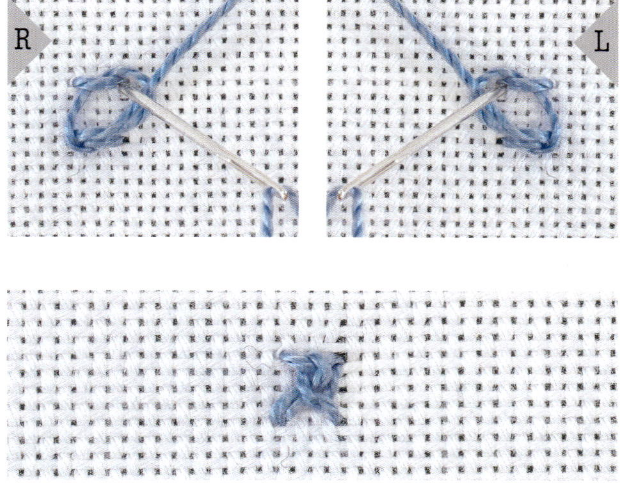

◊ Finished knot

◊ Ukrainian square knots worked in perle cotton #5 thread

Wave Stitch

Wave stitch is a simple, quick, filling stitch that is worked row upon row to fill an area. When worked in a shaded manner, it is also known as *looped shading stitch.*

Worked in a traditional manner, wave stitch is evenly spaced, but if you want to work it free-form or change the spacing and heights of the rows, it can become a stitch with a very contemporary feel.

1. Work a line of evenly spaced small vertical straight stitches.

2. Bring your needle out at the base of the first row and pass the needle under the first straight stitch. Pull the needle through to thread your yarn under the stitch.

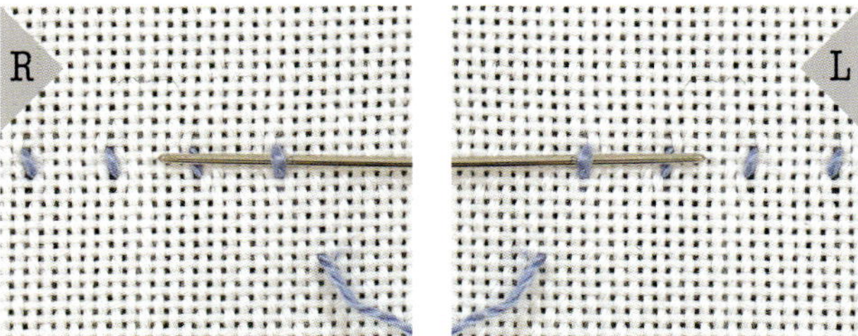

3. Insert your needle at the base of the row to the left so that the yarn forms an inverted V shape.

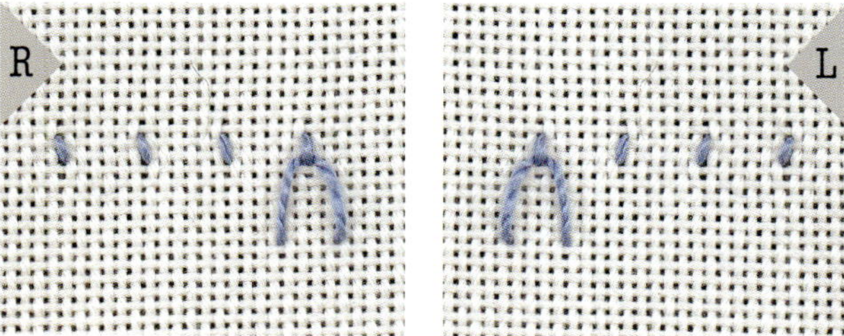

4. To start the next stitch, bring your needle out close to where it entered the fabric. Continue threading the straight stitches to work the first row.

5. On the second and following rows, bring your needle out at the base of the row and work in the opposite direction along the row, threading your yarn through the feet of the inverted V stitches made on the previous row.

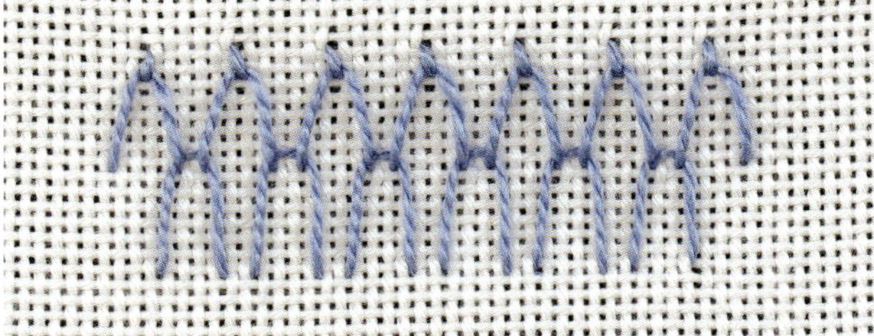

6. Continue in this back-and-forth manner until the area is filled with wave stitches.

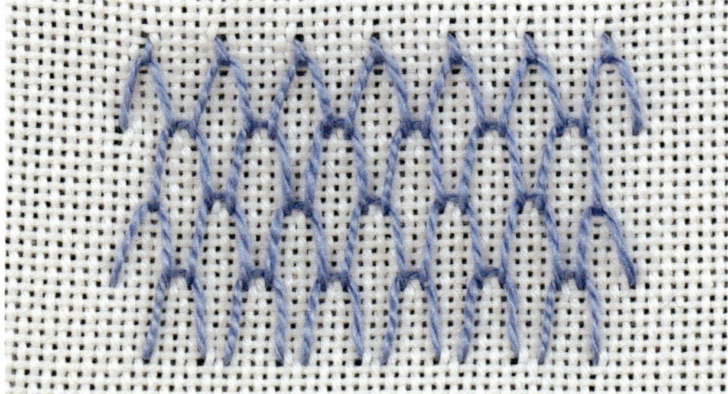

Wave stitch worked in variegated thread on hand-painted background

Wheat Ear Stitch (Chained)

Chained wheat ear stitch is similar to wheat ear stitch, except it has an extra chain stitch, which means it creates a thicker textured line. It follows a curve well and lends itself to organic designs.

1. Work this stitch vertically. Start with 2 straight stitches worked at a 45° angle to form a V.

2. Bring your thread out a little below the base of the V.

3. Pass your needle under the bars of the V stitch.

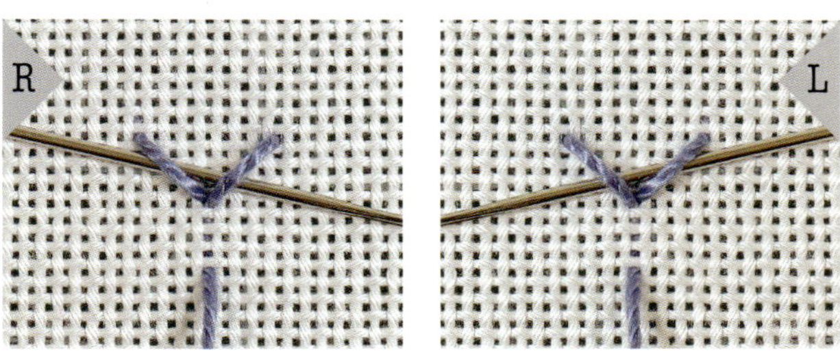

4. Pull your needle through and have your needle emerge from the fabric just below the chain loop you created.

5. To make a second loop that chains the wheat ear stitch, pass your needle once again under the V stitch.

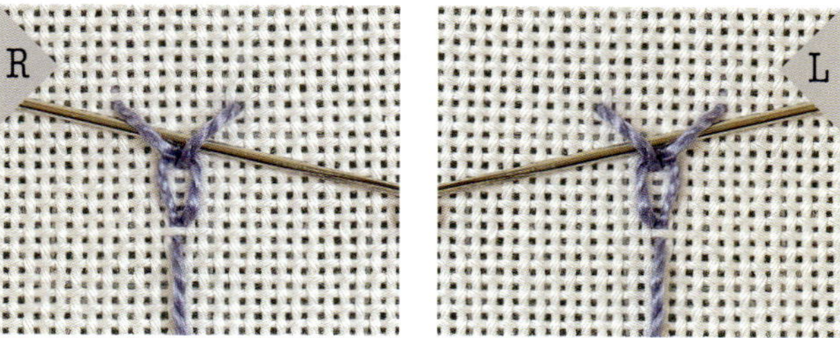

6. Take your needle back into the fabric at the point where your thread emerges.

7. Continue these steps down the line, but pass your needle under the previous chained loops of each stitch.

◊ Finished line of chained wheat ear stitch

◊ Chained wheat ear stitch worked in slow-stitch project

Wheat Ear Stitch (Double)

Double wheat ear stitch is a versatile, easy variety of wheat ear stitch that can be used to depict wild grasses or in other designs that have an organic theme. It follows a curve well.

1. Work this stitch vertically. Start by working a set of 2 stitches sitting at a 45° angle, mirrored, to form a V shape. Bring your thread out a little below the base of the V. You will have 2 nested V shapes.

2. Pass your needle from right to left under both V stitches.

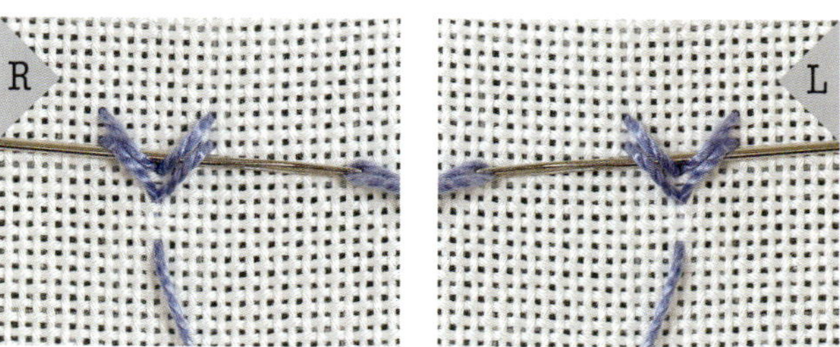

3. Pull your needle through and take it to the back of the fabric so that the thread loops to form a single chain. This is a single detached double wheat ear stitch.

4. Add another set of V-shaped stitches to start repeating the stitch down the line.

Line of double wheat ear stitch

Double wheat ear stitch worked in hand-dyed variegated perle cotton #5 thread

Wheat Ear Stitch (Double Whipped)

Whipped double wheat ear stitch is worked in two journeys. First, you lay down a line of double wheat ear stitch (page 177); then you whip both sides of the chain stitches that run up the middle. To whip the stitch, use a blunt tapestry needle to avoid splitting the foundation stitches.

1. Work a foundation row of double wheat ear stitch (page 177).

2. Bring your needle out at the base of the line, pass it under 1 side of the first chain stitch, and with your needle under the side of the stitch and pointing toward the centerline, pull your needle through. Avoid picking up any of the fabric.

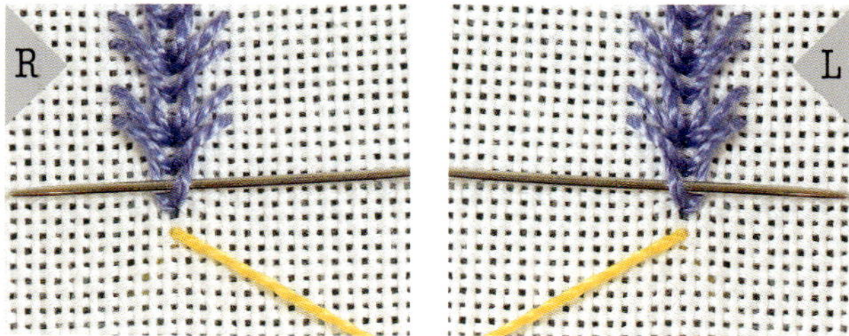

3. Take the needle up to the second double wheat ear stitch and repeat to continue whipping. Make sure that you pick up only 1 side of the chain stitch.

4. Finish the line by tying the thread off at the back of your work.

5. For the next journey, bring your needle out at the base of the line.

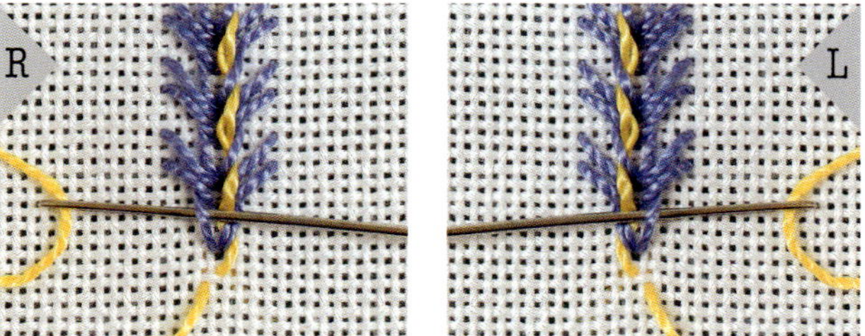

6. Repeat the same whipping action up the other side of the foundation row of double wheat ear stitches.

◊ Whipped double wheat ear stitch used in slow-stitch project

Wheat Ear Stitch (Zigzag)

Zigzag wheat ear is an interesting variety of wheat ear stitch that looks good worked in a precise fashion on even-weave fabric, particularly when combined with other even-weave canvas stitches. Or it can be worked in a free-form fashion in organic curves to create prickly-looking grass heads and the like.

Work this stitch downward in a vertical direction.

1. Start with a straight horizontal stitch.

2. Add a vertical stitch. Bring your thread out on the diagonal and lower than the 2 straight stitches.

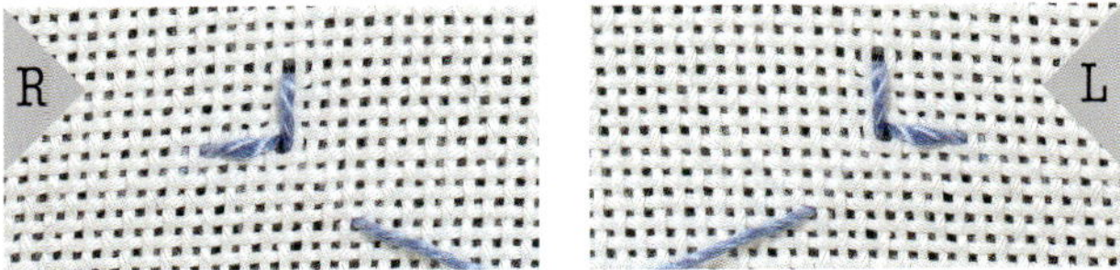

3. Pass your needle under the 2 straight stitches.

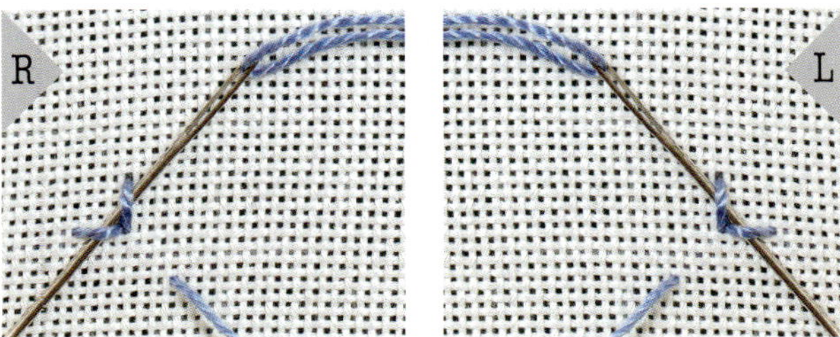

4. Take your needle back into the fabric where your thread emerged. This produces a loop to complete a slanting wheat ear stitch. Bring your thread out in line with your first horizontal stitch.

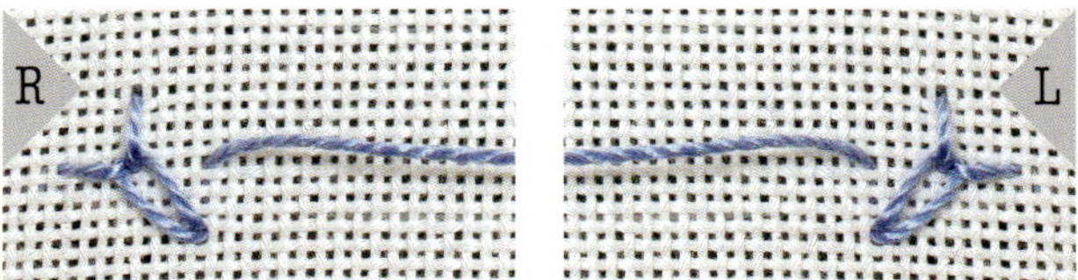

5. Work 2 straight lines, 1 horizontal and 1 vertical.

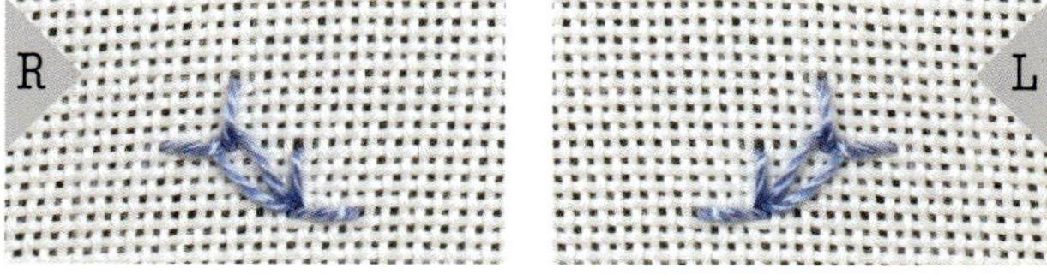

6. Work a second loop to create a second wheat ear stitch slanting in the opposite direction.

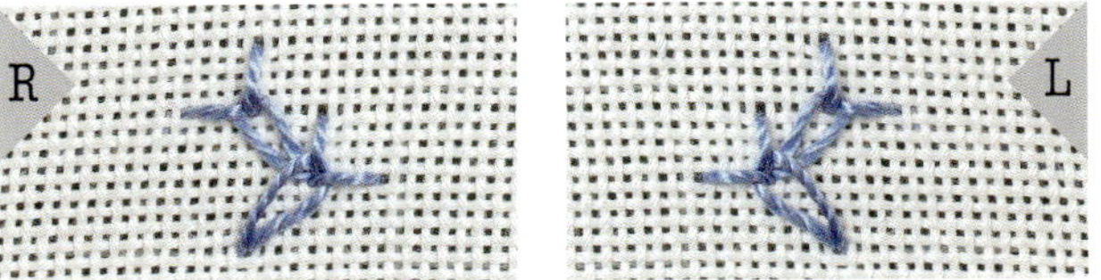

7. Continue in this zigzag manner to complete the line.

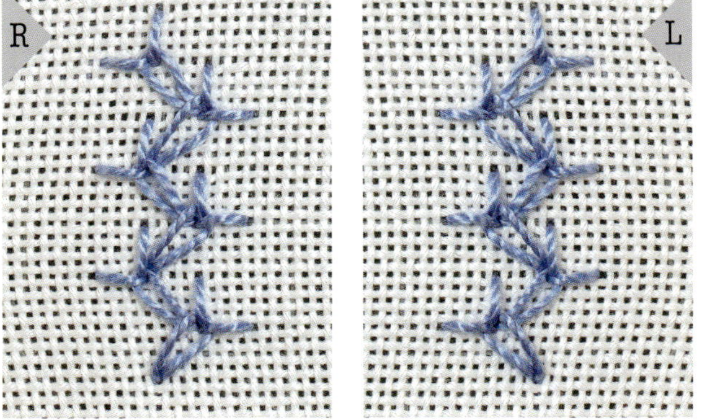

Zigzag wheat ear stitch worked between lines of satin stitch to form pattern

Zigzag Whipped Backstitch

Zigzag whipped backstitch follows a curve well and can be worked on even-weave and plain fabric. It also makes an interesting light border, or you can work row upon row to create a fill.

You can change threads at various points in the process. You can work the foundation rows in different colors, use a different color whipping thread, or select metallic threads. You can change the look of this stitch by varying how far apart the foundation rows are.

1. Zigzag whipped backstitch is worked on a foundation of 3 rows of backstitch (page 183). Work your foundation rows loosely because you have to whip them. The whipping will tighten the foundation stitches as you work.

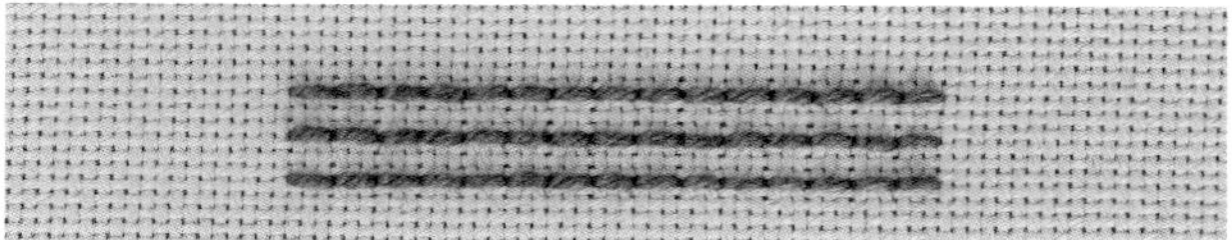

2. The pattern is: Whip 2 foundation stitches; then whip a single stitch. On the next line, whip a single stitch; then whip 2 stitches. Bring your needle out at the top of the line of backstitches and whip the first 2 stitches by passing your needle under 2 stitches. Pull your needle through to whip the 2 stitches together. Take care when whipping to pass your needle under the stitches, not through the fabric.

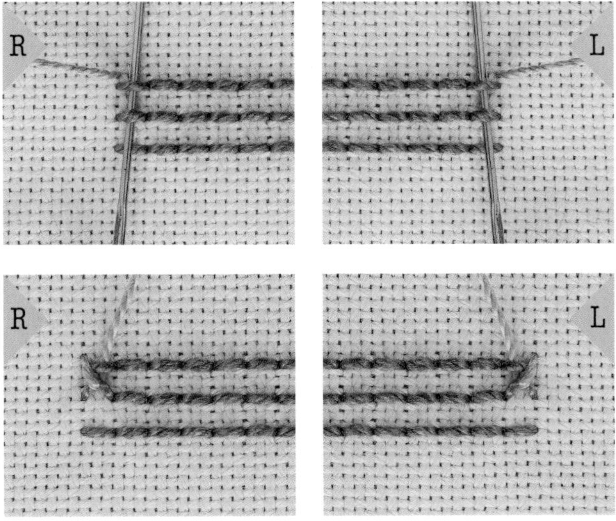

3. Move along a stitch and pass your needle under a single stitch. Whip that stitch.

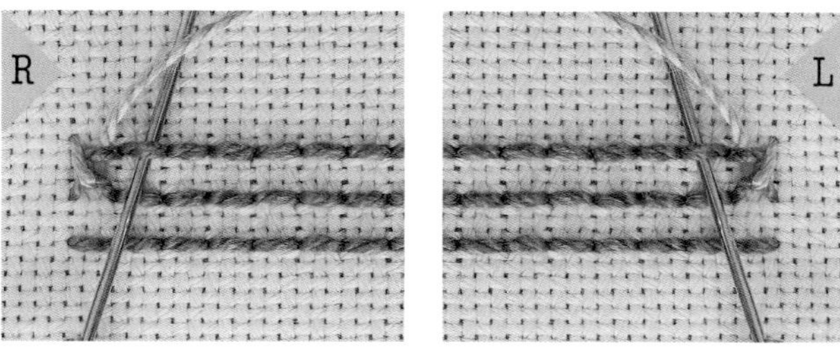

4. Next move along the line and whip 2 of the foundation stitches.

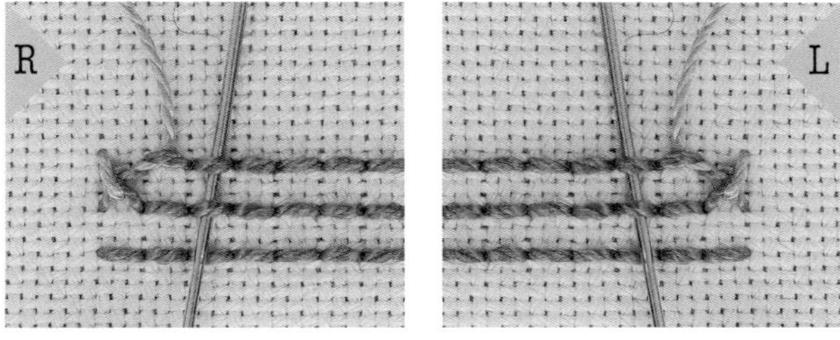

5. Repeat this pattern along the line to the end. As you can see, every second stitch is pulled to form a pattern. This is why it is important to work your foundation stitches a bit loose.

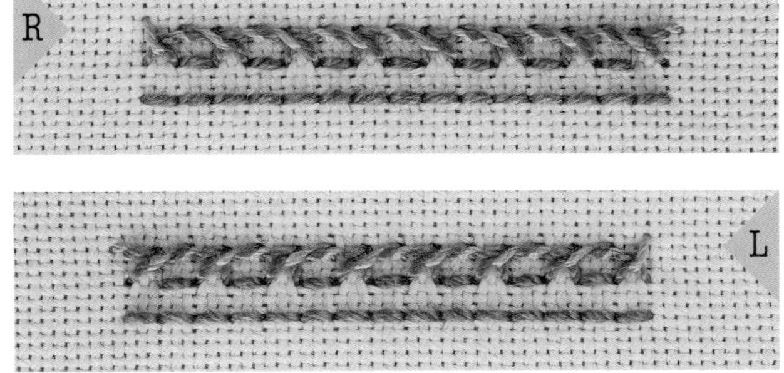

6. Move to the bottom line (turn your work if it is easier) and continue with the whip 1 and then whip 2 together pattern.

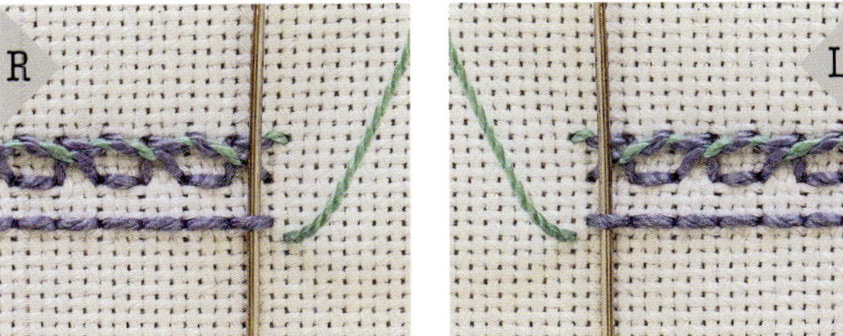

7. Make sure to offset the whipping pattern. Where you have whipped 2 stitches on the top 2 lines, whip 1 foundation stitch; where you have whipped 1 foundation stitch, whip 2. This pattern quickly builds up and is easier than it sounds.

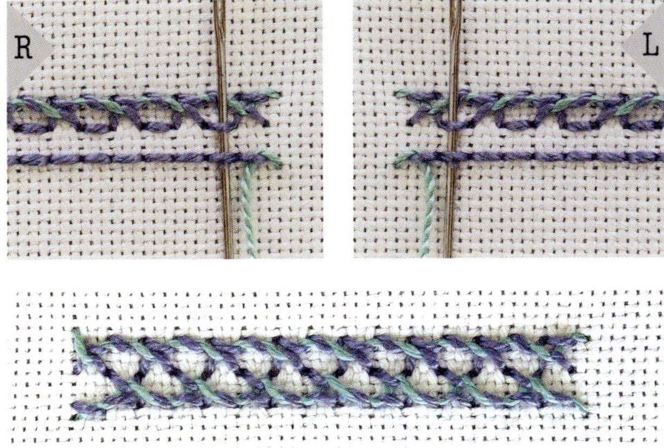

◊ Completed zigzag whipped backstitch

◊ Sample of zigzag whipped backstitch worked on foundation of variegated perle #8 thread whipped with metallic flecked thread

Foundational Stitches

Some of the stitches in this book are built on basic, foundational stitches. These stitches were originally presented in *Creative Stitches for Contemporary Embroidery* (C&T Publishing). You can find 120 more embroidery stitches, including the ones presented in this section in that first volume.

Backstitch

Backstitch is a good, basic linear stitch that forms a clean line in a design. Backstitch can be used as a delicate outline or as a foundation in composite stitches, such as Double Pekinese stitch (page 109). If you want to give blackwork patterns a modern twist, work the design in backstitch using over-dyed or variegated threads.

1. If needed, mark your line with a quilters pencil or soluble pen or pencil. Bring the thread up from the back of the fabric and make a backward stitch. Bring the needle out on the line, a little in front of the first stitch.

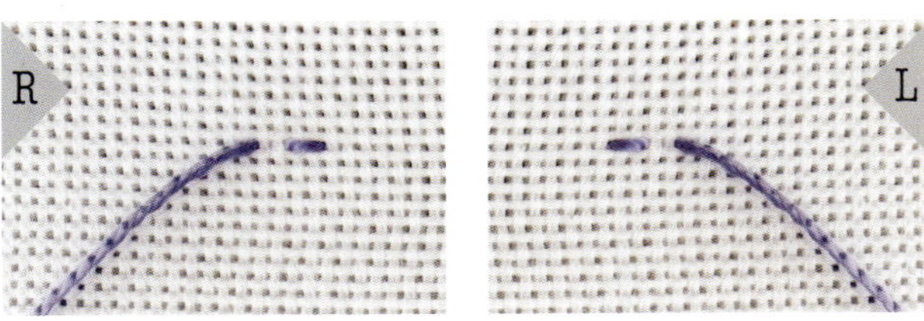

2. Make the second stitch backward, inserting the needle into the hole made by the first stitch. Bring the needle out in front of the second stitch. Repeat this back-and-forth movement along the line.

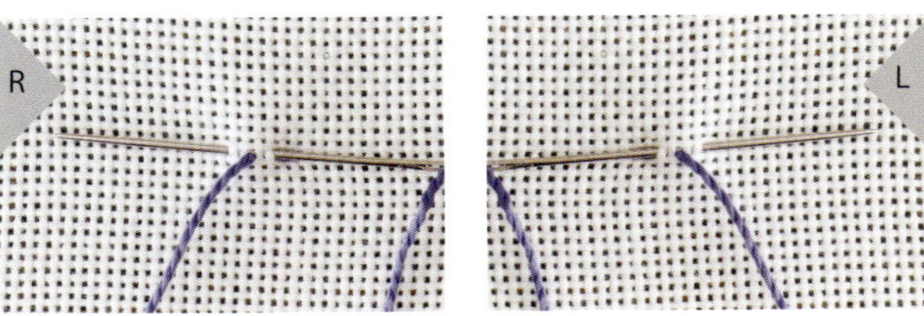

Buttonhole Stitch

1. Work from left to right (right to left if you're left-handed) along 2 imaginary horizontal lines. Bring the thread out on the lower line. Move to the right and make a vertical stitch, from upper line to lower line, looping the working thread under the point of the needle. Pull the thread through.

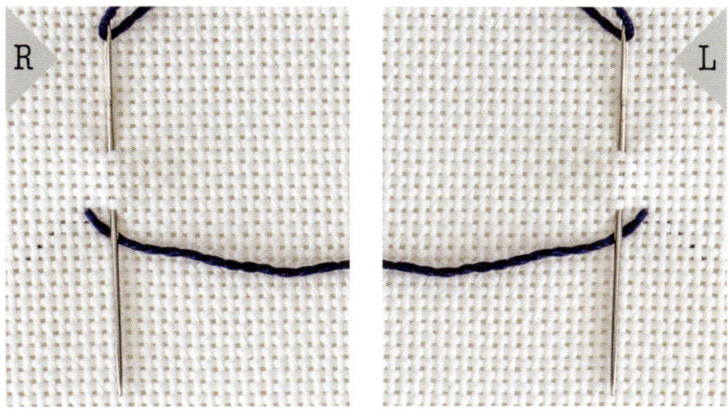

2. Repeat along the line.

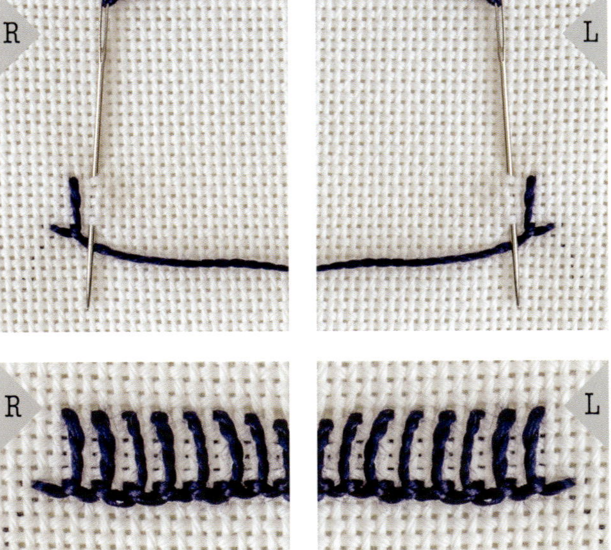

Cable Chain Stitch

1. Bring the needle up on the line you want to work. Slip the needle under the thread; then twist the thread around the needle once.

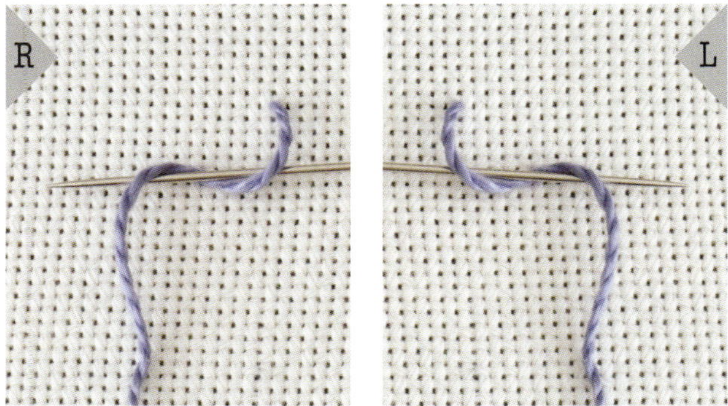

2. Point the needle back into the original hole. Push the thread down the shaft of the needle, so the loop sits close to the fabric. You want a firm but not tight loop around the needle. Bring the needle out below the loop and wrap the thread under the point of the needle as you would for basic chain stitch.

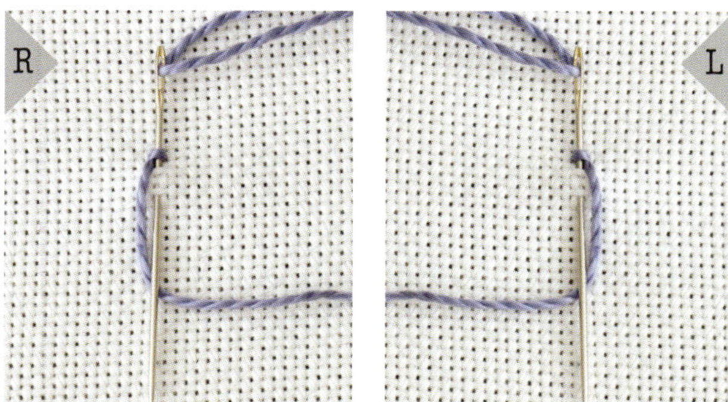

3. Pull the thread through the fabric and you have created your first cable chain stitch.

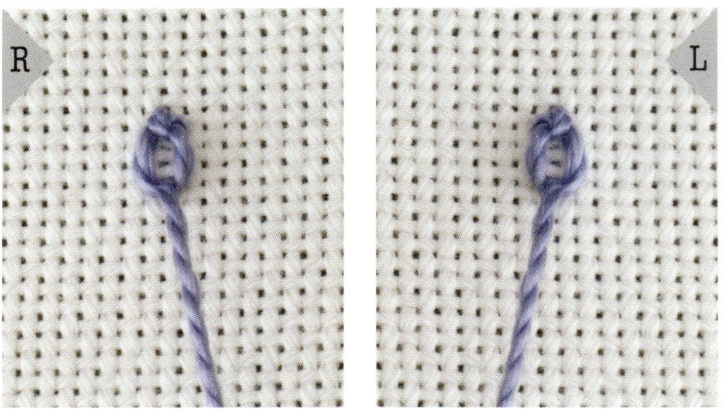

4. Repeat the pattern, creating a knot before moving on to the next chain stitch.

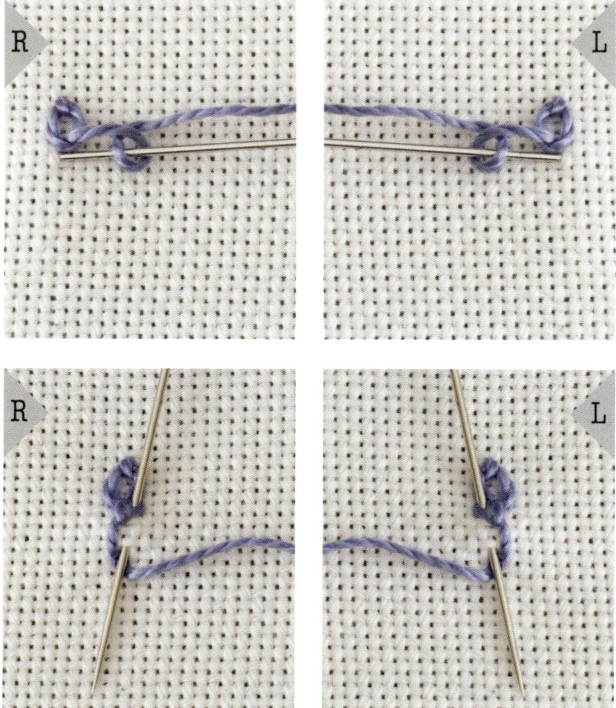

◊ Line of cable chain stitch

Chain Stitch

1. Bring the needle up through the fabric and insert the needle back into the original hole. With the thread wrapped under the needle, pull the needle through the fabric a short distance from the first point.

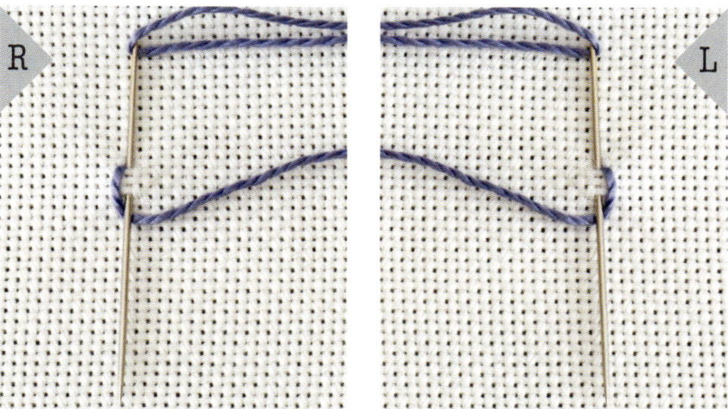

2. Insert the needle into where the thread emerges from the chain. With the thread wrapped under the point of the needle, pull the needle through the fabric to create the second chain stitch.

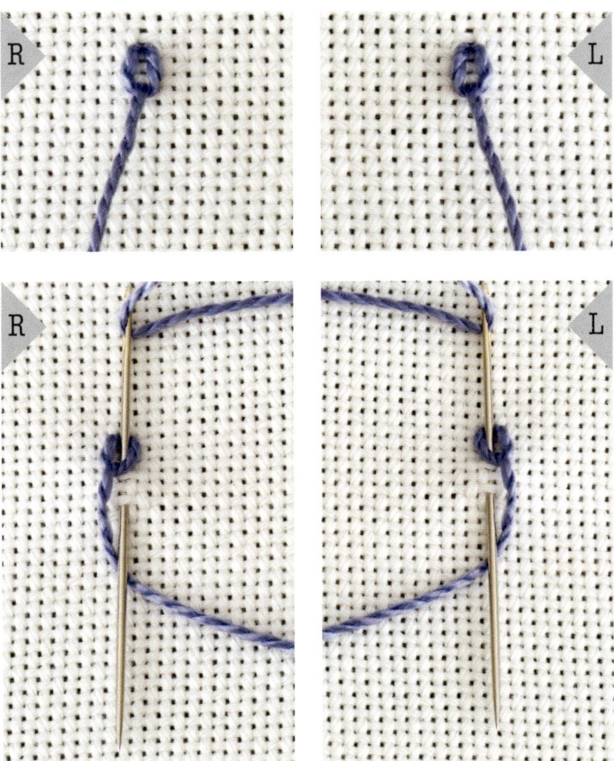

3. Continue the pattern. At the end of the line, tie off with a small straight stitch.

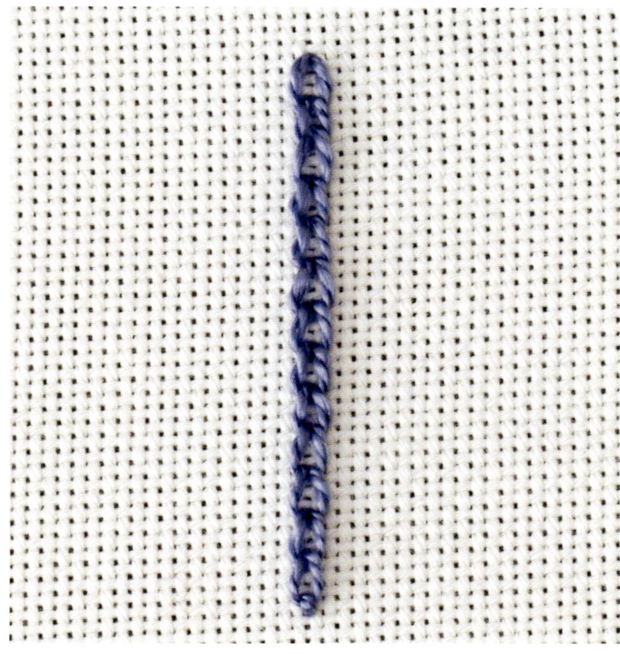

◊ A line of chain stitch

Coral Stitch

1. Follow an imaginary line or use a pen that will disappear to mark a line. Bring the thread from the back of the fabric. Take a stitch at a slight right angle, above the line to be worked. Wrap the thread over and then under the needle.

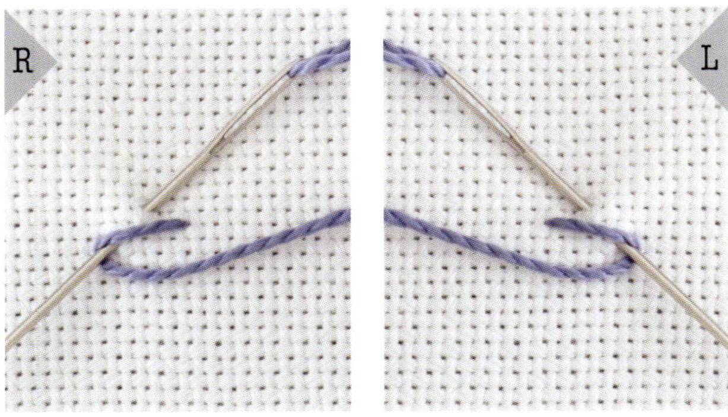

2. Pull the needle through the fabric to form a knot. Repeat the pattern along the line.

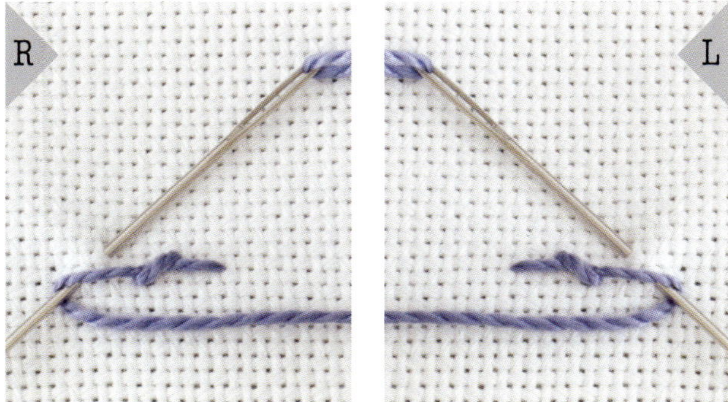

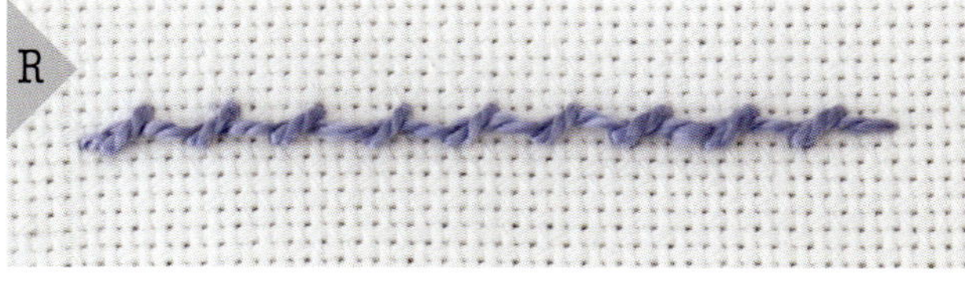

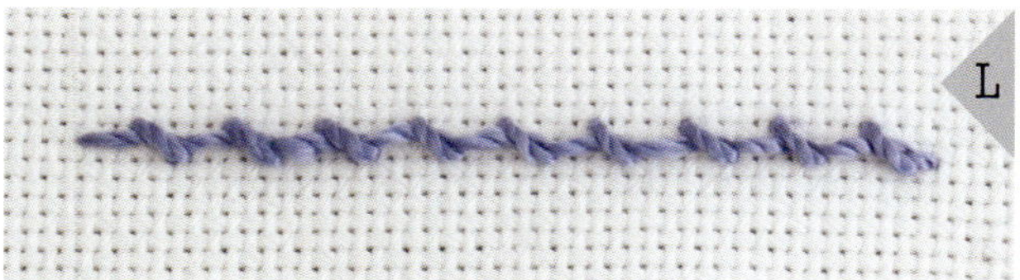

Line of coral stitch. This sample was worked using perle cotton #5. The effect created by coral stitch can be altered by using thicker threads or even a fine ribbon.

Cross-Stitch

Cross-stitch is extremely quick and easy to work. Work a diagonal straight stitch. Then work a second diagonal stitch laid in the opposite direction.

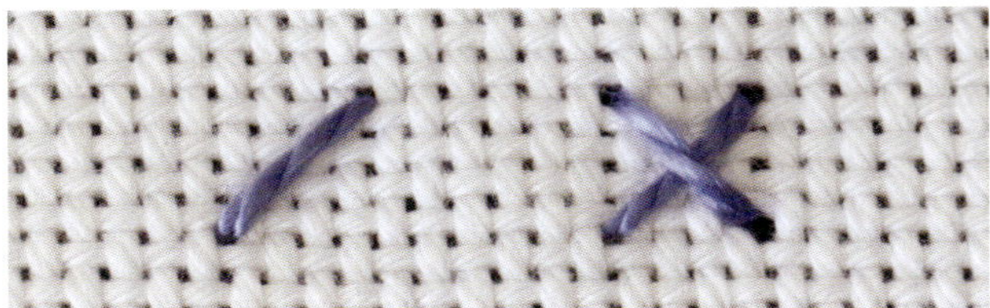

Although the construction of cross-stitch is the same, there are different ways of working. Cross-stitch can be worked individually, completing each cross before moving on to the next. Use this method if you are using a multicolored thread. Or you can work a line of half-cross-stitches and then finish the crosses on a return journey. No matter the method used, in traditional cross-stitch, one rule remains constant: The top diagonals should always lie in the same direction. (This rule is often deliberately broken by some contemporary embroiderers.)

Detached Chain Stitch

1. Bring the needle up through the fabric. Insert the needle so that the point emerges a short space away.

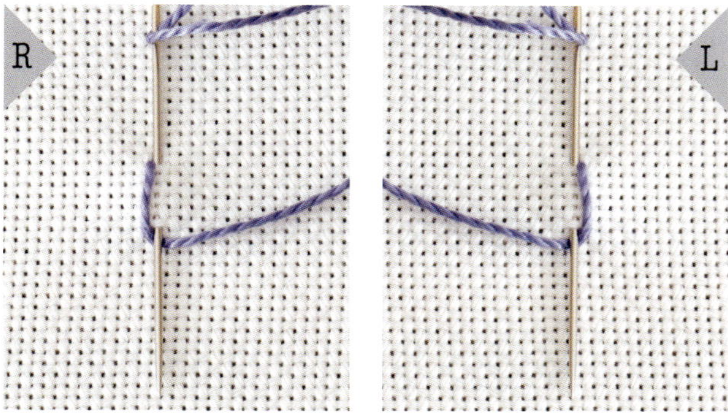

2. With the thread wrapped under the point of the needle, pull the needle through the fabric.

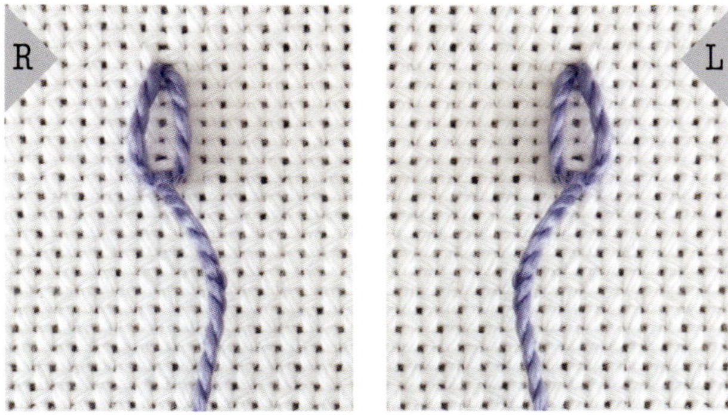

3. Take the needle to the back of the fabric by making a small straight stitch. This will secure and complete the stitch.

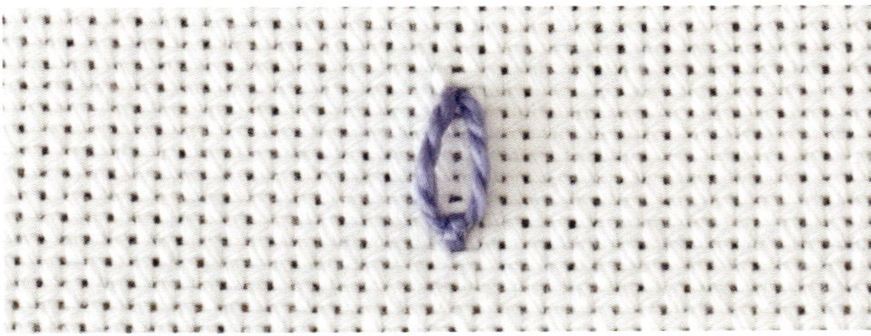

◊ Detached chain stitch

Feather Stitch

Tips

- To make sure this stitch sits neatly on a curve, keep the center of the stitch on the line you want to follow.
- You can vary feather stitch by changing the width between the tops of the Y, the angle of your needle, and the spacing in the length of stitches.

1. Bring the thread up at the top left (right if you're left-handed). Insert the needle to the right (left) and make a downward stitch so that the needle emerges between the 2 points. With the thread wrapped under the needle, pull it through the fabric. It should make a V.

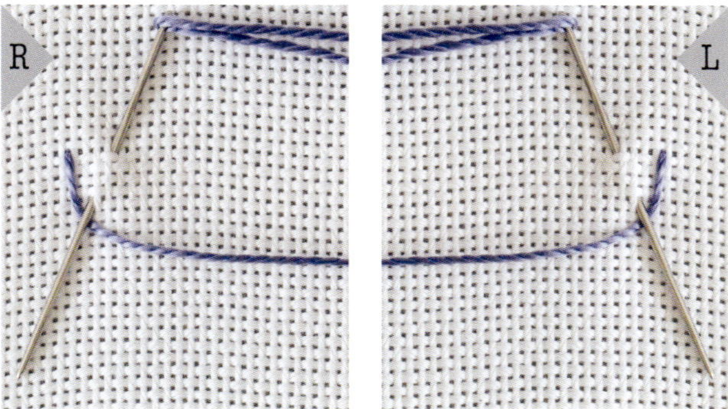

2. Insert the needle to the right (left) and make another downward diagonal stitch so that the needle emerges between the 2 points. With the thread wrapped under the needle, pull it through the fabric.

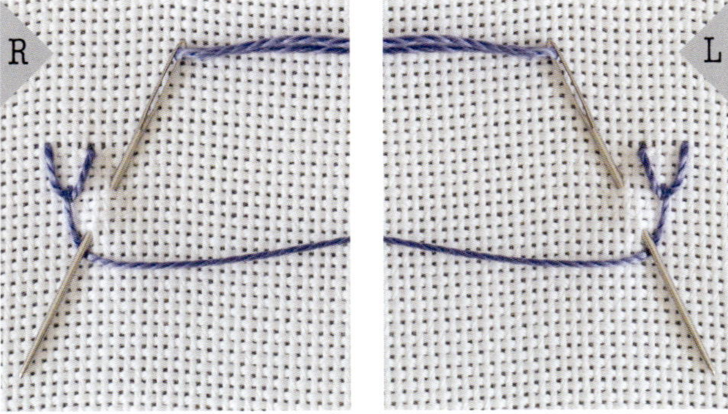

3. Continue working on alternate sides of the line, keeping the Vs aligned.

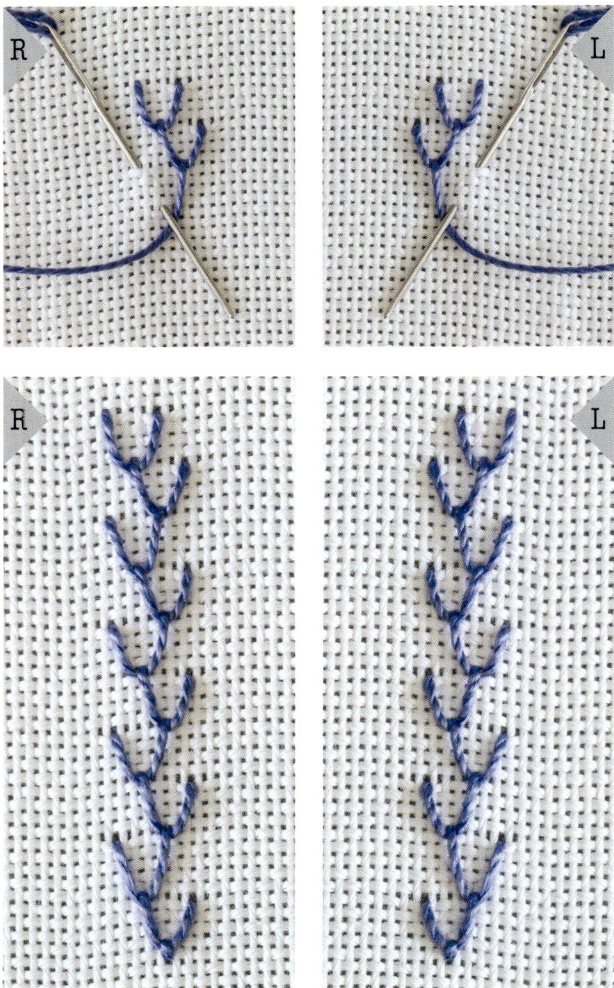

◊ Feather stitch

Fly Stitch

1. Bring the thread up at the top left (right if you're left-handed) and insert the needle to the right (left). Make a downward stitch between the top 2 points.

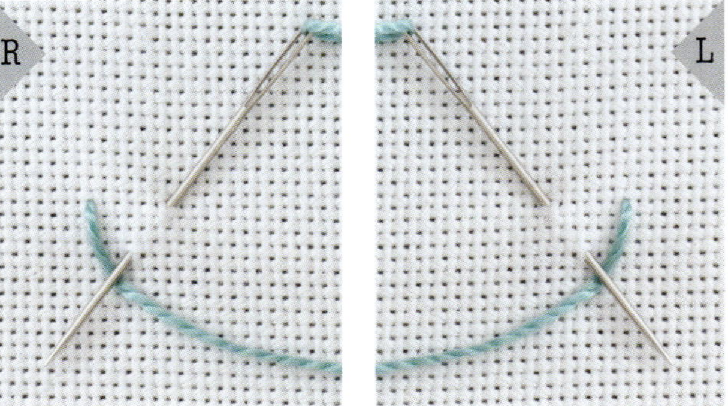

2. With the thread wrapped under the needle, pull it through the fabric. Secure the V in position with a small vertical straight stitch.

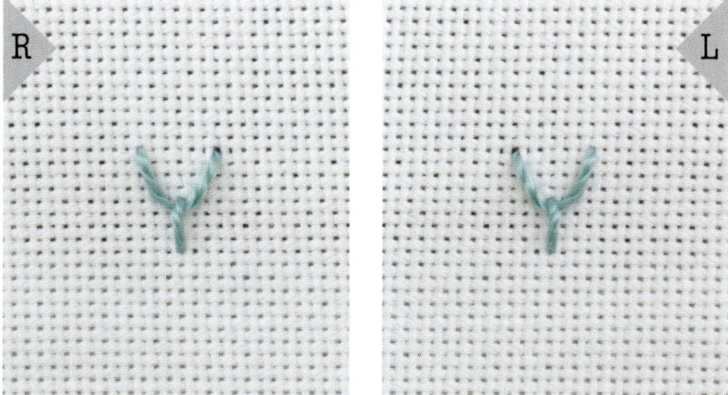

◊ Fly stitch

Herringbone Stitch

1. Work along 2 imaginary horizontal lines. Bring the needle out on the top left. Move diagonally to the lower line and make a small stitch.

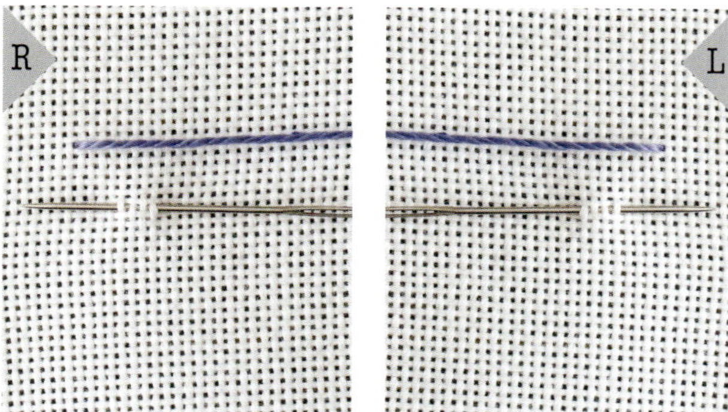

2. Insert the thread on the upper line, a little to the right (left), and make a small stitch.

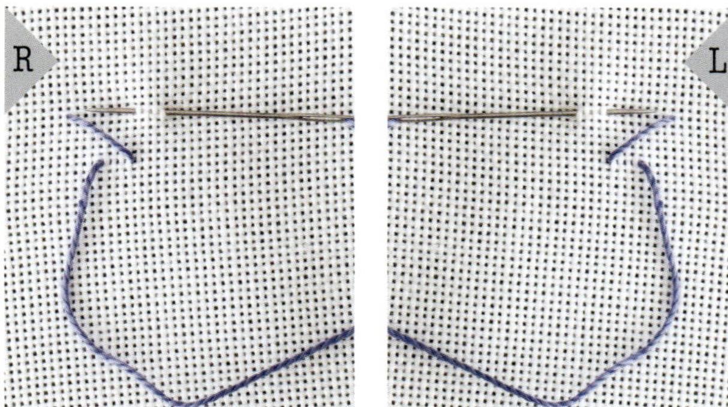

3. Continue the pattern along the line.

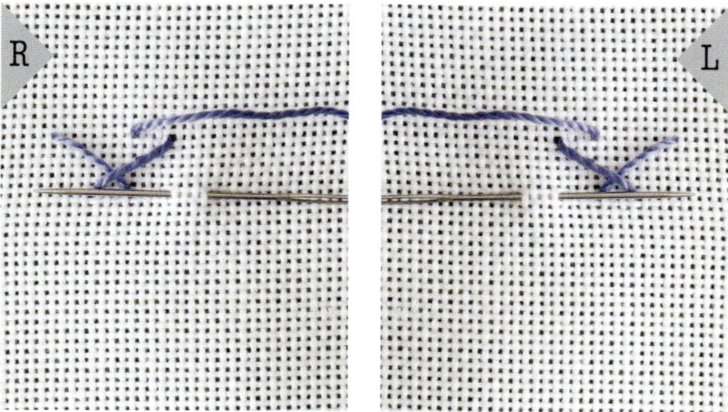

◊ A completed row of herringbone stitch

Index

About the Author

Sharon Boggon has been stitching since she was a little girl. She trained in fine arts in Perth, Western Australia, and holds a master's degree in textiles from the Australian National University. She has developed considerable skill in contemporary embroidery and crazy quilting and has taught crazy quilting internationally, including in the United States and online, and was a lecturer in the Textiles Department at the Canberra School of Art at the Australian National University. She lives in Canberra, Australia's "bush capital," with her husband of 45 years. They have one adult daughter and a young grandson.

Visit Sharon online and follow on social media!

Website/Blog: pintangle.com

Facebook: /facebook.com/pintangle

Facebook group: TAST - Take a Stitch Tuesday

Instagram: @sharonboggon

Pinterest: /sharonboggon

YouTube: /sharonboggon

◊ Trailing stitch used in detail of book cover